Stateness and Democracy in East Asia

Democratization and state building are fundamental political processes, yet scholars cannot agree on which process should be prioritized in order to put countries on a positive path of institutional development. Where much of the existing literature on the state-democracy nexus focuses on quantitative cross-national data, this volume offers a theoretically grounded regional analysis built around in-depth qualitative case studies. The chapters examine cases of successful democratic consolidation (South Korea, Taiwan), defective democracy (Philippines, Indonesia, East Timor), and autocratic reversal (Cambodia, Thailand). The book's evidence challenges the dominant "state first, democracy later" argument, demonstrating instead that stateness is neither a sufficient nor a necessary condition for democratic consolidation. The authors not only show that democratization can become trapped in path-dependent processes, but also that the system-level organization of informal networks plays a key role in shaping the outcome of democratic transitions.

Aurel Croissant is Professor of Political Science at Heidelberg University. His research focuses on comparative democratization, comparative authoritarianism, civil-military relations, and Asian politics. He also serves as the co-editor of the journal *Democratization*. Recent publications include *Civil-Military Relations in Southeast Asia* (Cambridge Elements, 2018), *Comparative Politics of Southeast Asia* (2018), and *Civil-Military Relations: Control and Effectiveness across Regimes* (co-edited with Tom Bruneau, Lynne Rienner, 2019).

Olli Hellmann is Senior Lecturer in Political Science and International Relations at the University of Waikato, Aotearoa/New Zealand. He specializes in the comparative analysis of political institutions with a special focus on Northeast and Southeast Asia. Recent relevant publications include a co-edited special issue of *International Political Science Review* (with Aurel Croissant), examining the link between state capacity and autocratic regime resilience, and an article in *Crime, Law and Social Change* that addresses the historical origins of different corruption types.

Stateness and Democracy in East Asia

Edited by
AUREL CROISSANT
Heidelberg University

OLLI HELLMANN
University of Waikato

CAMBRIDGE
UNIVERSITY PRESS

University Printing House, Cambridge CB2 8BS, United Kingdom

One Liberty Plaza, 20th Floor, New York, NY 10006, USA

477 Williamstown Road, Port Melbourne, VIC 3207, Australia

314-321, 3rd Floor, Plot 3, Splendor Forum, Jasola District Centre, New Delhi - 110025, India

103 Penang Road, #05-06/07, Visioncrest Commercial, Singapore 238467

Cambridge University Press is part of the University of Cambridge.

It furthers the University's mission by disseminating knowledge in the pursuit of education, learning and research at the highest international levels of excellence.

www.cambridge.org
Information on this title: www.cambridge.org/9781108797382
DOI: 10.1017/9781108862783

© Aurel Croissant and Olli Hellmann 2020

This publication is in copyright. Subject to statutory exception and to the provisions of relevant collective licensing agreements, no reproduction of any part may take place without the written permission of Cambridge University Press.

First published 2020
First paperback edition 2022

A catalogue record for this publication is available from the British Library

Library of Congress Cataloging in Publication data
Names: Croissant, Aurel, 1969- editor. | Hellmann, Olli, 1979- editor.
Title: Stateness and democracy in East Asia / edited by Aurel Croissant, Olli Hellmann.
Description: Cambridge, United Kingdom ; New York, NY : Cambridge University Press, 2020. | Includes bibliographical references and index.
Identifiers: LCCN 2019058892 | ISBN 9781108495745 (hardback) | ISBN 9781108797382 (ebook)
Subjects: LCSH: Democratization--East Asia. | Democracy--East Asia. | Institution building--East Asia. | East Asia--Politics and government--21st century.
Classification: LCC JQ1499.A91 S73 2020 | DDC 320.95--dc23
LC record available at https://lccn.loc.gov/2019058892

ISBN 978-1-108-49574-5 Hardback
ISBN 978-1-108-79738-2 Paperback

Cambridge University Press has no responsibility for the persistence or accuracy of URLs for external or third-party internet websites referred to in this publication, and does not guarantee that any content on such websites is, or will remain, accurate or appropriate.

Contents

List of Figures		*page* vii
List of Tables		ix
List of Contributors		xi
Acknowledgements		xv
1	Introduction: Rethinking Stateness and Democracy in East Asia *Aurel Croissant and Olli Hellmann*	1
2	State-Building and Democratization: The Sequencing Debate and Evidence from East Asia *Tuong Vu*	25
3	South Korea's Democracy and the Legacies of the Developmental State *Olli Hellmann*	47
4	After Hegemony: State Capacity, the Quality of Democracy and the Legacies of the Party-State in Democratic Taiwan *Kharis Templeman*	71
5	Democratization Interrupted: The Parallel State and the Demise of Democracy in Thailand *Paul W. Chambers*	103
6	Weak State and the Limits of Democratization in Cambodia, 1993–2017 *Kheang Un*	133
7	The Institutional Roots of Defective Democracy in the Philippines *Erik Martinez Kuhonta and Nhu Truong*	153

8 Stateness and State Capacity in Post-Authoritarian Indonesia: Securing Democracy's Survival, Entrenching Its Low Quality   179
   Marcus Mietzner

9 As Good as It Gets? Stateness and Democracy in East Timor   204
   Aurel Croissant and Rebecca Abu Sharkh

10 Stateness and Democracy: Evidence from East Asia and Cross-Regional Comparisons   233
   Aurel Croissant and Olli Hellmann

Index   263

Figures

1.1	Electoral democracy and state capacity in East and Southeast Asia	*page* 5
1.2	The partial regimes of embedded democracy	11
3.1	South Korea's civil society	60
3.2	Seat share in per cent of the president's party (based on legislative election results)	63
7.1	Perception of the Philippine electoral integrity and sub-dimensions, 2016	158
7.2	Voice and accountability estimate, 1996–2014	160
7.3	Country estimate on rule of law, 1996–2014	162
7.4	Philippine trend in income inequality, 1961–2015	166
9.1	Average state capacity (capacity1 measure) in East and Southeast Asia, 2002–2010	209
9.2	Petroleum sector in percentage (%) of total GDP and public revenues, 2004–2015	212
10.1	Autocratic reversions and democratic transitions according to BTI, 2006–2018	239
10.2	Consolidating, defective and failed democracies worldwide	240
10.3	Development in state capacity in seven Asian societies, 1960–2009	242

Tables

1.1	Three waves of democratization in East and Southeast Asia	page 2
1.2	Electoral and liberal democracy in East Asia	3
7.1	Journalists killed in Southeast Asia, 2000–2015	161
9.1	Regional differences and inequalities	214
9.2	Freedom of the press in East Timor and other Southeast Asian nations	217
9.3	Freedom of organization and association (Freedom House, 2006–2016)	218
10.1	BTI criteria, indicators and the partial regimes of embedded democracy	235
10.2	Third-wave democracies and current regime category (BTI, 2018)	236
10.3	BTI scores for the partial regimes of the embedded democracy in East and Southeast Asia	238
10.4	BTI scores for five partial regimes of the embedded democracy by region, 2006 and 2018	241
10.5	Cross-regional comparison of three BTI stateness indicators, 2006 and 2018	244
10.6	BTI stateness indicators in East and Southeast Asia	246

Contributors

Rebecca Abu Sharkh studied at University of California–Santa Cruz, University of California–Berkeley and University of Cape Town before she joined Heidelberg University as a research assistant and graduate student at the Institute of Political Science. She has interned with the Freeman Spogli Institute for International Studies at Stanford University, the United Nations Information Center in Washington, DC, and the Committee on Human Rights and Humanitarian Aid at the Bundestag in Berlin. Her main research interests include democratization studies and peace and conflict research.

Paul W. Chambers is Lecturer and Special Advisor on international affairs at the Center of ASEAN Community Studies, Naresuan University (Thailand). He is a fellow at the Peace Research Institute Frankfurt and the German Institute of Global Area Studies. His research focus is civil-military relations, democratization and Southeast Asian politics. He is executive editor of the journal *Asian Affairs: An American Review*. Recent publications include his co-edited volume *Khaki Capital: The Political Economy of the Military in Southeast Asia* (NIAS, 2017) and his co-edited special issue "Conflict in the Deep South of Thailand: Never-ending Stalemate" (*Asian International Studies Review*, 2019).

Aurel Croissant is Professor of Political Science and Dean of Faculty of Economics and Social Sciences at Heidelberg University. His research focus is comparative democratization, comparative authoritarianism, civil-military relations and Asian politics. He is co-editor of the journal *Democratization*. Recent publications include *Civil-Military Relations in Southeast Asia* (Cambridge Elements, 2018), *Comparative Politics of Southeast Asia* (Springer, 2018) and *Civil-Military Relations: Control and Effectiveness across Regimes* (edited with Tom Bruneau, Lynne Rienner Publishers, 2019).

Olli Hellmann is Senior Lecturer in Political Science and International Relations at the University of Waikato, Aotearoa/New Zealand. He has published on questions of both democratization – in particular, on political parties and party systems – and state-building, including on corruption and the effect of state capacity on autocratic regime resilience. His current work explores how dictatorships employ visual storytelling to construct legitimacy narratives.

Erik Martinez Kuhonta is Director of the Institute for the Study of International Development and Associate Professor of Political Science at McGill University. He is the author of *The Institutional Imperative: The Politics of Equitable Development in Southeast Asia* (Stanford University Press, 2011), which was short listed for the Canadian Political Science Association Prize in Comparative Politics. He is co-editor of *Party System Institutionalization in Asia: Democracies, Autocracies, and the Shadows of the Past* (Cambridge University Press, 2015) and of *Southeast Asia in Political Science: Theory, Region, and Qualitative Analysis* (Stanford University Press, 2008). Kuhonta has also published in numerous academic journals and edited books. He received his PhD from Princeton University.

Marcus Mietzner is Associate Professor at the Department of Political and Social Change, Coral Bell School of Asia Pacific Affairs, Australian National University, Canberra. His research focus is Indonesian politics, including the role of the armed forces, presidentialism, populism and the rising influence of Islamic conservatism. Recent publications include *Reinventing Asian Populism: Jokowi's Rise, Democracy, and Political Contestation in Indonesia* (East-West Center, Hawaii, 2015) and *The Yudhoyono Presidency: Indonesia's Decade of Stability and Stagnation* (co-edited with Edward Aspinall and Dirk Tomsa, ISEAS, 2015).

Kharis Templeman is the project manager of the Taiwan Democracy and Security Project and a social science research scholar at the Shorenstein Asia-Pacific Research Center (APARC) at Stanford University. He is also a teaching affiliate at Stanford's Center for East Asian Studies, where he teaches a regular course on Taiwan politics and advises undergraduate and master's students. He is the editor (with Larry Diamond and Yun-han Chu) of *Taiwan's Democracy Challenged: The Chen Shui-bian Years* (Lynne Rienner Publishing, 2016). Other peer-reviewed work has appeared in *Comparative Political Studies*, *Ethnopolitics*, *The Taiwan Journal of Democracy* and *The APSA Annals of Comparative Democratization*. From 2016 to 2018, Templeman served as coordinator of the American Political Science Association's Conference Group on Taiwan Studies (CGOTS). He holds a BA (2003) from the University of Rochester and a PhD (2012) in political science from the University of Michigan.

List of Contributors xiii

Nhu Truong is PhD candidate in comparative politics at the Department of Political Science of McGill University. Her research addresses questions of authoritarian responsiveness, political institutionalization, law and legal institutions and political legitimation, with a regional focus on Southeast Asia and East Asia. Her current research aims to explain the variation in authoritarian responsiveness to land-related unrest in Vietnam and China.

Kheang Un is Associate Professor of political science and an associate of the Center for Southeast Asian Studies at Northern Illinois University. Un served as visiting fellow at the Royal Netherlands Institute for Southeast Asian and Caribbean Studies, the University of Louisville Center for Asian Democracy and the Center for Khmer Studies, Cambodia, and as a Fulbright Fellow at the Royal University of Phnom Penh. From 2008 to 2011, he was a researcher for Tracking Development, a multi-disciplinary and multi-country project based at Leiden University, examining the trajectory of development in Southeast Asia and sub-Saharan Africa under the sponsorship of the Netherland's Ministry of Foreign Affairs. Un's journal articles appear *Democratization*, *Journal of Asian Studies*, *International Political Science Review*, *Pacific Affairs*, *Asian Survey* and *Development and Change*, among others. His latest publication includes *Cambodia: Return to Authoritarianism* (Cambridge University Press, 2019).

Tuong Vu is Director of Asian Studies and Professor of Political Science at the University of Oregon. He has held visiting appointments at Princeton University and National University of Singapore and taught at the Naval Postgraduate School. Vu is the author and editor of four books including *Vietnam's Communist Revolution: The Power and Limits of Ideology* (Cambridge University Press, 2017), *Paths to Development in Asia: South Korea, Vietnam, China, and Indonesia* (Cambridge University Press, 2010), *Dynamics of the Cold War in Asia: Ideology, Identity, and Culture* (Palgrave, 2009) and *Southeast Asia in Political Science: Theory, Region, and Qualitative Analysis* (Stanford University Press, 2008). He has also authored numerous articles on the politics of nationalism and state-building in East and Southeast Asia. Currently, he is working on a book about the historical processes of imperial and state formations in East Asia.

Acknowledgements

The foundation for this edited volume was laid at a workshop at McGill University in September 2015, made possible by a grant from the UK's Economic and Social Research Council (ESRC) (award number: ES/L00061X/1). We would like to thank Erik Martinez Kuhonta and Nhu Truong for hosting and organizing the workshop. We are also grateful to a number of colleagues who attended the workshop as discussants, providing valuable feedback on each of the papers: Joseph Wong, Netina Tan, Juan Wang, Manuel Balan and Philip Oxhorn. And of course, this volume would not have seen the light of the day without the hard work put in by the authors. Thank you for contributing such rich and insightful analyses and for enduring our Germanic approach to getting things done.

At Heidelberg University, a number of people gave indispensable assistance at various stages in the preparation of the manuscript: Anton Fromageot, Ozan Emre Akbas, Djordje Mancev, Carmen Wintergerst and Anna Hengge. At the University of Sussex, Paul Grant was as helpful as ever when it came to the financial management of the ESRC grant. Thank you all.

We are also very thankful to the two anonymous reviewers for their constructive and extremely helpful comments on earlier versions of the manuscript as well as to the Cambridge University Press team in New York, Sara Doskow and Joshua Penney, not only for taking our proposal forward but also for their professional guidance throughout the production process.

Finally, and most importantly, we want to thank our spouses, Suli and Abby, for supporting us in everything we do and for enriching our lives in their unique ways. It is to them that we dedicate this volume.

1

Introduction: Rethinking Stateness and Democracy in East Asia

Aurel Croissant and Olli Hellmann

The relationship between stateness and democracy has attracted a great deal of attention in comparative politics. This is related not only to the "historical turn in democratization studies" (Cappocia and Ziblatt, 2010) but also to the improved availability and quality of data with regard to the measurement of democracy and stateness. A similar trend has taken place in the political economy and development economics literature, where, in the late 1980s, the call to "bring the state back in" (Evans et al., 1985) heralded the development of a variety of new research agendas. While political economists have been intensively researching the role of the state in Asia's industrialization and development processes since the 1980s, democratization research on East Asia has so far largely ignored the "state-democracy nexus" (Møller and Skaaning, 2014). In contrast to the prevalence of economic, cultural, and class-based approaches, stateness-related explanations for democracy in the region are exceedingly rare.[1]

This volume examines the relationship of stateness and democracy in East and Southeast Asian nations. Specifically, we focus on polities that introduced democratic structures during the so-called third wave of democratization, which swept much of the world between the mid-1970s and the mid-2000s. The seven case studies represent the full universe of *third wave* democracies in the region. While the first wave of democratization before and after World War I barely touched the shores of Pacific Asia, the second wave that followed World War II and decolonization resulted in only one case of consolidated democracy: Japan. Democracy has thus long been an exception in Asia; instead, the political landscape has historically been dominated by authoritarian systems of government – especially military dictatorships

---

[1] Notable exceptions are Hutchcroft (2000) and Seeberg (2014).

TABLE 1.1. *Three waves of democratization in East and Southeast Asia*

	First Wave	Second Wave	Third Wave
Brunei	–	–	–
Burma/Myanmar		1953–1961	–
Cambodia			1993–1997
China	–	–	–
East Timor			2002–
Indonesia			1999–
Japan	1912–1932 ("Taisho Democracy")	1947–	
Laos	–	–	–
Malaysia	–	–	–
North Korea	–	–	–
Philippines		1946–1972	1986–
Singapore	–	–	–
South Korea	–	–	1988–
Taiwan	–	–	1996–
Thailand	–	1946–1947	1975–1976, 1988–1991, 1992–2006, 2008–2014
Vietnam	–	–	–

Source: Woodall (2018) and the chapters in this volume. Classification as democracy based on the Electoral Democracy Index of the Varieties of Democracy (V-Dem) Project. Only political regimes with an EDI score of 0.45 or higher for at least three consecutive years have been classified as "democratic" in one of the three waves.

and one-party regimes. It was only with the third wave of democratization that a number of authoritarian regimes were replaced with democracies: the Philippines (1986), South Korea (1988), Thailand (1992), Cambodia (1993), and Taiwan (1996). Moreover, in the wake of the 1997 Asian financial crisis, Indonesia (1999) and East Timor (2002) were also swept up by the region's most recent wave of democratization (see Table 1.1).

Nevertheless, while the third wave of democratization was remarkable in its impact and reach, the ensuing reform processes resulted in great variation in terms of political regime outcomes across East Asia. While South Korea and Taiwan are often celebrated as resounding success stories of the third wave of democratization (Diamond, 2016; Hellmann and Templeman in this volume), other democracies such as Indonesia, the Philippines, and East Timor continue to face debilitating challenges – including political polarization, the rapid political mobilization of diverse groups, a deinstitutionalizing role of political leaders, and the failure of democratic structures to respond to growing social demands. In addition, a large number of studies and data from

TABLE 1.2. *Electoral and liberal democracy in East Asia*

	Electoral Democracy Index			Liberal Democracy Index		
	2017	2007	Change	2017	2007	Change
Burma/Myanmar	0.39	0.1	0.29	0.26	0.02	0.24
Cambodia	0.24	0.35	-0.11	0.08	0.15	-0.07
China	0.09	0.1	-0.01	0.06	0.06	0
East Timor	0.72	0.64	0.08	0.51	0.49	0.02
Indonesia	0.63	0.72	-0.09	0.48	0.53	-0.05
Japan	0.83	0.85	-0.02	0.76	0.79	-0.03
Laos	0.09	0.09	0	0.09	0.09	0
Malaysia	0.32	0.33	-0.01	0.21	0.21	0
North Korea	0.09	0.09	0	0.01	0.01	0
Philippines	0.51	0.5	-0.01	0.36	0.38	0.02
Singapore	0.45	0.4	-0.05	0.36	0.32	0.04
South Korea	0.79	0.85	-0.06	0.71	0.77	-0.06
Taiwan	0.8	0.77	-0.03	0.69	0.69	0
Thailand	0.14	0.18	-0.04	0.1	0.19	-0.09
Vietnam	0.26	0.18	0.06	0.19	0.11	0.08

Source: Coppedge et al. (2018). *V-Dem Dataset v8*. V-Dem Project. https://doi.org/10.23696/vdemcy18.

various democracy barometers[2] show that, in most new democracies in East Asia, a persistent gap exists between the electoral components of democracy – or what Robert A. Dahl (1971) terms *polyarchy* – on the one hand, and the enforcement of civil liberties, judicial independence, and horizontal accountability, which represents the *liberal* aspect in the concept of liberal democracy, on the other hand (Shin and Tusalem, 2009; Croissant and Bünte, 2011). Moreover, with the exception of Taiwan, the quality of (liberal) democracy seems to be eroding (see Table 1.2).

The extent of erosion varies from country to county, but overall, the data suggests that East Asia has joined the global wave of democratic backsliding (Lührmann et al., 2018). The clearest examples of this alarming trend are the cases of Cambodia and Thailand. In both countries, already-defective democracies were subjected to full autocratic reversal and replaced by authoritarian regimes (see Chapter 5 by Chambers and Chapter 6 by Un in this volume).

This trend of democratic erosion still has momentum in Asia, despite the fact that, more recently, a number of autocratic regimes in the region appear to have embarked on processes of political liberalization. In Malaysia, an alliance

---

[2] Such as Freedom House (www.freedomhouse.org), the Economist Intelligence Unit (www.eiu.com/public/topical_report.aspx?campaignid=Democracy0814), the Bertelsmann Transformation Index (www.bti-project.org/en/home/), and the Varieties of Democracy (V-Dem) dataset (www.v-dem.net/en/data/data-version-8/).

of opposition parties won a historic election victory in the general elections of May 2018 and toppled the *Barisan Nasional* (National Front) coalition, which had been in power since 1957. In Myanmar, the military (*Tatmadaw*) initiated a process of gradual disengagement from day-to-day politics that led to the election of a civilian government in 2015. This process of military-controlled reform "should not be understood simply as an exit strategy by the military to retreat from national politics" (Hung, 2012: 2); instead, the ratification of a new constitution, together with the disbanding of the military junta and the organization of reasonably free elections in November 2015, constitute remarkable achievements in a long process of transition from direct military rule toward "something else" (Croissant, 2015). Still, at the time of preparing this volume, it was too early to assess the direction and magnitude of political reforms in Malaysia and Myanmar and judge whether the end of autocratic rule would give way to democratic regimes, thereby balancing the trend of democratic decline.

In short, the third wave of democratization produced three different types of regime outcomes in East and Southeast Asia: consolidated democracies, defective democracies, and autocratic backsliders. Moreover, and of crucial importance for a systematic analysis of the state-democracy nexus, the seven cases with which the contributions in this volume are concerned exhibit a remarkable variation in the degree of stateness. To begin with, Cambodia and East Timor experienced simultaneous state-building and democratization as part of post-conflict reconstruction under the authority of United Nations (UN) interim administrations. Nonetheless, they are often considered *weak* states that display very little capacity to regulate social and economic relations. At the other end of the spectrum, we find Taiwan and South Korea: both represent *strong* and high-capacity states and seem to add credence to the *stateness first* argument (Wilson, 2018), which maintains that positive political development is more likely when effective state institutions had been put in place prior to democratization.

However, for reasons that we elaborate in this volume, the Asian experience challenges some of the key tenets of the prominent *sequencing* approach to the state-democracy nexus and *stateness first* arguments more specifically. As the cases studies in this volume demonstrate, there is no linear or clear-cut relationship between levels of stateness, on the one hand, and the robustness or *quality* of democracy, on the other. Certainly, South Korea and Taiwan rank high in terms of both the strength of their states and the qualities of their democracies, while Cambodia combines a weak state with weak democratic structures. However, as the respective contributions in this volume show, existing state-democracy theories struggle to account for specific mechanisms beyond this broad comparative pattern: Why do democracies in South Korea and Taiwan continue to suffer from path-dependent impairments? Why did autocratic reversal in Cambodia unfold in the time and the way that it did? Even more damningly, the "stronger states facilitate democratization" argument collapses completely when the focus is widened beyond these three cases. For example, despite the fact that both Indonesia and Thailand

Introduction: Rethinking Stateness and Democracy in East Asia

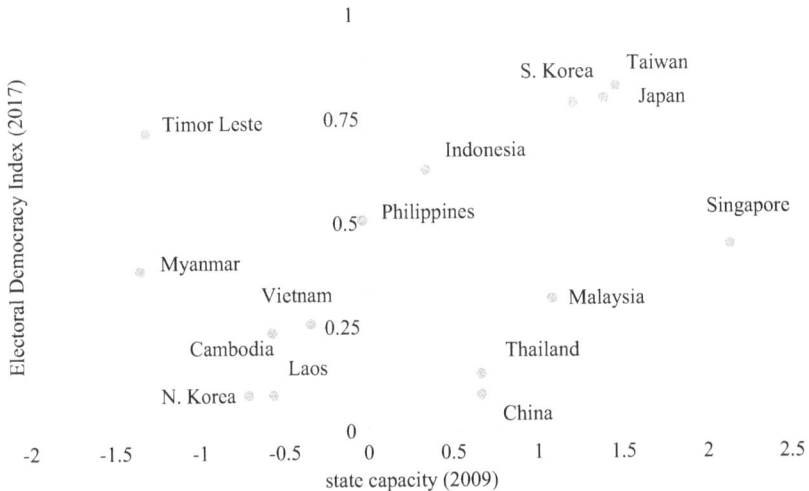

FIGURE 1.1. Electoral democracy and state capacity in East and Southeast Asia.
Source: Electoral Democracy Index of the V-Dem Project and State Capacity Index (Hanson and Sigman, 2013). Higher scores indicate higher levels of electoral democracy/ state capacity.

exhibit medium-level state capacity, the two political systems differ markedly in terms of their institutional features: whereas democratic structures have endured in Indonesia, they have collapsed in Thailand. Similarly, while both the Philippines and East Timor struggle with anemic state capacity, the quality of democracy diverges significantly: the Philippines have, under the presidency of Rodrigo Duterte (elected in 2016), witnessed a dismantling of key democratic institutions and a trend toward regime hybridization; East Timor, in contrast, is regularly ranked as the top Southeast Asian country in most democracy barometers (see also Figure 1.1).

THE AIM OF THIS VOLUME

This variation calls for explanations and makes Asia an excellent region for studying the complex relationship of stateness and democracy. Specifically, we will approach the state-democracy nexus in East Asia from two complementary perspectives: while the first one is focused on the impact of state-building on the development of post-authoritarian democracies, the second considers the effect of democratic reforms on the state's infrastructural power and state-society relations. As explained in more detail in the remainder of this chapter, the resulting dual focus allows us to make at least four distinct contributions to the literature.

First, through a set of qualitative case studies, our volume addresses three weaknesses in existing research on the state-democracy nexus: (1) Up until now, the relevant academic literature has dealt mostly with the question of how stateness and state capacity affect the likelihood that the breakdown of autocratic rule will result in consolidated democracy; we know much less about how the installment of democratic structures affects the subsequent development of stateness. (2) Existing work on the state-democracy nexus, especially the *stateness first* strand of the literature, makes the mistake of applying the mechanism drawn from the historical experience of first wave democracies in Europe and North America to third wave democracies in non-Western regions. (3) Attempts to test arguments about the state-democracy nexus through quantitative means are fraught with problems of measurement.

Second, by disaggregating the multidimensional concepts of stateness and democracy into a number of different components or *partial regimes* (Schmitter, 1995), the case studies in this volume are able to make more nuanced arguments about how different elements of stateness affect different facets of democracy.

Third, our own argument on the relationship between stateness and the quality of democracy places particular focus on the relationship between the state and particularistic networks and the distribution of power between particularistic networks. We broadly agree with the sequentialist approach that the chances of democratic consolidation are greatest in new democracies where the state – because of its infrastructural properties – has a strong ability to fend off particularistic demands. However, we go beyond the sequentialist approach to show that political systems characterized by lower levels of state autonomy can develop into electoral democracies, depending on the systemic properties of particularistic networks.

Fourth, taken together, our case studies show that stateness does not exert a linear effect on the quality of democracy. The reasons include not only the properties of particularistic networks – as an intervening factor – but also path-dependent effects and mechanisms of circular causality. The case study approach chosen in this volume is particularly appropriate because it allows the researcher to accommodate bidirectional and reverse causalities.

The rest of this chapter proceeds with two sections that discuss the meaning and content of the key theoretical concepts of this study: stateness, state capacity, and democracy. Next, we identify the primary strands in the literature on the stateness-democracy nexus before we lay out our own argument. The final section presents an overview of the rest of the volume.

STATENESS AND STATE CAPACITY

There is well-established, rich literature in social science on how to define the state. Other core concepts in the state-building literature, such as state capacity and stateness, are of more recent origin. In *Politics as Vocation*, Max Weber famously defined the state as "a human community that (successfully) claims the monopoly of the legitimate use of physical force within a given territory" (Weber, 1992: 158–59). While the empirical realities to which the terms *state* and *political regime* refer to are tightly interwoven, they constitute conceptually distinct concepts: whereas a political regime concerns the access to and exercise of political power, the state provides political power holders with an instrument to implement policies and other interventions. The state "is a (normally) more permanent structure of domination and coordination including a coercive apparatus and the means to administer a society and extract resources from it" (Fishman, 1990: 428), whereas a political regime "designates the institutionalized set of fundamental formal and informal rules identifying the political power holders [and] regulates the appointments to the main political posts [...] as well as the [...] limitations on the exercise of political power" (Skaaning, 2006: 15).

While fundamentally shaped by this Weberian understanding of the state, empirical studies differ in what exactly constitutes stateness. Without fully entering the theoretical debate, we can establish that the literature on the stateness-democracy nexus typically highlights three key components or dimensions of stateness (cf. Linz and Stepan, 1996; Andersen et al., 2014; Carbone and Memoli, 2015; Andersen, 2017): (1) political order and the monopoly on violence; (2) basic administration and administrative effectiveness; and (3) the dimension of citizenship agreement – that is, the attachment of citizens to the state. The first component refers to the core of the Weberian definition of the state as the source of legitimate physical force and the monopoly over the means of violence within a given territory. The second constitutive dimension concerns the presence of a basic infrastructure for the exercise of state power, or a "usable bureaucracy" (Linz and Stepan, 1996: 11). The third dimension refers to the extent to which the members of a political community are attached to the state as the legitimate public authority and agree about citizenship.

The concepts of stateness and state capacity overlap to some extent; however, the latter concept is more specific and concerns the ability of state institutions to implement official goals and policies (Skocpol, 1985: 8). It is related, in particular, to the projection of state authority over the national territory and the administrative dimension of stateness. But since many scholars assume state capacity "to require a degree of legitimacy and trust in state institutions" (Carbone and Memoli, 2015: 7), state capacity is also connected to the third constitutive dimension of stateness.

In order to operationalize a state's capacity to implement official policy goals, scholars propose a broad range of criteria and indicators. Based on the existing literature and inspired by Michael Mann's typology of state powers (Mann, 1984), we distinguish three forms of state capacity: coercive, administrative (the quality of the bureaucracy), and the state's social embedding.[3]

---

[3] A fourth capacity is a state's ability to raise revenues (extractive capacity). While extractive capacity is essential for funding state activities of all types, it is highly dependent on the ability of the state to enforce its monopoly on the use of force over a population/territory and the capacity to gather and maintain information, which depends on the presence of administrative agents to carry out these functions ably (Hanson, 2018).

The three capacities overlap but are not identical to Michael Mann's typology of state power.[4]

Coercive capacity refers to the state's ability to maintain the monopoly over the legitimate use of force, including both the ability to maintain order within the borders of the state and to defend the territory against external threats. Of course, coercive capacity is not a "binary, on-off condition" (Fukuyama, 2014: 1329). Instead, the extent to which a state is able to provide security to its population can be measured as a continuous variable that ranges from near-absolute security to the complete breakdown of state authority. In authoritarian regimes, in particular, the state's coercive capacity is frequently used to suppress civil and political opposition and can be an important tool to compensate for lacking administrative capacities and weak social embedding (Seeberg, 2014; White, 2018).

Administrative capacity is broadly defined as "the ability to develop policy, […] to produce and deliver public goods and services and […] to regulate commercial activity" (Hanson and Sigman, 2013: 4). Similar to coercive capacity is the scalar concept, indicating the degree to which public state organizations are governed by meritocratic recruitment and formally institutionalized rules, rather than by forms of particularism, such as corruption, clientelism, nepotism, cronyism, or patronage (Hanson, 2018). It indicates whether a state sits closer toward the legal-rational type or the patrimonial type in Weber's framework of legitimate authority. As Andersen et al. (2014: 1208) note, coercive and administrative capacities are closely related, as states seldom exhibit strong administrative capacity without also having the capacity to exercise a monopoly on violence (see also Fortin-Rittberger, 2014: 1245).

The capacity of the state is not just a function of the state's institutional properties. The ability of the state to implement official policies also depends on the degree of citizenship agreement, or put differently, the extent to which citizens accept the state's exercise of political power as legitimate. The state can derive legitimacy from a number of sources, including economic performance, social factors (such as ethnic homogeneity) and the design of participatory processes (see Gilley, 2009). What matters more for the discussion here, however, is that – once the state has achieved a certain level of legitimacy, citizens will support the state's action on a quasi-voluntary basis, thus boosting public organizations' capacity to implement policy goals (Uslaner and Rothstein, 2016: 240). In contrast, when the state lacks legitimacy, citizens will be incentivized to evade the control of the state – for example, by refusing to pay taxes (Bräutigam, 2008) or by participating in the informal rather than the formal economy (Rothstein and Teorell, 2008: 165–66). In short, low levels of citizen agreement undermine the state's capacity to enforce official laws and regulations.

---

[4] According to Mann, *despotic* power refers to the "range of actions which the elite is empowered to undertake without routine, institutionalized negotiation with civil society groups," whereas infrastructural power highlights the state's capacity to "penetrate civil society and to implement logistically political decisions throughout the realm" (Mann, 1984: 88).

While this three-component framework doubtlessly covers key aspects of stateness, we believe that the existing literature on the state-democracy nexus has neglected *the role of informal institutions and networks in shaping state capacity*. To a large extent, this has to do with the fact that informal political structures are difficult to measure quantitatively, thus making them unavailable for statistical inquiry. As will be discussed in more detail in the following section, it is precisely large-N research designs that have dominated existing work on the state-democracy nexus.

To begin with, states that score high on quantitative capacity measures can get hijacked by informal, particularistic networks. For example, if we apply the most common indicator of coercive capacity (armed forces personnel per capita), Myanmar ranks very high in global comparison. However, what this obscures is that military units have often been *privatized* by high-ranking military officers, who employ this supposedly public organization to further their own private goals (e.g. Holliday, 2012: 68). Similarly, South Korea's high-capacity *developmental state*, was – during military rule (1963–1988) – under firm control of informal networks between political and business elites, which were employed to organize the distribution of public loans in exchange for kickbacks and bribes (e.g. Kang, 2002; also see Chapter 3 by Hellmann in this volume). In other words, as in the case of Myanmar, infrastructurally strong state organizations were misused to facilitate self-interested predatory practices.

Conversely, just because a state is infrastructurally weak does not mean that political elites do not possess the ability to deliver public goods. As a growing body of literature shows, informal networks, depending on their organization and resources, may possess the capability to perform functions that we usually associate with the state. For instance, academic work on neopatrimonialism shows that centralized patron-client networks can help to *buy* peace and thus provide security to the population (Le Billon, 2003). Meanwhile, the so-called "Asian puzzle" literature demonstrates that many autocratic regimes in Southeast Asia successfully coordinated industrial development without a high-capacity *developmental state* at their disposal. Instead, scholars highlight how specific configurations of particularistic networks not only incentivized political elites to pursue developmental goals but also boosted their ability to implement growth-enhancing policies (e.g. MacIntyre, 2000; Rock and Bonnett, 2004). Likewise, there is evidence that particularistic networks can be used to secure the agreement of social groups regarding the question of citizenship – for example, by co-opting community leaders into distributive arrangements (e.g. Kimenyi, 2006).

As will be explained in more detail in this chapter, we argue that these informal aspects of state-society relations matter to explain why there is no linear relationship between stateness and the quality of democracy: not only do states differ in their ability to fend off hijacking attempts by particularistic networks, which is largely a function of their infrastructural power, but particularistic networks also display differences in their organizational and relational properties.

DEMOCRACY AND ITS PARTIAL REGIMES

The age-old political science debate on what democracy is or should mean fills more than one library. For the purpose of this volume, it is sufficient to acknowledge that, despite the nature of democracy as an "essentially contested concept" (Collier et al., 2006), actual empirical research on democratization and the quality of democracy relies on a procedural understanding of democracy (Diamond and Morlino, 2006; Munck, 2016). Still, the debate is whether a minimal and essentially electoral understanding of democracy (*polyarchy*; cf. Dahl, 1971) is sufficient or whether democracy should also include the presence of more substantial elements such as the rule of law and constitutionalism (Diamond, 1999, 2008; Diamond and Morlino, 2006; Merkel, 2004).

Our approach rests on the assumption that a minimal, electoral conception of democracy will not suffice for the study of the relationship between state-building and democracy. What do we really *know* when we *know* that Taiwan and the Philippines or Indonesia and South Korea are all democracies despite evident differences in the integrity of elections, effectiveness of civil liberties or levels of political participation, not to mention the strength (or weakness) of the rule of law in these countries? Furthermore, the global spread of democracy in the last quarter of the twentieth century has not been a triumph of democratic liberalism but of an often quite *illiberal* electoralism (Zakaria, 1997). Even before the recent debate about the backsliding of democracies (Lührmann et al., 2018), it had become clear that many transitions from authoritarian rule in the third wave were stuck in a gray zone between (minimal) democracy and (open) autocracy (Carothers, 2002).

The case studies in this volume adopt the model of "embedded democracy" developed by Wolfgang Merkel and his coauthors (Merkel and Croissant, 2000; Merkel, 2004; Croissant and Merkel, 2019). It systematizes the relationship between the different partial regimes of liberal democracy in order to distinguish it from the various types of less-than-liberal forms of democracy and autocratic rule. Embedded democracy, as a root concept of democracy, thereby includes the necessary components of a liberal democracy. Defective democracies, on the other hand, are political regimes that fulfil some, but not all, of the criteria of this root concept (Croissant and Merkel, 2019). According to the concept of embedded democracy, a contemporary democracy is akin to an institutional superstructure, being composed of highly complex yet additive *partial regimes* (Schmitter, 1995). The partial regimes themselves are as follows (see Figure 1.2).

A. The *electoral regime* is the central piece among the five partial regimes, and it operates by filling the principal state power positions through regular, free, general, equal, and fair elections. Such a regime fulfils the minimal requirements for electoral democracy.
B. The *political rights* regime facilitates the democratic right to political communication and organization by entitling people to free speech/opinion as well as free association, demonstration, and petition. It also

Introduction: Rethinking Stateness and Democracy in East Asia

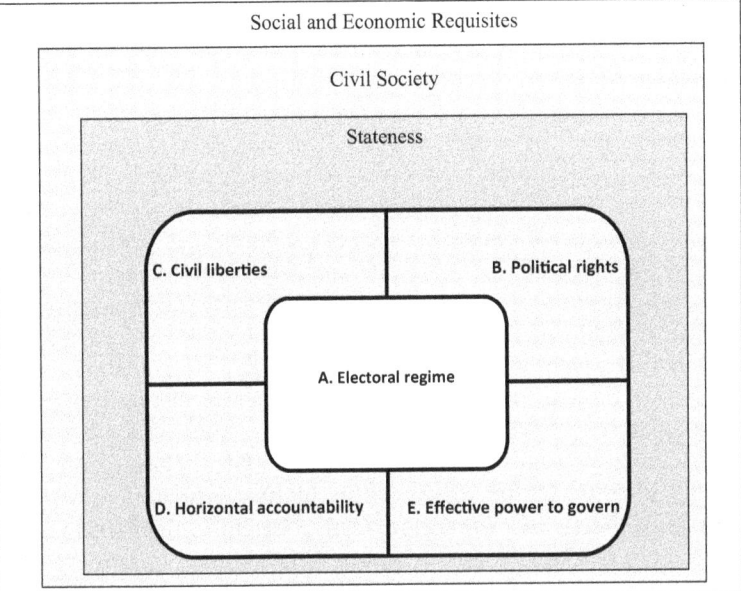

FIGURE 1.2. The partial regimes of embedded democracy.
Source: Adapted from Merkel (2004: 37).

includes freedom of the press and the free formation of interest groups and democratic political parties.

C. The *civil liberties* regime functions through the democratic requirement of the rule of law. The rule of law guarantees constitutional rights to protect the individual from state infringements on his/her rights. Moreover, there must be constitutional equality under the law and independent courts.

D. The partial regime of *horizontal accountability* emphasizes the need for the executive, legislative, and judicial branches to engage in mutual checks and balances, without one body dominating or interfering with the constitutionally defined core sphere of the other bodies. As such, horizontal accountability is a key ingredient of liberal democracy: it buttresses constitutionalism, legality and the deliberative process.

E. Lastly, *the effective power to govern*, "stresses[es] the necessity that the elected representatives are the ones which actually govern" (Merkel, 2004). This regime encompasses the requirement that militaries, both formally and actually, obey the orders of civilian governments. It is essential in a democracy that popularly elected representatives, rather than appointed bureaucrats, control the ultimate levers of power.

These analytically distinct sets of norms, rules, and practices interact with each other, with each partial regime mutually influencing and balancing the functions and effects of the other partial regimes. Yet, the *partial regimes* are only fully functional if they are mutually embedded (Croissant and Merkel, 2019). Furthermore, the model embeds these five partial regimes in a wider context, arguing that the different layers of the external embedding "represent the conditions of possibility and impossibility that raise or lower the quality of a liberal democracy" (Merkel, 2004: 44). The most important components of democracy's embeddedness are the socioeconomic context, civil society, and stateness. Although Merkel et al. note that *stateness* is a prerequisite for democracy, they do not explain how much stateness democracy requires and how exactly differences in state capacity affect the robustness and functioning of any of its partial regimes. In this regard, Møller and Skaaning demonstrate that whether stateness is a necessary condition for democracy depends on the conception of democracy: while it is neither a logical prior step to democratization nor a necessary precondition for minimalist democracy, for thicker conceptions of democracy (liberal instead of electoral democracy), the stateness criteria are perhaps more demanding (Møller and Skaaning, 2011b: 99).

STATENESS AND DEMOCRACY: RESEARCH DIRECTIONS

The relationship between stateness and democracy is complex. Scholars have tried to cut through this complexity from two different directions: (1) from the perspective of the state-building literature and (2) from the perspective of the democratization literature.

Within the state-building literature, two opposing arguments have emerged regarding the state-democracy nexus. Essentially, scholars cannot agree on whether state-building is possible under democratic conditions: whereas *nexians* (Vu in this volume) argue that democracy creates incentives for political elites to strengthen the capacity of state institutions, *stateness first* arguments (Wilson, 2018) are based on the assumption that state-building is harder to achieve under democratic rules and that authoritarian regimes are better able to develop state institutions. As Fukuyama (2014) prominently argues, the introduction of democracy in a context where an effective state does not yet exist risks engendering clientelistic practices in which political contenders offer government positions and rents in exchange for votes. Similarly, D'Arcy and Nistotskaya (2017) maintain that the installment of democracy will lock states into the predemocratic level of state capacity, meaning that state-building should come before democratization.

Since stateness is a variable that influences the stability and inner workings of every type of political regime (Snyder, 2006: 222–24), scholars within the democratization literature have approached the state-democracy nexus with different research questions in mind. Some scholars have explored whether lower levels of state capacity make the *introduction* of democracy more likely, or put differently, whether higher levels of state capacity increase the resilience and durability of autocratic regimes (Way, 2006; Slater and Fenner, 2011; Seeberg, 2014; Van Ham and Seim, 2018). Another group of scholars has investigated whether, once democratic elections have been introduced, the further *deepening* of democracy depends on the level of stateness (e.g. Rose and Shin, 2001; Bratton and Chang, 2006; Møller and Skaaning, 2011a, 2011b). This body of academic work – termed *sequentialism* by Carothers (2007) – is consistent in its findings: strong stateness and a high level of state capacity are necessary conditions for higher-quality democracy to emerge. In other words, sequencers arrive at the same prescriptive conclusion as the *stateness first* proponents in the state-building literature: state-building should come before democratization (Andersen et al., 2014). However, the sequentialist argument suffers from three important problems.

First, the argument is often based on a few historical cases and a contestable reading of the historical sequence of state-building and democratization in Northwest Europe (see Møller and Skaaning, 2011b; Wilson, 2018). As Møller (2018) notes, the medieval institution of self-government and self-organization in Europe resulted in a *bottom-up* process of state-building that did not occur in other regions. On the one hand, "involvement of the communal groups increased infrastructural power while it limited despotic power" (Møller, 2018: 309), while the state, on the other hand, could incorporate the existing communal structures. In the end, protest by social groups against the centralization of power led to a more efficient and more centralized state than in other regions. *Bottom-up* state-building fostered a system of checks and balances with a high degree of institutional diffusion, ending in the modern, law-bound, and democratic European state (Møller, 2015: 112). In contrast, in Asia and other non-Western regions, state-building after World War II was a *top-down* process. Sometimes, *top-down* state-building resulted in high coercive capacities of the state, either because independence had to be achieved through revolutionary struggle, or because new nations were challenged by communal and/or class-based insurgencies. In such a scenario, militaries played a prominent role in suppressing internal unrest. Consequently, countries such as Indonesia, Burma, Laos, Cambodia, and South Korea (in the 1950s) ended up with coercive but administratively weak states and fragile political institutions (Croissant, 2018). Such developments created the impression that the failure of state-building was a key reason for the failure of democracy in many emerging nations in Africa and Asia during the 1950s and 1960s. However, it is anything but clear whether weak states did contribute to the failure of democracy or whether the lack of inclusion of communal groups and democratic practices impaired state-building.

Second, sequencers and proponents of the *stateness first* thesis tend to neglect the role of "democracy as a state-building mechanism" (Carbone, 2015). That is to say, to some extent – "things may work backward," as the implementation of democratic elections may foster state-building, which in turn can contribute to the deepening of democracy (Mazucca and Munck, 2014). For example,

Carbone and Memoli (2015: 21) show that the extent to which a country's political system is democratized is indeed a key variable in explaining progress toward state consolidation: more democratic countries are more likely to develop stronger and more effective states. Their work suggests that democracy can contribute to stronger stateness through mechanisms of political and social inclusion, political competition and accountability, and electoral institution-building.

Third, it is not easy to quantitatively test sequentialist or *stateness first* arguments. Small contingent events and the timing of events can exert long-lasting effects on future trajectories and forms of political institutions. To account for those factors, contextualized knowledge and a focus on causal processes rather than causal effects are required (Wilson, 2018). To balance the large number of quantitative studies in the literature on state-building and democratization, this volume follows the case study approach, which, we believe, is particularly appropriate to further our understanding of the state-democracy nexus because it allows the researcher to accommodate bidirectional and reverse causalities in state-building and democratization.

CONCEPTUALIZING THE RELATIONSHIP OF STATENESS AND DEMOCRACY IN ASIA

The dominant sequentialist approach assumes a linear relationship between stateness and democratic quality: the higher the degree of stateness, the more likely that new democracies consolidate political reforms and reach a higher level of democratic quality. However, as we just highlighted, this approach suffers from a number of theoretical and methodological weakness. And, in fact, the sequentialist model does not go very far in explaining differing levels of democracy in East Asia. Certainly, the two political systems with the highest-capacity states – South Korea and Taiwan – are the two new democracies in the region that have advanced furthest on the path of democratic consolidation (cf. also Figure 1.1). Yet, beyond these two cases, the sequentialist approach offers very little insight into the stateness-democracy nexus. In particular, sequentialists fail to offer an explanation as to why, from a cluster of four political systems with similar levels of state capacity, two developed into minimal electoral democracies (the Philippines and Indonesia), while the other two lapsed back into authoritarian rule (Thailand and Cambodia). Similarly puzzling, East Timor is characterized by a lower-quality state than Thailand or Cambodia but a better level of democracy compared to the Philippines and Indonesia. In short, the relationship between stateness and democratic quality is much less clear-cut than assumed by the sequentialist approach.

We argue that complexity arises due to how informal institutions and networks structure state-society relations. This occurs on two dimensions: (1) the extent to which the state is autonomous from particularistic demands and (2) the organizational and systemic properties of informal networks competing over access to the state's resources.

We concur with the sequentialist approach that coercive capacity, administrative capacity, and citizen agreement are important factors in the consolidation of new democracies. Without a certain level of infrastructural power and legitimacy, the state and its organizational entities will not be able to properly enforce the laws and institutions that constitute democracy's partial regimes. Moreover, we agree that, as the process of state-building – that is, the process by which the state's capacity to implement public policies is increased – progresses, the role of informal networks and institutions will decrease vis-à-vis formal organizations and institutions (also see North et al., 2009; Mungiu-Pippidi, 2015; Rueschemeyer, 2005). However, while we acknowledge that state capacity facilitates the consolidation of new democracies, we do not assume a linear relationship between state capacity and the quality of democracy – for four reasons.

First, particularistic networks can also play an important role in political systems that feature a high-capacity state. In the East Asian context, scholars have, for example, put the focus on cartel-like networks that connect political and business elites in South Korea (e.g. Johnston, 2008) and highlighted the mobilizational capabilities of local factions in Taiwan (e.g. Bosco, 1992).

Second, the introduction of free and fair elections can strengthen these networks versus formal state organizations. In South Korea, the increase in campaign finance demand meant that particularistic relationships between politicians and business came to assume more importance than under autocratic rule (e.g. Kang, 2002). Similarly, in Taiwan, the *Kuomintang* (KMT) – being exposed to increased electoral competition from opposition parties – strengthened its connections with local factions, thereby elevating the latter to key-player status in post-autocratic politics (e.g. Wu, 2003). In both cases, this had, at least in the earlier stages of the democratization process, negative implications for the functioning of the *electoral regime* (partial regime A): in South Korea, electoral competition was skewed heavily toward those politicians who were able to secure illegal campaign funding from business; in Taiwan, clientelistic benefits distributed to voters through local factions not only gave the KMT a significant advantage over opposition parties but also perverted the vertical accountability mechanism built into elections. Put differently, there is a case to be made for circular causality, as democratization may undermine state capacity, which in turn may negatively affect the functioning of democracy.

Third, the process of state-building under autocratic rule can have long-term path-dependent effects. For example, as Chapter 3 on South Korea in this volume shows, the military regime made no investments in mediating organizations between state and society when constructing the *developmental state*. As a result, South Korean democracy – still to this day – continues to be plagued by problems of consolidation: while the inchoate nature of the party system means that *horizontal accountability* (partial regime D) is stymied, the organizational weakness of interest groups regularly forces *civil society* to resort to undemocratic means to further its goals.

Fourth, the stateness-democracy nexus is further complicated by differences in how particularistic networks are organized at the systemic level. Following the literature on informal governance, it is possible to distinguish political systems based on whether the horizontal distribution of power between networks is concentrated or fragmented (also see Khan, 2010). We argue that these differences help to explain why countries with similar levels of state capacity took different paths of political trajectories, either developing into electoral democracies (the Philippines, Indonesia, and East Timor) or slipping back into autocratic rule (Thailand and Cambodia). In the latter, power between networks is unevenly distributed and the structure of the dominant network largely overlaps with hierarchies in formal organizations – the military and the Cambodian People's Party (CPP), respectively. As the chapters by Chambers and Un in this volume show, these centralized networks reach into every corner of the state and allowed elites to coordinate a return to non-democratic forms of governance. Both the Thai and the Cambodian state display characteristic features of what Reno calls the *shadow state*, defined as an informal state that "is constructed behind the facade of laws and government institutions" and in which "authority that is based upon the decisions and interests of an individual, not a set of written laws and procedures, even though these formal aspects of government may exist" (2000: 434). In the Philippines, Indonesia, and East Timor, in contrast, the distribution of power between networks is considerably more fragmented. In such a context, *elections* (partial regime A) serve as an institutionalized mechanism to govern the competition between particularistic networks. As Case argues about the introduction of elections under US colonial rule in the Philippines, local elites "discovered these procedures could be operated in ways that met their interests, enabling them peacefully to share access to state positions and resources" (2002: 213–14). While the electoral regime, given the elites' shared interest in ensuring political competitiveness, may function relatively well, the same cannot be said about the partial regimes of *civil liberties* (C) and *horizontal accountability* (D). This has to do with the fact that, to maximize their predatory yield, particularistic networks will seek to weaken the rule of law as well as constitutional checks on their rent-seeking activities. Strategies that help to 'switch off' partial regimes C and D include patron-clientelism, patronage, and intimidation (e.g. Rogers, 2004; Tomsa, 2015).

To sum up, we agree with the sequentialist approach that coercive capacity, administrative capacity, and citizenship agreement are important factors that shape the process of democratic consolidation. However, as briefly outlined in this section, these three dimensions are not sufficient to fully elucidate the stateness-democracy nexus in East Asia. Instead, we argue that analyses need to pay closer attention to relationships between the state and particularistic networks and the distribution of power between particularistic networks. These features of state capacity are difficult to measure quantitatively and thus call for a qualitative case study design.

Introduction: Rethinking Stateness and Democracy in East Asia   17

OVERVIEW OF THE VOLUME

The rest of this book comprises a comparative historical analysis, seven country case studies, and a concluding chapter that compares our findings with the developing world as a whole. In selecting the sample for the case studies, we chose countries in East and Southeast Asia according to two simple selection rules: first, we limited inclusion in the sample to those cases that had made the transition from authoritarianism to democracy during the so-called third wave of democratization. Consequently, our sample does not include Japan, which became a democracy after World War II (see Table 1.2). Second, since we are also interested in the impact of democratization on stateness and state capacity, we excluded from the sample those countries that did not experience a transition to democracy during the time frame of the third wave of democratization.

In Chapter 2, Tuong Vu provides a fundamental review of the different sides of the state-democracy debate: the *sequencers* (stateness first, then democracy) and the *nexians* (democracy can benefit state-building *at any level* of political development). From a comparative historical analysis of state-building and democracy in East Asia's three waves of democratization, his chapter draws four conclusions. First, Vu shows that sequencers may be somewhat naïve in their arguments: in many cases, state-building under autocratic rule strengthened nondemocratic government and impeded transitions to democracy. Second, historical evidence from Asia shows that, in line with nexian arguments, democratization can aid state-building – not only when embedded in negotiated peace settlements and internationally supported post-conflict peace-building projects but also when societies are confronted with deep and persistent communal conflicts. Third, however, Vu also demonstrates that the robustness of democracy in such contexts is largely a function of foreign involvement and is thus likely to decline when international support is withdrawn. Fourth, Vu notes that the choice on how to sequence state-building and democratization is largely theoretical. East Asian history suggests that, in reality, these sequences are largely shaped by global economic and political pressures.

The seven country case studies are organized into three blocks, reflecting the different regime outcomes of the third wave of democratization: the first block focuses on East Asia's consolidated democracies (South Korea and Taiwan), the second block discusses cases of autocratic reversal (Thailand and Cambodia), and the third block places the focus on defective democracies (the Philippines, Indonesia, and East Timor).

The cases of South Korea (Chapter 3) and Taiwan (Chapter 4) – analyzed by Olli Hellmann and Kharis Templeman, respectively – share much in common. Both political systems feature high-capacity *developmental* states and comparatively well-consolidated democracies. At first glance, the two cases seem to support *stateness first* arguments – in fact, the two case studies show that the state's infrastructural power and legitimacy played an important role in enforcing key democratic processes and institutions. However, both Hellmann and Templeman also highlight that the democratic regimes continue to be challenged by persistent path-dependent problems: while South Korea's democracy displays deficits in partial regime D (horizontal accountability) and the development of civil society, Taiwan's democracy is hampered by issues relating to the enforcement of civil liberties (partial regime C) as well as horizontal accountability. As both case studies explain, these path-dependent defects can be traced back to the process of state-building under autocratic rule: in South Korea, state-building was achieved through repressive means, while in Taiwan, state-building was strongly intertwined with the KMT's party-building efforts. This means that the outgoing autocratic regimes left contrasting legacies: an under-institutionalized party system in South Korea and an unevenly institutionalized party system in Taiwan – with important consequences for the consolidation of democracy. In short, the cases of South Korea and Taiwan demonstrate that a high level of stateness is by no means a sufficient condition for successful democratic consolidation.

In addition, both Hellmann and Templeman reveal that the introduction of free and fair elections initially triggered a decline in state capacity, mainly because the sudden jump in electoral competition strengthened incentives for politicians and parties to engage in corruption and other particularistic activities. Yet, after a phase of maturation, democratic institutions – as the nexian approach would have predicted – strengthened the state's ability to fend off particularistic demands from political elites. That is to say, the cases of South Korea and Taiwan make it clear that the relationship between stateness and democracy needs to be understood in cyclical, not linear, terms.

The finding that stateness is not a sufficient condition for positive democratic development is further corroborated by the case of Thailand (Chapter 5): as Paul Chambers outlines, Thailand experienced autocratic reversal despite the fact that the state exhibits similar levels of infrastructural power as Taiwan's developmental state. To explain this puzzle, Chambers highlights the role of the *parallel state* – a tight informal network that connects military, bureaucratic, and monarchic elites. This network, as Chambers explains, has provided conservative actors with the administrative, coercive, and symbolic power to overthrow electoral democracy – whenever they felt that their interests were threatened by elected governments, such as in 1991, 2006, and 2014.

Interestingly, Kheang Un puts forward a similar argument to explain the breakdown of Cambodia's democratic regime (Chapter 6). Un claims that, irrespective of the introduction of democratic political institutions in 1993 under the auspices of the international community, the Cambodian state continues to be subject to a neopatrimonial logic: political power is not equated with formal positions of authority but is, instead, determined by informal patron-client relationships, control over which is monopolized by the leadership of the CPP and Prime Minister Hun Sen. Not only has neopatrimonialism created an unlevel playing field in the electoral arena, but it has also allowed Hun Sen and the CPP to orchestrate a creeping return to authoritarian rule, in particular because the neopatrimonial state has politicized public organizations tasked with enforcing democracy's partial regimes, such as the civil service, law enforcement agencies, and the judiciary.

The evidence from Thailand and Cambodia suggests that informal networks – if they are organized in a centralized fashion and control strategically relevant resources – can be deployed by nondemocratic elites to hijack key democratic institutions and implement processes of autocratization. As the Thai case evidences, this mechanism of autocratic reversal can even be observed in the political contexts of high state capacity. Put differently, a strong state does not guarantee the democratization of a political system.

East Asia's cases of defective democracy, on the other hand, throw up a different question entirely: How much stateness is required for democracy to survive? Importantly, all three cases – the Philippines, Indonesia, and East Timor – display the same pattern of democratic consolidation: while partial regime A (elections) and partial regime B (political rights) function relatively well, democracy's other partial regimes – in particular, partial regime C (civil rights) and partial regime D (horizontal accountability) – are severely impaired. All three political systems, while not meeting the requirements of embedded democracy, can thus be classified as Schumpeterian minimalist democracies. What is striking is that such democratic regimes appear to be compatible with a broad range of states. The case of East Timor (Chapter 9), in particular, presents a puzzling case for *stateness first* theories. As Aurel Croissant and Rebecca Abu Sharkh show, Asia's youngest sovereign nation displays an unusual combination of fragile stateness and a relatively well-developed and robust democracy. States in the Philippines (Chapter 7) and Indonesia (Chapter 8), meanwhile, are stronger; however, they are still a far cry from the high-capacity developmental states of South Korea and Taiwan.

The organization of particularistic networks at the systemic level can help explain the resilience of minimalist democracy under conditions of low state capacity, as in the Philippines. In contrast to Thailand and Cambodia, control over particularistic networks is more fragmented, with networks competing against each other for access to the state's resources: family clans in the Philippines, henchmen of the former Suharto regime in Indonesia, and guerrilla command structures in East Timor. To prevent a monopolized control over rent-seeking opportunities, elites have institutionalized systems of minimalist democracy that provide competition over access to public office (partial regimes A and B) but do not impose strong constraints on predatory behaviour (partial regimes C and D). This mechanism is most visible in the Philippines. As Erik Kuhonta and Nhu Truong argue in Chapter 7, sequencing of democratization and state-building in the mid-twentieth century gave Filipino elites the opportunity to design public organizations in such a way that these could easily be hijacked for the particularistic extraction of public resources. Similarly, in Chapter 8, Marcus Mietzner claims that Indonesian democracy has endured because former elements of the Suharto regime – in particular, military and bureaucratic elites – have come to understand that elections provide them with a relatively secure mechanism to maintain their rent-seeking activities.

While East Asia's minimalist democracies thus indicate that stateness is not a necessary condition for democracy to take hold, they also pose a strong challenge to the nexian approach to the state-democracy nexus. What all three case studies show is that the introduction of elections has not created incentives for politicians to invest in the infrastructural power of the state – in particular, the state's administrative capacity. One reason for this is that the weakness of judicial authorities and law enforcement agencies (partial regimes C and D) allows elites to mobilize voters through illicit means, such as vote buying and clientelism, thereby undermining democracy's vertical accountability mechanism. As a result, it appears as if East Asia's minimalist democracies are caught in a *predatory state* trap, whereby both state capacity and democratization are 'frozen' at current levels.

In the conclusion (Chapter 10), we place these findings in comparative perspective. Specifically, by comparing East Asia to other parts of the developing world (Latin America, Africa, and South Asia), we demonstrate that our findings are generalizable. That is to say, the mechanisms that govern the state-democracy nexus in East Asia also help to explain differing regime outcomes in other regions that were swept up in the third wave of democratization.

References

Andersen, D. (2017). *Stateness and Democratic Stability*. Aarhus: Forlaget Politica.
Andersen, D., Møller, J., and Skaaning, S. E. (2014). The State-Democracy Nexus: Conceptual Distinctions, Theoretical Perspectives, and Comparative Approaches. *Democratization*, 21(7), 1203–20.
Bosco, J. (1992). Taiwan Factions: Guanxi, Patronage, and the State in Local Politics. *Ethnology*, 31(2), 157–83.
Bratton, M., and Chang, E. C. C. (2006). State-building and Democratization in Sub-Saharan Africa Forwards, Backwards, or Together? *Comparative Political Studies*, 39(9), 1059–83.
Bräutigam, D. A. (2008). Introduction: Taxation and State-building in Developing Countries – Taxation and State-Building. In D. A. Bräutigam, O.-H. Fjeldstad, and M. Moore, eds., *Developing Countries: Capacity and Consent*. Cambridge: Cambridge University Press, pp. 1–33.
Cappocia, G., and Ziblatt, D. (2010). The Historical Turn in Democratization Studies: A New Research Agenda for Europe and Beyond. *Comparative Political Studies*, 43(8–9), 931–68.
Carbone, G. (2015). Democratisation as a State-Building Mechanism: A Preliminary Discussion of an Understudied Relationship. *Political Studies Review*, 13(1), 11–21.

Carbone, G., and Memoli, V. (2015). Does Democratization Foster State Consolidation? Democratic Rule, Political Order, and Administrative Capacity. *Governance*, 28(1), 5–24.
Carothers, T. (2002). The End of the Transition Paradigm. *Journal of Democracy*, 13(1), 5–21.
Carothers, T. (2007). The Sequencing Fallacy. *Democratization*, 18(1), 12–27.
Case, W. (2002). *Politics in Southeast Asia: Democracy or Less*. London and New York: Curzon Press.
Collier, D., Hidalgo, F. D., and Maciuceanu, A. O. (2006). Essentially Contested Concepts: Debates and Applications. *Journal of Political Ideologies*, 11(3), 211–46.
Coppedge, M., et al. (2018). V-Dem Codebook v8. Varieties of Democracy (V-Dem) Project. Available at: https://doi.org/10.23696/vdemcy18 [Accessed 22 June 2019].
Croissant, A. (2015). Southeast Asian Militaries in the Age of Democratization: From Ruler to Servant? In W. Case, ed., *Routledge Handbook of Southeast Asian Democratization*. London: Routledge, pp. 314–32.
Croissant, A. (2018). *Civil-Military Relations in Southeast Asia*. Cambridge: Cambridge University Press.
Croissant, A., and Bünte, M., eds. (2011). *The Crisis of Democratic Governance in Southeast Asia*. Basingstoke: Palgrave.
Croissant, A., and Merkel, W. (2019). Defective Democracy. In R. Kollmorgen, W. Merkel, and H.-J. Wagener, eds., *Handbook of Political, Social, and Economic Transformation*. Oxford: Oxford University Press, pp. 437–46.
D'Arcy, M., and Nistotskaya, M. (2017). State First, Then Democracy: Using Cadastral Records to Explain Governmental Performance in Public Goods Provision. *Governance*, 30(2), 193–209.
Dahl, R. A. (1971). *Polyarchy*. New Haven: Yale University Press.
Diamond, L. (1999). *Developing Democracy: Toward Consolidation*. Baltimore: Johns Hopkins University Press.
Diamond, L. (2008). *The Spirit of Democracy: The Struggle to Build Free Societies Throughout the World*. New York: Times Books/Henry Holt & Company.
Diamond, L. (2016). *In Search of Democracy*. London and New York: Routledge.
Diamond, L., and Morlino, L., eds. (2006). *Assessing the Quality of Democracy*. Baltimore: Johns Hopkins University Press.
Evans, P. B., Rueschemeyer, D., and Skocpol, T. (1985). *Bringing the State Back In*. Cambridge: Cambridge University Press.
Fishman, R. (1990). Rethinking State and Regime: Southern Europe's Transition. Review Article. *World Politics*, 42, 422–40.
Fortin-Rittberger, J. (2014). Exploring the Relationship between Infrastructural and Coercive State Capacity. *Democratization*, 21(7), 1244–64.
Fukuyama, F. (2014). State and Democracy. *Democratization*, 21(7), 1326–40.
Gilley, B. (2009). *The Right to Rule: How States Win and Lose Legitimacy*. New York: Columbia University Press.
Hanson, J. K. (2018). State Capacity and the Resilience of Electoral Authoritarianism: Conceptualizing and Measuring the Institutional Underpinnings of Autocratic Power. *International Political Science Review*, 39(1), 17–32.
Hanson, J. K., and Sigman, R. (2013). Leviathan's Latent Dimensions: Measuring State Capacity for Comparative Political Research. APSA 2011 Annual Meeting Paper. SSRN. Available at: https://ssrn.com/abstract=1899933 [Accessed 22 June 2019].

Holliday, I. (2012). *Burma Redux: Global Justice and the Quest for Political Reform in Myanmar*. New York and Chichester: Columbia University Press.
Hung, R. L. (2012). Re-thinking Myanmar's Political Regime: Military Rule in Myanmar and Implications for Current Reforms. *Contemporary Politics*, 19(3), 247–61.
Hutchcroft, Paul. (2000). *Booty Capitalism: The Politics of Banking in the Philippines*. Quezon City: Ateneo de Manila University Press, reprint.
Johnston, M. (2008). Japan, Korea, the Philippines, China: Four Syndromes of Corruption. *Crime, Law and Social Change*, 49(3), 205–23.
Kang, D. C. (2002). Bad Loans to Good Friends: Money Politics and the Developmental State in South Korea. *International Organization*, 56(1), 177–207.
Khan, M. H. (2010). Political Settlements and the Governance of Growth-Enhancing Institutions. Unpublished manuscript.
Kimenyi, M. S. (2006). Ethnicity, Governance and the Provision of Public Goods. *Journal of African Economies*, 15(suppl_1), 62–99.
Le Billon, P. (2003). Buying Peace or Fueling War: The Role of Corruption in Armed Conflicts. *Journal of International Development*, 15(4), 413–26.
Linz, J. J., and Stepan, A. (1996). *Problems of Democratic Transition and Consolidation: Southern Europe, South America, and Post-Communist Europe*. Baltimore: Johns Hopkins University Press.
Lührmann, A., et al. (2018). State of the World 2017: Autocratization and Exclusion? *Democratization*, 25(8), 1321–40.
MacIntyre, A. (2000). Funny Money: Fiscal Policy, Rent-Seeking and Economic Performance in Indonesia. In M. H. Khan and J. K. Sundaram, eds., *Rents, Rent-Seeking and Economic Development: Theory and Evidence in Asia*. Cambridge: Cambridge University Press, pp. 248–73.
Mann, M. (1984). The Autonomous Power of the State: Its Origins, Mechanisms and Results. *European Journal of Sociology*, 25(2), 185–213.
Mazucca, S., and Munck, G. (2014). State or Democracy First? Alternative Perspectives on the State-Democracy Nexus. *Democratization*, 21(7), 1221–43.
Merkel, W. (2004). Embedded and Defective Democracies. *Democratization*, 11(5), 33–58.
Merkel, W., and Croissant, A. (2000). Formal Institutions and Informal Rules in Defective Democracies. *Central European Political Science Review*, 1(2), 31–48.
Møller, J. (2015). The Medieval Roots of Democracy. *Journal of Democracy*, 26(3), 110–23.
Møller. J. (2018). Medieval Roots of the Modern State: The Conditional Effects of Geopolitical Pressure on Early Modern State-building. *Social Science History*, 42(2), 295–316.
Møller, J., and Skaaning, S. E. (2011a). *Requisites of Democracy: Conceptualization, Measurement, and Explanation*. London and New York: Routledge.
Møller, J., and Skaaning, S. E. (2011b). Stateness First? *Democratization*, 18(1), 1–24.
Møller, J., and Skaaning, S. E. (2014). *The State-Democracy Nexus: Special Issue of Democratization*. Abingdon and New York: Routledge.
Munck, G. (2016). What Is Democracy? A Reconceptualization of the Quality of Democracy. *Democratization*, 23(1), 1–26.
Mungiu-Pippidi, A. (2015). *The Quest for Good Governance: How Societies Develop Control of Corruption*. Cambridge: Cambridge University Press.

North, D., Wallis, J. J., and Weingast, B. R. (2009). *Violence and Social Orders: A Conceptual Framework for Interpreting Recorded Human History*. Cambridge: Cambridge University Press.

Reno, W. (2000). Clandestine Economies, Violence and States in Africa. *Journal of International Affairs*, 53(2), 433–59.

Rock, M. T., and Bonnett, H. (2004). The Comparative Politics of Corruption: Accounting for the East Asian Paradox in Empirical Studies of Corruption, Growth and Investment. *World Development*, 32(6), 999–1017.

Rogers, S. (2004). Philippine Politics and the Rule of Law. *Journal of Democracy*, 15(4), 111–25.

Rose, R., and Shin, D. C. (2001). Democratization Backwards: The Problem of Third-Wave Democracies. *British Journal of Political Science*, 31(2), 331–54.

Rothstein, B., and Teorell, J. (2008). What Is Quality of Government? A Theory of Impartial Government Institutions. *Governance*, 21(2), 165–90.

Rueschemeyer, D. (2005). Building States: Inherently a Long-Term Process? An Argument from Theory. In M. Lange and D. Rueschemeyer, eds., *States and Development*. New York: Palgrave Macmillan, pp. 143–64.

Schmitter, P. C. (1995). Democracy's Future: More Liberal, Preliberal or Postliberal? *Journal of Democracy*, 6(1), 15–22.

Schmitter, P. C. (1997). Civil Society: East and West. In L. Diamond, et al., eds., *Consolidating Third Wave Democracies: Themes and Perspectives*. Baltimore: Johns Hopkins University Press, pp. 239–62.

Seeberg, M. B. (2014). State Capacity and the Paradox of Authoritarian Elections. *Democratization*, 21(7), 1265–85.

Shin, D. C., and Tusalem, R. (2009). East Asia. In C. Haerpfer, et al., eds., *Democratization*. Oxford: Oxford University Press, pp. 356–74.

Skaaning, S. E. (2006). Political Regimes and Their Changes: A Conceptual Framework, Working Paper No. 55. Stanford University Center on Democracy, Development, and the Rule of Law, Stanford, CA.

Skocpol, T. (1985). Bringing the State Back In: Strategies of Analysis in Current Research. In P. B. Evans, D. Rueschemeyer, and T. Skocpol, eds., *Bringing the State Back In*. Cambridge: Cambridge University Press, pp. 3–38.

Slater, D., and Fenner, S. (2011). State Power and Staying Power: Infrastructural Mechanisms and Authoritarian Durability. *Journal of International Affairs*, 65(1), 15–29.

Snyder, R. (2006). Beyond Electoral Authoritarianism: The Spectrum of Nondemocratic Regime. In A. Schedler, ed., *Electoral Authoritarianism: The Dynamics of Unfree Competition*. Boulder: Lynne Rienner Publishers, pp. 219–31.

Tomsa, D. (2015). Local Politics and Corruption in Indonesia's Outer Islands. *Bijdragen tot de Taal-, Land- en Volkenkunde/Journal of the Humanities and Social Sciences of Southeast Asia*, 171(2–3), 196–219.

Uslaner, E. M., and Rothstein, B. (2016). The Historical Roots of Corruption: State-building, Economic Inequality, and Mass Education. *Comparative Politics*, 48(2), 227–48.

Van Ham, C., and Seim, B. (2018). Strong States, Weak Elections? How State Capacity in Authoritarian Regimes Conditions the Democratizing Power of Elections. *International Political Science Review*, 39(1), 49–66.

Way, L. A. (2006). Authoritarian Failure: How Does State Weakness Strengthen Electoral Competition? In A. Schedler, ed., *Electoral Authoritarianism: The Dynamics of Unfree Competition*. Boulder: Lynne Rienner Publishers, pp. 167–80.

Weber, M. (1992). Wissenschaft als Beruf/Politik als Beruf (MWG, I/17). In W. J. Mommsen and W. Schluchter, eds., *Max Weber-Gesamtausgabe: Band I/17: Wissenschaft als Beruf 1917/1919/Politik als Beruf 1919*. Tübingen: Mohr Siebeck.

White, D. (2018). State Capacity and Regime Resilience in Putin's Russia. *International Political Science Review*, 39(1), 130–43.

Wilson, M. C. (2018). The Value of Descriptive Sequences in Historical Institutionalist Research. *Comparative Democratization Newsletter*, 16(2), 9–13.

Woodall, B. (2018). Democratization in East Asia. In S. Hua, ed., *Routledge Handbook of Asian Politics*. London and New York: Routledge, pp. 15–25.

Wu, C. L. (2003). Local Factions and the Kuomintang in Taiwan's Electoral Politics. *International Relations of the Asia-Pacific*, 3(1), 89–111.

Zakaria, F. (1997). The Rise of Illiberal Democracy. *Foreign Affairs*, 76(6), 22–43.

2

State-Building and Democratization
The Sequencing Debate and Evidence from East Asia

Tuong Vu

INTRODUCTION

Should a well-functioning state be a precondition for democratization? Can democratization nevertheless contribute to state-building? What does the evidence from East Asia say about the so-called sequencing debate? This chapter first reviews the debate on the relationship between state-building and democratization to identify major issues of contention. Both sides of the debate now acknowledge that it is not possible to implement democracy in a failed state or where no state exists. At the same time, it has recently been claimed that democratization may assist state-building through various mechanisms, but these claims have not been tested.

The second part of this chapter examines the historical relationship between state-building and democratization in East Asia. This exercise serves both to test the arguments of the two camps of the sequencing debate and to generate insights specific to East Asia. In fact, the evolving relationship between state-building and democratization in East Asia has not been systematically studied. State-building in this region is precocious in the sense that defining elements of the modern state – such as bureaucratic centralization – emerged in China about two millennia ago. Other parts of East Asia lagged behind China in terms of state consolidation but were at levels comparable to Western Europe five hundred years ago. When it comes to democracy, however, the region is a follower. Yet democratization has spread widely in the region in the late twentieth century with diverse trajectories and outcomes.

Analysing the three 'waves' of democratization since the early twentieth century yields three important insights. First, privileging state-building over democracy has (good and bad) consequences but does not preclude the possibility of eventual democratization. Second, democratization can contribute to state-building in most cases of new states or old ones with deep and persistent ethnic or political cleavages. Democratization can help end civil wars, bring international legitimacy and nurture new national identities. Despite such benefits, democratization in such contexts requires costly foreign intervention to implement and enforce, and the process may not result in viable democracies. One final insight can be gained if we place the East Asian historical experience in the larger picture of world politics. Namely, where pressure from the West and from society exists, as well as the ruling elites' willingness to adopt democratic ideas on their own will, the question of whether state-building or democratization must be prioritized is rendered moot.

THE SEQUENCING DEBATE

In an early and influential study of third-wave democratic transitions, Juan Linz and Alfred Stepan claim that democracy 'is a form of governance of a modern state. Thus, without a state, no modern democracy is possible' (Linz and Stepan, 1996: 17). Linz and Stepan's idea that a well-established state is a precondition for democracy can be traced back to Dankwart Rustow (1970), Samuel Huntington (1968) and Robert Dahl (1989; see also Mazzuca and Munck, 2014). Other scholars who share this view include Jack Snyder (2000), Andreas Wimmer (2013), Robert Bates (2008) and Fareed Zakaria (2003). Following the setbacks of third-wave transitions, these authors have been deeply pessimistic about the prospects of democracy and democratization. They have spoken emphatically of the 'dark side of democracy', arguing that democratization in many contexts has unleashed violent conflicts over identity and power. Zakaria (2003: 248) flatly declares, 'What we need in politics today is not more democracy but less'.

In response to 'sequencers' like Linz and Stepan, many scholars have attempted to show that democracy can benefit state-building *at any level* of political development. This group, which we call 'nexians', based on the term 'the state-democracy nexus' used by some of them, does not deny that in certain contexts democratization must wait for state-building. As Thomas Carothers (2002: 19) – who criticizes sequencers for going too far – admits, 'the state will need to have at least minimal functioning capacity as well as something resembling a monopoly of force before such a country can pull itself onto the path of sustainable, pluralistic political development'. Carothers nonetheless argues that a *well-functioning* state is not needed for democratization to succeed, as Linz and Stepan claim. At the same time, prioritizing state-building may delay democratization indefinitely. An effective state apparatus may well help an authoritarian regime to deflect or suppress pressures for democratization (Carothers, 2002; see also Bratton and Chang, 2006: 1072).

Nexians argue that democracy can strengthen the state via three main mechanisms. First, democracy potentially increases participation and inclusion. As Carbone and Memoli (2015: 9) explain, opportunities to participate in political activities allow 'individuals and groups to feel that they are now taking part and have a stake in the system. Rather than feeling politically excluded, people more likely identify with the state and accept the legitimacy of its authority'. In a related argument, Sebastian Mazzuca and Gerardo Munck (2014: 1255–56) view democracy as a conflict management and power-sharing device that contributes to state-building by helping to resolve, avert or reduce the chance of civil war.

The second mechanism by which democracy may contribute to state consolidation is through strengthening its administrative capacity. Political competition, nexians argue, forces state leaders to be more responsive and effective in providing public services or otherwise risk losing elections (Carbone and Memoli, 2015: 10; Bratton and Chang, 2006: 1075). In addition, democracy allows the opposition, the media and the public to monitor government activities. This can mitigate corruption and other abuses of power, ultimately enhancing state effectiveness and legitimacy (Carothers, 2007: 20).

Strengthening the rule of law is the third mechanism in some nexian accounts. For example, Michael Bratton and Eric Chang believe that democratization, by instituting checks and balances, can 'help to tame a lawless state' by imposing limits on elites 'who would otherwise prefer to abrogate power and privileges for themselves and to rule by arbitrary, even violent, means' (Bratton and Chang, 2006: 1074, 1077). In other words, state-building and democratization are mutually reinforcing and do not necessarily require sequential implementation.

Nexian arguments about the benefits of democracy as a measure to avert civil war and curb excessive abuse of power are generally convincing – with an important caveat. The arguments seem most convincing in cases where states are on the verge of collapse because of impending or ongoing civil war or where the state machinery is highly vulnerable to complete capture by a small group of elites. Democratization is not just beneficial here but seems necessary to save these states from breakup or collapse. In these cases, however, it is obvious that democratization requires external intervention. It would be difficult, if not impossible, to persuade elites bent on slaughtering each other to accept sharing power under a democratic framework in the context of an impending or ongoing civil war. It would be similarly hard to persuade greedy and violent elites to accept the rule of law that would restrict their power. This raises questions about the necessity, costs and length of external intervention for the implementation and sustainability of power-sharing agreements and the rule of law.

In contrast, in cases where states are not close to breakup or collapse, the benefits of democratization for the state are less obvious. Democratization can certainly help mediate social conflicts, reduce political confrontations and make the bureaucracy cleaner and more responsive. These benefits of democratization are for citizens to enjoy, but they hardly matter to state-building in the Weberian sense.[1]

As scholars debate the advantages and disadvantages of democratization for state-building, they evoke European experiences of state-building, nation building and democratization to back up their respective arguments. Sequencers frequently allude to these to make the case that state-building is needed prior to democratization. In their accounts, European states experienced centuries of state consolidation before the idea of the nation emerged and before the political system opened up to democratic pressures (Linz and Stepan, 1996: 20–24). In response, Jorgen Møller (2014) re-examines European history to show that, throughout the centuries-long process of state-building there, rulers were in fact constrained by many medieval institutions, in particular the Church and the estates. Møller (2014: 29) claims that the existence of corporate groups and representative institutions prior to the state-building wave enabled government authority to be channelled into impersonal institutions and laws instead of into patron-client relations. The lesson of medieval Europe for today, Møller argues, is not to privilege state-building over democratization but to empower social groups to check the power of state elites.

While Møller's revisionist account is convincing, it was absolutist rulers, not the Church or the estates, that built European states. Where the estates became too powerful, as in Poland, state-building lagged behind, leaving the country to be carved up by greedy neighbours (Van Creveld, 1999). In the same vein, empowering social groups, in and of itself, does not guarantee that state-building will take place. The European story is certainly more complex than sequencers would have it, and Møller does have a point in stressing that building a cohesive and effective state does not eventually bring about democratization or ensure successful democratization. Yet this does not refute the fact that prior state-building contributed to later successful democratization in Europe.

The consensus in the sequencing debate is that a certain level of state-building must be achieved prior to democratization to sustain the latter. The

---

[1] According to Weber (1947: 156), 'The primary formal characteristics of the modern state are as follows. It possesses an administrative and legal order subject to change by legislation, to which the organized corporate activity of the administrative staff, which is also regulated by legislation, is oriented. This system of order claims binding authority, not only over the members of the state, the citizens, most of whom have obtained membership by birth, but also to a very large extent, over all action taking place in the area of its jurisdiction. It is thus a compulsory association with a territorial basis. Furthermore, today, the use of force is regarded as legitimate only so far as it is either permitted by the state or prescribed by it [...]. The claim of the modern state to monopolize the use of force is as essential to it as its character of compulsory jurisdiction and of continuous organization'. For an extended discussion of Weber's definition, see also Bendix (1997: 418–19).

question is at what level. Those who advocate democratization in tandem with state-building point out various mechanisms for the former to enhance the latter. However, their arguments appear to only apply to states facing breakup or collapse, and they assume external intervention for the implementation of democratization. The case of historical Europe on the whole supports sequencers more than nexians, with the caveat that successful democratization there was the result of factors other than just long periods of previous state-building.

Scholars in the sequencing debate have not paid attention to East Asian experiences, even though they are arguably more relevant to the debate because they have taken place in the modern era. The remainder of the chapter will turn to historical patterns of state-building and democratization in the region by systematically comparing cases in each of the three waves of liberalization and democratization.

STATE-BUILDING AND DEMOCRATIZATION
IN MODERN EAST ASIAN HISTORY

This section focuses on the historical relationship between state-building and democratization in East Asia since the pre-modern era. The purpose is not only to test various arguments in the sequencing debate but also to draw out new insights from East Asian cases. Democratization in East Asia can be grouped into three 'waves' that took place in the 1900–1930s, in 1945–1960 and 1985–2000. This chapter will not discuss all countries for each wave but focus on certain cases with important insights for the state-building democracy relationship. The method of analysis involves, first, reconstructing the historical context by chronology and, second, contrasting the process of political change between pairs of countries or in small groups in the region.

East Asia is home to one of the oldest great empires in human history. The Chinese empire was first unified in 221 BCE and consolidated under the Han dynasty during the next several centuries. While China continued to battle threats from nomadic tribes along its northern and western borders, and occasionally fell under their rule, by the fourteenth century the empire reached its zenith in terms of economic and political development. Its size, wealth, population, technological sophistication and military strength were perhaps unmatched by any other country at the time.

Much later than China but long before modern times, absolutist kingdoms that would later become Korea, Japan, Cambodia, Myanmar (Burma), Thailand and Vietnam emerged between the seventh and fifteenth centuries. Each of these kingdoms was built around a dominant creole group and exercised control over smaller tributary states in their vicinity. For example, Ayudhya (a predecessor of Siam) dominated Nakhonsimrat, Lan Na, Lan Xang (Laos) and others (Kasetsiri, 1976). Toungoo and then Konbaung (later Burma) dominated ethnic Shan states, Arakan and others (Koenig, 1990).

Victor Lieberman (2003) sees parallels in terms of state consolidation between mainland Southeast Asia and Western Europe, suggesting roughly comparable levels of political development around the fifteenth century.

Another parallel with Europe is found in archipelagic East Asia. Many trading kingdoms and city-states, such as the Ryukyus, Mataram/Majapahit (Java), Aceh, Ternate, Bali, Melaka, etc., emerged or were consolidated between the fourteenth and seventeenth centuries – the 'Age of Commerce' in the words of Anthony Reid (1993). These trading kingdoms and city-states emerged at around the same time as European city-states. They were less cohesive, complex and powerful than the mainland states and Japan, however, and they began to decline as Europeans arrived and vied for the control over trade routes. By the nineteenth century, most had been annexed into larger territories as colonies of Western powers.

Two legacies of pre-modern state-building can be identified. First, territorial frontiers and relatively cohesive communities were created around major centres of power in China, Korea, Japan, Vietnam, Cambodia, Siam and Burma. Some of these were strong enough to resist Western threats. In particular, Japan was able to modernize, while China and Siam escaped colonization. Moreover, Koreans, Vietnamese, Cambodians and Burmese did not lose their identity despite being colonized. The pre-modern territories did not have fixed borders, and the communities that inhabited those territories were not homogenous, but some degrees of both were achieved. Second, bureaucratic institutions emerged in China during the Han dynasty and were later imported into Korea, Japan and Vietnam. The predecessor states of today's Burma, Cambodia, Thailand and parts of Malaysia and Indonesia also were no strangers to bureaucratic institutions and practices, which were borrowed from India. These legacies undoubtedly contributed to state-building during and after the colonial period, although it is difficult to trace specific legacies over time.

Overall, however, not much can be said about the relationship between state-building and democratization in this period, except for the fact that absolutist rulers in pre-modern East Asia faced little societal constraint on their power. Among the pre-modern polities, only ancient China (Zhou period) and medieval Japan (between eleventh and sixteenth centuries) shared aspects of feudalism with Europe (Gernet, 1982; Jansen, 2000). Unlike in Europe, nowhere in pre-modern East Asia did corporate groups and representative institutions exist or have enough power to constrain absolutist rulers.[2] Buddhism, Hinduism and Islam, the three most important religions in East Asia, did not have a centralized system either or were fully under the control of monarchs.

---

[2] Medieval Japan, Korea and early modern Siam had a powerful nobility, but they were not unified as estates in the European contexts that could formally restrain the power of absolutist monarchs.

State-Building and Democratization   31

THE FIRST 'WAVE'

In the late nineteenth century to the early twentieth century, most of East Asia was colonized by Western powers. Colonial regimes undertook limited state-building projects primarily to serve the goals of economic exploitation and political pacification. A short but significant 'wave' of liberalization and democratization took place in two contexts. The first context involved Japan, Siam and China – countries that were not colonized. There, rulers embarked on modernizing the state and the economy to survive. In the process, some elites willingly adopted Western ideas and institutions, including representative government, universal suffrage and even socialism. State consolidation preceded limited democratization, which would be ultimately suspended. The second context was the Philippines, where US rule allowed partial democratization to prepare for future self-rule. The paired comparisons of Japan and China and Siam and the Philippines in this section are instructive for the sequencing debate.

Japan and China

Japan, the East Asian country most successful at modernization, also went farthest in terms of democratization. Under Emperor Meiji, the ruling oligarchy oversaw massive reforms that succeeded in creating a powerful modern state and an industrial economy. In the 1880s, less than two decades after modernization began, a movement advocating liberty and people's rights (*jiyu-minken*) emerged. The ruling oligarchs soon formally split into two political parties: one strongly attracted to English constitutional thought, and the other influenced by the rhetoric of the French Revolution (Jansen, 2000: 377–95, 414–23). The first national elections for parliament were held in 1890, but franchise was confined to propertied men. During the 1910s and 1920s, and especially during the rule of Emperor Taisho, further democratization ensued with universal male suffrage instituted in 1924.

Yet one should not exaggerate the scope and impact of the so-called Taisho democracy. The fruits of democracy were still elusive for lower classes (workers, tenant farmers), while the new middle classes gained significant political influence 'not by joining in partisan politics but by assuming public roles in alliance with the state bureaucracy' (Garon, 2000: 170–71). This close state-society partnership under bureaucratic supervision suggested a corporatist rather than a liberal democratic system. In any case, the democratic experiment in Japan could not sustain. It ended when the regime drifted back towards oligarchic rule in the 1930s.

In sum, the Japanese experience both validates and challenges the nexian camp. On the one hand, privileging state-building not only shaped the character of Taisho democracy but may eventually have also doomed it. On the other hand, the willingness of the Japanese oligarchy to support democratization is a missing factor in nexian accounts, which assume that ruling elites in a dictatorship would oppose democratization and rely on the state apparatus to block the process. This assumption, however, is not borne out in the Japanese case.

Voluntary democratization from above also took place in Qing China, although the ruling elites there started from a position of weakness. In the late 1890s, Qing China followed Meiji Japan in instituting reforms in the aftermath of military defeat at the hands of European powers. The central goal of the Qing reforms was the modernization of China's state and economy. Yet these reforms tended to be haphazard, and their impacts insignificant when compared to similar efforts in Japan (Bergere, 1968: 230–42; Spence, 1990: 216–19, 238–44). Despite such limitations, Western and Japanese liberal and republican ideas also gained support in Qing China, resulting in the official plan to replace the absolute monarchy with a constitutional government by 1917. As a first step, provincial assemblies were elected and met for the first time in 1909 (Fincher, 1968: 189–93; Spence, 1990: 238–49).

The reforms came too late to save the Qing and perhaps even contributed to its collapse in 1911 as a result of a revolution led by an alliance between rebellious provincial militaries and Sun Yat-sen's Revolutionary League. As a compromise, Yuan Shikai, a Qing general, instead of Sun Yat-sen, was made the provisional president of the first republican government in China. A parliament was democratically elected in 1913 by an all-male electorate, who were required to be above twenty-one years of age, possess an education and own property (Spence, 1990: 280). The republic was short-lived, however, with Yuan seeking to resurrect absolutism by proclaiming himself emperor. When Yuan died in 1916, central authority fell apart as regional warlords rose up in revolt.

Although Qing China appears to vindicate the nexian argument against privileging state-building, this is not the case. China's modernizing reforms under the Qing decentralized rather than centralized the state, which led to the rise of provincial armies and later warlords. Viewed in their historical context, Chinese reforms were undertaken as last-minute attempts to save the Qing state from nearly a century of decay and disintegration. Democratization in this case not only failed but also contributed to state collapse.

Siam and the Philippines

If nexians fail to account for voluntary democratization from above in Japan and China, they are correct regarding Siam, where the ruler rejected democracy. Siam was the only Southeast Asian country able to retain formal independence. In pre-modern times, the direct rule of the Siamese Chakri kings did not extend beyond a hundred kilometres from Bangkok, and the kings' authority at the court was checked by a group of powerful noble families (Pasuk and Baker, 2002: 226, 236–43). Under Kings Mongkut (1851–1867) and Chulalongkorn (1868–1910), Bangkok embarked on broad projects to create a modern and centralized bureaucracy and military. These projects were relatively successful in transforming Siam into a modern state with a vibrant economy based primarily on trade and agricultural exports.

As in Japan, albeit to a lesser degree, modernization created new urban classes that began to demand democratization in the 1920s (Pasuk and Baker, 2002: 117–24, 259–65). These demands were rejected by the Court, leading to several coup attempts. In 1932, a group of young civilian and military officials successfully launched a coup that replaced absolutism with a constitutional government (Terwiel, 2005). Following the coup, popular elections were held in 1933 to elect district representatives, who in turn selected one half of all members of the newly created National Assembly (Terwiel, 2005: 265–66). However, the new parliament did not have much authority, and the post-coup government was dominated by a shifting alliance between royal, military and bureaucratic cliques. In this case, the democratic movement failed to create a democratic regime, and the traditional dictatorship (absolutist monarchy) was replaced by a modern one (oligarchic rule). The nexian warning about the danger of privileging state-building proves true in this case.

In the rest of East Asia outside of Japan, China and Siam, colonial rulers privileged state modernization and consolidation over democratization, the only exception being the Philippines.[3] Under Spanish rule from the late sixteenth century to late nineteenth century, the Philippines served as a mere way station connecting Spain and the Americas. The colonial government based in Manila was weak and had little power over provincial governors (Steinberg, 2000: 54–62; see also Hutchcroft, 2000: 283). US rule starting in 1899, in contrast, promoted administrative decentralization and representative government at local levels. In 1907, an indigenous National Assembly was elected by limited suffrage and shared power with the US-dominated executive council.

The American Philippines was clearly the most 'democratic' among the Asian colonies at the time. Yet the early creation of representative institutions enabled local elites and their patronage networks to penetrate the state bureaucracy at all levels when the latter took shape (Hutchcroft, 2000: 290–92). The Philippines was, therefore, the mirror image of Siam. In the former, democracy was prioritized, in the latter, state-building was. If democratic institutions were quickly usurped by royal, military and bureaucratic elites in Siam after the 1932 coup, state institutions in the Philippines were captured by elected elites as soon as they were established. If Siam ended up with a sham democracy, the Philippines suffered from a sham state. To the extent that an effective state is as much a worthy goal as is democracy, privileging democracy creates equally undesirable consequences as does privileging state-building.

[3] Local elections were also held in British Burma and French Cochinchina, but these were much more limited than in the American Philippines.

THE SECOND 'WAVE'

Between 1945 and 1985, East Asia witnessed relentless state modernization and consolidation. Together with decolonization, democratic institutions to varying extents were revived or adopted in a large number of countries, including not only Japan, Thailand (formerly Siam) and the Philippines but also South Korea, Burma, Malaysia and Indonesia. Both foreign sponsorship and local elites' voluntary adoption of democracy were responsible for this 'wave'. With one exception (Japan), this wave ebbed within a decade with personal or military dictatorships becoming the predominant form of non-communist regimes. This section discusses Japan and three particular pairs of countries that, as this chapter argues, yield important lessons. The pair of South Korea and Indonesia represented two polar experiences: in the former, state-building was privileged; whereas in the latter, democratic achievements were significant despite certain failures. The second pair of British Malaya and Burma underlined the role of foreign sponsorship. The third pair of Thailand and the Philippines witnessed democracy, which was quickly thwarted in one case while persisting in the other.

South Korea and Indonesia

Under US occupation (1945–1948) and later during the Korean War (1950–1953), US forces suppressed popular revolts and helped build a new Korean state out of the remnants of the colonial state. The United States then helped this fragile state defeat southern Communists and the North Korean attempt at conquest (Vu, 2010). The South Korean state, especially its coercive apparatus, was greatly consolidated through these events (Kim, 1971; also see Chapter 3 in this volume). South Korea witnessed its first national elections in 1948, but these took place against the backdrop of leftist revolts. Although South Korea enjoyed competitive elections and a relatively free private media, the state was powerful and for decades was dominated by strongmen (Rhee Syngman, 1948–1960; Park Chung Hee, 1961–1979; and Chun Do Hwan, 1980–1988; the latter two were backed by the military). Democracy in South Korea was not a sham but was nevertheless severely compromised and effectively overturned in 1972, when Park installed martial law and the Yushin Constitution.

In contrast with South Korea, Indonesian elites of the Left and Right and of secular and religious proclivities were willing to work together in their struggle for independence against the returning Dutch in late 1945 (Vu, 2010). Communists launched an unsuccessful coup in 1948 but were not subsequently banned from political participation. Various coalitions of political parties took turns governing the central government after independence was achieved in 1949. Political mobilization through party and personal networks thoroughly permeated the national bureaucracy, the military and local governments. The first free elections were held in 1955, yet elite bickering, social unrest and regional revolts nearly destroyed the weak state and broke up the nascent country. At this point, Indonesia began to repeat the South Korean story, with President Sukarno seizing power in 1959. Under Sukarno's 'guided democracy', the Indonesian military succeeded in restoring order and defeating the rebels. In 1966, General Suharto took advantage of a communist-inspired coup to oust Sukarno and kill or imprison communists. He not only established military rule but also successfully revamped the state.

Up until the late 1950s, the overall Indonesian experience was marked by broad elite inclusiveness, in stark contrast to South Korea (Aspinall, 2005: 894). Power-sharing and democratic elections enabled Indonesia's native elites to work together for a decade and helped prevent the immediate and violent breakup of the former Dutch colony following the Second World War. Nevertheless, without an effective core of state institutions, and in the face of massive problems confronting the young country, democracy fell short and was eventually not sustainable. It is clear that democracy in the particular sense of political and ethnic inclusiveness helped preserve territorial unity and build the national identity of post-colonial Indonesia. Despite these contributions, democratization in the context of a fragile state hindered the creation of a professional and cohesive bureaucracy and contributed to the breakdown of order. To the extent that Indonesia's primary and immediate needs in the post-colonial period were territorial unity and identity construction (South Korea did not have these needs), democratic institutions, for all their defects, were arguably the most appropriate choice. Also, it is worth noting that the US occupiers chose to prioritize state-building in South Korea, whereas the Indonesian elites opted for political inclusiveness of their own will – just like their Japanese and Chinese counterparts during the first wave.

British Burma and Malaya

The pair of British Burma and Malaya parallel the Korea and Indonesia pair in the sense that they also experienced a mixture of state-building and democratization. But the two British colonies offer different lessons for the sequencing debate. Burma experienced far greater destruction during the war, and its complex geography posed a greater challenge to state-building than it did in Malaya. Returning after having defeated the Japanese, British authorities had much weaker control over the situation on the ground in Burma than in Malaya.[4] They also had much less interest in restoring colonial rule in Burma. The Burmese groups that negotiated with the British for independence were divided along ideological and ethnic lines. The extremely contentious process of negotiation witnessed significant unrest and threatened to descend into war at several points.

---

[4] My account in this and the next paragraph relies on Cady (1958), Callahan (2003) and Charney (2009).

Burmese elites willingly adopted democratic institutions, but they were ultimately not able to work together as in the case of Indonesia. Communists gradually broke away and launched a revolt in 1948, a few months after the country became independent. The Karens, a major ethnic group who feared domination by the Burman majority in the new country, also rebelled at the same time. Burmese leader U Nu and his socialist collaborators led the country through two free elections in 1951 and 1956. Continuous war against rebellions, factional bickering within the ruling coalition and a weak and corrupt bureaucracy caused the government to break down in 1958, and the military was invited to run the country as a caretaker government for eighteen months. Another democratically elected government took office in 1960, only to be overthrown in a military coup in 1962. General Ne Win, the coup leader, would rule Burma until 1988.

British Malaya did not experience pre-modern state-building as intensively as Burma, and the ethnic tension between ethnic Malays and Chinese would seem just as susceptible to violence as that between the dominant Burmans and Burma's ethnic minorities. The key differences were in British policy and their longer post-colonial involvement.[5] On their return to the colony after the war, the British initially sought to form a much more centralized government than under previous colonial rule. They later yielded to the Malay elites' demand for independence. It was agreed that the country would be a federation with a strong centralized government. As the negotiation was in progress, communists, who were well-armed and ethnically mostly Chinese, broke away and launched an insurgency in 1948. The revolt was dealt with and eventually defeated under British direction by the mid-1950s.

Under British tutelage, ethnic Malay, Chinese and Indian leaders were able to negotiate power-sharing constitutional agreements. Non-communist Malay and Chinese elites also willingly adhered to democratic institutions. These institutions were to lose much of their vitality in the 1980s and 1990s under Prime Minister Mohammad Mahathir (see Slater, 2003). Nevertheless, Malaysia never experienced military rule as Burma did. Opposition parties have occasionally won local elections and challenged the ruling party in national polls, and an active civil society has always existed. The contrast with Burma clearly points to the role of the British in defeating radical movements while facilitating territorial unity and ethnic power sharing. Without British involvement during 1945–1963, Malaysia would no doubt have become a very different country. Democratic institutions created by Malayan elites under British sponsorship clearly contributed to nation and state formation, as in Indonesia. At the same time, British emphasis on – and direct involvement in – early post-colonial state-building gave those institutions, however limited they were, the chance to survive even as military dictators arose throughout Southeast Asia.

---

[5] My account for this and the next paragraph relies on Ongkili (1985) and Andaya and Andaya (1982).

Thailand and the Philippines

These two countries broadly followed the pre-war trends analysed in the previous section. In Thailand, a democratic government was established following the Second World War, only to be replaced in 1948 by military rule under Phibun Songkhram, the strongman who had ruled Thailand during the war. Like the quick collapse of democracy after the 1932 coup, the fate of Thai democracy in the 1940s once again points to the problem of democratic transition in a cohesive state where oligarchic rule was entrenched.

The Philippines gained independence from the United States in 1946 and enjoyed a powerful legislature and independent judiciary from the beginning (Wurfel, 1988). Elections were competitive, and no restrictions on basic freedoms existed. However, the state was deeply decentralized with power significantly vested in provincial governments. The central bureaucracy was thoroughly penetrated by personal relationships, while the national military was small in size and ineffective in broadcasting state power across the archipelago. The rule of law and protection of civil liberties were weak not only because of its unconsolidated democracy but also because of an incoherent and ineffectual state.

As mentioned previously, the plight of the post-colonial Philippine state, a legacy of US rule, validates the sequencers' warning about the dangers of instituting democracy too early. Yet nexians should not be totally dismissed. Limited but stable democratic institutions as a mechanism for most elites to share power may have helped the Philippines avoid the regional revolts that wrecked Burma and threatened Indonesia. In addition, democracy arguably assisted subsequent state-building in a limited way. The strength of citizens' groups contributed to successful electoral reform in the late 1960s, which significantly reduced fraud as well as political violence (Wurfel, 1988: 105–6). Nevertheless, the problems of a weak state continued to beset the Philippines with, first, a communist insurgency in the 1950s, and second, an ethnic and religious secessionist revolt in the 1970s. The latter lent the justifications for President Ferdinand Marcos to declare martial law and establish a dictatorship in 1972. Whereas the Thai experience, again, vindicates the nexian fear of an entrenched state blocking democratization, the Philippine example in this period suggests that democratization may help state-building in a limited way – although it is doomed to fail without prior or concurrent effective state-building.

Japan

Similar contradictory implications for the sequencing debate can also be drawn from Japan, the most successful case of democratization in the second wave. In Japan, the pre-war state was kept mostly intact but democratized. During the occupation, the United States not only imposed a new constitution that established formal democracy but also dismantled key oligarchic institutions, including the military, the Home Ministry and some of the largest economic monopolies (*zaibatsu*) (Jansen, 2000). Together with newly instituted political freedoms and competitive elections, these measures tamed the pre-war state, placed pro-democratic forces on more equal footing with anti-democratic ones and contributed to the eventual consolidation of democracy in Japan (Krauss and Ishida, 1989).

Democratic consolidation was undoubtedly helped by the Taisho experience, which witnessed the debut of political parties and civic groups on the political stage as socially sanctioned forms of political organizations. Nevertheless, the Japanese state, while tamed under US occupation, still had profound influence on the character of Japanese democracy to the extent that the pre-war corporatist system remained largely intact under the cover of liberal democracy (Johnson, 1982; Campbell, 1989; Gordon, 2010). Until the 1990s, Japanese politics was dominated by a single conservative party, the Liberal Democratic Party. State bureaucrats maintained significant clout over civil society, albeit less than the extent they had enjoyed before the war.[6] The Japanese case suggests the need for an external occupation force to 'domesticate' a powerful state for democracy to be established (or restored) and consolidated. Even so, the legacies of privileging state-building ensured that formal democratic institutions, once consolidated, were fundamentally shaped by the pre-existing state structure and character.

Overall, the diverse set of East Asian cases in the second wave of democratization contributes several insights to the sequencing debate. First, privileging state-building has consequences and legacies for later democratization, as shown in the cases of Japan, South Korea and Thailand. Second, democratic institutions can contribute to state and nation building in newly formed states but frequently require foreign sponsorship in addition to native elites' voluntary adoption. Finally, democracy cannot survive in weak states for long without giving adequate attention to or making critical progress in state-building.

THE THIRD 'WAVE' AND BEYOND

From the late 1980s to the late 1990s, a third wave of democratization swept through East Asia.[7] To draw out implications for the sequencing debate, I will juxtapose cases of successful democratization (South Korea, Taiwan and Indonesia) against those that have democratized but are still struggling (the Philippines, Burma, Cambodia and Timor-Leste) and those that have effectively resisted democratization (Malaysia, Singapore, Thailand, China and Vietnam).

---

[6] Some have even labelled the system 'soft authoritarianism'. See Johnson (1987).
[7] For an earlier discussion of the outcomes of this wave in East Asia, see Croissant (2004).

Successful Democratizers

As previously mentioned, some nexians argue that privileging state-building may impede and delay democratization indefinitely. It is true that democracy was seriously curtailed or blocked for decades in South Korea, Taiwan and Indonesia under one-party or military rule. Nevertheless, all three eventually became democratic (with Indonesia behind the other two by a decade) and successfully consolidated their democracy. This is not the place to go into detail about how and why these three countries democratized, but the usual suspected factors include changes in the external environment,[8] rapid and sustained economic growth,[9] robust domestic demand for democracy,[10] the collapse of the authoritarian regime[11] and broad elite acceptance of democratic rule as legitimate.[12] The simple fact is that state-building did not foreclose the possibility of democratization and even contributed to the successful consolidation of democracy. For all its violations of human rights, the Indonesian military has been quite effective in combating religious terrorism that could have destabilized Indonesia's young democracy.

Although the experiences of the three countries support the case for privileging state-building, it should be noted that democracy has contributed to legitimacy and political stability, thereby also strengthening the state, in South Korea, Taiwan and Indonesia. Democracy has thus far bred greater toleration between deeply hostile domestic factions in South Korea (the Left vs. the Right) and in Taiwan (mainlanders vs. native Taiwanese). Democracy offered a mechanism for Indonesia to solve the long-standing conflict in East Timor (see Chapter 9 in this volume), which had seriously eroded the international legitimacy of the Indonesian state, and the civil war in Aceh that had threatened the unity of the country. Democracy also greatly enhances the international legitimacy of the Taiwanese state in the face of intense military pressure from China (Chu and Lin, 2001).

Struggling Democracies

Turning to the group of struggling 'democracies', democratization has contributed to state-building in Burma, Cambodia and Timor-Leste but not the Philippines. The military in Burma took over in 1962 and just recently returned power to a democratically elected government in 2016. Throughout

---

[8] Taiwan was internationally isolated after the United States and the United Nations (UN) switched their recognition to communist China. The end of the Cold War sharply reduced the communist threat to South Korea and Taiwan.
[9] For an astute analysis of this issue, especially concerning Southeast Asia, see Bertrand (1998).
[10] See Lee (2007), Chao and Myers (1998), Hsiao (1992) and Aspinall (2005).
[11] The Suharto regime collapsed in 1998 as a result of the financial crisis in 1997–1998.
[12] Elections continued to take place throughout the decades under authoritarian rule in South Korea and Indonesia. They were quite competitive in South Korea. For Indonesian elites' embracing of democratic values, see Bitar and Lowenthal (2015).

the period of military rule until today, Burma has never been free from civil war. Military rulers failed to solve the conflicts with various political and ethnic insurgent groups. Their crackdown of social protests and of the democracy movement led by Aung San Suu Kyi earned them worldwide condemnation and harsh sanctions by the West. Democratization, which began in 2014, has not yet helped Burma to stop these long-standing civil wars, but the country has gained international legitimacy just like Taiwan. Democratization has also brought Suu Kyi's group into the government, closing a major fissure within the state for the time being.

Like Burma, Cambodia also suffered from civil war. From 1979–1992, the Cambodian government backed by Vietnam and the Soviet Bloc, on the one hand, and a guerrilla government supported by China, the Association of Southeast Asian Nations (ASEAN) and the United States, on the other, were engulfed in fighting. The former controlled most of the country but was regarded as illegitimate by the UN. When all sides to the civil war agreed to a UN-brokered peace agreement in 1992, a democratic regime with regular free and fair multi-party elections was imposed at a cost of about US$2 billion. Democratization contributed to state-building in the sense that the war stopped, and foreign occupation ended, with the state acquiring international legitimacy and territorial integrity in the process.

Yet war almost broke out again five years later between the two major political factions led by the two co-prime ministers, Hun Sen and Prince Ranariddh. After Hun Sen's forces quickly defeated those of Ranariddh and averted a war, the regime became much more authoritarian. Nevertheless, a new opposition party, the Cambodia National Rescue Party (CNRP), emerged and came close to winning the last two elections. In response, in late 2017, Hun Sen arrested his opponents and dissolved the CNRP. At the time of writing, the future of Cambodian democracy appears bleak. If democratic power sharing was a means to end the civil war, it served its purpose, but it has not brought about a stable or viable democracy in the country. In hindsight, accepting democratization by imposition turned out to be only a temporary price for the Hun Sen regime to pay as it clawed its way back to international legitimacy, which it had been denied prior to 1993.

Timor-Leste was similar to Cambodia in the sense that its democracy was established under UN supervision after the Indonesian government under President Habibi allowed a referendum for independence in 1999. The new Timor-Leste government has been led mostly by former guerrilla leaders. Much smaller and as poor as Cambodia, Timor-Leste did not experience a civil war as Cambodia did; the struggle for independence against Indonesia united most Timorese. That is arguably a main reason why its democracy, except for a political crisis in 2006, has not faced a reversal as in Cambodia. Despite its limited state capacity, Timor-Leste's democracy has functioned relatively smoothly; some scholars even consider it a successful case of democratization (Aspinall et al., 2018; Croissant and Lorentz, 2018). Even more than

Cambodia, democratic government has brought Timor-Leste international legitimacy and critical material assistance for state-building.

If democratization has made some contributions to state-building in Burma, Cambodia and Timor-Leste, it has not done so in the Philippines. There, democracy returned in 1986 after Marcos was forced to resign in the wake of massive street protests. Yet democratization has not been beneficial to state-building. To use just one measure, democratic elections have brought as many incompetent and corrupt as effective and honest leaders into the presidency.[13] None of them, including the effective and honest ones, have contributed much to state-building. This case does not lend any support to nexians' claim that democratization can help make the state more cohesive and less corrupt.

Successful Resisters

Besides the mentioned two groups, the third wave has also rattled other authoritarian, or hybrid, regimes in East Asia, yet these have been able to count on their effective states to resist democratization. Malaysia, Singapore, Thailand, China and Vietnam are cases that bolster arguments against privileging state-building. Malaysia and Singapore preside over the most effective non-communist states in Southeast Asia. If the establishment of democratic regimes helped these countries to avoid bloody breakups when they gained independence, democratic institutions were later gradually restricted to protecting the ruling party or coalition. Despite the presence of sometimes viable opposition, elections have not been fair, enabling the long-standing dominance of a single political party since independence. As these countries successfully developed their economies and became wealthy, pressures for democratization from below have intensified, just as many democracy theorists would predict. Yet the effective Singaporean and Malaysian states have thus far successfully co-opted or suppressed the opposition (Rodan, 2011).[14]

Like Malaysia and Singapore, Thailand offers a cautionary tale about privileging state-building. Thailand's democratization has progressed in fits and starts in the 1970s. Mass protests in the streets of Bangkok forced the resignation of General Thanom Kittikachorn in 1973 and General Suchinda Kraprayoon in 1992. Regular and relatively free elections occurred between

---

[13] The former included Joseph Estrada and Gloria Macapagal-Aroyo. The latter included Fidel Ramos and Benigno Aquino III. Corazon Aquino was honest but not effective. See Hutchcroft and Rocamora (2011) and Abinales (2015).

[14] In the most recent general election of 2018, the ruling coalition, the National Front, which had dominated Malaysia since independence, lost to the opposition coalition, the Alliance of Hope. In this victory the Alliance benefited from a massive corruption scandal involving Prime Minister Najib Rajak, which caused former prime minister Mahathir Mohammad to defect from the ruling coalition and support the Alliance. If the Alliance succeeds in holding on to power in the next election, then Malaysia can be placed among the 'struggling democracies' instead of 'successful resisters'.

1980 and 2013. However, oligarchic forces, including the monarchy, the military and the state bureaucracy, have often resisted those electoral outcomes they did not favour. The ongoing conflict between the 'yellow shirts' (supporters of deposed Prime Minister Thaksin Shinawara) and the 'red shirts' (opponents of Thaksin) since the mid-2000s has resulted in the return of military rule in Thailand at the time of writing.

Communist China and Vietnam are also contexts in which state-building has thus far precluded democratization. These are hard-core dictatorships that were built on effective states based on the Stalinist-Maoist model. In the last several decades, China and Vietnam have liberalized their economies, resulting in more open societies and rising pressures from below for greater political freedoms. Despite having undergone significant decay, the communist parties of China and Vietnam still maintain tight control over their respective society and resist any political reforms that may threaten their rule.[15] These cases clearly highlight the difficulty of democratic transition where authoritarian rule is bolstered by an effective state.

For all the setbacks (Croissant, 2004), the third wave of democratization has made greater progress on democratization than previous waves. Back in the mid-1980s, it would have been unthinkable that the seemingly hard-core dictatorships of South Korea, Taiwan and Indonesia would one day become democracies. Privileging state-building delayed but did not preclude the possibility of democratization. Democratization has bridged deep domestic social and political cleavages as well as enhanced the international legitimacy of those countries including Cambodia and Burma.

CONCLUSION

This chapter has attempted to analyse and contribute to the sequencing debate with insights from East Asia. The East Asian region has experienced a long history of state-building, while its track record in democratization is much shorter. Our analysis has provided evidence in support of three important propositions that can be summarized as follows: first, while we found that privileging state-building impeded democratization in some cases, it needs not preclude the possibility of democratization. Japan in the 1920s, Thailand, South Korea and Taiwan in the 1980s–1990s and Indonesia in the 2000s suggest such possibilities even though in two of these cases (Japan and Thailand) democratization was reversed. We also found in the case of post-war Japan that the prior experience of successful state-building did indeed cast a long shadow on state-society relations after the country democratized.

Second, in concurrence with the nexian camp in the sequencing debate, we found that democratization is beneficial to new *and* old states that confront deep and persistent ethnic or political cleavages. In Indonesia, the Philippines,

---

[15] See Pei (2008) and Vu (2015).

Burma and Cambodia, democratization helped to end civil war and build national identity. Taiwan and Cambodia are cases where democratization also boosted the international legitimacy of struggling regimes or isolated states. However, democratization did not always result in viable democracies. In addition, for democratization to work as a conflict-solving mechanism, as in Cambodia (but not in Timor-Leste), costly external intervention and occupation is required.

Finally, the East Asian experience calls for placing the sequencing debate in the broader picture that takes into account the state system and the global trend of democratization. Modern states are units in a state system. The system is anarchic in the sense that there is no world government, but it does have a structure shaped by the distribution of power capabilities and by international norms accepted by most states. Western states have dominated the system since the nineteenth century. The West is also where democratic ideas and institutions first emerged. Throughout the past century, we have seen that this state system has offered opportunities while creating intense pressure on Asian elites to modernize and democratize. Political development in the region since the late nineteenth century provided clear evidence of that pressure. This pressure was one of the reasons why ruling elites in many East Asian countries willingly adopted democratic reforms. The other main reason was their belief in democratic values. This elite behaviour goes against the assumption that successful state builders must be against democratization.

Significantly, this pressure has not abated, as belief in democratic ideals has spread widely in East Asia today. Economic competition is as fierce as ever, while security rivalries are escalating with the recent rise of China. Pressure for economic growth continues to force ruling elites to strengthen state capacity, and where high growth is achieved, authoritarian or illiberal democratic regimes face increasing pressures from below for democratization. The theoretical choice between favouring state-building or democratization may no longer exist in reality. Of course, democratization should not be expected to lead straight to liberal democracy, so the quality of democracy remains an outstanding issue.

References

Abinales, P. (2015). Aquino's Mixed Presidential Legacy. East Asia Forum. Available at: www.eastasiaforum.org/2015/12/30/aquinos-mixed-presidential-legacy/ [Accessed 22 June 2019].

Andaya, B. W., and Andaya, L. (1982). *A History of Malaysia*. London: Macmillan Education.

Aspinall, E. (2005). *Opposing Suharto: Compromise, Resistance, and Regime Change in Indonesia*. Stanford: Stanford University Press.

Aspinall, E., et al. (2018). Timor-Leste Votes: Parties and Patronage. *Journal of Democracy*, 29(1), 153–67.

Bates, R. (2008). *When Things Fell Apart: State Failure in Late-Century Africa.* New York: Cambridge University Press.

Bendix, R. (1997). *Max Weber: An Intellectual Portrait.* Berkeley: University of California Press.

Bergere, M. C. (1968). The Role of the Bourgeoisie. In M. C. Wright, ed., *China in Revolution: The First Phase, 1900–1913.* New Haven: Yale University Press.

Bertrand, J. (1998). Growth and Democracy in Southeast Asia. *Comparative Politics,* 30(3), 355–75.

Bitar, S., and Lowenthal, A. F., eds. (2015). *Democratic Transitions: Conversations with World Leaders.* Baltimore: Johns Hopkins University Press.

Bratton, M., and Chang, E. (2006). State Building and Democratization in Sub-Saharan Africa: Forwards, Backwards or Together? *Comparative Political Studies,* 39(9), 1059–83.

Cady, J. (1958). *A History of Modern Burma.* Ithaca: Cornell University Press.

Callahan, M. (2003). *Making Enemies: War and State Building in Burma.* Ithaca: Cornell University Press.

Campbell, J. C. (1989). Democracy and Bureaucracy in Japan. In T. Ishida and E. Krauss, eds., *Democracy in Japan.* Pittsburgh: University of Pittsburgh Press, pp. 113–38.

Carbone, G., and Memoli, V. (2015). Does Democratization Foster State Consolidation? Democratic Rule, Political Order, and Administrative Capacity. *Governance,* 28(1), 5–24.

Carothers, T. (2002). The End of the Transition Paradigm. *Journal of Democracy,* 13(1), 5–21.

Carothers, T. (2007). The 'Sequencing' Fallacy. *Journal of Democracy,* 18(9), 12–27.

Chao, L., and Myers, R. (1998). *The First Chinese Democracy: Political Life in the Republic of China on Taiwan.* Baltimore: Johns Hopkins University Press.

Charney, M. (2009). *A History of Modern Burma.* New York: Cambridge University Press.

Chu, Y. H., and Lin, J. W. (2001). Political Development in 20th-Century Taiwan: State building, Regime Transformation and the Construction of National Identity. In R. L. Edmonds and S. Goldstein, eds., *Taiwan in the Twentieth Century: A Retrospective View.* New York: Cambridge University Press, pp. 102–29.

Croissant, A. (2004). From Transition to Defective Democracy: Mapping Asian Democratization. *Democratization,* 11(5), 156–78.

Croissant, A., and Lorentz, P. (2018). *Comparative Politics of Southeast Asia: An Introduction to Governments and Political Regimes.* Cham, Switzerland: Springer.

Dahl, R. A. (1989). *Democracy and Its Critics.* New Haven: Yale University Press.

Fincher, J. (1968). Political Provincialism and the National Revolution. In M. C. Wright, ed., *China in Revolution: The First Phase, 1900–1913.* New Haven: Yale University Press, pp. 185–226.

Garon, S. (2000). State and Society in Interwar Japan. In M. Goldman and A. Gordon, eds., *Historical Perspectives on Contemporary East Asia.* Cambridge: Harvard University Press, pp. 155–82.

Gernet, J. (1982). *A History of Chinese Civilization,* 2nd ed. New York: Cambridge University Press.

Gordon, A. (2000). Society and Politics from Transwar through Postwar Japan. In M. Goldman and A. Gordon, eds., *Historical Perspectives on Contemporary East Asia*. Cambridge: Harvard University Press, pp. 272–96.
Hsiao, H. H. M. (1992). The Rise of Social Movements and Civil Protests. In T. J. Cheng and S. Haggard, eds., *Political Change in Taiwan*. Boulder: Lynne Rienner Publishers, pp. 57–72.
Huntington, S. (1968). *Political Order in Changing Societies*. New Haven: Yale University Press.
Hutchcroft, P. (2000). Colonial Masters, National Politicos and Provincial Lords: Central Authority and Local Autonomy in the American Philippines. *Journal of Asian Studies*, 59(2), 277–306.
Hutchcroft, P., and Rocamora, J. (2011). Patronage-Based Parties and the Democratic Deficit in the Philippines: Origins, Evolution, and the Imperatives of Reform. In R. Robison, ed., *Routledge Handbook of Southeast Asian Politics*. New York: Routledge, pp. 97–119.
Jansen, M. (2000). *The Making of Modern Japan*. Cambridge: Harvard University Press.
Johnson, C. (1982). *MITI and the Japanese Miracle*. Stanford: Stanford University Press.
Johnson, C. (1987). Political Institutions and Economic Performance: The Government-Business Relationship in Japan, South Korea, and Taiwan. In F. Deyo, ed., *The Political Economy of the New Asian Industrialism*. Ithaca: Cornell University Press, pp. 136–64.
Kasetsiri, C. (1976). *The Rise of Ayudhya: A History of Siam in the Fourteenth and Fifteenth Centuries*. Kuala Lumpur: Oxford University Press.
Kim, S. J. (1971). *The Politics of Military Revolution in Korea*. Chapel Hill: University of North Carolina Press.
Koenig, W. (1990). *The Burmese Polity, 1752–1819: Politics, Administration, and Social Organization in the Early Kon-baung Period*. Ann Arbor: University of Michigan, Center for South and Southeast Asian Studies.
Krauss, E., and Ishida, T. (1989). Japanese Democracy in Perspective. In T. Ishida and E. Krauss, eds., *Democracy in Japan*. Pittsburgh: University of Pittsburgh Press, pp. 327–42.
Lee, N. (2007). *The Making of Minjung: Democracy and the Politics of Representation in South Korea*. Ithaca: Cornell University Press.
Lieberman, V. (2003). *Strange Parallels: Southeast Asia in Global Context, c. 800–1850. Volume 1*. New York: Cambridge University Press.
Linz, J., and Stepan, A. (1996). *Problems of Democratic Transition and Consolidation: Southern Europe, South America, and Post-Communist Europe*. Baltimore: Johns Hopkins University Press.
Mazzuca, S., and Munck, G. (2014). State or Democracy First? Alternative Perspectives on the State-Democracy Nexus. *Democratization*, 21(7), 1221–43.
Møller, J. (2014). Democracy First or State First? A Historical Perspective on the Sequencing Debate. APSA 2014 Annual Meeting Paper. SSRN. Available at: http://papers.ssrn.com/sol3/papers.cfm?abstract_id=2451896 [Accessed 22 June 2019].
Ongkili, J. (1985). *Nation-Building in Malaysia, 1946–1974*. Singapore: Oxford University Press.

Pasuk, P., and Baker, C. (2002). *Thailand: Economy and Politics*, 2nd ed. Kuala Lumpur: Oxford University Press.

Pei, M. (2008). *China's Trapped Transition: The Limits of Developmental Autocracy.* Cambridge: Harvard University Press.

Reid, A. (1993). *Southeast Asia in the Age of Commerce 1450–1680. Volume 2.* New Haven: Yale University Press.

Rodan, G. (2011). Consultative Authoritarianism and Regime Change Analysis: Implications of the Singapore Case. In R. Robison, ed., *Routledge Handbook of Southeast Asian Politic*. New York: Routledge, pp. 120–34.

Rustow, D. (1970). Transition to Democracy: Toward a Dynamic Model. *Comparative Politics*, 2(3), 337–63.

Slater, D. (2003). Iron Cage in an Iron Fist: Authoritarian Institutions and the Personalization of Power in Malaysia. *Comparative Politics*, 36(1), 81–101.

Snyder, J. (2000). *From Voting to Violence: Democratization and Nationalist Conflict*. New York: Norton.

Spence, J. (1990). *The Search for Modern China.* New York: W. W. Norton & Company.

Steinberg, D. J. (2000). *The Philippines: A Singular and Plural Place*, 4th ed. Boulder: Westview Press.

Terwiel, B. J. (2005). *Thailand's Political History: From the Fall of Ayutthaya to Recent Times.* Bangkok: River Books.

Van Creveld, M. (1999). *The Rise and Decline of the State*. New York: Cambridge University Press.

Vu, T. (2010). *Paths to Development in Asia: South Korea, Vietnam, China, and Indonesia*. New York: Cambridge University Press.

Vu, T. (2015). The Making and Unmaking of the Communist Party and Single-Party System of Vietnam. In A. Hicken and E. Kuhonta, eds., *Party System Institutionalization in Asia: Democracies, Autocracies, and the Shadows of the Past.* New York: Cambridge University Press, pp. 136–61.

Weber, M. (1947). *The Theory of Social and Economic Organization.* New York: The Free Press.

Wimmer, A. (2013). *Waves of War: Nationalism, State-Formation, and Ethnic Exclusion in the Modern World.* New York: Cambridge University Press.

Wurfel, D. (1988). *Filipino Politics: Development and Decay.* Ithaca: Cornell University Press.

Zakaria, F. (2003). *The Future of Freedom: Illiberal Democracy at Home and Abroad.* New York: W. W. Norton & Company.

3

South Korea's Democracy and the Legacies of the Developmental State

Olli Hellmann

INTRODUCTION

In comparison with other newly democratizing polities in East Asia and other parts of the developing world, South Korea is generally considered a success story. For example, Diamond describes South Korea along with Japan and Taiwan as the only 'consolidated and liberal democracies' in East Asia (2013:x), while Merkel and Croissant (2004:204) place South Korea in a small group of 'non-defective liberal democracies' in the global South. Similarly, Freedom House has consistently rated the South Korean political system as 'free' since 1989, while the Bertelsmann Transformation Index (BTI) has, since its inception, ranked South Korea among the top fifteen developing countries in terms of *democracy status*. Given that the autocratic regime that preceded South Korea's democratic transition invested heavily in a high-capacity, 'developmental state', the case of Korea seems to confirm the sequentialist argument that high levels of stateness facilitate democratic consolidation.

However, as this chapter will show, such an inferred causal link is too simplistic. Certainly, high state capacity has to a considerable extent contributed to the successful consolidation of democratic institutions and practices. However, as observers of Korean politics point out, South Korea's democracy continues to be plagued by two significant problems. For one, the effectiveness of *horizontal accountability* institutions is severely constrained. In particular, parliament's capacity to provide an independent check on the executive branch is not well developed (e.g. Park, 2000; Croissant, 2002, 2003; Asaba, 2013). Moreover, scholars have criticized that, by adopting highly contentious strategies of mobilization and engagement, *civil society* fails to perform its Tocquevillian function of socializing citizens into civil behaviour (e.g. Kim, 2004, 2009a, 2009b; Oh, 2012; Ku, 2014).

This chapter argues that these weaknesses stem from *the particular institutional choices that were made during the state-building process under autocratic rule*. In other words, the analysis will show that high state capacity does not automatically translate into high-quality democracy; instead, the historical process of state-building and path-dependent effects are key intervening variables that shape the quality of democracy in transition polities.

The argument is based on a conceptualization of state capacity that includes two dimensions: the state's infrastructural power and its social embeddedness. When focusing largely on the second dimension, it will be shown that, although there are various ways in which states can command loyalty from society and increase their capacity to implement policy goals, Korea's military-bureaucratic regime opted for a repression approach. The regime thus invested heavily into coercive instruments rather than building institutions of mass incorporation. For Korea's democratic development after the end of autocratic rule, these strategic choices have had significant consequences, since the architecture of state-society relations remains severely affected by structural weaknesses. Specifically, the under-institutionalization of political parties has contributed to 'hyper-presidential government' (Croissant, 2003), and citizens – largely due to the limited capacity of interest groups to influence political outcomes through formal channels – continue to rely on militant action and popular protest as the main forms of civic engagement.

The chapter proceeds in three steps. First, the chapter outlines the state-building process under autocratic rule. Second, it discusses how this process has shaped the institutional state-society architecture of the post-autocratic political system. And third, the chapter demonstrates how structural weaknesses in the state-society architecture negatively affect the quality of democracy.

THE ORIGINS OF KOREA'S DEVELOPMENTAL STATE

State-Building in a Comparative Perspective

State capacity can be defined as the ability 'to implement official goals, especially over the actual or potential opposition of powerful social groups or in the face of recalcitrant socioeconomic circumstances' (Skocpol, 1985: 8). The concept consists of two components. First, the effective implementation of policy goals depends on the state's physical and institutional base, or what Mann (1984) refers to as *infrastructural power*. As outlined in the introductory chapter, this component can be disaggregated into two analytically distinct dimensions: (1) the state's ability to maintain a monopoly of force (coercive capacity) and (2) the state's organizational competence and bureaucratic quality (administrative capacity). Second, state capacity is also a function of *social embeddedness*. As Migdal (2001) explains, the state is part of an environment of conflict in which a multitude of organizations struggle for social control of the population. Put differently, depending on the distribution of social control, other groups may be able to prevent the enforcement of policy goals. The state, for its part, has – broadly speaking – two strategies available to increase its levels of social control (cf. Migdal, 2001; Vu, 2007; Grzymala-Busse, 2008): punish non-compliance with sanctions (i.e. repress social groups) or promote compliance with rewards (i.e. incorporate social groups). Each of these strategies requires an investment in particular institutions: the state's coercive apparatus and redistributive channels, respectively. The latter may include formal (e.g. political parties, legislatures) and informal institutions (e.g. patron-client networks).

Developmental states are high-capacity states. Not only do they generate extensive infrastructural capacity, but they also possess the ability to command compliance from their citizens (Leftwich, 1995; Evans, 1995). The distinctive feature of South Korea's developmental state, which reached the peak of its ability to co-ordinate industrial transformation between the mid-1960s and the early 1980s, was that it achieved social compliance mainly through repressive means. This sets the Korean developmental state apart from neighbouring developmental states in Japan and Taiwan, where dominant political parties had invested heavily in redistributive institutions: the Liberal Democratic Party (LDP) maintained both close relationships with social interest organizations and a dense network of patron-client machines, while the *Kuomintang* (KMT) organized itself into branches and cells to penetrate key sectors of society.

As argued elsewhere (Hellmann, 2013), these differences can be explained by contagion effects. In the mid-twentieth century, both the LDP and the KMT saw themselves exposed to fierce competition from left-wing political parties, prompting party leaders to implement reforms that were aimed at emulating their respective competitors' *mass party* model of internal organization. In Japan, the introduction of democracy under US supervision gave a significant boost to political forces on the left – most importantly, the Japan Socialist Party (JSP) and the Japanese Communist Party (JCP). Alarmed by these developments, the two major conservative parties merged to form the LDP. The new leadership subsequently took measures to create a 'mass personalized-network party' (Richardson, 2001) that integrated local clientelistic machines into formal organizational structures borrowed from leftist parties. The KMT, on the other hand, had been forced off the Chinese mainland by Mao Zedong's communist forces and withdrew to Taiwan to re-gain strength for a counterattack. After reviewing the reasons behind this catastrophic defeat, the leadership around Chiang Kai-shek concluded that the KMT's organizational weaknesses had contributed considerably to the party's loss of support among the Chinese population. Consequently, it was decided to copy the Communist Party of China and reconstitute the KMT on the Leninist model of party organization (also see Chapter 4 in this volume).

In South Korea, in contrast, the military-bureaucratic regime inherited a political system that – as will be outlined in more detail in the next section – had ruthlessly crushed left-wing groups. Certainly, the regime found itself under threat from the Stalinist North. However, the Korean War (1950–53) had made clear that military capabilities would be key to deterring aggression and ensuring South Korea's security in the future. In short, the military-bureaucratic regime did not experience contagion effects regarding political party organization. Hence, rather than investing in redistributive party channels, the regime focused on strengthening its coercive apparatus as a means to exercise social control.

As will be discussed in this chapter, the developmental state's instruments of repression – although initially highly effective at securing social compliance – increasingly struggled to pressure citizens into acting upon policy decisions. The reason for this was that society grew stronger as the process of industrialization deepened. To counter the state's declining ability to command loyalty, the military-bureaucratic regime began to invest in redistributive institutions. However, this strategic shift came too late, as the regime found itself constrained by two factors: the growing urban parts of society were expensive to buy off, and the strategy of industrialization – which was based on encouraging private savings and extreme debt financing of the corporate sectors – meant that there were no resources available for forging a broad redistributive coalition. Hence, eventually, the regime had to concede to demands for democratization, leaving in its wake a state-society architecture without significant mediating institutions.

The Development of Infrastructural Power

Although the Korean state experienced its most significant boost in infrastructural power in the early years of the Park Chung-hee regime (1961–1979), important groundwork had been laid earlier in the twentieth century – more specifically, under Japanese colonial rule (1910–1945) and the post-World War II regime of Rhee Syngman (1948–1960).

When the Japanese took possession of the Korean peninsula, the local state was showing signs of disintegration. For almost five centuries, the Yi monarchy had ruled Korea in a highly patrimonial fashion without ever extending centralized bureaucratic control beyond the capital. Instead, monarchs relied on the landowning *yangban* class to exercise governmental authority over the population (Palais, 1975). Hence, Japanese colonial authorities, driven by the long-term objective of eventually integrating Korea into an expanded Japan, immediately set out to increase state capacity. Their institution building focused on three different areas (see Kohli, 1994: 1273–75). First, patrimonial elements of the monarchical state were replaced with a depersonalized, hierarchical bureaucracy staffed by colonial officials and Japanese-trained Korean civil servants. Second, the Japanese set up a well-organized, highly disciplined police force. Third, not only were the state's bureaucratic and coercive capacities strengthened, but 'the new state also achieved considerable downward penetration: both the civil and police bureaucracies reached into the nooks and crannies of the society'. To achieve direct bureaucratic penetration, the *yangban* class was incorporated into local governance structures, not without, however, first subordinating it to the new state through an extensive land survey.

The end of colonial rule – precipitated by Japan's surrender in World War II – and the division of the Korean peninsula along the 38th parallel undoubtedly marked a critical juncture in the process of state-building. The implications for the South Korean state in terms of the quality of its institutions were mixed. On the one hand, bureaucratic capacity declined considerably. This was mainly because of the fact that the Japanese withdrawal left a great void in civil service personnel, which the US-backed regime of Rhee Syngman proceeded to fill with politically motivated patronage appointments rather than well-trained technocrats (Haggard et al., 1997: 873). On the other hand, in other aspects of state-building, the Rhee regime produced a more positive impact. In particular, the state's security organs saw a dramatic increase in capacity. As Vu argues, the extreme ideological polarization among political elites incentivized the right-wing Rhee regime to 'revive [...] coercive institutions, reorganize them under Korean command, test them in battles, and re-orient them toward repressing communism' (2007: 35).

However, at the same time as heavily investing in the state as a coercive instrument, Rhee politicized the security apparatus for his own strategic purposes (Kim, 1971: 75–76; Huer, 1989: 13). Critically, by promoting loyal supporters to the highest ranks of the officer corps and playing off rival factions against one another, Rhee succeeded in achieving effective control over the military, which – fuelled by US military aid and the exigencies of the Korean War – had emerged as the most significant organization in the political system. In particular, Rhee used his influence over high-ranking officers to mobilize military units as voters in elections and funnel public funds earmarked for military purposes into his party's coffers. Over time, however, Rhee's meddling in the military's internal affairs was met with increasing opposition from younger officers, eventually contributing to a military coup under the leadership of Park Chung-hee in 1961.

As one of his first priorities, Park purged loyalists of the Rhee regime from the military leadership and then went on to further strengthen the coercive capacities of the state. Most significantly, only a few weeks after taking charge, the new regime set up the Korean Central Intelligence Agency (KCIA), which – equipped with far-reaching authority and placed directly under presidential control – would become 'Park's favorite instrument of power' (Kim, 2011a: 144; also see Kim, 1971: 111–21). Equally important for the state-building process, if not more so, was the regime's decision to re-establish the bureaucracy based on Weberian principles of public administration. As Kim H. A. explains:

The junta also sought to rejuvenate the *haengsi* [administrative entrance examination] system in 1961 by dramatically increasing the number of successful examinees with an eye to recruiting the best of the younger generation in their early twenties, with college and graduate degrees, into the state bureaucracy at the mid-level, and through the establishment of a new Ministry of Government Affairs (MGA) to promote on the basis of merit rather than on the existing tradition of seniority. (2011b: 93–94)

Another important piece in the construction of the developmental state was the centralization of economic decision-making in a powerful Economic Planning Board (EPB). Staffed with highly trained technocrats and bestowed with the power to independently raise capital for industrial projects through foreign loans and investments, the EPB would move on to become *the* key pilot agency responsible for co-ordinating Korea's economic transformation (e.g. Cheng et al., 1998). Finally, by reorganizing the taxation system, the Park regime significantly increased the state's extractive capacity, as reflected in the fact that tax collections – with little change in the tax structure or rates – increased 18.6 per cent in 1964, 44.5 per cent in 1965 and 68.7 per cent in 1966 (Haggard et al., 1991: 864).

To explain why the Park regime engaged in reforms that pushed the Korean state towards the *developmental* type, scholars generally emphasize the belligerent threats posed by North Korea and the scarcity of natural resources in the southern part of the Korean peninsula (e.g. Woo-Cumings, 1998; Doner et al., 2005). Together, these factors created incentives for the Park regime to achieve rapid industrialization, with the developmental state acting as the primary vehicle for transformation.[1]

State-Society Relations: Domination through Repression

As explained in previous chapters, infrastructural power alone is not sufficient for states to be able to extract resources and implement policy effectively; states also need to be equipped with the ability to command loyalty from their citizens. The Korean developmental state performed strongly on this dimension, evidenced by the observation that 'state-society relations in South Korea from 1953 to 1980 were largely devoid of contention' (Vu, 2007: 39). The state's domination over society was a function of two factors: society's own weakness and the state's powerful repressive apparatus. Redistributive institutions, on the other hand, only played a minor role in generating social compliance. The regime attempted to broaden the redistributive coalition in the 1970s; however, its policies for industrialization (and the success of these policies) prevented the regime from buying off urban middle and working classes. Crucially, these classes became the main driving force for democratization in the 1980s.

---

[1] Other scholars disagree, arguing that 'the birth of the developmental state was anything but technocratic. Despite their effectiveness, the administrative reforms carried out by Park and his junta derived from no blueprint or master plan prepared at the outset of the coup [....] On the contrary, the junta's programs were preoccupied with the issue of political control rather than with the question of how to use a strengthened control mechanism for other goals, including economic growth' (Kim, 2011b: 86).

The weakness of Korean society had its origins in colonialism. Not only did Japanese authorities, as briefly mentioned earlier, weaken the landowning elites through a land survey, but they also engaged in systematic repression of the peasantry and urban labour. After World War II, civil society experienced an unprecedented boost in its ability to mobilize support for action, manifested in a wave of protests by peasants and workers. However, the flourishing of civil society did not last long, as the US military government – and later the Rhee regime – 'crushed and mutilated' (Koo, 1993: 135) all organized left-wing movements. The Korean War (1950–53) did the rest to drive these movements into oblivion.

Moreover, the upheaval caused by the war with North Korea undermined the economic and social position of the landholding class. This, in turn, allowed the Rhee regime – pressured by US military authorities – to implement a far-reaching programme of land reform. In the long run, land reform would prove important because, by considerably weakening the *yangban* elite, it increased the autonomy of the state from social actors, thereby establishing the basis for the developmental state's ability to co-ordinate and carry out programmes of industrial transformation (Cumings, 1984). At the same time, the Korean War – and the subsequent reconstruction effort – gave rise to a new economic elite of industrial manufacturing entrepreneurs. Rhee Syngman co-opted this elite into the regime through an informal rent distribution system, which was based on the exchange of public resources (undervalue sale of Japanese-owned property, government and US military contracts, loans at below-market rates) for political support (Han, 1972: 133; Haggard and Moon, 1993: 62–64).

Apart from these informal networks, the Rhee regime did not invest in redistributive institutions. Most notably, investment in political party structures was extremely low. Instead, to win elections, the regime relied mainly on fraud and the mobilization of military personnel as voters (Han, 1974: 27–28). From a rational perspective, these strategic choices make sense (cf. Vu, 2007). Rhee had inherited a highly efficient police force from the Japanese and received considerable US military aid to further increase the state's coercive capacity. Given the relative weakness of society, there were no incentives for Rhee to incorporate the masses into a broader redistributive coalition.

The architecture of state-society relations did not change under Park Chung-hee – at least not initially. However, what did change was that the Park regime, as outlined previously, strengthened the administrative and extractive capacities of the state. The regime then used the state's improved infrastructural power to implement a successful programme of export-oriented industrialization.[2]

More specifically, the regime co-ordinated industrialization through three policy instruments. First, the EPB – as the developmental state's pilot agency – adopted a series of policy measures to manipulate the foreign trade

---

[2] For detailed accounts of the process of industrialization under the Park regime see Amsden (1989), Haggard et al. (1991), Chang (1993) and Kohli (2004: Ch. 3).

regime, such as pegging the Korean won to the US dollar and imposing restrictions on imports. Second, having nationalized the banking sector, the Park regime came to exercise a monopoly on the provision of credit to private business. To generate the necessary capital, the regime took measures to attract foreign loans – in particular from Japan – and encourage private savings. Third, through state-corporatist structures, the regime put tight restrictions on the organization of labour unions, weakening their bargaining power to raise wages and improve working conditions.

Taken together, these interventionist instruments helped the developmental state to deliberately 'get the prices *wrong*' and move the economy through different stages of industrialization. At first, the regime created incentives for private entrepreneurs to focus on low-skilled, labour-intensive manufactured goods such as textiles, footwear and toys. Then, towards the end of the 1960s, the EPB also promoted diversification into high-skilled goods such as electronic products. However, while fuelling rapid economic growth, the success of the export-oriented industrialization programme increasingly undermined Korea's global competitive advantage in labour-intensive manufacturing. In particular, economic expansion had led to a shortage of skilled workers, which – in combination with rising inflation – caused a sharp rise in real wages. As a consequence, in the early 1970s, the regime decided to forge a new niche in the world economy by promoting heavy and chemical industries such as iron and steel, shipbuilding, machinery, electronics and petrochemical processing. The EPB encouraged monopolistic production in some of these industries, based on the calculation that this would strengthen companies' competitiveness through economies of scale. As a result, during this stage of the industrialization process, the level of industrial concentration increased significantly with large conglomerates (the so-called *chaebol*) growing rapidly at the expense of small and medium-sized companies. This fast expansion fuelled by government loans – and this is important for the argument to be made later – meant that the *chaebol* came to have very high debt-to-equity ratios.

However, given that the development of heavy and chemical industries was supplied entirely by energy fuel imports from abroad, the second *oil shock* in 1979 dealt a heavy blow to the government's industrial policy. Consequently, and also partly due to the assassination of Park Chung-hee in October by his own head of security and a disastrous agricultural harvest in the same year, the Korean economy plunged into a severe economic crisis, manifested in a 2 per cent decline in gross domestic product (GDP) in 1980 and the accumulation of US$22 billion in foreign debt during 1979–1982. The successive regime leadership around Chun Doo-hwan reacted to this slump with measures aimed at improving the competitiveness of the *chaebol* – in particular, by opening the domestic market to foreign competition, eliminating market monopolies and allowing the *chaebol* to tap international capital markets for investment. In addition, the government sought to restore macroeconomic stability through fiscal adjustment and budgetary discipline.

Of key importance to the discussion here is that the process of industrialization just outlined significantly reshaped state-society relations – in particular, by strengthening labour's ability to organize collective action. In the late 1960s, when the crisis of the low-skilled, export-oriented manufacturing sectors galvanized workers' grievances, labour protests were largely spontaneous and localized, aimed primarily at improving working conditions at the factory level. However, as industrialization expanded and economic growth transformed the class structure, the organizational capacity of the working class increased dramatically – for mainly two main reasons (see Koo, 1993: 139–41). First, the shift to heavy industrialization in the early 1970s led to a concentration of factory workers in large units of production, which, in turn, helped create working-class communities. Second, parts of the rapidly expanding middle class – especially church groups and students – came to play an important role in raising workers' collective consciousness. As a result, over time, labour activism became more assertive and larger in scale.

The military-bureaucratic regime reacted to labour's growing organizational capacity through repression. In 1972, Park Chung-hee implemented the so-called *Yushin* (Revitalization) constitution, which equipped the regime with even wider powers to restrict protest activity and placed the Federation of Korean Trade Unions – the umbrella movement for all labour unions – under tight corporatist control. When, after Park's assassination, social movements used the ensuing climate of uncertainty to voice their grievances through concerted political action, the Chun regime responded with the full force of the state's coercive apparatus, illustrated most starkly by the new leadership's response to an uprising in the southwestern city of Kwangju in May 1980, which left hundreds of protesters dead.

Despite these advancements in social collective action, the regime never invested in institutions to incorporate the urban middle and working classes into a redistributive coalition. The regime's redistributive coalition was only ever extended to include the *chaebol* and the rural population. The *chaebol* were co-opted through an institutionalized system of corruption, whereby senior regime officials provided privileged access to public resources (credit, import licenses, etc.) in exchange for a kickback (Kang, 2002). The rural population was included in the coalition through the launch of the *Saemaŭl* (New Village) programme in 1970, which showered farmers with generous subsidies. These subsidies were distributed through patron-client machines of individual regime party candidates, thereby effectively turning farmers into loyal voters (Lee, 2011a; Chon, 2000).

It may be argued that the urban middle and working classes were never incorporated into the regime's redistributive coalition for two reasons. First, they were relatively expensive to buy off compared to other social actors and groups. Second, the regime's industrialization policies relied on *extracting* resources out of these classes (savings, labour at globally competitive wage rates) and on aggressively financing growth through debt. Thus, the industrialization strategy did not provide excess resources that the regime could have used to make political side payments to urban middle and working classes. This latter point receives further support when one considers that, during the 1979–1980 economic crisis, the regime saw itself forced to significantly cut down on subsidies to rural sectors in order to ensure macroeconomic stability. The result was declining support for the regime and a strengthening of opposition groups in rural areas (Haggard and Moon, 1993: 87).

In short, it can be concluded that two factors placed the military-bureaucratic regime on a path-dependent route by which repression emerged as the main instrument for organizing state-society relations: (1) the immediate availability of an effective coercive state apparatus after de-colonization and (2) the decision of the Park regime to adopt policies for the promotion of industrialization that were based on financing growth through debt (rather than equity) and squeezing the population for productivity gains. Once set on this trajectory, the regime had no resources available to invest in redistributive institutions.

THE EFFECT OF DEMOCRATIZATION ON THE STATE AND ITS SOCIAL EMBEDDING

As it is widely known, the state's repressive instruments ultimately failed to stem the tide of social unrest. In June 1987, the military-bureaucratic regime conceded to the opposition's demands for constitutional reforms, paving the way for democratization. The state's institutional features, as will be shown in this section, remained largely unaffected by the political changes that ensued.

Certainly, there is evidence that, in the initial stage of the transition, Korea saw an increase in political corruption – driven largely by surging demand for electoral campaign finance – which, in turn, weakened administrative capacity and undermined the state's autonomy from business actors (Kang, 2002; Wad, 2002). However, it appears that the stricter anti-corruption legislation passed under the Roh Moo-hyun administration was able to disrupt the black money market, thereby re-strengthening the state's administrative capabilities (Ko and Cho, 2015).

Moreover, despite significant improvements in terms of political and civil rights that the democratic reforms brought to Korea, the path-dependent development of state-building under autocratic rule left lasting institutional legacies that continue to shape state-society relations. Specifically, by primarily relying on repression as a means to generate social compliance, the military-bureaucratic regime did not equip the post-autocratic political system with institutionalized organizations for state-society mediation – in particular, political parties and interest organizations. In addition, and of critical importance for the development of democracy, such organizations – as the following section will show – have not emerged since.[3]

Generally speaking, political parties can be considered institutionalized when 'they are not subordinated to the interests of ambitious leaders; they acquire an independent status and value of their own' (Mainwaring and Scully, 1995: 5). This condition of autonomy from individual interests, in turn, will only be satisfied 'if parties have firmly established structures; if they are territorially comprehensive; if they are well organized; if they have clearly defined internal structures and procedures; and if they have resources of their own' (Mainwaring, 1999: 28).

Political parties in Korea's new democracy have generally failed to tick any of these boxes. During the 'three Kims' era – which refers to the first generation of post-autocratic politicians who dominated politics until the 2002 presidential elections – party bosses literally ran their parties 'as if they were feudal lords' (Im, 2004: 189): 'Essentially, whenever Kim Dae-Jung, Kim Young-Sam or Kim Jong-Phil [...] founded a party, they brought with them their own leadership group, funding and popular support base. When one of these personalities left to form another party, they gutted the organization, leaving it to wither on the vine' (Heo and Stockton, 2005: 676).

The main mechanism through which the 'three Kims' controlled their political parties was their relatively easy access to political finance. Crucially, the arrival of democracy did not disrupt the 'cosy relationship between top business and political leaders' (Ferdinand, 2003: 62). Quite the opposite happened: as briefly mentioned previously, the introduction of free elections meant that politicians' scramble for money became more intense with the *chaebol* channelling financial contributions to those politicians with the best odds of winning presidential office (see Kang, 2002; Park, 2008). In other words, the 'three Kims', as the strongest contenders for the top executive post, attracted the lion's share of political funding. In contrast, political parties, as abstract organizations, were unable to generate their own sources of income – in particular, because they lacked local organizational structures supported by fee-paying members. Instead, local party branches were the *property* of individual candidates or lawmakers, 'based [...] on personal and particularistic bonds between a political boss and followers' (Park, 1988: 1051).

---

[3] It should be noted, however, that some parts of the state-society architecture *did* change. Most significantly, the *chaebol* – due to the fact the demand for election campaign finance increased considerably – were able to increase their influence over the developmental state's economic planning. In fact, for many scholars of Korean political economy (e.g. Kang, 2002; Kim, 1999), this loss of autonomy marked the end of the developmental state.

To effectively perform their vote-gathering functions, these machines at the local level largely depended on financial resources provided by the party leader, which, in turn, undermined any project of party institutionalization from below (see Hellmann, 2011, 2013). To begin with, due to their near monopoly over the provision of funding, party leaders were able to successfully resist the implementation of institutionalized rules for party internal decision-making. For example, candidate nomination for public election was entirely determined by personal loyalty to the party leader rather than by formal rules of career advancement. The parties of the 'three Kims' thus saw continuous competition for the leader's favour, structured along factional networks that provided individual politicians with a degree of protection in an organizational setting otherwise characterized by high uncertainty. More importantly, the very survival of political parties – and local bosses' machines as their basic organizational units – was inextricably tied to the political career of their respective leaders: if the leader failed to win the election or reached his term limit, the party would simply disintegrate and cease to exist.

With the last of the 'three Kims' having left office, a number of things changed regarding the organization of political parties. First, whereas during the era of the 'three Kims' party leaders were automatically nominated as presidential candidates for their respective parties, parties have since 2002 moved towards more democratic procedures for nominating presidential front-runners, who generally also assume the party leadership. It needs to be stressed, however, that these nomination procedures have not yet become institutionalized; instead, they are renegotiated before every election with the final outcome reflecting the preferences and negotiating power of each pre-candidate (see Hellmann, 2014: 68). Second, in 2004, the Roh Moo-hyun government passed the aforementioned reforms to the campaign funding system, which were aimed at reducing the influence of money in politics. The main components of these reforms were to (1) outlaw corporate contributions to electoral campaigns, (2) set strict campaign spending limits and (3) increase the amount of public funding available to political parties. It appears as if these reforms have been successful at decreasing political corruption and making it more difficult for presidential candidates to attract the same funding streams as the 'three Kims' did (see Ko and Cho, 2015).

However, in other important aspects, the organization of Korean political parties has remained unchanged. First of all, political parties have not made any effort towards developing a formally institutionalized membership organization. Instead, party *branches* continue to depend on the local candidate's own resources for their electoral functions. Moreover, the authority structure remains highly centralized. One reason for this is that parties have still not institutionalized internal career paths. Instead, the selection of candidates remains firmly in the hands of party leaders. Hence, as during the 'three Kims' era, personal loyalty and membership in informal networks are the main criteria shaping party internal hierarchy – a feature that clearly manifests itself before every parliamentary election, when politicians' personal ties to the party leader become a strong predictor for nomination.[4] Finally, party leaders control access to the cabinet and other executive posts, providing yet another mechanism to encourage internal party loyalty.

In short, although political finance structures have become more transparent and party leaders are now selected through competitive means, Korean parties still get 'hijacked' by ambitious leaders for their own ends. This is because, in violation of the necessary conditions for institutionalization outlined in previous sections, they lack formal bureaucratic procedures and a formal rank-and-file membership that could help to *emancipate* the organization from the leader's control. Thus, the case of Korea confirms Hicken and Kuhonta's (2015) argument that party systems in new democracies are unlikely to develop a high level of institutionalization unless the prior autocratic regime had invested in political parties as vehicles of mass mobilization and elite co-optation. Due to their formative history, 'Korean parties are trapped in a vicious cycle of organizational instability' (Lee, 2014). This is primarily due to the fact that those leaders who have succeeded in hijacking a political party are not interested in strengthening its organizational structure – simply because it was the weakness of the organizational structure that allowed them to hijack the party in the first place (Hellmann, 2011, 2013).[5]

However, the party system is not the only part of the state-society architecture that is fragile and failing in its mediating function; interest organizations are also characterized by low levels of institutionalization. In particular, scholars of Korean politics have highlighted two significant problems with civil society. First, interest organizations 'suffer from a lack of financial, human, and organizational resources' (Kim, 2009a: 885). This also applies to the labour movement, which – as explained earlier – was one of the main motors driving the democratization process. Koo (2000: 248) sums up the state of South Korea's trade unionism as follows: 'Although the solidarity demonstrated in [...] labor protests has been impressive, the organizational structure needed to maintain and enhance it remains weak and underdeveloped'. More precisely, the rate of unionization is relatively low, and unionized workers are

---

[4] For example, before the 2008 parliamentary elections, the Grand National Party (GNP) – then dominated by President Lee Myung-bak and his faction – refused to nominate a large number of supporters of Lee's main rival, Park Geun-hye. These supporters then formed a splinter party, winning a considerable number of seats in the election. Before the 2012 parliamentary elections – after Park Geun-hye succeeded in taking control of the party – nomination patterns were reversed: of the sixteen lawmakers who were refused re-nomination, eleven were outspoken Lee loyalists.

[5] The presidential system certainly also plays a role in explaining the under-institutionalization of Korean political parties – mainly because it encourages personality-centred over party-centred electoral competition. However, the comparison with Taiwan, which combines a highly institutionalized party system with a semi-presidential system of government, suggests that the factor of historical party formation weighs more heavily than institutional factors.

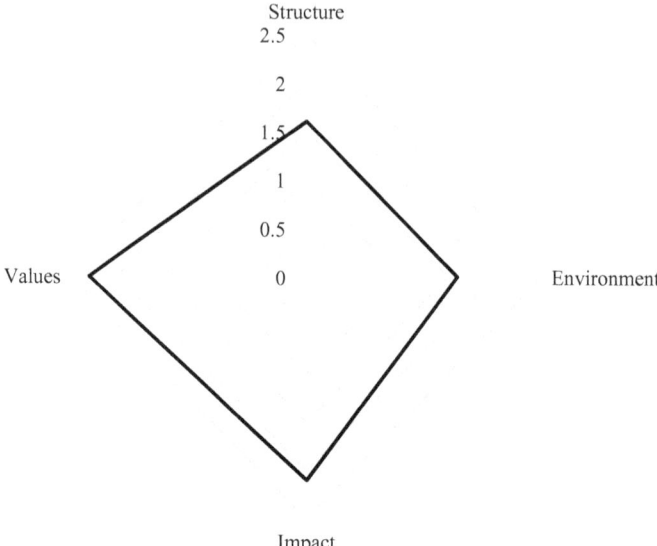

FIGURE 3.1. South Korea's civil society.
Source: CIVICUS Civil Society Index.

predominantly organized in smaller unions at the enterprise level. Second, studies of Korean civil society have drawn attention to the fact that interest organizations are not formally integrated into the policy-making process. As Oh observes, 'Politicians and state actors are not prepared to interact with interest groups, which undermines the groups' potential (and perhaps sole) channel of systematic influence' (2012: 539). A similar and more specific conclusion can also be drawn for the inclusion of trade union organizations into formal structures of consultation: despite anti-labour laws having been lifted at the end of autocratic rule, 'a stable institutionalized industrial order based on compromise with management did not emerge' (Rowley and Bae, 2013: 210).

These weaknesses of the Korean interest-group sector are clearly reflected in the CIVICUS Civil Society Index (see Figure 3.1): Korean interest organizations score relatively low on the dimensions of *structure* (which captures such features as breadth and depth of citizen participation, organizational infrastructure and endowment with resources) and *environment* (which assesses the political and legal context as well as the attitudes and behaviour of state and private-sector actors towards civil society).

Arguably, the weaknesses of Korean interest organizations stem to a large extent from the under-institutionalization of the party system.[6] In many

---

[6] This is not to say that high party system institutionalization is a sufficient explanation for the emergence of strong civil society organizations. As the case of Taiwan shows (see Chapter 4 in this volume), political systems can also combine a highly institutionalized party system with a weak civil society.

established democracies, party-interest group relationships are characterized by shared long-term policy goals and close organizational interaction with political parties providing interest groups with institutionalized access to political power (Allern and Bale, 2012). However, given the low systemness and routinization of Korean political parties, such party-group structures have not emerged in post-autocratic South Korea. Oh (2012: 540) concurs with this argument when she states: 'Effective interest group politics is contingent on the capacity of political parties to serve as a channel between state and society. Political parties should respond to interest group pressure by channelling their demands to the state and also carry state demands back to interest groups. Yet, Korean political parties fulfil neither of these functions'. Likewise, Lee Yoonkyung (2011b: 151) argues that 'for Korean unions, these inchoate and shallow political parties could not be regarded as stable and reliable agents for the representation of labor interests'.

Given the lack of institutionalized party-interest group structures, Korean interest organizations' incorporation into the policy-making process depends on whether this aligns with the strategic interests of the government of the day. Generally speaking, political parties and interest organizations tend to co-operate only on an ad hoc basis, facilitated by interpersonal relationships between party and interest group leaders. In many cases, such co-operation has taken the form of recruiting civil-society leaders into government and state positions. Interest organizations are cut off from political support, including public funding provided through the Law on Promotion of Nonprofit Organizations passed in 2000, at the government's will (Lee and Arrington, 2008). More institutionalized mechanisms for civil society participation were only implemented under the Roh Moo-hyun administration's *collaborative governance* programme – driven by Roh's need to broaden his support basis in the face of strong opposition from within the National Assembly and his own party. Yet, the programme was largely top-down and limited to certain stages in the policy-making process (Kim, 2010).

To citizens, party-interest group relations look a lot like *vertical co-optation*, reducing civil society organizations to mere 'handmaidens of the government'. This is clearly reflected in declining public trust in interest organizations and partly explains why interest organizations struggle to attract members and donations as a means to strengthen their organizational capacity (Kim, 2009a). In other words, civil society associations – just like political parties – appear to be stuck in a vicious circle: because of their institutional weakness, they are easily hijacked for politicians' own political gains, which, in turn, further undermines their ability to engage citizens in their organizational activities.

To sum up this section, the military-bureaucratic regime – by relying mainly on repression to generate social compliance with its policies – implanted state-society structures that were only weakly institutionalized. These structures have changed very little since the introduction of free and fair elections in the late 1980s. Political parties, lacking formal rules for career advancement and rank-and-file organizations, remain easy prey for ambitious politicians. Similarly, interest organizations, due to their low organizational capacity, have struggled to play an independent role in the political process.

STATE-BUILDING'S PATH-DEPENDENT EFFECTS AND THE QUALITY OF DEMOCRACY

There is no doubt that high levels of state capacity have contributed to the relatively high quality of democracy in South Korea. For example, as outlined earlier, the state-building process strengthened the state's authority over other social actors – in particular landowners. Moreover, reforms implemented under Japanese colonial rule and the Park regime significantly boosted the state's administrative and coercive capacity, effectively shielding the bureaucracy against particularistic practices such as corruption and patron-clientelism and introducing a high degree of professionalism into all branches of the state. The final outcome of these processes was a state characterized by high bureaucratic competence and a high degree of autonomy from social interests. For the newly democratizing polity, these state features proved to be extremely beneficial. For example, based on high state capacity, the Korean economy – except during the 1997 financial crisis – continued to enjoy respectable levels of economic growth, which has translated into wide social support for democratic rule (Park and Chu, 2014). Moreover, the state's autonomy has allowed for the effective enforcement of the political institutions that constitute the new regime. Most importantly, elections are performed in stringent consistency with electoral laws (Norris, 2018), and there are no *brown* areas in which citizens' civil rights could be systematically violated by non-state actors. In addition, high levels of state capacity also indirectly helped to establish civilian supremacy over the military, which had arguably been the largest threat to democratic consolidation in Korea. As Croissant et al. (2013) argue, the relationship between democratic consolidation and civilian supremacy is circular. That is to say, all the factors just discussed – democracy's socio-economic embeddedness, the legitimacy accorded to democratic processes and the strength of democratic institutions – have played a crucial role in preventing the military from re-intervening in politics.

Yet, a review of the relevant academic literature reveals that South Korea's democracy, despite showing an overall positive development since the end of autocratic rule, continues to face two problems. First, the dimension of *horizontal accountability* – defined by Merkel (2004: 40) as the condition 'that elected authorities are surveyed by a network of relatively autonomous institutions' – is notably impaired. More specifically, the National Assembly does not effectively check the executive, thus shifting the equilibrium of the balance of power unilaterally in favour of the president. Second, *civil society* associations largely fail to perform their function of socializing citizens into democratic and civil

South Korea's Democracy and the Legacies of the Developmental State

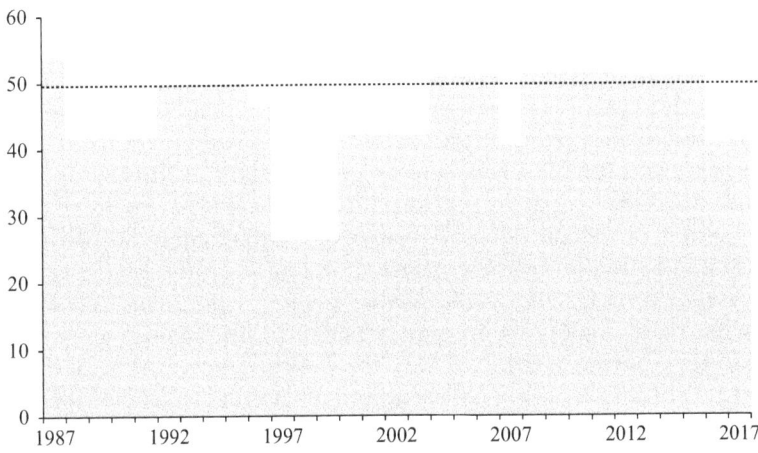

FIGURE 3.2. Seat share in per cent of the president's party (based on legislative election results).
Source: Author's own calculation.

behaviour. Instead, civil society has, even with the military-bureaucratic regime removed, largely retained its *uncivil* approach to engaging in the political process. As the following section will show, both of these problems can be linked to the under-institutionalization of the state-society architecture and thus to the process of state-building under autocratic rule.

Executive-legislative relations in South Korea's new democracy have been described as 'hyper-presidential government' (Croissant, 2003) and 'imperial presidency' (Shin, 2003: 233). At least, this is the case when a single party maintains unified control of the presidency and the National Assembly. As can be seen from Figure 3.2, since the Korean party system consolidated around two main parties in the early 1990s, periods of unified government – measured as the legislative seat share of the president's party – have been more prevalent than periods of divided government. Moreover, in cases where the president's party failed to win an outright majority of seats, governments have often been able to construct post-election majorities, facilitated by the fluid nature of the party system. In particular, governments have been benefitting from the common practice of party switching, the ephemeral nature of smaller parties and the relatively large number of independent legislators.

During periods of unified government, the National Assembly and individual lawmakers do not play an independent role in the political process, meaning that the constitutional checks and balances for limiting executive power are undermined. The resulting 'majority terror' (Croissant, 2002: 16) by the government manifests itself in a number of ways. Regarding the lawmaking process, it can be observed that opposition parties are passed over in the allocation of parliamentary committee chairs, most legislative initiatives originate in the executive branch, and proposed bills are typically whipped through the National Assembly without consultation or debate (Croissant, 2003: 87). Moreover, unconstrained by parliamentary control, executives have, in the past, enjoyed great discretion in using authoritarian-era laws, such as the defamation law and the National Security Law, against political opponents (Haggard and You, 2015).

There is considerable agreement among scholars of Korean politics that this executive-heavy distribution of political power is not so much the result of the design of the presidential system per se but more so of the under-institutionalization of political parties. Similar to Shin (2003: 232; also see Croissant, 2003: 81; Kim, 2008; Asaba, 2013: 47–48), many scholars argue that 'what really makes the Korean presidency 'hegemonic' or 'imperial' is not statutory power at all [....] It is the political power that derives from the top position in a highly coherent and disciplined ruling party'. As outlined in some detail earlier, presidential candidates, due to the low systemness of party organization, are able to hijack political parties for their own personal interests. They secure the loyalty of individual politicians within the party mainly through the mechanisms of political finance, candidate selection and executive post allocation, which, at the same time, provide formidable *sticks* for punishing National Assembly members who do not toe the official party line.

In line with these arguments, since the end of the 'three Kims' era and the implementation of stricter political funding laws, it has been observed that party discipline in the National Assembly has been somewhat weaker (e.g. Jaung, 2005: 56–58). However, although individual national assemblymen have come to rely more on their own efforts to raise campaign money than in the past, career paths continue to be shaped by loyalties to political leaders. In other words, political finance reforms have done little to counteract hyper-presidentialism. For instance, the presidency of Lee Myung-bak (2008–2013) was characterized by repeated bursts of majority terror such as the ratification of a free-trade agreement with the United States in December 2008 and the passing of new media laws in July 2009 – both of which were pushed through parliament against the strong resistance from opposition parties, provoking the latter to resort to violent means to disrupt the voting. Similarly, under the Park Geun-hye (2013–2017) administration, the opposition at times saw no other option but to engage in contentious action as a means to influence legislative proceedings. Most notably, in August 2014, opposition parties staged a sit-in when the government refused to set up an independent commission to investigate the Sewol ferry disaster.

While physical violence is only a strategy of last resort in the legislative process, the same cannot be said about the extra-parliamentary arena. Outside of formal institutional channels, civil society groups regularly use militant tactics to achieve their goals. In fact, as quantitative data available until 2009 shows (see Kim, 2009b), the level of popular protest has not declined significantly since the autocratic regime relinquished power. What is more, the proportion of large-sized protests (2,000 people or more) has been increasing, and almost three-fourths of protests are either violent (e.g. resulting in physical harm or property damage) or disruptive (e.g. occupation of public space, strikes) in nature. Hence, the general consensus in the relevant academic literature is that 'civic groups in Korea are more inclined to employ militant strategies than to see compromises and consensus when dealing with social and economic conflicts' (Lim and Tang, 2002: 574; also see Oh, 2012; Kim, 2004).

These strategies have, in many cases, proven effective. For example, one policy area that is regularly referred to when discussing civil society's ability to influence political decision-making is that of environmental politics, where social movements have, since the early 1990s, repeatedly been successful in putting up resistance against infrastructure projects perceived to be environmentally harmful (e.g. Heo, 2013; Lim and Tang, 2002). However, because of the frequent use of violent and disruptive strategies, it is questionable whether civil society groups perform their function as *schools of democracy*. By fomenting militant action against the state and the political class, civil society does not provide a favourable space for cultivating civic virtues and socializing citizens into accepting democratic norms.

The under-institutionalization of the state-society architecture plays an important part in explaining the prevalence of violent and disruptive conflicts between civil society and the state. First, formal interest groups do not provide citizens with institutionalized access to the political process. This is due to their own organizational weaknesses and the unwillingness – or inability – of political parties to engage with interest groups in a regularized format. As Lee (2006: 732) argues in the case of labour politics, 'The unions, being unable to effectively influence either the electoral space or the centralized policy making process, have resorted to disruptive activities outside of institutionalized politics'. Second, political parties do not enable citizen participation in politics either. As outlined earlier, Korean parties are highly elitist organizations, characterized by the lack of mass membership organizations. The consequences of this for civil society activism are perfectly summed up by Kim (2009b: 20): 'Frustrated by amorphous political parties with unclear visions and options, South Korean citizens continue to rely on civic engagement focused on direct action and popular protest'.

CONCLUSION

When the military-bureaucratic regime gave way to democratization in the late 1980s, it left behind a high-capacity developmental state characterized by strong infrastructural power and a large degree of autonomy from society. While the state's infrastructural power has undoubtedly helped to consolidate certain partial regimes of Korea's new democracy (such as the all-important electoral regime), the architecture of state-society relations continues to pose problems for democratic consolidation.

In other words, this chapter has argued that the problems of South Korea's new democracy can be traced back to the *state-building process* under autocratic rule. To construct the developmental state – specifically, to generate social compliance with the state's transformational programmes – the military-bureaucratic regime relied primarily on coercive means. Investment in redistributive channels, such as political parties or clientelistic networks, remained low. Two factors, in particular, explain these strategic choices: the regime inherited a well-oiled repressive state apparatus from the Japanese colonialists, and the programme of industrialization adopted under Park Chung-hee's leadership was based on a debt-and-extraction model. Taken together, these two factors locked the state-building process on a path-dependent trajectory, making it impossible to switch to a redistribution strategy when, from the mid-1970s onwards, the state's coercive instruments increasingly struggled to contain social pressure for democratic reform.

The autocratic regime's over-reliance on repression as a compliance mechanism has left Korea's new democracy with a lasting legacy. Most importantly, the state-society architecture lacks significant mediating institutions that could play an independent role in the political process: political parties are only weakly institutionalized and thus easy prey for ambitious politicians, while interest groups struggle with a lack of organizational resources and institutionalized access to the political decision-making process. The consequences for the quality of democracy are considerable. The under-institutionalization of political parties means that parliament fails to provide an effective check on executive power, while the structural weakness of formal interest groups explains why civil society continues to engage in militant tactics when pushing for its demands.

Overall, the findings presented here suggest that high state capacity does not automatically translate into high-quality democracy. Rather, researchers need to pay more attention to the historical process of state-building and the mechanisms through which state capacity has been built. Moreover, this chapter highlighted how important it is to analyse the state's social embeddedness if we want to further our understanding of the relationship between state capacity and the quality of democracy. The architecture of state-society relations, however, is not a concept that is easily measurable in quantitative terms. Thus, future research on the state-democracy nexus is well advised to combine large-N analyses with qualitative, in-depth case studies.

References

Allern, E. H., and Bale, T. (2012). Political parties and interest groups: Disentangling complex relationships. *Party Politics*, 18(1), 7–25.

Amsden, A. H. (1989). *Asia's Next Giant: South Korea and Late Industrialization*. New York: Oxford University Press.

Asaba, Y. (2013). Presidentialism in Korea: A strong president and a weak government. In Y. Kasuya, ed., *Presidents, Assemblies and Policy-making in Asia*. Basingstoke and New York: Palgrave Macmillan, pp. 40–58.

Chang, H. J. (1993). The political economy of industrial policy in Korea. *Cambridge Journal of Economics*, 17(2), 131–57.
Cheng, T. J., Haggard, S., and Kang, D. (1998). Institutions and growth in Korea and Taiwan: The bureaucracy. *The Journal of Development Studies*, 34(6), 87–111.
Chon, S. (2000). The election process and informal politics in South Korea. In L. Dittmer, H. Fukui, and P. N. S. Lee, eds., *Informal Politics in East Asia*. Cambridge: Cambridge University Press, pp. 66–81.
Croissant, A. (2002). Strong presidents, weak democracy? Presidents, parliaments and political parties in South Korea. *Korea Observer*, 33(1), 1–45.
Croissant, A. (2003). Legislative powers, veto players, and the emergence of delegative democracy: A comparison of presidentialism in the Philippines and South Korea. *Democratization*, 10(3), 68–98.
Croissant, A. et al. (2013). *Democratization and Civilian Control in Asia*. Basingstoke: Palgrave Macmillan.
Cumings, B. (1984). The origins and development of the Northeast Asian political economy: Industrial sectors, product cycles, and political consequences. *International Organization*, 38(1), 1–40.
Diamond, L. (2013). Introduction. In L. Diamond, M. F. Plattner, and Y. H. Chu, eds., *Democracy in East Asia: A New Century*. Baltimore: Johns Hopkins University Press, pp. ix–xxx.
Doner, R. F., Ritchie, B. K., and Slater, D. (2005). Systemic vulnerability and the origins of developmental states: Northeast and Southeast Asia in comparative perspective. *International Organization*, 59(2), 327–61.
Evans, P. B. (1995). *Embedded Autonomy: States and Industrial Transformation*. Princeton: Princeton University Press.
Ferdinand, P. (2003). Party funding and political corruption in East Asia: The cases of Japan, South Korea and Taiwan. In R. Austin and M. Tjernström, eds., *Funding of Political Parties and Election Campaigns*. Stockholm: International Idea, pp. 55–70.
Grzymala-Busse, A. (2008). Beyond clientelism: Incumbent state capture and state formation. *Comparative Political Studies*, 41(4–5), 638–73.
Haggard, S., and Moon, C. I. (1993). The state, politics, and economic development in postwar South Korea. In Koo, H., ed., *State and Society in Contemporary Korea*. Ithaca: Cornell University Press, pp. 51–93.
Haggard, S., and You, J. S. (2015). Freedom of expression in South Korea. *Journal of Contemporary Asia*, 45(1), 167–79.
Haggard, S., Kim, B. K., and Moon, C. I. (1991). The transition to export-led growth in South Korea: 1954–1966. *The Journal of Asian Studies*, 50(4), 850–73.
Haggard, S., Kang, D., and Moon, C. I. (1997). Japanese colonialism and Korean development: A critique. *World Development*, 25(6), 867–81.
Han, S. (1974). *The Failure of Democracy in South Korea*. Berkeley: University of California Press.
Han, Y. C. (1972). Political parties and elections in South Korea. In S. J. Kim and C. H. Cho, eds., *Government and Politics of Korea*. Silver Spring: The Research Institute on Korean Affairs, pp. 127–47.
Hellmann, O. (2011). *Political Parties and Electoral Strategy: The Development of Party Organization in East Asia*. Basingstoke: Palgrave Macmillan.

Hellmann, O. (2013). The developmental state and electoral markets in East Asia: How strategies of industrialization have shaped party institutionalization. *Asian Survey*, 53(4), 653–78.

Hellmann, O. (2014). Party system institutionalization without parties: Evidence from Korea. *Journal of East Asian Studies*, 14(1), 53–84.

Heo, I. (2013). Changing aspects of government–society relations in South Korea: Evidence from the evolution of environmental-policy governance. *Contemporary Politics*, 19(4), 459–73.

Heo, U., and Stockton, H. (2005). The impact of democratic transition on elections and parties in South Korea. *Party Politics*, 11(6), 674–88.

Hicken, A., and Kuhonta, E. M. (2015). Introduction: Rethinking party system institutionalization in Asia. In A. Hicken and E. M. Kuhonta, eds., *Party System Institutionalization in Asia: Democracies, Autocracies, and the Shadows of the Past*. New York: Cambridge University Press, pp. 1–24.

Huer, J. (1989). *Marching Orders: The Role of the Military in South Korea's 'Economic Miracle', 1961–1971*. New York: Greenwood Press.

Im, H. B. (2004). Faltering democratic consolidation in South Korea: Democracy at the end of the 'three Kims' era. *Democratization*, 11(5), 179–98.

Jaung, H. (2005). Foreign policy and South Korean democracy: The failure of party politics. *Taiwan Journal of Democracy*, 1(2), 49–68.

Kang, D. C. (2002). Bad loans to good friends: Money politics and the developmental state in South Korea. *International Organization*, 56(1), 177–207.

Kim, B. K. (2011a). The labyrinth of solitude: Park and the exercise of presidential power. In B. K. Kim, and E. F. Vogel, eds., *The Park Chung Hee Era: The Transformation of South Korea*. Cambridge: Harvard University Press, pp. 140–67.

Kim, E. (2009a). The limits of NGO-government relations in South Korea. *Asian Survey*, 49(5), 873–94.

Kim, H. A. (2011b). State building: The military junta's path to modernity through administrative reforms. In B. K. Kim and E. F. Vogel, eds., *The Park Chung Hee Era: The Transformation of South Korea*. Cambridge: Harvard University Press, pp. 85–111.

Kim, S. (2004). South Korea: Confrontational legacy and democratic contributions. In M. Alagappa, ed., *Civil Society and Political Change in Asia: Expanding and Contracting Democratic Space*. Stanford: Stanford University Press, pp. 138–63.

Kim, S. (2009b). Civic engagement and democracy in South Korea. *Korea Observer*, 40(1), 1–26.

Kim, S. (2010). Collaborative governance in South Korea: Citizen participation in policy making and welfare service provision. *Asian Perspective*, 34(3), 165–90.

Kim, S. J. (1971). *The Politics of Military Revolution in Korea*. Chapel Hill: University of North Carolina Press.

Kim, Y. (2008). Intra-party politics and minority coalition government in South Korea. *Japanese Journal of Political Science*, 9(3), 367–89.

Kim, Y. T. (1999). Neoliberalism and the decline of the developmental state. *Journal of Contemporary Asia*, 29(4), 441–61.

Ko, K., and Cho, S. Y. (2015). Evolution of anti-corruption strategies in South Korea. In Y. Zhang and C. Lavena, eds., *Government Anti-Corruption Strategies: A Cross-Cultural Perspective*. Boca Raton: CRC Press, pp. 103–22.

Kohli, A. (1994). Where do high growth political economies come from? *The Japanese lineage of Korea's 'developmental state'*. World Development, 22(9), 1269–93.

Kohli, A. (2004). *State-Directed Development: Political Power and Industrialization in the Global Periphery*. Cambridge: Cambridge University Press.

Koo, H. (1993). The state, minjung, and the working class in South Korea. In H. Koo, ed., *State and Society in Contemporary Korea*. Ithaca: Cornell University Press, pp. 131–62.

Koo, H. (2000). The dilemmas of empowered labor in Korea: Korean workers in the face of global capitalism. *Asian Survey*, 40(2), 227–50.

Ku, J. H. (2014). The decline of political participation in Korea between 2000 and 2011. In G. M. D. Dore, J. H. Ku, and K. Jackson, eds., *Incomplete Democracies in the Asia-Pacific: Evidence from Indonesia, Korea, the Philippines and Thailand*. Basingstoke and New York: Palgrave Macmillan, pp. 119–42.

Lee, S. J., and Arrington, C. (2008). The politics of NGOs and democratic governance in South Korea and Japan. *Pacific Focus*, 23(1), 75–96.

Lee, Y. (2006). Varieties of labor politics in Northeast Asian democracies: Political institutions and union activism in Korea and Taiwan. *Asian Survey*, 46(5), 721–40.

Lee, Y. (2011a). *Militants or Partisans: Labor Unions and Democratic Politics in Korea and Taiwan*. Palo Alto: Stanford University Press.

Lee, Y. (2014). Diverging patterns of democratic representation in Korea and Taiwan. *Asian Survey*, 54(3), 419–44.

Lee, Y. J. (2011b). The countryside. In B. K. Kim and E. F. Vogel, eds., *The Park Chung Hee Era: The Transformation of South Korea*. Cambridge: Harvard University Press, pp. 345–72.

Leftwich, A. (1995). Bringing politics back in: Towards a model of the developmental state. *The Journal of Development Studies*, 31(3), 400–27.

Lim, J. H., and Tang, S. Y. (2002). Democratization and environmental policy-making in Korea. *Governance*, 15(4), 561–82.

Mainwaring, S. (1999). *Rethinking Party Systems in the Third Wave of Democratization: The Case of Brazil*. Stanford: Stanford University Press.

Mainwaring, S., and Scully, T. R. (1995). Introduction: Party systems in Latin America. In S. Mainwaring and T. R. Scully, eds., *Building Democratic Institutions: Party Systems*. Stanford: Stanford University Press, pp. 1–34.

Mann, M. (1984). The autonomous power of the state: Its origins, mechanisms and results. *European Journal of Sociology*, 25(2), 185–213.

Merkel, W. (2004). Embedded and defective democracies. *Democratization*, 11(5), 33–58.

Merkel, W., and Croissant, A. (2004). Conclusion: Good and defective democracies. *Democratization*, 11(5), 199–213.

Migdal, J. S. (2001). *State in Society: Studying How States and Societies Transform and Constitute One Another*. Cambridge: Cambridge University Press.

Norris, P. (2018). Electoral integrity in East Asia. In T. J. Cheng and Y. H. Chu, eds., *Routledge Handbook of Democratization in East Asia*. Abingdon and New York: Routledge, pp. 405–24.

Oh, J. S. (2012). Strong state and strong civil society in contemporary South Korea: Challenges to democratic governance. *Asian Survey*, 52(3), 528–49.

Palais, J. B. (1975). *Politics and Policy in Traditional Korea*. Cambridge: Harvard University Press.

Park, C. H. (2008). A comparative institutional analysis of Korean and Japanese clientelism. *Asian Journal of Political Science*, 16(2), 111–29.

Park, C. M., and Chu, Y. H. (2014). Trends in attitudes toward democracy in Korea and Taiwan. In L. Diamond, and D. Shin, eds., *Institutional Reform and Democratic Consolidation in Korea*. Stanford: Hoover Institution Press, pp. 27–67.

Park, C. W. (1988). Legislators and their constituents in South Korea: The patterns of district representation. *Asian Survey*, 28(10), 1049–65.

Park, C. W. (2000). Legislative-executive relations and legislative reform. In L. Diamond and D. Shin, eds., *Institutional Reform and Democratic Consolidation in Korea*. Stanford: Hoover Institution Press, pp. 73–96.

Richardson, B. (2001). Japan's '1955 system' and beyond. In L. Diamond, and R. Gunther, eds., *Political Parties and Democracy*. Baltimore: Johns Hopkins University Press, pp. 143–69.

Rowley, C., and Bae, K. S. (2013). Waves of anti-unionism in South Korea. In G. Gall, and T. Dundon, eds., *Global Anti-Unionism: Nature, Dynamics, Trajectories and Outcomes*. Basingstoke and New York: Palgrave Macmillan, pp. 207–22.

Shin, D. C. (2003). Democratic governance in South Korea: The perspectives of ordinary citizens and their elected representatives. *Japanese Journal of Political Science*, 4(2), 215–40.

Skocpol, T. (1985). Bringing the state back in: Strategies of analysis in current research. In P. B. Evans, D. Rueschemeyer, and T. Skocpol, eds., *Bringing the State Back In*. Cambridge: Cambridge University Press, pp. 3–37.

Vu, T. (2007). State formation and the origins of developmental states in South Korea and Indonesia. *Studies in Comparative International Development*, 41(4), 27–56.

Wad, P. (2002). The political business of development in South Korea. In E. Gomez, ed., *Political Business in East Asia*. London: Routledge, pp. 182–215.

Woo-Cumings, M. J. E. (1998). National security and the rise of the developmental state in South Korea and Taiwan. In H. S. Rowen, ed., *Behind East Asian Growth: The Political and Social Foundations of Prosperity*. London: Routledge, pp. 319–40.

4

After Hegemony: State Capacity, the Quality of Democracy and the Legacies of the Party-State in Democratic Taiwan

Kharis Templeman

INTRODUCTION

Taiwan is one of the resounding success stories of the third wave of democratization. Beginning in 1986, it transitioned over a ten-year span from a repressive autocracy to one of Asia's most liberal and vibrant democracies. Although it has faced some challenging moments since, today Taiwan's democracy appears to be of high quality and well-consolidated. In 2017, Taiwan was ranked 'free' by Freedom House (2018) with an overall score of 93/100, second in East and Southeast Asia only to Japan's score of 96 and significantly better than Mongolia (85), South Korea (84), the Philippines (62), Indonesia (64), East Timor (69), Hong Kong (59), Singapore (52), Thailand (31), Myanmar (31) and Cambodia (30). Findings are similar for other democracy barometers such as the Polity IV project (2016), the Varieties of Democracy (Huang, 2017) and the Bertelsmann Transformation Index (2018). Taiwan also scores high to very high on rule of law (World Bank, 2015; GAN, 2019) and freedom of media indicators (Reporters without Borders, 2019), consistently leading the region on the latter.

As both a 'late developer' and an even later democratizer, Taiwan is a case that appears to fit nicely with the sequentialist argument laid out in the introduction and Chapter 2 of this volume: to get high-quality democracy, it is beneficial to first build state capacity and then (and only then) introduce popular elections.[1] The consolidation of Taiwan's democracy has clearly been aided by the prior existence of a high-capacity state. Most notably, well-run elections, the unquestioned supremacy of elected civilian leaders over unelected ones

---

[1] Or at least, elections for the central government. The regime in Taiwan allowed contested elections for local offices beginning in the early 1950s, even as the central level remained off-limits.

and a highly institutionalized party system are major strengths of the contemporary democratic regime on Taiwan that can be directly linked back to the character of the state in the pre-democratic era. But the Taiwan case does not necessarily contradict the alternative, nexian perspective, either. The high capacity of the state appears to have had at best no effect on and, at worst, actively undermined the establishment of a robust rule of law and protections for civil liberties. These have improved in Taiwan despite, not because of, the legacies of the authoritarian era and for the most part have trailed – rather than preceded and facilitated – democratic deepening. Indeed, arguably the most important lesson to be taken from the Taiwan experience is the power of initial conditions to shape the quality of democracy over the long run. There is remarkable path-dependence in the Taiwanese regime's democratic evolution: most of the prominent strengths and enduring weaknesses of Taiwan's democracy can be traced directly back to the survival of the former hegemonic party, the Chinese Nationalist Party or Kuomintang (KMT), at the advent of democratization over thirty years ago and to the gradual, legacy-preserving way that the transition unfolded.

At the beginning of the democratic era, the state in Taiwan had at least four distinct features that set it apart from the other cases in this volume: a 'bifurcation' between a high capacity, high autonomy central government and deeply socially embedded local governments, a fused 'party-state' regime, a vibrant but fragmented and shallowly rooted civil society sector and a business community with only limited influence over the central government. These features have together shaped a distinct kind of democratic political regime in Taiwan. On the positive side, the comprehensive extension of state authority into the furthest reaches of Taiwanese territory during the early martial law years in the 1950s, along with the high professional capacity of the state's agents and its population registration system, combined to enable the development of a very high-quality system of election management even under martial law (1949–1987). In addition, the Leninist-style fusion of party and state ensured the thorough penetration of and control over military and security agencies by the civilian (party) leadership, so that at the advent of the transition to democracy the top leaders of the KMT regime enjoyed uncircumscribed authority over all parts of the state. And while these leaders were unaccountable to Taiwanese citizens until the 1990s, the introduction of full, direct elections for the legislature (in 1992) and the president (in 1996) settled this matter for good; national elections now confer on their winners the fully effective right to rule with no reserved domains for unelected officials.

The gradual nature of the transition to democracy, and especially the survival of the hegemonic ruling party into the democratic era, also had some surprisingly salutary consequences for the quality of the subsequent regime. The KMT was able to preserve the vast organizational and financial resources it built up during the pre-democratic era for use in fully contested elections, giving it a systematic advantage over opposition party challengers and helping it stay in power (cf. Hellmann, 2013). While this legacy presented an obvious stumbling block to democratic consolidation, it also had some beneficial effects (cf. Loxton, 2015). Chief among these was the institutionalization of the party system: the KMT was willing to allow open contestation for elections that it expected to win, and unlike in Korea, opposition to the regime was channelled into electoral mobilization rather than mass protests (Cheng and Hsu, 2015; Hellmann, 2011: 67–96; Mobrand, 2014). The opposition also prioritized expansion of political rights and a relaxation of restrictions on campaigns, and the KMT leadership acceded to these reforms because of its electoral strength (cf. Slater and Wong, 2013). As a consequence, Taiwan's democracy now exhibits broad respect for the full array of political rights, including freedoms of speech and assembly, the right to start new political parties, to organize and demonstrate for political goals and to campaign for office unhindered.

On the less positive side, Taiwan's civil rights regime, while well-regarded today, continues to suffer from weak legal foundations. In the pre-democratic era, the KMT and the state dominated the judiciary and subsumed legal decisions under party and bureaucratic control (Chisholm, 2014). The transition to democracy occurred well before the consolidation of an impartial rule of law regime, and as a consequence, reform of the judicial branch has continued to lag behind progress in other areas (Chang, 2018). Likewise, horizontal accountability has been incompletely institutionalized, despite the regime's formal separation of powers. The main check on the executive branch in practice comes from the legislature, not the judiciary, and legislators in turn are motivated mostly by partisan concerns rather than institutional ones. When the same party controls both branches, as has been the case since 2008, horizontal accountability is significantly weakened. Thus, Taiwan's highly developed state at the beginning of the democratic era appears to have had at best no effect and at worst actively undermined establishment of a robust rule of law and protections for civil liberties. These have improved in Taiwan despite, not because of, its state capacity, as partisan influence over the judiciary has gradually waned.

THINKING ABOUT TAIWAN'S DEMOCRACY AS 'PARTIAL REGIMES'

Rating the 'Partial Regimes' of Taiwan's Democracy

In a 2004 piece in the journal *Democratization,* Wolfgang Merkel (2004) criticized the then-prevailing tendency of scholars to treat democracy and autocracy as a simple dichotomy and of some global rankings organizations to focus on narrow, procedural definitions of democracy over broader, richer and multifaceted ones. As an alternative to the minimalist approach, Merkel proposed what he termed 'embedded democracy'. In this formulation, liberal democracy consists of five 'partial regimes' that depend upon and reinforce one another: *elections, political rights participation, civil rights, horizontal accountability* and *effective power to govern*. Merkel argues that high-quality democracies meet best practices in all five of these areas, ensuring that elections are meaningful and that those who win elections will govern in accordance with constitutional principles. When democracies fall short in one or more of these components, they are 'defective' in some way.

One can use this five-part framework to assess Taiwan's contemporary democracy. To do so, this chapter draws on the latest Freedom House's Freedom in the World 2018 country report,[2] supplemented with other quantitative and qualitative evidence from the literature on democratic practice in Taiwan. The Freedom House aggregate democracy score for Taiwan was 93/100 for 2017, an increase from 91 in 2016 and 89 in 2015. That result puts Taiwan's democracy among the most democratic in Asia, second only to Japan's 2017 score of 96/100. If we drill down into the five partial regimes, we can get a better sense of the strengths and remaining weaknesses of embedded democratic practice in Taiwan.

First, what of Taiwan's electoral regime? Freedom House gives a perfect score for electoral processes, noting that direct elections for the president and legislature have generally been free and fair since their introduction in the 1990s and that these elected representatives hold real authority in their respective branches of government. Likewise, the most recent Electoral Integrity Project report rates Taiwan at the top of the region, tied with South Korea for the best electoral processes and pluralism in East Asia (Norris et al., 2018). An important reason for the high integrity of elections is that the Central Election Commission, Taiwan's election management body, was professionalized and given significant autonomy well before the end of the martial law era (Su, 2020; Templeman, 2017). Today, it remains independent of control by any political party, and election irregularities are rare. Since the transition to democracy, the one persistent threat to electoral integrity – one that shows up in comparative ranking systems such as the Varieties of Democracy Project as well as in Taiwan case studies – is vote buying. But that, too, has waned since the mid-2000s thanks to increased media scrutiny, an aggressive campaign by prosecutors' offices and tighter enforcement of anti-corruption laws (Göbel, 2016; Huang, 2017; Wang, 2016).

Freedom House is also quite positive overall about Taiwan's political rights regime, as are most scholars who evaluate Taiwan comparatively.[3] Citizens 'have the right to organize in different political parties', and the political system is 'free of undue obstacles to the rise and fall of these parties…'. There is vigorous electoral competition between the KMT and Democratic Progressive Party (DPP) throughout most of Taiwan's jurisdictions, and smaller parties have been able to operate 'without interference' and have contested both the most recent

---

[2] Available at https://freedomhouse.org/report/freedom-world/2018/taiwan.
[3] Rigger, 2018: 153. For other recent work that assesses Taiwan's democracy against comparative benchmarks and finds it generally compares well, see Dickson 2018; Chang et al., 2011; McAllister, 2016; Mobrand, 2014; and Sanborn, 2015.

presidential and legislative elections. The opportunity for opposition parties to increase their support and take power through elections was powerfully demonstrated in 2016, when the DPP won a decisive victory over the KMT in the presidential election and captured a majority in the legislature for the first time. Taiwan's media 'reflect a diversity of views and report aggressively on government policies and corruption allegations'. Freedoms of assembly, speech and the academy are all consistently respected and non-governmental organizations and other civil society groups can organize and operate without government interference. One concern about political rights highlighted in the Freedom House report, and in recent writings about democracy in Taiwan, is the threat that mainland Chinese influence poses to the public sphere; some media owners have significant business interests in China, 'leaving them vulnerable to pressure and prone to self-censorship' on sensitive topics.[4] But media regulators have also blocked proposed mergers that would have concentrated media outlets in the hands of China-friendly ownership (Rawnsley et al., 2016).

Taiwan's civil rights regime appears to be the most problematic of the five 'partial regimes', although it has in recent years followed a 'nexian'-style trajectory of gradual, piecemeal improvements pushed via civil society activism, media reporting and electoral campaigns. Recent critiques of civil rights practices in Taiwan note several continuing areas of concern related to the rule of law, including inconsistent application of eminent domain laws to seize property, poor legal protections for foreign migrant workers and inadequate enforcement of special protections for the land rights of indigenous peoples (Freedom House, 2018). Violence against women remains a 'serious problem', although Freedom House notes gradual improvement in procedures for reporting and punishing rape and sexual assault. Following a constitutional court decision in 2017, the legislature finally implemented legal recognition of same-sex marriage in 2019, but the rights of same-sex couples remain more circumscribed than heterosexual ones. On the positive side, a number of scholars have noted that Taiwan's judiciary is now reasonably independent and its rulings generally are free of political interference; that violations of criminal defendants' rights have decreased in frequency in recent years; and that constitutional protections for due process and safeguards against arbitrary police detention are largely respected (e.g. Garoupa et al., 2011; Ma, 2015; Lewis and Cohen, 2013; Wang, 2010). The role of the Council of Grand Justices, Taiwan's constitutional court, has been especially positive in moving the country towards a more liberal civil rights regime over the last twenty years (Chang, 2015; Chen, 2010; Chen and Hsu, 2016; Ginsburg, 2002), although there remains considerable debate over how to reform other aspects of the judicial system to improve citizen trust in its decisions (e.g. Chang, 2015; Lewis, 2017; Su, 2017).

---

[4] In addition to the Freedom House Report, see the Reporters Without Borders Press Freedom Index (available at: https://rsf.org/en/world-press-freedom-index) and Hsu, 2014.

What of horizontal accountability in Taiwan? Here, the picture is also mixed. As Freedom House notes, the executive and legislative branches are elected separately, generally operate independently of one another and often come into conflict over policy changes and budget politics. The constitutional court has in the past issued important interpretations that have clarified the balance of power between the other branches, and these decisions have in most cases been respected and followed in subsequent interactions (Ginsburg, 2003: 106–57; Huang, 2005; Lin, 2016). The prosecutoriate and the rest of the judiciary have become increasingly independent and professional and have been particularly aggressive in recent years about combatting vote buying and public corruption (Wu and Huang, 2004; Chen and Hsu, 2016; Göbel, 2016; Wang, 2006; cf. Lo, 2008). On the downside, one potential weakness in horizontal accountability is that the legislature and president are now elected concurrently: since the change to a more majoritarian electoral system for legislative elections, this feature has greatly increased the chances that both branches are controlled by the same party, as has indeed been the case since 2008 (Chu et al., 2016: 10). In addition, the conduct of legislative business within the Legislative Yuan remains under-institutionalized – in particular, the minority parties routinely violate the normal rules of order to enhance their own bargaining power in inter-party negotiations (Huang and Sheng, 2020; cf. Diamond, 2001). A particularly serious breach of regular order occurred in 2014 when student protestors occupied the legislative floor for two weeks in response to a dispute over the procedures used to consider a trade agreement with the People's Republic of China (PRC). While interpretations of this event, which came to be known as the Sunflower Movement, vary widely, it clearly demonstrated weak institutionalization of the legislative process and reflected poorly on the Taiwanese political system's ability to resolve confrontations through regular institutional channels.[5] The legislature as a whole also lacks the professional capacity to effectively monitor the executive branch or to draft detailed legislation on its own, instead relying on government ministries to propose the bulk of new bills (Templeman, 2020: 25).

On the final dimension, effective power to govern, Taiwan's democracy looks very good. Since 1996, when the president was directly elected by the Taiwanese electorate for the first time, the executive and legislative branches have been fully under control of elected representatives. There are no reserved domains for unelected bodies such as the military (Croissant et al., 2012; Kuehn, 2008) or religious authorities. Moreover, the power of the state extends to all corners of Taiwan's territory (though the Republic of China regime has not renounced its now-symbolic claims to mainland China, which it does not control). The one element of this partial regime that might be considered defective is Taiwan's limited recognition in the inter-state system. Pressure from the PRC, combined with Taiwan's need to

[5] For two contrasting views, see Chu, 2015, and Ho, 2015.

maintain good relations with the United States, places significant practical limits on the country's sovereignty; for instance, Taiwan is formally recognized today by only fifteen other countries, and efforts to adopt a new constitution or hold a referendum on Taiwanese independence from China have in the past been strenuously opposed not only by the PRC but also by the United States.

Taiwan's Democracy in a Nutshell

To sum up, democracy in Taiwan today is excellent on Merkel's electoral and political rights partial regimes, good and improving on civil rights, good but with enduring weaknesses on horizontal accountability and excellent on effective right to rule. The democratic defects that global rankings organizations such as Freedom House are able to identify are fairly minor: inconsistent respect for due process in eminent domain, some remaining concerns about vote buying and political corruption, under-institutionalized horizontal accountability and the possible chilling effects of Chinese influence over the public sphere, especially media.

These concerns look rather trivial when contrasted with the obvious democratic defects in most other regimes in the region. These include restrictions on freedom of speech, campaigning and assembly in the Republic of Korea (You, 2017), media self-censorship due to government pressure in Japan (Fackler, 2016), widespread extra-judicial killings and threats against journalists and activists in the Philippines (Human Rights Watch, 2017) and a disputed presidential election in Mongolia (Organisation for Security and Cooperation in Europe, 2018). From this perspective, the real question raised by the state of Taiwan's contemporary political regime is not why minor defects remain, but instead why Taiwan has developed and retained enough strengths across all of Merkel's partial regimes to support a robust liberal democracy.

The central motivation of this volume is to explore whether, and to what extent, features of the state affect the quality of democracy across Asia. To answer that question in the Taiwanese case, the state in Taiwan needs to be considered in more detail.

CHARACTERISTICS OF THE TAIWANESE STATE IN THE POST-WAR ERA

Origins of the Taiwanese State

In comparison to most of the other case studies in this volume, the Taiwanese state stands out for its especially high capacity and autonomy from society. It is also a counterexample to claims that the most effective modern states in the developing world rest on the legacies of older, pre-modern ones (Bockstette et al., 2002; Comin et al., 2010; Michalopoulos and Pappaioanou, 2013).

Taiwan's state has a weak pre-modern foundation. For most of its history as a possession of the Qing Empire in China, Taiwan was on the periphery – a frontier land where traditional Chinese social order and bureaucratic authority were weak. Although Qing rule was strengthened and extended by the 1800s, it was in practice limited mostly to the western plains of the island and never fully reached the indigenous tribes that inhabited the mountains and east coast. Nor was the power of local Han clan-based groups ever completely subjugated by Qing administrators.[6]

Yet in the post-WWII era, the Taiwanese state was strong enough to oversee the transformation of the island's economy and society and catapult it into the developed world within thirty years. So, where did this vaunted 'developmental state' come from?

The first part of the answer is the island's Japanese colonial legacy.[7] Taiwan was a Japanese colony from 1895 until 1945, when the Republic of China assumed control, and the intensive efforts by the Japanese to transform Taiwanese society, economy and administrative systems during this period dramatically strengthened the 'stateness' of Taiwan. The Japanese colonial administration established a civil police service, conquered and pacified the indigenous mountain tribes and created modern systems of administrative control. The colonial authorities also fundamentally reshaped Taiwan's infrastructure, founding new cities, building rail lines and paved roads around the island and setting up telegraph and telephone service. They instituted a full primary education system, so that by the end of the colonial era a majority of Taiwanese below the age of twenty could read, write and speak Japanese. And they transformed Taiwan's economy, creating modern joint-stock corporations and state-run enterprises, improving irrigation systems and introducing cash crops and eventually constructing heavy industrial plants as the Japanese empire ramped up for military expansion in WWII. The colonial legacy left by the Japanese created a sturdy foundation for a capable state where there had previously been none.[8]

The second part is the lasting legacy of an uprising against KMT rule and the subsequent military crackdown on Taiwan.[9] After Taiwan came under the control of the KMT-led Republic of China in 1945, public opinion quickly turned against

---

[6] For more on the territorial limits of Qing-era rule on Taiwan, see Barclay, 2018.

[7] For a succinct introduction to the Japanese colonial origins of the Taiwanese state, see Lamley, 1999. Chang and Myers, 1963, describe the policy motivations of and resources used by the first colonial leaders to quickly build up the state's administrative and security capacity. Kohli, 1994, makes a similar argument about the Japanese colonial impact on Korea. For a comparison of the systems of political control employed by the Japanese in the two colonies, see Chen, 1970.

[8] A carefully researched study from the early post-war era of the Japanese colonial legacy is Barclay, 1954. See also Ka, 1995 (2018); Lamley, 1999; Morgan and Liu, 2007; and Myers and Ching, 1964.

[9] Philips, 1999, provides an overview of this period. On the post-war economic boom and its relation to the *benshengren*-mainlander divide during this time, see Gold, 1986: 122–34.

the deeply corrupt and venal KMT officials who arrived to rule the island. Local grievances erupted in 1947 into a violent riot against KMT authorities, known colloquially as the 2–28 Incident, which grew into an island-wide revolt that was ruthlessly suppressed by troops sent from mainland China. Somewhere between 6,000 and 30,000 people were killed in the uprising – many of them among the pre-1945 Taiwanese elite. The remaining Taiwanese, known as 'local provincials' (*benshengren* in Mandarin Chinese), were intimidated into silence. This division between mainlanders and *benshengren* persisted for decades afterwards and fundamentally shaped the nature of state-society relations well into the transition to democracy in the 1990s: the mainlander-dominated state remained highly insulated from domestic social forces and thus was able to devise and execute policy changes opposed by local interests (Gold, 1986: 47–55).

The third source of the strong Taiwanese state was the reorganization of the ruling KMT and institutions of the Republic of China in Taiwan.[10] The KMT retreated to Taiwan in 1949 after losing the Chinese civil war to the Chinese Communist Party, bringing more than a million refugees from the mainland to the island. Once its survival appeared ensured by the United States – the outbreak of the Korean War in 1950 drastically changed US policy towards Chiang Kai-shek's regime, and US aid again started to flow after having been cut off the previous year – the KMT gained breathing room to set about rebuilding itself. Chiang reasserted firm control over the party and institutions of the Republic of China, and with most of his rivals in the party either in exile or sidelined, he had a free hand to reshape the regime. The KMT was fundamentally reorganized and its membership reconstituted, and key Republic of China institutions reformed with new appointees. Under Chiang's rule, the regime on Taiwan enjoyed unusual autonomy from both Taiwanese *benshengren* and mainlander emigres, and as a consequence, the operations of state institutions were far removed from the corrupting personal networks that had brought about the KMT's demise on the mainland. That, along with substantial US assistance and pressure,[11] enabled the regime to undertake a far-reaching land reform that greatly improved the distribution of wealth and income on the island (You, 2014), and it also provided the political basis for a switch to an export-oriented development strategy that drove Taiwan's sustained economic boom from the 1960s through the 1990s (Gold, 1986; cf. Greene, 2008).

Features of the Taiwanese State at the Advent of the Democratic Era

These historical patterns of state-building in Taiwan left at least four distinct legacies at the advent of the democratic era that have shaped the regime's

---

[10] On the reorganization of the KMT in the early 1950s, see Dickson, 1993, and Myers and Lin, 2007. For the broader set of reforms and their consequences, see Wang, 1999.
[11] On the US role, see Lee, 2020.

subsequent evolution in ways both good and bad. The first is an unusual 'bifurcation' of the institutions of the state between central (*zhongyang*) and local (*difang*) governments (cf. Lerman, 1977). Before the transition to democracy began, the highest offices in the Republic of China regime were not subject to direct elections from Taiwanese constituencies. Instead, both the Legislative Yuan, which confirmed the premier (the formal head of government), and the National Assembly, which chose the president, were filled with permanent representatives elected from mainland constituencies before 1949 – the vast majority of them loyal supporters of the KMT.

As a consequence, the central government was effectively walled off from direct accountability to the population over which it held sway. 'Technocrats' trusted by Chiang Kai-shek (and later, his son and successor Chiang Ching-kuo) were granted broad autonomy to shape economic and social policy and, at key moments, were able to shift policy in the face of opposition from business interests (Booth, 2011; Greene, 2013; Cheng and Chu, 2002). The recruitment and promotion of civil servants, ranging from policemen to schoolteachers to foreign service officers, was done through a standardized, impartial system of civil service examinations that precluded opportunities to use personal connections or bribery to get ahead. And this system was supplemented by a variety of internal monitoring bodies that kept tabs on civil servants and limited opportunities for abuse of public office for private ends (Greitens, 2016: 75–111). The overall effect was to sustain a central state with impressive capacity and autonomy.

At the same time, a large number of positions within local government were directly elected, ranging from county-level mayors and magistrates, city councillors, township heads and representatives, down to village and city ward chiefs and even farmer's association and irrigation council representatives. These elected politicians were by and large KMT members, but they varied a great deal in their dependence on, and loyalty to, the ruling party. In many cases, the election winners belonged to or derived critical support from local *benshengren* factions – groups of individuals with some kind of personal ties who worked with one another in informal, loosely hierarchical groups to capture and retain local power. Because of the KMT's origins on the mainland and need to extend its control across Taiwan, its leadership sought to incorporate these local power brokers into the party hierarchy. To this end, local elections provided an effective way to identify new political talent, channel and regulate political ambition and encourage co-operation with the KMT regime. To make participation in elections worthwhile, however, the offices had to provide something of value to the winners. As a result, local elected officials could exert influence over budgets, deciding what government projects to prioritize in their districts. These offices also provided opportunities for rent-seeking in domains under local government control, particularly via bids for construction projects and decisions about land-use regulation (Kuo, 1995).

Thus, at the beginning of the democratic era, the quality and character of the state in Taiwan varied significantly between the central and local governments. At the central level, and in ministries that exercised full, vertical control over local civil servants, the professionalism, competence and impartiality of the bureaucracy was relatively high. But at the local level, and in state ministries such as agriculture that had limited authority over local institutions like farmer and irrigation associations, bureaucratic quality varied a great deal. In many localities, the exploitation of local public resources for private ends was ubiquitous.[12]

Second, it is quite difficult in the pre-democratic era to distinguish between 'the state' as a set of independent institutions, on the one hand, and the regime created and led by the KMT, on the other. The ruling party was founded on a Leninist model: its leaders sought to penetrate and ultimately control all state institutions as well as non-state, 'independent' organizations, typically by ensuring that the power-holders in these institutions were loyal party members who would follow KMT orders and discipline (Cheng, 1989). In practice, many if not most of the 'state' personnel in Taiwan in the post-war era were also KMT personnel. Thus, much like the Chinese Communist Party in the PRC today, it is hard to pinpoint precisely where the party ended and the state began in the pre-democratic era. A key issue of contention in the transition to democracy was precisely this issue: drawing a sharp line between the interests, personnel and resources of the ruling KMT and between those of the nominally non-partisan state apparatus.[13] One unfortunate legacy of this opaque intermingling of party and state personnel, interests and resources can be seen today, as a DPP-created committee is currently investigating KMT-controlled assets that may have been transferred illegitimately from the state to the party during the martial law era (Brown, 2017; cf. Loxton, 2015).

Nevertheless, the most important post-transition consequence of the fusion of party, regime and state was the development of a well-institutionalized party system. The KMT's massive resource advantage, combined with its long experience running in and winning contested local elections, helped ensure its survival in power through the transition to democracy and beyond. In this, it is unusual among authoritarian ruling parties (Hicken and Kuhonta, 2014) – it not only permitted democratization but succeeded in retaining power in the new regime and successfully survived as a major political force even after it lost the presidency in 2000. In order to challenge the KMT's formidable political organization in elections, the DPP built its own centralized, hierarchical and relatively disciplined party organization, one that, in an ironic twist, copied its basic form and incentives from the KMT (Rigger, 2001: 55).

[12] For a good overview of this system's political consequences, see Wu, 1987.
[13] This was a special challenge in the military and security sectors; see Tzeng, 2016.

Together, these two political parties have dominated the Taiwanese political scene since democratization. One or the other has always controlled the presidency and/or the legislature, and almost all local elected mayors and county magistrates belong to either the KMT or DPP. Partisanship has grown rapidly in Taiwan as well.[14] While political polarization has at times threatened to bring the political system to a halt, the rise of partisan attachments has also increased the responsiveness of the two main political parties to shifts in public opinion, since national elections are increasingly decided by shifts among a relatively small group of swing voters. Thus, party system institutionalization brought about by the authoritarian legacy of the KMT has aided the development of electoral accountability during the democratic era (Cheng and Hsu, 2015; Templeman, 2019).

The third legacy of the pre-democratic state is related to its effect on civil society. Because of its Leninist origins, the KMT sought to control and manipulate all major civil society groups or, in some cases, to create its own as substitutes – prominent examples of KMT-founded 'civic' organizations include the Republic of China Red Cross, the China Youth Corps, the National Women's League and the Republic of China Public Service Association. The party's penetration of most other large organizations, from industrial unions to university professors associations, effectively prevented civil society from developing as a major force outside the state under martial law (Cheng, 1989).

As the regime began to liberalize in the late 1980s, this pattern changed: a huge number of new, independent groups sprang up to challenge state policies and advocate for all manner of causes, from women's and labour rights to environmental protection. Many of these organizations were loud, confrontational and ambitious, and in some cases, they achieved major changes in state policy or practice (Ho, 2010; Hsiao, 1990, 2011). But these apparent successes overshadow the important fact that civil society as a whole was quite fragmented: most groups were small, dominated by a handful of elite activists and had few or no grassroots branches or other ways to connect to the broader public (Huang, 2016; Wright, 1999). Instead of developing these connections, most of these activist groups tended in the early transition years to make common cause with the DPP, which in turn developed its *own* local branches and grassroots networks. Particularly notable is the weakness of labour unions, which struggled to overcome the enervating legacy of KMT penetration during the authoritarian era and never developed into a significant independent political force in Taiwanese politics (Lee, 2011).

The reorientation of Taiwanese politics from a pro- versus anti-regime cleavage to one centred on the China question – what Taiwan's relationship with mainland China should be – also hampered the development of broader civil society coalitions with deep roots in local communities. By the end of the

---

[14] For a recent data-rich study of this growth in partisanship and its consequences for Taiwan's political system, see the chapters in Achen and Wang, 2017.

transition to democracy in 1996, civil society groups had ended up in a secondary political role, sometimes working in concert with the DPP and sometimes at cross purposes, but operating almost always at the elite rather than the mass level. Those groups that did have large memberships and extended their organizational reach across most of the island, by contrast, tended to be apolitical – religious organizations, for instance, such as Protestant or Catholic churches or the Tzu-chi Buddhist foundation (Madsen, 2007).

This pattern of shallow, fragmented and elite-driven civil society groups has persisted. In notable contrast to Korea, today it is still the major political parties rather than autonomous civil society groups that continue to serve as the primary organizations linking ordinary citizens to the democratic political process (Lee, 2014). Even the recent Sunflower Student movement, which in March 2014 succeeded in mobilizing hundreds of thousands of Taiwanese to take to the streets of Taipei to protest a trade agreement with the PRC, has had its most lasting impact via electoral politics and the party system. The protests were converted into a groundswell of electoral activity that swept the KMT out of power in local elections across the island in late 2014, and some of the movement's leaders then founded the New Power Party, which won five seats in the 2016 election and became the third-largest party in the legislature.

Fourth, at the beginning of the democratic era, the Taiwanese state was unusual in how limited its connections were to large business groups and how little influence private (as opposed to party- or state-controlled) businesses had over the central government (Cheng et al., 1998). Taiwan's economic take-off was due in large part to the incorporation of small and medium-sized Taiwanese firms into multi-national production chains, where their remarkable dynamism and adaptability allowed them to thrive as contract manufacturers (Hamilton and Kao, 2018; Lam and Clark, 1994; Skoggard, 1996). Yet the KMT-led state had limited interest in actively supporting these firms, even though they came from the most efficient sectors of the Taiwanese economy; for instance, most family-level firms could not secure bank loans (banks, too, were under state control). Instead, state economic planners pursued a top-down industrial policy that focused on promoting high-tech industry, including electronics manufacturing and, later, semi-conductors (Greene, 2013). As a consequence, most private business groups did not get very big and wielded much less collective influence over the central state than, for instance, *chaebols* in South Korea or *keiretsu* in Japan. The commanding heights of the economy remained under central government control via state-owned enterprises, and the civil servants who regulated most industries were able to resist lobbying from private businesses and pursue policies with much longer time horizons (Cheng et al., 1998; Gold, 1986: 97–111; Greene, 2013; Kuo and Myers, 2012).

This pattern of 'arms-length' relations between state agents and private business stems from a couple different sources. One is simply the small size of the median Taiwanese firm, which typically operated at the level of the family or the community; with so many firms competing for market share, no single company could exercise disproportionate influence on the central state. But a second is the ethnic divide between mainlanders and *benshengren* (Kang, 1995: 571). Under the regime that the KMT set up in the early 1950s, the Taiwanese *benshengren* land-holding elite were initially denied access to political power, and in many cases, much of their land was confiscated and redistributed as part of the KMT's land reform project. In return, however, they received compensation in the form of stock in state-owned enterprises (SOEs) or cash payments. This capital served as the basis for starting new enterprises, and a number of *benshengren* built up large business groups in the post-war era, including the founders of Formosa Plastics and Evergreen Corporation (Gold, 1986: 71–72). This growth was tolerated but not favoured by state regulators, and it often brought them into conflict with SOEs specializing in the same areas. The privately owned Formosa Plastics Group, for instance, struggled for two decades to win government approval for construction of a naphtha cracker plant, which would have competed with the state-controlled China Petroleum Corporation's existing plants (Chen and Ku, 1999: 84–85).

The Evolution of the State after Democratization

As the KMT-led regime in Taiwan gradually liberalized and then transitioned to full democracy between 1986 and 1996, some of these features of the state changed dramatically. Among the most important was state-business relations, which became more symbiotic but in a rather peculiar way. In particular, KMT-owned or controlled business groups grew rapidly in the 1990s as part of a fundamental shift in the political economy of the regime. The introduction of competitive elections for the National Assembly, the legislature and the presidency vastly increased the KMT electoral organization's demand for resources that could be used to win these elections – primarily via vote buying, payoffs to local factions and promises of patronage or preferential contracts. This increase in demand, in turn, spurred the creation and growth of KMT-linked businesses that could help fund the party's campaign activities (Fields, 2002). Some non-KMT business groups that had previously been kept at arms-length also were willing to provide funding to the ruling party in return for special benefits and treatment from state agents, who were ultimately accountable to the KMT leadership and thus had to made accommodations. Many of the KMT-linked businesses became highly profitable because of these special arrangements. The money these businesses made, or at least some of it, was then ploughed back into the party organization and used to help win the next elections – increasingly with the involvement of organized crime groups as well in a pattern that became known in the local parlance as 'Black Gold' (*heijin*). Thus, Taiwan's scores on most anti-corruption and rule of law indicators actually show a decline during this period, as the strict wall between the state, business and electoral politics broke down, and the judiciary and civil society were too weak or divided to effectively counteract this trend (Chin, 2003).

The surprise victory of the DPP candidate Chen Shui-bian in the 2000 presidential election put a stop to this pattern and set off a mad scramble among KMT-linked businesses to protect their interests. With the executive branch now actively hostile to many of these businesses, their profitability declined dramatically – five of seven major KMT holding companies suffered losses of at least US$40 million after tax in 2001 (Wang et al., 2016: 252). Most of these companies eventually became a political and financial liability for the KMT and were sold off in the following years. Chen Shui-bian also sought to break the broader clientelist system that had grown up around KMT rule: in state-owned and state-controlled enterprises, the DPP government managed over its eight years in office to replace more than 7,000 appointed positions with its own supporters, including presidents, general managers, boards of directors and boards of trustees. In some cases, these changes brought improved performance – in 2002, for instance, several prominent SOEs reported substantial profit growth. Chen's efforts to foster closer ties between the DPP and private business conglomerates, however, were less successful, and in his second term, especially, he alienated the leaders of many large internationally oriented firms with his increasingly strident rhetoric about cross-Strait relations and a policy that favoured domestic protectionism over cross-Strait trade and investment (Lee and Chu, 2008; Wang et al., 2016: 254–57).

The election of the KMT's Ma Ying-jeou as president in 2008 marked another clear shift in the state-business relationship. Ma advocated a largely 'neo-liberal' approach to economic development, emphasizing the dismantling of trade and investment barriers and relaxation of other regulatory requirements imposed on Taiwanese firms. The central piece, albeit the most controversial one, in this approach was achieving a rapprochement in cross-Strait relations, including signing free-trade agreements with the PRC. However, Ma also sought to reinvigorate bureaucratic capacity and autonomy and restore the state's previous arms-length relationships with big business – most of his appointees to key economic policy positions were either academics or career bureaucrats rather than party officials or business leaders (Wang et al., 2016: 257–60). Ma's vision for a more rationalized, professional economic bureaucracy that would respect free markets and regulate based on the rule of law was a significant departure from any of his predecessors, and it was only partially met (Chu, 2013). As became clear towards the end of the Ma era, the state no longer had wide latitude to design and execute policy changes without first taking into account the preferences of other political actors (Chiang, 2015; cf. Booth, 2011). For instance, even though Ma's own KMT held a large majority in the legislature, his government's efforts to lift barriers to investment by private equity firms and to imports of US beef and pork – both sensitive issues in the US-Taiwan relationship – were repeatedly blocked by the Legislative Yuan (Dai and Wu, 2015). The Ma administration's plan to impose new business taxes was also shot down by legislators from his own party. And most prominently, the long string of agreements with the PRC finally crashed up against a rising tide of public opinion that opposed new trade deals with Beijing for fear of the threats to Taiwan's economic prosperity and political system (Chen, 2016). By the end of the Ma era, it was clear that the state could no longer direct economic policy with a free hand – the legislature, the media and civil society groups all had to be won over to implement major changes. Taiwan's state appeared more constrained by social and political forces than at any previous time in the last seventy years (Chu, 2015).

Yet in other ways, the state has maintained its formidable capacity since democratization. The recruitment and promotion of civil servants continues to be based on professional qualifications and performance on tests, ensuring a high level of impartiality (though it does not necessarily reward innovation). The core institutions of the state – the military and police, the central bank, the economic policy planners, the ministries of transportation, education and foreign affairs – all continue to function at a reasonably effective level and to enact policy that is impartial and intended to benefit the public interest rather than particular and private. What has changed for the bureaucracy is vastly increased scrutiny of its decisions: by opposition parties, the media and the civil society groups who have incentives to play up possible malpractice and criticize state actions or policies for political gain. This constant scrutiny has resulted in a bureaucracy that is timid, cautious and limited in its ability to carry out controversial policies (Chu, 2006, 2015). But it is also one that is highly attuned to public opinion and shifts in the partisan environment.

STATE CAPACITY AND DEMOCRACY QUALITY IN TAIWAN

So what can be said about the relationship between state capacity and democratic quality in Taiwan? Does this generally high capacity state have much to do with Taiwan's reasonably successful democracy?

Before this question is tackled in more depth, it should first be acknowledged that the existence of a democratic regime in contemporary Taiwan is overdetermined. It is consistent, for instance, with a modernization argument: Taiwan has an advanced industrialized economy, a high per-capita income and a relatively low level of inequality. Its population is very well-educated, and many of the island's political, economic and cultural leaders spent significant time in North America, Europe or Japan and continue to be powerfully influenced by democratic practices in those places. The international system in which it is embedded is another factor: Taiwan has had an especially close relationship with and dependence on the United States since the early 1950s, which has provided the United States tremendous leverage over the island's political leaders, helped diffuse democratic ideals and practices and strengthened the hand of the political opposition in its battles with the KMT to liberalize the regime.

Nevertheless, if the fact that the current regime in Taiwan meets the minimal standards for electoral democracy is considered along with its *quality*, the distinctive features of the authoritarian era party-state do appear to explain some of the strengths and weaknesses of the current regime. For greater analytical clarity, the next sections will take each of Merkel's partial regimes in order and consider how Taiwan's 'stateness' has shaped these aspects of its democracy.

STATE CAPACITY AND THE ELECTORAL REGIME

Part of Taiwan's high-quality electoral regime is clearly attributable to its high-capacity state that is evident at every step of the electoral process (Templeman, 2017). For instance, electoral rolls are generated before each election from the state's household registration system, or *huji zhidu*. This system, originally set up by the Japanese colonial government and retained by the KMT, ties each citizen of the Republic of China in Taiwan to a household registered at an official address; that address, in turn, is linked to one's national identification card and other official documents. In this way, the voting rolls are updated to account for citizens who move their official household registration, die or become eligible to vote between elections.[15]

Polling stations are typically located in state facilities, often schools or civic centres – and because these exist in any official town or village, no matter how small or remote, access to them is equally convenient across the island. Poll workers are volunteers, but traditionally have been public schoolteachers – that is, employees of the state. Much is asked of these workers on Election Day: they are responsible for setting up the polling station, checking IDs against registrations and ensuring voters receive the right ballots. As soon as the polls close, these same poll workers are responsible for counting the ballots at the polling place in view of the public and then reporting the official totals. The whole process is remarkably transparent, efficient, accurate and fast – final election results are routinely announced for the whole island less than four hours after the polls close. All these features of the electoral regime depend on having a comprehensive, effective system of registering and organizing citizens' formal relationships with the state, as well as a competent, trustworthy group of volunteers to serve as poll workers (Su, 2020).

The high-capacity state has also helped ensure the integrity of the electoral regime in Taiwan through its effect on election-related violence. In short,

---

[15] It also has so far precluded the introduction of absentee voting – all ballots have to be cast in person on Election Day at one's assigned polling place.

there is none. Physical intimidation of voters, to say nothing of actual violence against elected officials or candidates, is exceptionally rare – it is possible only one politically motivated murder has happened in the last twenty years. In part, this is because violent crime itself is so rare. But it is also due to a well-managed and independent national police administration, which is responsible for ensuring the safe conduct of elections. Policemen are rotated across counties with some regularity (Martin, 2013) and therefore are unlikely to end up supporting local attempts to disenfranchise or intimidate voters, unlike in some of the other country cases in this volume. Candidates for local office have often tried underhanded tactics to come out ahead on Election Day, but the strength of the state has eliminated all these practices except vote buying; ballot stuffing, voter intimidation or impersonation and fraudulent vote counts are virtually non-existent in Taiwan today.

'STATENESS' AND RESPECT FOR POLITICAL RIGHTS

Taiwan's broad respect for political rights is one of the more impressive aspects of its democratic regime. There are few practical limits on the ability to discuss politics in public, to found new political parties or other organizations, to demonstrate in the streets or to publish and disseminate political writing. Media regulators operate with a very light touch: lively debates among partisans from all sides can be found almost every night on the cable news channels, and news outlets pull no punches in reporting on political news – the more scandalous and salacious, the better. Election campaigns also take place in a remarkably permissive environment – as anyone who has visited Taiwan during election campaign season can attest. Candidates from all political parties and for all political offices can freely post banners, hold election rallies, run sound trucks through residential neighbourhoods, appear in public spaces to ask for votes and advertise on TV, radio, television and the Internet.[16]

This partial regime was first established by the end of the transition to democracy in 1996, and it has barely changed in the more than twenty years since. On this dimension, it is difficult to locate explanations for the broad respect for political rights in the character of the Taiwanese state. Indeed, given their impressive capacity to crack down on all these activities, which they demonstrated repeatedly during the martial law era, the considerable restraint of state actors after the transition to democracy is surprising and a bit puzzling.

Jong-sung You has put forward one plausible explanation: the incentives of the opposition camp in the transition. In a startling comparison of Taiwan with Korea, You documents how much more lenient Taiwan's

---

[16] For compelling documentation of these practices, see the Asian Network for Free Elections (ANFREL) report on the 2004 legislative election, at: http://aerc-anfrel.org/country/taiwan/mission-reports/.

campaign regulations are despite sharing a broadly similar pre-democratic history and transition process (You, 2017). He explains this difference by highlighting the role of incumbency: all else equal, challengers need much more media coverage than do incumbents to make the electorate familiar with them and their positions; thus, restrictions on campaigning work to the incumbent's advantage. In Taiwan before 1996, most incumbents in most elections were members of the ruling KMT, while most DPP candidates were exposure-starved challengers. Thus, the DPP had a strong collective incentive to focus on liberalizing media and campaign regulations as much as possible – and they largely succeeded in associating regulation of any kind with the bad old days of martial law. Moreover, part of the regime's control over the media was exercised through its permit system for TV, radio stations and newspapers. The only print and broadcast media that were issued licenses to operate were owned by the state or the KMT. Thus, liberalization of this licensing system was one of the first objectives of the pro-democracy forces, and they pushed to eliminate all restrictions on speech content. As a consequence, the state in Taiwan went from incessant state interference with political communication to virtually none at all as the regime transitioned to full democracy.[17]

By contrast, in Korea, a significant number of incumbents were from the opposition camp, and they also had some incentive to support restrictions on political communication because of worries about facing their own challengers. Korea's more fragmented and volatile party system also made this threat more acute than in Taiwan, where the two major parties could better regulate challenges to their incumbents via their internal party nomination procedures. Whereas the DPP pushed hard for the liberalization of campaign regulations, the Korean opposition did not. (You argues that Japan's situation is somewhere in between.) To the extent one can attribute characteristics of the state in Taiwan to the broad respect for political rights during the democratic era, then, it is only indirectly – through the legacy of an increasingly competitive and highly institutionalized party system.

THE STATE AND TAIWAN'S CIVIL RIGHTS REGIME

The protection of life, liberty and property from arbitrary action by the state – sometimes called 'negative freedom' – is a cornerstone of modern liberal democracy. But respect for the rule of law, including due process and equal application of the law regardless of an individual's social status, has long been the weak leg of Taiwan's liberal democratic 'tripod' (cf. Ginsburg, 2002). The other two legs are much stronger: existence of high-capacity impartial state

[17] Feng, 2016, provides a good overview of Taiwan's media and political speech landscape. Because of market pressures on media companies, this unfettered environment has not necessarily resulted in especially high-quality journalism.

long predates the democratic era, and democratic accountability via regular elections has been well-established since the first direct presidential election in 1996.

The transition to democracy coincided with significant improvements in Taiwan's civil rights regime, including the ending of prosecution of civilians in military courts, the elimination of the feared and extra-legal Taiwan Garrison Command and the cessation of labour camps and torture of suspects held in police captivity (Lewis and Cohen, 2013). The security apparatus was also reformed, streamlined and placed more firmly under a civilian chain of command (Kuehn, 2008; Tzeng, 2016). Most of these improvements, however, occurred as the result of media coverage, passage of new laws, changes in professional lawyer organizations and via executive orders or changes in bureaucratic protocol or personnel rather than being compelled by the judiciary itself. In fact, reforms of the courts and prosecutoriate for the most part trailed, rather than led, the transition to democracy (Wang, 2006, 2010; Winn and Yeh, 1995), and the judiciary as a whole remains a weak spot in Taiwan's democratic regime (Wang, 2008).

One of the reasons for this weakness, ironically, is the highly developed capacity of party and state accountability institutions. During the martial law era, there was little need for an independent court system to adjudicate interbranch disputes or check political leaders – the regime's internal systems of monitoring (such as the KMT's Sixth Division of the Central Committee or the Control Yuan) and its collective leadership bodies (such as the KMT's Central Standing Committee) served those roles instead. In short, party and bureaucratic authority in the executive dominated legal authority in the judicial branch and left judges and prosecutors with highly circumscribed institutional prerogatives (Greitens, 2016; Wang and Sung, 2017).

Halting but significant progress on the judicial front did occur after democratization in the 1990s and 2000s – in particular, two independent-minded ministers of justice, Ma Ying-jeou (in the 1990s) and Chen Ding-nan (in the 2000s), worked to promote younger, more independent, idealistic and professional prosecutors and to change the culture in many prosecutorial offices around the island. Chen Ding-nan also permitted district branch offices to open investigations into affairs that occurred outside their geographic jurisdictions, which set off a kind of competitive dynamic: if the local district prosecutor failed to look into allegations of serious criminal conduct in their own jurisdiction, prosecutors from other offices might still open their own investigations (Chen and Hsu, 2016).

Nevertheless, Taiwan's judicial practices still fall significantly short of the impressive results in other partial domains. Suspects who are an obvious flight risk still frequently are allowed to post bail and then flee the country, avoiding prosecution (Lo, 2008). Punishments handed down by judges tend to vary based on the social status of the defendant, with more influential people receiving much lighter sentences (Wu, 2019). Prosecutions, or the lack of prosecutions, of public officials still appear in some cases to be politically motivated (US State Department, 2016). And when property is seized by the state via eminent domain law, disputes are typically resolved in favour of the government agency (Chang, 2017).

These practices are the legacy of a hegemonic party-dominated state in which party leaders were the real decision makers in this realm, and judges and prosecutors operated as a branch wholly subservient to the executive branch of the central government and to the ruling KMT. Thus, further strengthening of the rule of law will require tough reforms that will probably take decades to play out (cf. Chang, 2018).

HORIZONTAL ACCOUNTABILITY IN THE TAIWANESE STATE

Formally, the Republic of China regime is set up to ensure horizontal accountability via a separation of powers system with an independent executive, legislative and judicial branches that are supposed to supervise and check one another. Beyond this standard configuration, there are also two other branches that have co-equal status under the constitution: the Control Yuan, which serves as a kind of auditor and ombudsman, and the Examination Yuan, which has responsibility for recruiting civil service personnel as well as designing and administering criteria for evaluation and promotion. The original 1947 constitution also provided for two other bodies: the president, who was intended to be a unifying, non-partisan figure with few formal powers, and the National Assembly, which selected the president, confirmed the members of the Judicial and Examination Yuans and passed constitutional amendments. In practice, however, the president enjoyed extraordinarily broad powers under the terms of martial law, and he also served as the de facto head of the executive branch via his power to appoint (with confirmation by the legislature) and remove the premier, the leader of the Executive Yuan. His position as chairman of the KMT, moreover, and the dominance of party over state institutions, ensured that the president could exercise unchallenged authority over the regime. After the transition to democracy, additional constitutional reforms introduced direct election of the president, legislature's investiture power while giving it the right to call a vote of no confidence in the premier, and abolished the National Assembly and transferred its confirmation powers to the legislature (Yeh, 2002; Wilson Center, 2004).

Thus, today, Taiwan has a regime that looks much closer to the standard three-power presidential model than it did twenty years ago. But it also shows signs of a system that is out of balance: the executive branch remains the most powerful, while the legislature wields veto power over much of the state's activities without having developed additional institutional capacity to handle its increased authority. Most successful legislation, for instance, is based on bills drafted by the executive branch and then modestly altered by legislators before they approve it, and the legislature still has no independent source of expertise about policy akin to the Congressional Research Service in the United States. Its ability to serve as an effective check on the executive has also been weakened since a more majoritarian electoral system was introduced in 2008 and presidential and legislative elections were made concurrent. These changes make it likely that the party of the president will also control a majority of the seats in the legislature, as has indeed been the case since 2008. The one saving grace for horizontal accountability to date has been the organization of the Legislative Yuan, which in practice gives minority parties disproportionate influence over the legislative agenda, including the ability to compel ministers to testify and the power to introduce their own bills. But if the legislature should ever become more streamlined in its operation – and it could, since much of the respect for minority party rights is based on convention, not law – the legislature could turn into even less of a check on the executive branch under most circumstances (Rigger, 2011; Huang and Sheng, 2020).

That said, the weakest link in the system of horizontal accountability is not the legislature, but the judiciary (and, perhaps, the Control Yuan). A key problem is the appointment procedure and length of terms of grand justices and Control Yuan members – they are nominated by the president and confirmed by the legislature, and they serve staggered eight-year terms and are not eligible for reappointment. As a consequence, if a president serves two full terms, as Ma Ying-jeou did from 2008 to 2016, the Council of Grand Justices can consist entirely of his appointees by the end of his time in office and can hardly be expected to act as a robust check on executive branch overreach. A similar problem bedevils the Control Yuan, which obtained a reputation during the Ma years for crassly partisan behaviour – for instance, four of its members opened an investigative case based on trumped-up accusations against then-candidate Tsai Ing-wen shortly before the 2012 presidential election, then closed it a year later, after President Ma had won re-election (Shih and Wang, 2013).

Overall, the picture of horizontal accountability in Taiwan remains mixed. The Control Yuan, a key institution of accountability prior to the 1990s, has fallen into considerable disrepute during the democratic era (cf. Caldwell, 2017). The legislature has risen in stature and authority, but it remains disproportional and under-institutionalized – in particular, the respect for minority party rights, including some veto rights over policy that is currently practiced, appears vulnerable to an aggressive one-party majority's efforts to streamline policymaking. The constitutional court in the Judicial Yuan has at key moments played a crucial role in adjudicating inter-branch disputes, but its impartiality, too, is threatened by the system of confirmation. Yet through the present, at least, the legislative branch has continued to function as an effective check on executive branch priorities even when the majority is of the president's party.

ELECTED OFFICIALS AND THE EFFECTIVE POWER TO GOVERN

Since the first direct presidential election in 1996, elected officials have de facto as well as de jure governed Taiwan. There are no longer reserved domains for unelected bodies, either military or party. This outcome was not foreordained in Taiwan: as noted earlier in the chapter, a huge issue in the transition was what to do about mainlander lifetime representatives in the National Assembly and Legislative Yuan. The entire central government effectively functioned as a reserved domain because these representatives continued to exist and could not be challenged or replaced from Taiwanese constituencies. But by 1996, this question was settled: the permanent mainlander representatives were retired and the president, National Assembly and legislature would henceforth be fully and directly elected by Taiwanese electorate.

This partial regime of Taiwan's democracy cannot be linked to state capacity per se. It is due instead to critical decisions made during the transition to democracy: that all Republic of China leaders would be chosen by the Taiwanese electorate; that only residents of territory under Republic of China control would be considered 'nationals' and therefore receive full citizenship rights (as opposed to the many more Chinese living in territory outside of Republic of China control); and that the regime's institutions would be reformed in practice to reflect the reality of a Taiwan-based Republic of China, while not jettisoning its symbolic ties to mainland China. Nevertheless, the precedent of a very effective state with tradition of civilian partisan control laid the foundation for the current supremacy of elected officials in Taiwan's political system.

CONCLUSION: TAIWAN'S LESSONS FOR THEORIES
ABOUT STATE CAPACITY AND DEMOCRACY

Taiwan is a broadly successful, high-quality democracy: it enjoys an efficient, effective and trusted electoral regime, broad respect for political rights, a good and improving civil rights regime, reasonable horizontal accountability and elected leaders who have an uncircumscribed right to rule. This outcome is a bit miraculous, given where Taiwan started out decades earlier. In the 1950s, the Republic of China on Taiwan was, in effect, a police state – its many overlapping security and intelligence agencies had little respect for civil liberties or the rule of law, its leadership was unelected and spent 80 per cent of the central government budget on the military, opposition parties were banned, and no other institution dared challenge Chiang Kai-shek's dictatorial rule. In addition, it was a very poor and insecure country in a dangerous neighbourhood. Its existence as an independent state was threatened by the communist People's Republic of China across the Taiwan Strait, and it gradually lost diplomatic recognition from the vast majority of the world, so that today it has official relations with only fifteen countries. For Taiwan to end up as a significantly higher-quality democracy, with far fewer defects than the Philippines, Thailand or even South Korea, is impressive.

But to what degree can this success be attributed to the characteristics of the Taiwanese state? This chapter has argued that the high-capacity, high-autonomy state of the pre-democratic era in Taiwan can account in part, but only in part, for the nature of its democracy. State capacity appears to have made a significant positive contribution in four of Merkel's five partial regimes: the electoral regime, the effective right to rule, and indirectly via the institutionalized party system, to political rights and horizontal accountability. On the other hand, Taiwan's highly developed state capacity appears to have at best had no effect and at worst actively undermined establishment of a robust rule of law and protections for civil liberties. These have improved in Taiwan despite, not because of, its state capacity, as partisan influence over the judiciary has gradually waned.

Finally, how can the Taiwan case illustrate the central debate between 'sequencers' and 'nexians' described in this volume's Introduction and Chapter 2 (Tuong Vu)?[18] That is, must one have decent state capacity before the introduction of democracy or else be locked into a clientelist equilibrium of low-quality state institutions and defective democratic practices? Or can democracy itself enhance state capacity over the long run? On this question, Taiwan provides considerable support for the sequencers: a high-capacity state made it much easier to establish a fair electoral and political rights regime and ensure that policies supported by a broad majority of the public could be articulated, adopted and executed in an effective way. Nevertheless, one can also find evidence that is consistent with a nexian view: the rise of a vibrant media, institutionalized party system and regular, competitive elections were effective at exposing and punishing the shift towards clientelism under KMT dominance that occurred in the late 1990s as well as the political corruption that Chen Shui-bian and the DPP engaged in during his second term. And the combination of media scrutiny, civil society activism and electoral incentives to spotlight legal injustices have helped nudge Taiwan's civil rights regime towards greater transparency, procedural consistency and equal protection under the law. Arguably the most important lesson to be taken from the Taiwan experience is the power of initial conditions to shape the quality of democracy over the long run. There is remarkable path-dependence in the Taiwanese regime's democratic evolution: most of the prominent strengths and enduring weaknesses of Taiwan's democracy can be traced directly back to the survival of the former hegemonic party, the KMT, at the advent of democratization over thirty years ago, and to the gradual, legacy-preserving way that the transition unfolded.

---

[18] For an introduction, see Andersen et al., 2014.

References

Achen, C. H., and Wang, T. Y. (2017). *The Taiwan Voter.* Ann Arbor: University of Michigan Press.
Andersen, D., Møller, J., and Skaaning, S. E. (2014). The State-Democracy Nexus: Conceptual Distinctions, Theoretical Perspectives, and Comparative Approaches. *Democratization*, 21(7), 1203–20.
Barclay, G. W. (1954). *Colonial Development and Population in Taiwan.* Princeton: Princeton University Press.
Barclay, P. D. (2018). *Outcasts of Empire: Japan's Rule on Taiwan's 'Savage Border', 1874–1945.* Oakland: University of California Press.
Bertelsmann Transformation Index. (2018). Transformation Index 2018. Available at: www.bti-project.org/en/home/ [Accessed 22 June 2019].
Bockstette, V., Chanda, A., and Putterman, L. (2002). States and Markets: The Advantage of an Early Start. *Journal of Economic Growth*, 7(4), 347–69.
Booth, A. (2011). Is the Taiwan Model of Growth, Human Resource Development, and Equity Sustainable in the Twenty-First Century? In R. Ash, J. W. Garver, and P. B. Prime, eds., *Taiwan's Democracy: Economic and Political Challenges.* London: Routledge, pp. 101–24.
Brown, D. G. (2017). Governing Taiwan Is Not Easy: President Tsai Ing-wen's First Year. Brookings Institution op-ed. Available at: www.brookings.edu/opinions/governing-taiwan-is-not-easy-president-tsai-ing-wens-first-year/ [Accessed 22 June 2019].
Caldwell, E. (2017). The Control Yuan and Human Rights in Taiwan: Towards the Development of a National Human Rights Institution? In J. A. Cohen, P. A. William, and C.-F. Lo, eds., *Taiwan and International Human Rights: A Story of Transformation.* Singapore: Springer, pp. 155–72.
Chang, W.-C. (2015). Courts and Judicial Reform in Taiwan: Gradual Transformations towards the Guardian of Constitutionalism and Rule of Law. In J. R. Yeh and W. C. Chang, eds., *Asian Courts in Context.* Cambridge: Cambridge University Press, pp. 143–82.
Chang, W.-C. (2018). Institutional Independence of the Judiciary: Taiwan's Incomplete Reform. In H. P. Lee and M. Pittard, eds., *Asia-Pacific Judiciaries: Independence, Impartiality, and Integrity.* New York: Cambridge University Press, pp. 330–53.
Chang, Y. C. (2017). Eminent Domain Law in Taiwan: New Law, Old Practice? In I. Kim, H. Lee, and I. Somin, eds., *Eminent Domain: A Comparative Perspective.* Cambridge: Cambridge University Press, pp. 93–117.
Chang, H. Y., and Myers, R. H. (1963). Japanese Colonial Development Policy in Taiwan, 1895–1906: A Case of Bureaucratic Entrepreneurship. *The Journal of Asian Studies*, 22(4), 433–49.
Chang, Y.-T., Chu, Y.-H., and Huang, M.-H. (2011). Procedural Quality Only? Taiwanese Democracy Reconsidered. *International Political Science Review*, 32(5), 598–619.
Chen, C.-J. J. (2016). The Social Basis of Taiwan's Cross-Strait Policies, 2008–2014. In G. Schubert, ed., *Taiwan and the 'China Impact': Challenges and Opportunities.* London: Routledge, pp. 151–73.

Chen, I. T. E. (1970). Japanese Colonialism in Korea and Formosa: A Comparison of the Systems of Political Control. *Harvard Journal of Asiatic Studies*, 30, 126–58.
Chen, T. J., and Ku, Y. H. (1999). Second-Stage Import Substitution: The Taiwan Experience. In G. Ranis, S. C. Hu, and Y. P. Chu, eds., *The Political Economy of Taiwan into the 21st Century: Essays in Memory of John C.H. Fei*. Cheltenham: Edward Elgar, pp. 79–107.
Chen, W.-T., and Hsu, C.-H. (2016). Horizontal Accountability and the Rule of Law. In Y.-H. Chu, J. Diamond, and K. Templeman, eds., *Taiwan's Democracy Challenged: The Chen Shui-bian Years*. Boulder, CO: Lynne Rienner Publishers, pp. 145–72.
Chen, Y. J. (2010). One Problem, Two Paths: A Taiwanese Perspective on the Exclusionary Rule in China. *New York University Journal of International Law & Politics*, 43(3), 713–28.
Cheng, T. J. (1989). Democratizing the Quasi-Leninist Regime in Taiwan. *World Politics*, 41(4), 471–99.
Cheng, T. J., and Chu, Y.-H. (2002). State Business-Relationship in Taiwan: A Political Economy Perspective. In P. C. Y. Chow, ed., *Taiwan's Modernization in Global Perspective*. Westport: Praeger, pp. 195–214.
Cheng, T. J., Haggard, S., and Kang, D. (1998). Institutions and Growth in Korea and Taiwan: The Bureaucracy. *The Journal of Development Studies*, 34(6), 87–111.
Cheng, T. J., and Hsu, Y.-M. (2015). Long in the Making: Taiwan's Institutionalized Party System. In A. Hicken and E. M. Kuhonta, eds., *Party System Institutionalization in Asia: Democracies, Autocracies, and the Shadows of the Past*. New York: Cambridge University Press, pp. 109–35.
Chiang, M. H. (2015). *China-Taiwan Rapprochement: The Political Economy of Cross-Straits Relations*. London: Routledge.
Chin, K. L. (2003). *Heijin: Organized Crime, Business, and Politics in Taiwan*. New York: M. E. Sharpe.
Chisholm, N. (2014). The Faces of Judicial Independence: Democratic versus Bureaucratic Accountability in Judicial Selection, Training, and Promotion in South Korea and Taiwan. *American Journal of Comparative Law*, 62(4), 893–950.
Chu, Y.-H. (2013). Coping with the Global Financial Crises: Institutional and Ideational Sources of Taiwan's Economic Resiliency. *Journal of Contemporary China*, 22(82), 649–68.
Chu, Y.-H. (2015). Coping with the Challenge of Democratic Governance under Ma Ying-jeou. Taiwan's Democracy at a Crossroads, Stanford University, 26–27 October. Stanford: Center on Democracy, Development and the Rule of Law.
Chu, Y.-H., Diamond, L. J., and Templeman, K. eds. (2016). *Taiwan's Democracy Challenged: The Chen Shui-bian Years*. Boulder: Lynne Rienner Publishers.
Chu, Y.-P. (2006). The Mutinous Mutation of the Developmental State in Taiwan. In H. Hill and Y.-P. Chu, eds., *The East Asian High-Tech Drive*. Cheltenham: Edward Elgar, pp. 119–82.
Comin, D., Easterly, W., and Gong, E. (2010). Was the Wealth of Nations Determined in 1000 BC? *American Economic Journal: Macroeconomics*, 2(3), 65–97.

Croissant, A., Kuehn, D., and Lorenz, P. (2012). Breaking with the Past? Civil-Military Relations in the Emerging Democracies of East Asia. *Policy Studies*, 63), III.

Dai, S.-C., and Wu, C.-L. (2015). The Role of the Legislative Yuan under Ma Ying-jeou: The Case of China Policy Legislation and Agreements. In J. P. Cabestan and J. deLisle, eds., *Political Changes in Taiwan under Ma Ying-jeou: Partisan Conflict, Policy Choices, External Constraints, and Security Challenges*. London: Routledge, pp. 60–81.

Diamond, L. (2001). How Democratic Is Taiwan?: Five Key Challenges for Democratic Development and Consolidation. The Transition from One-Party Rule: Taiwan's New Government and Cross-Straits Relations, Columbia University, 6–7 April.

Dickson, B. J. (1993). The Lessons of Defeat: The Reorganization of the Kuomintang on Taiwan, 1950–52. *The China Quarterly*, 133, 56–84.

Dickson, B. J. (2018). The Quality of Democracy in Taiwan. In W. C. Lee, ed., *Taiwan's Political Realignment and Diplomatic Challenges*. Cham, Switzerland: Palgrave Macmillan, pp. 33–48.

Fackler, M. (2016). The Silencing of Japan's Free Press. *Foreign Policy*, May 27. Available at: http://foreignpolicy.com/2016/05/27/the-silencing-of-japans-free-press-shinzo-abe-media/ [Accessed 22 June 2019].

Feng, C.-S. (2016). Press Freedom and the Mass Media. In Y.-H. Chu, L. Diamond, and K. Templeman, eds., *Taiwan's Democracy Challenged: The Chen Shui-bian Years*. Boulder: Lynne Rienner Publishers, pp. 219–40.

Fields, K. J. (2002). KMT, Inc.: Liberalization, Democratization and the Future of Politics in Business. In E. T. Gomez, ed., *Political Business in East Asia*. London: Routledge, pp. 115–54.

Freedom House. (2018). Freedom in the World Report. Available at: https://freedomhouse.org/report/freedom-world/freedom-world-2018 [Accessed 22 June 2019].

GAN. (2019). GAN Taiwan Corruption Report. Available at: www.ganintegrity.com/portal/country-profiles/taiwan/ [Accessed 22 June 2019].

Garoupa, N., Grembi, V., and Lin, S. C. P. (2011). Explaining Constitutional Review in New Democracies: The Case of Taiwan. *The Pacific Rim Law & Policy Journal*, 20(1), 1–40.

Ginsburg, T. (2002). Confucian Constitutionalism? The Emergence of Constitutional Review in Korea and Taiwan. *Law & Social Inquiry*, 27(4), 763–99.

Ginsburg, T. (2003). *Judicial Review in New Democracies: Constitutional Courts in Asian Cases*. Cambridge: Cambridge University Press.

Göbel, C. (2016). Taiwan's Fight against Corruption. *Journal of Democracy*, 27(1), 124–38.

Gold, T. B. (1986). *State and Society in the Taiwan Miracle*. Armonk: M.E. Sharpe.

Greene, J. M. (2008). *The Origins of the Developmental State in Taiwan: Science Policy and the Quest for Modernization*. Cambridge: Harvard University Press.

Greene, J. M. (2013). KMT and Science and Technology, 1927–1980. In D. B. Fuller, and M. Rubenstein, eds., *Technology Transfer Between the US, China, and Taiwan: Moving Knowledge*. London: Routledge, pp. 7–24.

Greitens, S. (2016). *Dictators and Their Secret Police: Coercive Institutions and State Violence*. New York: Cambridge University Press.

Hamilton, G. G., and Kao, C.-S. (2018). *Making Money: How Taiwanese Industrialists Embraced the Global Economy.* Stanford: Stanford University Press.

Hellmann, O. (2011). *Political Parties and Electoral Strategy: The Development of Party Organization in Asia.* New York: Palgrave Macmillan.

Hellmann, O. (2013). The Developmental State and Electoral Models in Asia: How Strategies of Industrialization Have Shaped Party Institutionalization. *Asian Survey*, 53(4), 653–78.

Hicken, A., and Kuhonta, E. M, eds. (2014). *Party System Institutionalization in Asia: Democracies, Autocracies, and the Shadows of the Past.* Cambridge: Cambridge University Press.

Ho, M.-S. (2010). Understanding the Trajectory of Social Movement in Taiwan (1980–2010). *Journal of Current Chinese Affairs*, 39(3), 3–22.

Ho, M.-S. (2015). Occupy Congress in Taiwan: Political Opportunity, Threat, and the Sunflower Movement. *Journal of East Asian Studies*, 15(1), 69–97.

Hsiao, H. H. M. (1990). Emerging Social Movements and the Rise of a Demanding Civil Society. *The Australian Journal of Chinese Affairs*, 24(July), 163–80.

Hsiao, H. H. M. (2011). Social Movements in Taiwan: A Typological Analysis. In J. Broadbent and V. Brockman, eds., *East Asian Social Movements: Power, Protest, and Change in a Dynamic Region.* New York: Springer, pp. 237–54.

Hsu, C.-J. (2014). China's Influence on Taiwan's Media. *Asian Survey*, 54(3), 515–39.

Huang, T. W. (2005). Judicial Activism in the Transitional Polity: The Council of Grand Justices in Taiwan. *Temple International and Comparative Law Journal*, 19(1), 1–61.

Huang, C.-L. (2016). Civil Society and the Politics of Engagement. In Y.-H. Chu, L. Diamond, and K. Templeman, eds., *Taiwan's Democracy Challenged: The Chen Shui-bian Years.* Boulder: Lynne Rienner Publishers, pp. 195–218.

Huang, C. (2017). *Taiwan: A Country Report Based on Data 1900-2014. V-Dem Country Report Series, No. 16.* Gothenburg, Sweden: University of Gothenburg, Varieties of Democracy Institute.

Huang, S. H., and Sheng, S. Y. (2020). Legislative Politics. In K. Templeman, L. Diamond, and Y.-H. Chu, eds., *Dynamics of Democracy in Taiwan: The Ma Ying-jeou Years.* Boulder: Lynne Rienner Publishers, forthcoming.

Human Rights Watch. (2017). Philippines: Events of 2016. Available at: www.hrw.org/world-report/2017/country-chapters/philippines [Accessed 22 June 2019].

Ka, C. M. (2018) [1995]. *Japanese Colonialism in Taiwan: Land Tenure, Development, and Dependency, 1895-1945.* New York: Routledge.

Kang, D. (1995). South Korean and Taiwanese Development and the New Institutional Economics. *International Organization*, 49(3), 555–87.

Kohli, A. (1994). Where Do High Growth Political Economies Come From? The Japanese Lineage of Korea's 'Developmental State'. *World Development*, 22(9), 1269–93.

Kuehn, D. (2008). Democratization and Civilian Control of the Military in Taiwan. *Democratization*, 15(5), 870–90.

Kuo, J.-L. (1995). The Reach of the Party-State: Organizing Local Politics in Taiwan. Unpublished Dissertation, University of Chicago, Department of Political Science.

Kuo, T.-C., and Myers, R. H. (2012). *Taiwan's Economic Transformation: Leadership, Property Rights and Institutional Change 1949–1965*. London and New York: Routledge.
Lam, D., and Clark, C. (1994). Beyond the Developmental State: The Cultural Roots of 'Guerrilla Capitalism' in Taiwan. *Governance*, 7(4), 412–30.
Lamley, H. J. (1999). Taiwan under Japanese Rule 1895–1945: The Vicissitudes of Colonialism. In M. Rubinstein, ed., *Taiwan: A New History*. Armonk: M. E. Sharpe, pp. 201–6.
Lee, J. (2020). U.S. Grand Strategy and the Origins of the Developmental State. Journal of Strategic Studies, forthcoming.
Lee, K. (2011). *Militants or Partisans: Labor Unions and Democratic Politics in Korea and Taiwan*. Stanford, CA: Stanford University Press.
Lee, K. (2014). Diverging Patterns of Democratic Representation in Korea and Taiwan: Political Parties and Social Movements. *Asian Survey*, 54(3), 419–44.
Lee, P.-S., and Chu, Y.-H. (2008). The New Political Economy after Regime Turnover in Taiwan: An Assessment of the First Chen Shui-bian Administration. In S. Goldstein and J. Chang, eds., *Presidential Politics in Taiwan: The Administration of Chen Shui-bian*. Norwalk: EastBridge, pp. 143–66.
Lerman, A. (1977). National Elite and Local Politician in Taiwan. *American Political Science Review*, 71(4), 1406–22.
Lewis, M. K. (2019). Who Shall Judge? Taiwan's Exploration of Lay Participation in Criminal Trials. In J. A. Cohen, W. P. Alford, and C.-F. Lo, eds., *Taiwan and International Human Rights: A Story of Transformation*. Singapore: Springer, pp. 437–455.
Lewis, M. K., and Cohen, J. A. (2013). How Taiwan's Constitutional Court Reined in Police Power: Lessons for the People's Republic of China. *Fordham International Law Journal*, 37, 863.
Lin, C. C. (2016). The Judicialization of Politics in Taiwan. *Asian Journal of Law and Society*, 3(2), 299–326.
Lo, S. S. H. (2008). The Politics of Controlling Heidao and Corruption in Taiwan. *Asian Affairs: An American Review*, 35(2), 59–82.
Loxton, J. (2015). Authoritarian Successor Parties. *Journal of Democracy*, 26(3), 157–70.
Ma, D. (2015). Explaining Judicial Independence in the East Asian Developmental States: The Case of Taiwan. Dissertation, University of North Carolina, Department of Political Science.
Madsen, R. (2007). *Democracy's Dharma: Religious Renaissance and Political Development in Taiwan*. Berkeley: University of California Press.
Martin, J. T. (2013). Legitimate Force in a Particularistic Democracy: Street Police and Outlaw Legislators in the Republic of China on Taiwan. *Law & Social Inquiry*, 38(3), 615–42.
McAllister, I. (2016). Democratic Consolidation in Taiwan in Comparative Perspective. *Asian Journal of Comparative Politics*, 1(1), 44–61.
Merkel, W. (2004). Embedded and Defective Democracies. *Democratization*, 11(5), 33–58.
Michalopoulos, S., and Papaioannou, E. (2013). Pre-colonial Ethnic Institutions and Contemporary African Development. *Econometrica*, 81(1), 113–52.

Mobrand, E. (2014). South Korean Democracy in Light of Taiwan. In L. White, K. Zhou, and S. Rigger, eds., *Democratization in China, Korea, and Southeast Asia: Local and National Perspectives*. New York: Routledge, pp. 19–36.

Morgan, S. L., and Liu, S. (2007). Was Japanese Colonialism Good for the Welfare of Taiwanese? Stature and the Standard of Living. *The China Quarterly*, 192, 990–1013.

Myers, R., and Lin, H.-T. (2007). *Breaking with the Past: The Kuomintang Central Reform Committee on Taiwan*. Stanford: Hoover Institution Press.

Myers, R. H., and Ching, A. (1964). Agricultural Development in Taiwan under Japanese Colonial Rule. *The Journal of Asian Studies*, 23(4), 555–70.

Norris, P., Wynter, T., and Cameron, S. (2018). Corruption and Coercion: The Year in Elections 2017. Electoral Integrity Project annual report. Available at: www.electoralintegrityproject.com [Accessed 25 August 2018].

Organisation for Security and Cooperation in Europe. (2018). "Mongolia – Presidential Election, 26 June and 7 July 2017: OSCE/ODIHR Limited Election Observation Mission – Final Report." www.osce.org/odihr/elections/mongolia/101349 [Accessed 10 December 2019].

Philips, Steven. (1999). Between Assimilation and Independence: Taiwanese Political Aspirations under Nationalist Rule, 1945–1949. In M. Rubinstein, ed., *Taiwan: A New History*. Armonk: M.E. Sharpe, pp. 275–319.

Rawnsley, M. Y., Smyth, J., and Sullivan, J. (2016). Taiwanese Media Reform. *Journal of the British Association for Chinese Studies*, 6(6), 66–80.

Reporters without Borders. (2019). World Press Freedom Index. Available at: https://rsf.org/en/ranking [Accessed 22 June 2019].

Rigger, S. (2001). *From Opposition to Power: Taiwan's Democratic Progressive Party*. Boulder: Lynne Rienner Publishers.

Rigger, S. (2011). The Politics of Constitutional Reform in Taiwan. In R. Ash, J. W. Garver, and P. Prime, eds., *Taiwan's Democracy: Economic and Political Challenges*. New York: Routledge, pp. 37–50.

Rigger, S. (2018). Studies on Taiwan's Democracy and Democratisation. *International Journal of Taiwan Studies*, 1(1), 141–60.

Sanborn, H. (2015). Democratic Consolidation: Participation and Attitudes toward Democracy in Taiwan and South Korea. *Journal of Elections, Public Opinion & Parties*, 25(1), 47–61.

Shih, S.-C., and Wang, C. (2013). Tsai Gets Censured over Yu Chang Case. *Taipei Times*, 3 October.

Skoggard, I. A. (1996). *The Indigenous Dynamic in Taiwan's Postwar Development: The Religious and Historical Roots of Entrepreneurship*. Armonk: M. E. Sharpe.

Slater, D., and Wong, J. (2013). The Strength to Concede: Ruling Parties and Democratization in Developmental Asia. *Perspectives on Politics*, 11(3), 717–33.

Su, K.-P. (2017). Criminal Court Reform in Taiwan: A Case of Fragmented Reform in a Not-Fragmented Court System. *Pacific Rim Law and Policy Journal*, 27(1), 203–40.

Su, Y.-T. (2020). Angels Are in the Institutional Details: Voting System, Poll Workers, and the Integrity of Electoral Administration in Taiwan. In W. Chen and H. Fu, eds., *Authoritarian Legality in Asia: Formation, Development, and Transition*. Cambridge: Cambridge University Press, forthcoming.

Templeman, K. (2017). Why the KMT Eliminated Electoral Fraud during Martial Law in Taiwan. American Political Science Association, San Francisco, CA.

Templeman, K. (2019). Blessings in Disguise: How Authoritarian Legacies and the China Factor Have Strengthened Democracy in Taiwan. *International Journal of Taiwan Studies*, 2(2), 230–63.

Templeman, K. (2020). Politics in the Tsai Ing-wen Era. In H. Stockton and Y.-Y. Yeh, eds., *Taiwan: The Development of an Asian Tiger*. Boulder: Lynne Rienner Publishers, pp. 67–96.

Tzeng, Y. S. (2016). Depoliticizing Taiwan's Security Apparatus. In Y.-H. Chu, L. Diamond, and K. Templeman, eds., *Taiwan's Democracy Challenged: The Chen Shui-bian Years*. Boulder: Lynne Rienner Publishers, pp. 289–312.

United States Department of State. (2016). Country Report on Human Rights Practices for 2016: Taiwan. Available at: www.state.gov/j/drl/rls/hrrpt/humanrightsreport/index.htm?year=2016&dlid=265374 [Accessed 25 August 2018].

Wang, C.-S. (2006). Taiwan's Judicial Independence Reform and the Collapse of the KMT's Clientelist System. [in Chinese] *Taiwan Journal of Political Science*, 10(1), 103–62.

Wang, C.-S. (2008). Judicial Reform in Taiwan in the Past 20 Years: On the Road to Independence. [in Chinese] *Thought and Words*, 46, 113–74.

Wang, C.-S. (2010). The Movement Strategy in Taiwan's Judicial Independence Reform. *Journal of Current Chinese Affairs*, 39(3), 125–47.

Wang, C.-S. (2016). Democratic Progressive Party Clientelism: A Failed Political Project. In Y.-H. Chu, L. Diamond, and K. Templeman, eds., *Taiwan's Democracy Challenged: The Chen Shui-bian Years*. Boulder: Lynne Rienner Publishers, pp. 267–87.

Wang, C.-S., and Sung, Y.-H. (2017). The Decline of the Effectiveness of Vote-Buying as Electoral Mobilization Strategy in Taiwan. American Political Science Association, San Francisco, CA.

Wang, J. W. Y., Chen, S.-M., and Kuo, C.-T. (2016). Restructuring State-Business Relations. In Y.-H. Chu, L. Diamond, and K. Templeman, eds., *Taiwan's Democracy Challenged: The Chen Shui-bian Years*. Boulder: Lynne Rienner Publishers, pp. 241–66.

Wang, P. C. M. (1999). A Bastion Created, a Regime Reformed, an Economy Re-engineered, 1949–1970. In M. Rubinstein, ed., *Taiwan: A New History*. Armonk: M.E. Sharpe, pp. 201–6.

Wilson Center. (2004). Taiwan's Constitutional Reform: Domestic Inspiration and External Constraints. Asia Program Special Report, no. 125.

Winn, J. K., and Yeh, T.-C. (1995). Advocating Democracy: The Role of Lawyers in Taiwan's Political Transformation. *Law & Social Inquiry*, 20(2), 561–99.

World Bank. (2015). Worldwide Governance Indicators Database. Available at: https://databank.worldbank.org/source/worldwide-governance-indicators [Accessed 22 June 2019].

Wright, T. (1999). Student Mobilization in Taiwan: Civil Society and Its Discontents. *Asian Survey*, 39(6), 986–1008.

Wu, C.-L. (2019). Do the 'Haves' Come Out Ahead? Resource Disparity in Public-Land Usurpation Litigation in Taiwan. *Social Science Quarterly*, 100(4), 1215–27.

Wu, C.-L., and Huang, C. (2004). Politics and Judiciary Verdicts on Vote-Buying Litigation in Taiwan. *Asian Survey*, 44(5), 755–70.

Wu, N.-T. (1987). The Politics of a Regime Patronage System: Mobilization and Control within an Authoritarian Regime. Dissertation, University of Chicago, Department of Political Science.

Yeh, J.-R. (2002). Constitutional Reform and Democratization in Taiwan, 1945–2000. In P. Y. Chow, ed., *Taiwan's Modernization in Global Perspective*. Westport: Praeger, pp. 47–78.

You, J.-S. (2014). Land Reform, Inequality, and Corruption: A Comparative Historical Study of Korea, Taiwan, and the Philippines. *The Korea Journal of International Studies*, 12(1), 191–224.

You, J.-S. (2017). Liberal Taiwan versus Illiberal South Korea: The Divergent Paths of Electoral Campaign Regulation. American Political Science Association, San Francisco, CA.

5

Democratization Interrupted: The Parallel State and the Demise of Democracy in Thailand

Paul W. Chambers

INTRODUCTION

This chapter analyses the link between stateness and the tendency for democracy in Thailand to continuously collapse or fail to consolidate. More specifically, the chapter examines the baffling relationship between strong degrees of stateness and the failure to sustain democracy in the kingdom. It contends that this puzzling combination can be explained by the historical evolution of relatively well-developed stateness as a result of 'modernization from above' and authoritarian state-building since 1851. When traditional authoritarian actors felt that their interests were threatened by elected governments, they plotted to overthrow them. The result was a vicious cycle of coups across time and the failure of high-quality democracy to develop. Following democratization in 1992, state capacity remained relatively high compared to other 'new democracies' in Southeast Asia, such as the Philippines (1986), Indonesia (1998) and East Timor (1999). Such a high level of state capacity combined with renewed distrust of elected governments by the monarch-led 'parallel state' and resulted in the collapse of democracy in 2006 and again in 2014.

A brief glance at scholarly literature on Thai politics in the 1990s reveals a sense of unabashed optimism regarding the development of democracy in Thailand during that time, especially after the 1997 'people's constitution' (see, for example, Albritton, 2006: 140). In fact, Thailand represents a paradigmatic case of well-developed stateness alongside democratic backsliding: the erosion of democracy as a result of interventions by arch-royalist forces as well as elected Prime Minister Thaksin Shinawatra's own policy choices led to his ouster in a military coup, followed by a brief period of fragile, unstable, low-quality democracy and another coup in 2014 (against Thaksin's proxy Niwathamrong Boonsongpaisan). The 2014 coup and subsequent military rule represents simply the most recent stage in the vicious cycle of coup followed by election followed by coup as a result of a strong state and weak democracy. From 2014 until 2019 Thailand possessed almost the only official military junta on the globe and was one of only three military regimes worldwide (the others are Egypt and Mauritania, existing behind the fig leaf of 'democracy'). Since 2014, Freedom House has dropped Thailand to a combined rating of 5.5, labelling the country as 'Not Free' (Freedom House, 2017). Meanwhile, in the 2016 Bertelsmann Transformation Index, Thailand was ranked 111th (out of 129 countries) in terms of its 'democracy status' and classified as a 'hard-line autocracy' (BTI, 2016).

Using the concepts of stateness, state capacity and quality of 'embedded democracy' (Merkel, 2004), this chapter addresses the following three questions: How did the military and monarchy construct a high-capacity state and maintain control over it? Why did defective democracy arrive in 1992 despite continuing control over the state by the monarchy and military? How has the persistent domination of the state by the monarchy and military facilitated the vicious cycle of coups, eventually leading to the most recent democratic collapse?

The rest of this chapter is organized as follows: the next section explores the concept of a *parallel state*, clarifying its definition, origins and evolution as an influential actor related to autocracy, democracy and stateness in Thailand. The third section looks at the origins, contours and capacities of the state in Thailand, whereas the fourth section examines the rise and collapse of defective democracy from 1992 to 2014. The fifth section scrutinizes the link between well-developed stateness and fragile democracy. The final section offers conclusions.

THAILAND'S PARALLEL STATE

Overall, scholars studying stateness focus attention upon the strength of state[1] in three arenas: the monopoly of force, administrative effectiveness and citizenship agreement (the public's acceptance of the state and its body politic as legitimate; cf. Andersen et al., 2014; see also Chapter 10). However, to understand how and why Thailand has never succeeded in consolidating democracy, it is necessary to not only focus on the state and its capacity[2] as such

---

[1] The state itself is defined in terms of '1) a differentiated set of institutions and personnel, embodying 2) centrality, in the sense that political relations radiate outwards from a centre to cover a 3) territorially demarcated area, over which it exercises 4) a monopoly of authoritative binding rule-making, backed up by a monopoly of the means of physical violence' (Mann, 1984: 189). In this sense, military and civilian bureaucracies are state institutions while officers or soldiers and civilian bureaucrats are the personnel staffing them.

[2] State capacity, which concerns the implementation of official objectives and policies, represents the three arenas of coercive capacity (the state's possession of and capacity to utilize resources to uphold its monopoly of force, extractive capacity and administrative capacity, cf. Hanson and Sigman, 2013).

but also to comprehend Thailand's *parallel state* (Chambers and Waitoolkiat, 2016). Drawing partly on the work of Briscoe (2008: 6–8, 12–16), a parallel state is itself not an actual state. It is rather defined as a shadowy network or institutional arrangement that is connected to the state and possesses formal political, social and economic authority as well as informal clout, prerogatives and interests outside those of civilian leaders – who must acquiesce to the autonomy of the informal power structure because the parallel state is insulated from and can exert influence over them.

The linchpin of a parallel state is the informal structure's influence over 'experts in violence' – such as the military – to maximize the informal structure's interests. Parallel states are almost always found in political cultures characterized by neo-patrimonialism, and their origins tend to derive from traditional, entrenched authoritarian institutions that have survived across history as the most powerful and omnipresent institution (or have succeeded in resurrecting such clout) amidst the weaknesses of other institutions. Such institutions tend to be closely connected to national identity and state formation. This power corresponds with enormous extractive capacities, often derived through political patronage networks that formal state actors would be unable to (or too afraid to) oppose. The existence of parallel states moreover tends to correlate with stalled democratization or ousted democracy, given that the parallel state sometimes undermines, corrodes, captures or overthrows democracies for its own interests. Transactions between elected civilians and the informal structure, based upon context and institutional interest, determine the political equilibrium – which invariably favours the parallel state. Furthermore, where militaries cannot by themselves rule for long because of insufficient institutional legitimacy and where elected civilian governance is weak, this has resulted in vicious interchanges between militia rule and weak democratic rule. Such situations have benefited parallel states because they are entrenched actors associated with national identity that can control militaries and sway civilians. Ultimately, parallel states can indirectly influence the extent to which the formal state delivers public goods, as well as for whom and for what purposes. At the same time, parallel states can establish an 'accommodation' whereby they perpetuate their own power by allowing (leaders of) the military or elected civilian regimes to formally rule. In return, the latter do not hinder the interests of parallel states. Examples of such states include the Sicilian Mafia, Afghanistan warlords, the Rwandan Hutu tribe and the Thai monarchy.

The essence of Thailand's parallel state is an asymmetrical nexus centred upon a powerful, neo-patrimonial monarch, and primarily linked to the military but also the Privy Council and, to a lesser extent, civilian bureaucrats, judges and the urban middle and upper class, all of whom co-operate to sustain a palace-centred political order (Chambers and Waitoolkiat,

2016: 429–30).³ This order offers military guardianship for the monarch and legitimacy for the military, thus extending the broad interests of the monarch, military and Privy Council. This institutional grouping engages in vigorous transactions with elected governments, when they exist. It also works handily with military regimes. Thus, it is a highly influential, informal power structure that is embedded in Thai society, economy and bureaucracy. Hence, the notion of a *parallel state* does not refer to a 'type of state' but a type of political domination. The parallel state consists of a certain set of political actors (bureaucratic, military and royalist elites such as the members of the Privy Council), controlling and employing the coercive, bureaucratic and extractive capacities of the state – although elected governments could be 'formally' in charge, defining the terms of the 'citizenship agreement' or state acceptance.

The monarchy's institutional influence is politically, economically and culturally pervasive in Thailand (McCargo, 2005). Constitutionally, the monarch is considered to be above politics, but he has nevertheless engaged in it both publicly and privately. This has given the parallel state several mechanisms of control over Thai society. First, the king commands state coercive capacity operators as he is the nominal head of Thailand's armed forces. Moreover, the monarchy is the only institution that has succeeded in uniting Thailand's traditionally factionalized military. Second, the king's endorsement is necessary for all constitutions and the formation of all laws (including military and police reshuffles). Third, the king endorses all governments (including those derived from military takeover). Not since 1977 has a successful coup occurred without the king's endorsement. Fourth, the monarch can grant royal pardons for anyone at any time. Fifth, in terms of extractive capacity, through the king's Crown Property Bureau, he controls vast holdings and investments worth around US$30 billion (Reuters, 2017). Such enormous dividends have allowed the king substantial influence in the economy.

---

³ The concept of *parallel state* differs substantially from McCargo's 'network monarchy' and Merieau's 'deep state'. *Parallel state* prioritizes the asymmetrical connections primarily between a dominant partner – monarchy – and two junior partners – military and Privy Council, while other associated actors are more peripheral. 'Network monarchy' is a monarch-led arrangement across a coterie of arch-royalist elites, though it 'never achieved the conditions of domination' and had to work 'primarily through the elected parliament' (McCargo, 2005: 499–501). Merieau's monarch-centred 'deep state' is much more institutionalized and inclusive of civilian elites than either network monarchy or parallel state, with arch-royalist judges (supported by other multiple deep state actors) working as a 'surrogate king' (see Mérieau, 2016: 445–66). A related concept that needs clarification is that of 'bureaucratic polity'. It is a form of rule common in highly centralized regimes where civil servants possess enormous power. Such state-building is dominated mostly by the military but also by civilian bureaucratic elites. Any political competition tends to occur only within the parameters of the bureaucracy (Riggs, 1966). Bureaucratic polities also possess relatively well-developed stateness and fairly high state capacity.

Sixth, the monarch can make royal speeches, the interpretation of which can affect public policy. Seventh, undergirding all monarchical power are *lèse majesté* regulations long enshrined as Article 112 in the Criminal Code, which can land a person in jail for years for ambiguous insults to the king, queen, heir-apparent or regent.

So close is its subservient association with the monarchy that the military is best conceptualized as a 'monarchized military'. The association defines the military in terms of ideological dynamics, symbols, rituals and processes that enhance its legitimacy. The monarchized military derives the legitimacy of its authority from historical-cultural legacies, whereby soldiers secured a patrimonial monarchy that evolved to oversee a capitalist, centralized state (Chambers and Waitoolkiat, 2016). In this sense, the term should not be understood as turning the military into a monarch; instead, it reflects the extent to which the military has depended upon a discourse of 'royalism to maintain or extend their power' (Pathmanand, 2008: 129–30).

As the junior partner in the *parallel state*, Thailand's military holds a monopoly of force through enormous coercive capacities and acts as guardian of the monarchy, factors which have facilitated its repeated (palace-endorsed) interventions in democratic politics. The monarchy has appeared to welcome the continuing pivotal role of the military, if only to preserve monarchical primacy. Meanwhile, urban-, middle- and upper-class perceptions that civilian politicians are corrupt and self-interested have been beneficial to the popularity of the monarchy, Privy Council and military.

Yet though the coherent appearance of the parallel state is reflected in the unitary actor of monarchy, such singularity masks the divisions and rivalries among military factions that oscillate around it, competing for royal favour. Until the mid-1970s, military strongmen exerted enormous power across Thai society. Yet, by 1980, an intensified fission of factions in the armed forces helped to galvanize monarch-dominated hierarchical stability over them.

The origins and evolution of Thailand's parallel state have not been smooth. Before 1932, absolute monarchy was Siam's formal regime. Though monarchical absolutism was overthrown in 1932, monarchical clout was slightly resurrected in 1947–1951 and then again after 1957 through the efforts of military leaders in need of the palace to boost their political legitimacy. But the monarchy remained the junior actor in the military-monarchy political partnership. Not until 1980, when arch-royalist army General Prem Tinsulanonda was appointed premier, did the monarchy become the senior partner of parallel statehood. Indeed, with Prem's assistance (through his control over the military), monarchical influence soared higher than it had been since 1932. Though Thailand did not revert to monarchical absolutism, after 1980, the palace became the country's most powerful institution and remains so today. However, it continues to rely on military guardianship, a relationship that is assured because the military obtains its legitimacy from the monarchy. Prem's 1988 elevation to the Privy Council secured that body as a key nexus (led by a retired military man) between monarchy and the armed forces. This nexus worked to ensure that the military-monarchy dynamic, though previously at times fraught, would henceforth be assuredly under the monarch's control.

This chapter argues that in order to understand the failure and demise of democracy in Thailand, it is necessary to comprehend the logic, trajectories and results of the country's authoritarian state-building efforts. State-building from above (beginning in 1851 under the absolute monarchy) created a 'modern state' with an entrenched bureaucracy and standing army. In 1932, these bureaucratic forces overthrew the monarchy and established a 'bureaucratic polity'. After 1973, the political power of bureaucratic forces began to erode (suffering extreme erosion by 1988), while the military became highly factionalized. In 1980, an alliance between the monarchy and the Prem-dominated military paved the way for the establishment of Thailand's parallel state. During this period, stateness remained relatively high – at least compared to other Southeast Asian nations, such as Indonesia, the Philippines and Cambodia. At the same time, non-bureaucratic forces became more influential, either by forming political parties led by civilian capitalists or by forming coalitions with arch-royalist bureaucratic and societal forces. This process resulted in two outcomes: (1) the transition to electoral democracy in 1992; and (2) the emergence of an accommodation between democratic forces and the *parallel state* to ensure the sustainability of electoral democracy in return for unlimited (though indirect) monarchical tutelary clout over the political and economic system. When, in 2006, the parallel state perceived that this accommodation was not being maintained by the elected government, it endorsed the overthrow of democracy. A similar situation occurred in 2014. Since that year, Thailand has been under military authoritarianism as endorsed by the monarchy.

STATENESS IN THAILAND

Traditionally, though Siam (Thailand) was ruled by an absolute monarchy, power was decentralized into the hands of local bureaucrats. The 1851 ascension to power of King Mongkut saw the beginning of monarchical attempts to establish a modern 'state' – centralizing state-building so as to consolidate and entrench the power of the monarchy across the kingdom. In 1852, Mongkut created a permanent standing army that guarded the palace[4] and incrementally extended its sway across the feudal principalities that today constitute Thailand.[5]

---

[4] In this chapter, the words 'palace', 'monarch' and 'king' have the same meaning and are thus used interchangeably.
[5] Consolidation continued under the following three kings.

The monarch was formulator of state policy while state capacity was tasked to crown-employed security officials and civilian bureaucrats, who behaved as autocrats in their relations with ordinary people. A coup in 1932 ousted the absolute monarchy, and a military-dominated 'bureaucratic polity' overshadowed Thailand until 1944. The state spearheaded development projects, improved transportation to peripheral areas and built infrastructure in the countryside with defence spending rising to 33 per cent of the national budget – the highest amount ever attained (Samudavanija, 1982: 12). Civilian bureaucrats, answering to military directives, became significant actors in the formulation and implementation of numerous public policies. With state actors enjoying a monopoly of force through the heightened coercive capacities of the military and civilian bureaucrats exercising enormous authority, the degree of stateness and the strength of state capacity during this time reached a pinnacle.

Following a brief civilian interregnum from 1944 to 1947, the military resumed its leadership in state-building activities, the maintenance of internal security and monopoly of force, domination over the administration and civilian bureaucrats and control over social policy and the economy (Wilson, 1962: 277–78). In 1957 and 1958, the military again staged coups, after which its authoritarian control over Thailand became even more entrenched. To establish control, it used brute force and ideological support from the monarchy (Chaloemtiarana, 2007: 51–54, 181). By 1973, Thailand's state leaders – through the ease of dictatorship – had entrenched their power. Fifteen years of authoritarian dominance had facilitated the highest levels of stateness and state capacity since the 1930s. Regarding coercive capacity, the defence budget was the highest of all ministries. Meanwhile, junta leaders profited from an informal extractive 'apparatus' which was a form of rent-seeking, given that they owned multiple businesses and sat on the boards of numerous corporations (Waitoolkiat and Chambers, 2017). Administrative effectiveness under the bureaucratic polity was threatened, however, by problems of bureaucratic lethargy, corruption and inefficiency. Meanwhile, the military used violence to confront citizen disagreements in the form of ethnic or communist insurgencies. By the mid-1970s, the bureaucratic polity was severely eroding, and the military was becoming increasingly divided. The growing state fissures increased space for other political actors, briefly weakening authoritarian actors' control over state-building efforts. Yet, in 1976, the military (endorsed by the monarchy) again established direct autocratic rule.

From 1980 until 1988, arch-royalist General Prem Tinsulanonda was the appointed premier, dominating the armed forces. Prem utilized monarchical support to unite the armed forces while, at the same, also bringing bureaucrats, businesspeople and other civilian actors together in support of his authoritarian regime. In doing so, Prem helped to entrench Thailand's monarchical parallel state beginning in 1980.

In addition, under Prem, stateness and state capacity grew to even higher levels. Prem deftly demonstrated administrative effectiveness, overseeing military state-building efforts and the buoyant expansion of the Thai economy after 1986. He also used the military's monopoly of force to end the communist insurgency (Neher, 1992: 594).

Nevertheless, continuing problems of corruption and inefficiency under the bureaucratic polity were creating growing problems for policy makers and business groups that increasingly sought to penetrate bureaucratic policy making (Girling, 1981). Thus, the monarchy forged new alliances with non-bureaucratic actors, such as civilian capitalist-politicians and other societal forces. As Thailand's economy had expanded since the mid-1980s, these groups became increasingly influential across society.

Following a 1991 coup, military officials made a final, though unsuccessful, attempt to maintain control over the arenas of stateness. However, the unpopular coup leaders' forced resignation in 1992 opened up greater control over stateness for civilians. Nevertheless, given the overriding influence by Thailand's monarchical parallel state, civilian influence proved limited.

Contours of Stateness after 1991

After 1992, the erosion of the bureaucratic polity appeared to affect the contours of stateness: monopoly of force, administrative effectiveness and citizenship agreement. However, because authoritarianism, as overseen by the monarchy and military, had historically remained high, by 1992, the level of stateness looked set to continue at a well-developed level. However, the growing influence of civilian entrepreneurs and societal forces, paralleling a 1992 military massacre of protesters, led to pressures to work towards more civilian control over the military – a move supported by the king. As a result, the monarchy sustained the power of the armed forces but relied on Prem's Privy Council to ensure that civilian control over the military would remain archroyalist. When in 2006 and 2014, the monarchy felt threatened by civilians, military coups cemented the centralization of stateness under the parallel state.

During this latest period, Thailand has tended to possess a generally high level of stateness.[6] For example, on a 1–10 scale, from 2006 until 2016, Thailand averaged 7.1 in terms of stateness (Bertelsmann 2006–2016). With regard to the monopoly of force, Thailand's parallel state was always intent on ensuring its effectiveness. In the aftermath of the 1997 Asian Financial Crisis, it became imperative to reform the military as a means of making the monopoly of force more efficient. Under the guidance of former prime minister and privy council president Prem, the state began to press for security

---

[6] Measured by the Bertelsmann Transformation Index in terms of monopoly of force, state identity, no interference of religious dogmas and basic administration.

sector reform. In 1999, the army commander approved a plan to reform the military into a smaller and more credible, professional, capable and transparent armed forces over the following ten years. Yet some criticized these reforms as mere 'window dressing' designed to provide the military a better public image given the negative public perceptions of the military following the bloody 1992 massacre (Beeson and Bellamy, 2008: 119). Under Prime Minster Thaksin (2001–2006), security sector reforms continued in the form of reduced budgetary expenditure for the military. However, beginning in 2004 (when a deep south insurgency intensified; see following sections) and especially following the 2006 coup, budgeting was resurrected for even more troop numbers as well as military hardware and mission costs.

One of the greatest challenges in terms of enforcing Thailand's monopoly of force occurred from 2006 until 2014 (except during the 2006–2008 junta years) – a period during which politically aligned protest groups created havoc and pandemonium in different urban areas. The most disruptive demonstrator groups during this time were the anti-Thaksin People's Alliance for Democracy (PAD) 'Yellow Shirts', the pro-Thaksin United Front for Democracy against Dictatorship (UDD) 'Red Shirts' and the anti-Thaksin People's Democratic Reform Committee (PDRC). The state's monopoly of force was disaggregated during this period because most of the arch-royalist military opposed the UDD while most of the police supported it. The military refused to break up PAD demonstrations in 2006 and 2008 (Reuters, 2008) and did not repress the 2013–2014 PDRC protests (Bangkok Post, 2014). However, the armed forces did quell UDD protests in 2009 and 2010 (Associated Press, 2012). From this pattern of military reactions, it is clear that the parallel state perceived only UDD demonstrations as against its interests. As such, the military, as a junior partner in the parallel state, used state capacities to repress them. At the same time, the pro-Thaksin governments of 2001–2006; 2008; and 2011–2014, which resisted the parallel state, tended to utilize the police while maintaining distance from the military. Only with the 2014 putsch did the state unite the monopoly of force via martial law.

Aside from maintaining a monopoly of force to achieve parallel state-dominated order at the national level, a perhaps more critical threat to the state's monopoly of force came from Malay-Muslim secessionist insurgents in Thailand's Deep South borderlands. Separatist groups had long opposed Thai state control in that region. In 2004, the insurrection suddenly intensified.

From 2008 until 2014, the Thai state practiced a policy in the Deep South of combining repression and negotiations with insurgent leaders in order to maintain order and the monopoly of force. While four civilian governments atop the state[7] attempted negotiations with insurgents, on the ground, the

---

[7] These civilian governments were those of Samak Sundaravej (2008), Somchai Wongsawat (2008), Abhisit Vechachiwa (2008–2011) and Yingluck Shinawatra (2011–2014).

military continued to employ aggressive counterinsurgency tactics. In 2009, there was an upsurge in violence primarily because state counterinsurgency operations were committing more human rights violations, which exacerbated Malay-Muslim grievances against the state (Jitpiromsri and McCargo, 2010: 163).

In 2009, the coalition government of Democrat Abhisit Vechachiwa proclaimed that a new paradigm of 'Politics Leading the Military' would henceforth guide southern counterinsurgency policy. Elected civilians now sought to establish supremacy over administrative policy regarding the Deep South (Deep South Watch, 2009).

In 2013, the elected Yingluck government used its control over Deep South administrative policy to commence a formal dialogue with insurgents in the region. However, the military perceived Yingluck as meddling in its traditional supremacy over far southern affairs (ICG, 2015). By early 2014, amidst chaotic anti-government political demonstrations in Bangkok, the talks came to a standstill. Following the 2014 coup, the junta resurrected the military's complete control over the monopoly of force in Deep South policy.

From January 2004 – when the insurgency was exacerbated – until April 2017, there were 6,544 deaths and 12,963 non-fatal casualties (Deep South Watch, 2017). Though the Thai state managed to dominate the monopoly of force against insurgents, instability continued in the Deep South borderlands. However, unlike the military's stance regarding demonstrator groups, where it selected which protests to repress based upon the preferences of the parallel state, in the Deep South, the armed forces were simply unable to squelch the insurgency.

Turning to administrative effectiveness, while Thailand's administrative structures had traditionally been highly centralized, in 1994 the state implemented a decentralization law partly intended to improve the effectiveness of administrative structures at the sub-district, mayoral and provincial levels. From 1994 until 2014, the political space allowed by growing administrative and political decentralization increasingly seemed to indicate that local people's problems were better addressed by locally elected officials. Formerly, appointed bureaucrats had often seemed oblivious of local needs. Moreover, state policy became increasingly effective in guaranteeing one of the lowest levels of unemployment in the world (1.0 per cent in 2010 to 0.8 per cent in 2014; United Nations, 2016).

However, the administrative effectiveness of decentralization was weakened by the fact that most administrative tasks and budgetary allocations remained in the hands of provincial governors and the Ministry of the Interior. Moreover, the duties of appointed Interior Ministry officials and local elected representatives sometimes overlapped, leading to disputes. Third, by 2014, the administrative effectiveness of the Thai bureaucracy remained uneven, though it was strong relative to most countries in Southeast Asia. Fourth, in terms of budgeting national administrative capacities, according to a 2012 World Bank study, Thailand continued to possess 'an overconcentration on expenditure in Bangkok and inefficiency in budget distribution between the central government and local administrations nationwide, [resulting in] one of the world's widest discrepancies in public services between the capital and upcountry' (Fernquest, 2012). Fifth, there was a continuing problem of corruption and lethargy among some bureaucrats. Finally, the period 2008–2014, which was marked by prolonged violent and divisive political pandemonium, worked to diminish effective state capacities with civic engagement towards and trust in government dipping to historically low levels as people took to the streets to riot (Jukic, 2015).

Finally, regarding citizenship agreement, the Thai state has long sought to transform multiple ethnic and linguistic groups into a single nation-state while monopolizing control over nationalist ideology centralized under the monarchy – a strategy that has been backed by the parallel state as a means of enhancing its popular support. Thus, the state has continuously defined Thai nationality in terms of culture by means of three dimensions: the Thai language, loyalty to the Thai king and Buddhism. However, Buddhism has not been a requirement. Two conceptions of citizenship can be identified in Thailand today. The first, 'proprietary citizenship', permits the state to identify and register, maintain control and surveillance over and obtain taxes from its citizens as part of the kingdom of Thailand. Most Thais hold such citizenship. The second, 'contingent citizenship' in the form of a variety of different identification cards, has been utilized by ethnic minority peoples who cannot prove Thai citizenship but are allowed into Thailand only for limited 'contingent' purposes (Laungaramsri, 2015: 3). These conceptions are crucial with regard to ethnic minority groups along Thailand's borderlands.

A principal obstacle to citizenship agreement relates to the minority Malay-Muslims in the three Deep South provinces of the country, some of whom are separatists. Muslims represent close to 5 per cent of Thailand's total population nationwide but approximately 80 per cent of the population in the country's three southernmost provinces (with most being Malay), where Malay-Muslim insurgency has been extensive (Funston, 2008: 7). Yet continuing antagonisms in the Deep South have led to conflicting conceptualizations of citizenship. Where the Thai state has sought to impress upon southern Malay-Muslims their responsibilities as Thai citizens, these Malay-Muslims might be characterized as 'contingent' or 'informal citizens'. In this area of the country, citizenship is sometimes not necessarily sought or granted. In this sense, citizenship is a matter of degree (McCargo, 2011). Efforts by Thai state officials to find acceptance from southern Malay-Muslims of a national Thai ideology have been primarily hindered by entrenched differences in religion, ethnicity, culture as well as distinct regional identity. Though Bangkok has injected enormous amounts of aid and investment into the region since 2004, the military's simultaneous counterinsurgency campaign has not been conducive to encouraging citizenship agreement in the region.

A second obstacle to citizenship agreement involves 'hill tribe' ethnic minority groups, numbering almost two million (IOS, 2017). These groups mostly live in the far north of Thailand and along the Thai-Myanmar border with at least 337,000 lacking citizenship, preventing them from voting, buying land, obtaining legal employment, enjoying freedom of travel and receiving state welfare benefits (IOS, 2017). In 2008, the democratic regime enacted administrative changes, amending Thailand's Nationality Act to make it easier for members of 'hill tribes' to achieve citizenship. But the amendment still does not reduce the high administrative costs, years of processing forms and long, expensive journeys to state offices for those seeking citizenship (ISI, 2015). Because they lack sufficient evidence to prove proprietary citizenship, these ethnic minorities suffer from contingent citizenship (Laungaramsri, 2015: 6).

The legal challenges that contingent citizenship poses to southern Malay-Muslims and northern ethnic minorities has enhanced authoritarian policies towards them while also undermining their democratic rights. In the southern borderlands, because most Malay-Muslims live in a counterinsurgency zone and are often identified by the military as the enemy, they tend to fall victim to authoritarian abuses of power by the armed forces. Yet for the northern ethnic minorities, if they lack proper documentation of citizenship, they are often considered stateless and are deprived of democratic rights and therefore can easily fall prey to exploitation.

State Capacities after 1991

Thailand's growing political space after 1992 appeared to indicate that civilians were gaining supremacy over state capacity. Nevertheless, while after 1992 extra-bureaucratic forces (e.g. business) had enhanced power over the state, state actors maintained direct control over state capacity in terms of coercive capacity, extractive capacity and administrative capacity. Indeed, state capacity in Thailand from 2002 to 2010 averaged 0.796, slightly above average relative to other countries of Asia but quite high for Southeast Asia (only behind Malaysia and Singapore; Hanson and Sigman, 2013).[8] However, the 2014 coup placed soldiers and bureaucrats in charge of the country, enhancing their influence over Thailand's state capacity in the areas of coercive capacity, extractive capacity and administrative capacity.

Regarding Thailand's coercive capacity, the armed forces' troop strength grew from 290,000 under democracy in 1994 to 627,425 (335,425 active-duty and 292,000 reserves) under military rule in 2017 (globalfirepower.com, 2017). Given that the military is answerable to the monarchy rather than elected civilians, this expansion reflected a preference by the parallel state to ensure ample guardianship for itself as democratic forces sought enhanced political power.

---

[8] The score draws from the three measures of coercive, extractive and administrative capacities.

Looking specifically at coercive capacity in the Deep South counterinsurgency, the Thai state has invested heavily in troop strength in the region. Following Thaksin's 2001 election, he set in motion a dramatic change in coercive capacity whereby responsibility for southern security needs shifted from the military to the police. Thaksin also eliminated all civil-military coordinating mechanisms (e.g. the Southern Border Province Provincial Administrative Center) because he saw them as tools of his political rivals. His policies heightened tensions in the region such that insurgency became exacerbated in 2004, and more troops were sent to quell the insurrection. Following the 2014 coup, the junta again increased the amount of combat personnel in the area. In 2015–2016, it increased the 60,000 troops deployed in the region to over 70,000 security forces. These included approximately 32,500 soldiers (which included numerous paramilitary 'rangers') under army command as well as a small number of navy and marine corps officials. Within the total number there were also roughly 18,600 Royal Thai Police (though this number included Border Patrol Police under Royal Thai Police control). Finally, there were exactly 9,680 *Or Sor* Volunteers under the Ministry of the Interior (ISOC, 2016).

Regarding the extractive capacity of the state, though Thailand had experienced over 10 per cent annual economic growth rates each year from 1986 until 1996, with the advent of the 1997 financial crisis, the economy contracted from US$183 billion in 1996 to US$126.7 in 1999. Though the diminished finances hindered the ability of the state to extract resources, it also made it more difficult for the state to bankroll state organizations. Thailand's economy began to rebound in 2003. By 2008, domestic political chaos in Bangkok combined with a global recession again weakened the state's extractive capacity, lessening the finances available as part of state capacity. Since the 2014 coup, the economy has deteriorated.

Yet despite an unsteady economy, military budgetary spending increased from US$2.9 billion, or 2.6 per cent of gross domestic product (GDP), in 1992 under electoral democracy, to US$6.3, or 1.6 per cent of GDP, in 2016 under military rule (SIPRI, 2017). Meanwhile, though direct military businesses mostly disappeared shortly after the 1997 financial crisis, the indirect military extractive 'apparatus (a form of rent-seeking)' continued – many senior military officers maintained sinecures on the boards of state enterprises and military-led associations profited from the development of mega-projects (Waitoolkiat and Chambers, 2017).

A large amount of spending on military operations has gone to the Deep South counterinsurgency. From 2004 until 2016, such spending totalled around 264.9 billion baht (US$7.5 billion; INS, 2016). Despite this investment, the military was unable to establish sufficient state capacity to defeat the Deep South guerrillas.

Finally, in terms of administrative capacity, the post-1992 period witnessed civilian bureaucrats losing authority over state capacities to elected civilians. Elected civilians became patrons to civilian bureaucrats, sometimes purging those who refused to do their bidding. But elected politicians' rent-seeking behaviour weakened administrative effectiveness over public policy (Bowornwathana, 2005: 42–43). The politicization of state policy making by crony capitalist politico-business people was ultimately destructive to the state when state-building was eroded by the 1997 Asian financial crisis. In reaction, the state vastly reduced its budget, diminishing its extractive capacity, including appropriations for the military and administrative actors (Haggard, 2000: 143, 159).

In 2001, populist Thaksin was elected Prime Minister (and re-elected in 2005). Thaksin demonstrated enormous administrative capacity, implementing sound welfare programmes. Indeed, he used state capacity to implement his policy programmes. He also personally achieved administrative control over Thailand's police, parliament and courts (McCargo and Pathmanand, 2005: 137). Under Thaksin, the power of civilian bureaucrats vis-à-vis elected civilians plunged to its lowest levels (Bowornwathana, 2005: 43–44). Having led Thailand out of economic crisis, Thaksin embarked upon rapid state-building, constructing multiple infrastructure projects and streamlining Thailand's various ministries. Yet his policy choices included carving out a faction favouring him in the military (he appointed his cousin as army commander in 2003) as well as attempts at privatizing military-owned enterprises (TV Channel 5). Such policy choices helped convince the monarch-led parallel state that it was necessary to overthrow Thaksin in 2006 and Thaksin's sister in 2014. Thailand's 2006 and 2014 coups led to the re-centralization of administrative capacities under military and civilian bureaucrats alike.

THE RISE AND COLLAPSE OF DEFECTIVE DEMOCRACY IN THAILAND

The history of democracy in Thailand has been continuously interrupted by military coups, often supported by the monarchy. As a result, prior to 1992, Thailand experienced democracy only during three brief timeframes: the 1946–1947 electoral democracy (Ferrara, 2015: 127) as well as the 1975–1976 and 1988–1991 periods of extremely low-quality defective democracy.

Thailand's modern trajectory of democratization began in 1992 in response to a military tainted by massacre. The massacre united civilians against the military and compelled King Bhumipol to seek the military prime minister's resignation (Maisrikrod, 1992: 32–33). September 1992 saw new elections and the return of civilian rule with democracy, albeit defective, lasting for the next fourteen years. Democracy was defective because neither the monarchy nor military were under civilian control. Nevertheless, 1992 temporarily halted decades of state-building under direct autocratic control.[9]

---

[9] Prior to 1992, the control over state-building by authoritarian actors (military and monarchy) had helped the military carry out coups and exercise non-democratic rule.

The king and Prem's Privy Council backed civilian control rather than military rule, if only to solidify the palace's supremacy over the military. Prem's powerful position as chief advisor to the king (and continuing military influence) led him to be dubbed the post-1992 'surrogate strongman' of Thai politics (Samudavanija, 1997: 56). The greater political space during this period – as guided by the palace and Privy Council – allowed civilians to be elected and lead governments. It also permitted the enactment of the 1997 'People's constitution' that – though maintaining the king above Thai politics – produced relatively higher quality democracy with near-universal suffrage, an all-elected Senate, a strengthened judiciary and legally enshrined political rights and civil liberties.

The post-1992 period of elected civilian rule continued to be overshadowed by the *parallel state* dominated by the monarchy, Privy Council and military. After 1992, this informal nexus opposed consolidation of fully embedded democracy, allowing only domain (defective) democracy. The parallel state entered into an implied understanding with Thailand's new democratic polity: the former would utilize its influence over stateness and state capacity to undergird the democratic regime as long as democracy did not curb its power and privileges. This accommodation represented a bargain or equilibrium between political forces seeking greater democratization on one side, and authoritarian institutions that still could veto any expansions in the political space on the other. Thus, democracy could exist, and elected politicians could use the state as long as the privileges of entrenched aristocracy were respected. The result was defective 'royalist democracy' (Winichakul, 2008: 6). Indeed the 'problem' then and now with Thai democracy is that the monarchy 'does not operate to embrace the function of democracy but instead obstructs it' (Chachavalpongpun, 2011: 47).

Meanwhile, the post-1992 period witnessed the loss by the 'bureaucratic polity' of authority over stateness and state capacities to elected civilians, whose growing power was reflected in the expanding influence of the urban middle class and civilian business leaders. Thus, after 1992, military rule became unacceptable because democratic institutions, including decentralized elections, were in vogue and elected civilians were powerful, sometimes purging civilian bureaucrats who refused to do their bidding.

The 2001 landslide election of Thaksin Shinawatra (and re-election in 2005) brought to office the most powerful elected civilian leader in Thai history. Thaksin immediately embarked on implementing various populist policies while supporting the expansion of electoral decentralization. He made use of the 1997 constitution that buttressed the powers of political parties and prime ministers. Thaksin's landslide electoral victories, enormous popularity among the masses and successful competition against the traditionally powerful military and civilian bureaucrats allowed him to monopolize the political space once dominated by the bureaucratic polity (McCargo and Pathmanand, 2005: 1316–38). The advent of Thaksin awakened and mobilized the majority rural poor to increasingly participate in democracy, turning into Thaksin's loyal constituents. The resulting schism between anti- and pro-Thaksin groups created an enormous and lasting divide among Thais involving contention over control of state resources (Ferrara, 2015: 262).

In some cases, Thaksin proved to be a heavy-handed prime minister. His political party monopolized control over parliament, the courts and even competed with General Prem in terms of political influence. He placed his loyalists in key positions in the judiciary, in monitoring agencies and atop security agencies. By 2005, elements associated with Thailand's monarchy began to voice their irritation that Thaksin was violating the post-1992 accommodation that democratic forces had previously made with the parallel state. Thaksin appeared to be becoming too independent of the king and building up a popular support base independent of the monarchy. Though Thaksin's apparent threat to the existing power structure was already clear by 2005, the parallel state nevertheless allowed him to run for re-election in February that year. Surprised by Thaksin's massive landslide re-election victory, elites, senior military officials and others rapidly coalesced in favour of his downfall, by coup if necessary. With the aristocracy increasingly perceiving that Thaksin was challenging the monarchy, their resistance grew against any power-sharing role with him that might seem to push them into a secondary position. At the same, the overwhelming power of Thailand's monarchy and military over Thai society made any bargain between the parallel state and elected civilians unsustainable. Thus, both agency and structure doomed democratization in Thailand. By early 2006, Thais were becoming staunchly split over Thaksin. Amidst the growing divisions, the parallel state acted. The monarchy, using its supreme influence in the parallel state, endorsed a military coup that ousted Thaksin and Thailand's democracy, re-installing authoritarian control over state-building.

THE CONTOURS OF THAI DEMOCRACY FROM 1992 TO 2006

Having described the origins of democracy in post-1992 Thailand, we now must assess its democratic quality – after which we discuss democracy's decline and collapse in 2008–2014. Following Merkel's model of embedded democracy (2004), this section evaluates the quality of Thai democracy in five partial regimes: electoral regime, political rights, civil rights, horizontal accountability and effective power to govern. Overall, from 1992 until 2006, Thailand created a functional yet defective electoral democracy. Though the country saw a growth in formal political competitiveness and civil society participation, there remained serious defects in the areas of rule of law, human rights and civilian control.

In terms of its formal-institutional design, Thailand's 1992–2006 electoral regime was highly competitive (Croissant, 2007: 23). This owes to the fact that electoral rights and party stability grew between 1992 and 2000, as seen in (a) the introduction of electoral decentralization at the mayoral, sub-district and provincial levels starting in 1994; (b) the post-1992 requirement that prime ministers must be elected; (c) the 1997 strengthening of political parties following the adoption of a mixed plurality and proportional electoral system; and (d) the evolution of a fully elected senate, which was achieved in 2000. Nevertheless, the electoral regime had its share of weaknesses. First, the multi-party system within the electoral regime tended to be highly fragmented and factionalized – especially before 1997 (Croissant, 2007: 23). Second, despite government reforms aimed at reducing vote buying during the 1990s, it continued unabated (Chattharakul, 2010). Third, the 1997 constitution mandated that Thai parliamentary candidates must hold at least a bachelor's degree. Fourth, despite constitutional reforms, almost all parties continued to possess shallow structures dominated by wealthy financiers. The 1997 constitution succeeded in diminishing party switching by members of parliament. It also strengthened the status of parties, which diminished the pre-1997 propensity of unstable government turnovers (Chambers, 2008). Ultimately and overall, during the 1992–2006 period, 'elections remained regular, free and fair' (Case, 2015: 17).

In the area of political rights, after 1992, there was marked improvement. Indeed, from 1999 until 2005, Freedom House continuously gave Thailand a score of '2' in the measurement of 'political rights' (with '1' the best and '7' the worst; Freedom House 1999, 2000, 2001, 2002, 2003, 2004, 2005, 2006). Freedom of expression, freedom of the press, freedom of association, freedom of assembly and other freedoms all appeared to grow during the 1990s and became enshrined in the 1997 constitution, a charter with 67 provisions. Meanwhile, civil society became more vibrant. Yet Thailand's political rights were offset in 2004 by the promulgation of defamation provisions in the 2004 Thai penal and criminal code, which partly undermined the aforementioned legal provisions. As a result, in early 2006, Freedom House downgraded Thailand to a '3', reflecting a downturn in these freedoms caused partly by the Thaksin administration's growing restraints on the broadcast and print media. This lower score corresponded with a statement by Bertelsmann Transformation Index (BTI, 2006) that the 1997 constitution's 'liberal agenda' had been 'displaced by the increasing dominance of the Thai Rak Thai Party...centred on the personal authority of...Thaksin' (BTI, 2006). Meanwhile, when counterinsurgency commenced in Thailand's Deep South in 2004, the state imposed martial law, severely circumscribing the rights of assembly and association in the region (Freedom House, 2006). Finally, freedom of speech did not exist for anyone perceived to have committed *lèse majesté* crimes.

Turning to civil liberties, though 1992 witnessed an upturn in this area, by 2006, there was – similar to political rights – a noticeable regression. The initial upturn in civil liberties was reflected in the 1997 constitution, which enshrined into law numerous civil rights and human rights reforms. This included the establishment of a Human Rights Commission, an ombudsman and other monitoring agencies to scrutinize alleged violations of the law related to such liberties. Courts and the senate were also strengthened to pursue alleged abuses of office by bureaucrats and politicians. Though such institutions showed initial promise, as characterized by a growing number of prosecutions, by 2001, partisan interests had already begun interfering in the work of these agencies (Mérieau, 2016). Thailand's judiciary, though nominally independent, was, during the early 2000s, accused of growing corruption and bias (Bertelsmann, 2006: 6). Meanwhile, regarding *lèse majesté*, from 1992 until 2005, 3.7 cases were tried each year, and in 2005, 31 cases had been finished with those convicted receiving up to 15 years in prison for each count (Streckfuss, 2010: 317). Finally, few soldiers and military officials were punished by the judiciary for violations of civil and human rights, amounting to legal impunity for security officials (Fenn, 2015). Such impunity included security officials' involvement in a 2003 'drug war' massacre and two massacres of Malay-Muslims in the country's Deep South.

Regarding the area of horizontal accountability in Thailand after 1992, it incrementally expanded with an elected prime minister seeming to balance the legislature and judiciary. Partly because of concerns that elected politicians had colluded in contributing to the 1997 economic disaster, the 1997 constitution introduced more robust checks and balances together with a more representative and responsive democratic order (BTI, 2006). Nine important independent accountability institutions were created, of which the four most associated with horizontal accountability are the Elections Commission of Thailand, the National Counter Corruption Commission, the Constitutional Court and the Administrative Court (Maisrikrod, 2008: 105–9). Initially, these monitoring institutions appeared effective in checking the abuses of politicians and bureaucrats, including vote buying and corruption. However, after Thaksin became prime minister in 2001, horizontal accountability diminished as a result of several factors. First, Thaksin's Thai Rak Thai party dominated the lower house, while he succeeded in indirectly influencing the senate. Second, in 2002, Thaksin used the Anti-Money Laundering Office (AMLO), an independent monitoring agency, to investigate the assets of his political critics and intimidate them. Third, Thaksin attempted to influence the decisions of judicial bodies. Fourth, Thaksin promoted a concept called 'CEO Governors', who would help boost efficiency, though it was detrimental to decentralized electoral participation and the 'promotion of horizontal accountability' (Maisrikrod, 2008: 111–12). Ultimately, as prime minister, Thaksin 'weakened horizontal accountability – eroding press freedoms, dominating parliament and subverting the judiciary and independent watchdog agencies' (Case, 2015: 17).

Finally, regarding effective power to govern, this area was the weakest of the five partial regimes of democracy throughout 1992–2006. Though after 1992 the blossoming of elected civilian rule was a boon to public accountability and scrutiny, democracy was never able to resolve the traditionally dominant roles of the monarchy, Privy Council and military – in other words, the parallel state – over Thai politics. The parallel state, dominating Thailand since 1980, limited the extent of democratization from 1992 until 2006 (Chambers and Waitoolkiat, 2016). Though Thaksin was a strong elected leader, he could not compete with the parallel state. This is because no elected civilian could have any real effective power to govern without monarchical support, since the king endorsed and could countermand any government decision. Meanwhile, under Thai law, the monarch is answerable to no one, while the Privy Council and the military only obey the king. With such impunity, these three institutions continuously played important roles in ousting elected governments opposed by the monarchy. Examples included Privy Council Chair Prem's influence in pressuring the fall of the Chavalit Yongchaiyudh government in 1997 (McCargo, 2005), the monarch's speech to senior judges that led to their voiding of 2006 election results and the military's 2006 coup against Thaksin, which was supported by the palace and the Privy Council (Pathmanand, 2008).

In sum, the assessment of these areas of democratic quality demonstrates that Thailand witnessed an increasingly robust democracy between 1992 and 2006. This corresponds with the Polity Dataset IV scores for Thailand in this period, which classified the country as a 'democracy', before classifying it as an 'autocracy' in 2007–2008. Yet this score does not adequately examine the quality of Thai democracy during this period. Other assessments of Thailand's democracy have revealed that democracy began to worsen prior to the 2006 coup. Freedom House, in its first ranking, rated Thailand as 'free' from 1999 until 2005, diminishing that score to 'partly free' in 2006 (judging Thaksin's last year in office) and then 'not free' under the 2006–2008 military regime. Meanwhile, the 2006 Bertelsmann Transformation Index (using data before the 2006 coup), ranked Thailand 41st (out of 129) and as a defective democracy in terms of its 'democracy status', sandwiched between Peru and the Philippines above it and Bosnia-Herzegovina and Honduras below it. Ultimately, though Thailand did possess democracy from 1992 until 2006, it remained defective throughout the period.

THE COLLAPSE, RESTART AND FINAL DEMISE OF THAI DEMOCRACY BETWEEN 2006 AND 2014

By 2006, Thailand's monarch-led parallel state was no longer satisfied with the direction of the post-1992 accommodation between itself and democratic forces. This is because it perceived that Thaksin was threatening the equilibrium between electoral democracy and monarchical tutelary clout over the political and economic system. The palace was particularly miffed by Thaksin's growing control over the devices of stateness and state capacity. For example, Thaksin had developed influence over the military and police independent of that of the monarchy. Second, Thaksin's popularity with voters allowed him to use Thai democracy as a springboard for returning to office and dominating parliament, thus challenging the political longevity of the parallel state. Third, though Thaksin was already quite wealthy, he seemed to be using the Thai state to enrich himself and so challenge the parallel state's own economic dominion. Finally, Thaksin showed a willingness to think independently of the parallel state. For example, in June 2006, he denounced the interference by a 'charismatic, extra-constitutional figure [thought to refer to Prem]' in Thailand's democracy (Pinyorat, 2006).

The parallel state appeared intent on re-establishing control over the democracy, which it perceived had become too independent of monarchical supremacy under Thaksin. Thus, on September 19, 2006, the parallel state ousted Thaksin: the king and the Privy Council endorsed the putsch, while the military physically carried out the coup against the elected government. The result (until February 2008) was military rule under royalist hegemony. The junta voided the 1997 constitution, replacing it with a charter that weakened political parties, gerrymandered the electoral system and created a half-elected, half-appointed senate that gave a domain of seats to the military. Administrative changes included a new Defence Act that gave the military near control over armed forces reshuffles. In December 2007, the junta allowed an election to occur, unsuccessfully influencing its outcome (The Nation, 2007).

When the military returned to the barracks in 2008, a six-year long period followed during which the quality of democracy was extremely low and fragile, while the political situation was marked by divisive instability. During this period, the poor quality of democracy was reflected in the fact that parliament became even more chaotic (and almost non-functional) – as illustrated by the fact that there were three general elections and four successive civilian prime ministers. Meanwhile, elections during this time suffered from intervention by non-democratic forces. During the 2007 election, the then-ruling junta harassed a pro-Thaksin political party and sought to influence the electoral outcome (Freedom House, 2002; BTI, 2010). The 2011 election was deemed by most international observers, such as Freedom House, to be 'free and fair' (Freedom House, 2005). However, prior to the election, the military formed a task force designed to monitor the Red Shirts and sway votes (The Nation, 2011). During the 2014 election, demonstrators tried to intimidate Thais seeking to vote, while security forces did nothing to prevent the harassment (USIP, 2014). Turning to the post-2007 senatorial system, half of the senators were appointed and half were elected. Among the appointed senators, the armed forces were guaranteed a quota of senate seats for retired military personnel (Chambers, 2009: 26). Though political rights continued to be guaranteed after the enactment of a military-supported constitution in 2007, many of these rights were only enforced for those who were clearly opposed to Thaksin. *Lèse majesté* convictions skyrocketed by 2,000 per cent between the periods 1992–2005 and 2006–2009 (Streckfuss, 2010: 112). At the same time, the 2007 enactment of the Computer Crimes Act empowered the state to give harsh prison sentences for unwanted online social activities. A further obstacle to equitable rule of law was the extremely partisan (anti-Thaksin) nature of Thailand's courts (Hewison, 2013), demonstrating the weakness of institutional capacities in the judicial system. Moreover, there were arch-royalist interventions in the 2008–2014 democracy: in 2008, an anti-Thaksin coalition led by the Democrats was cobbled together in the home of the then-army commander under the direction of a representative of the Privy Council. This 'silent coup' occurred due to the influence of the palace, the Privy Council and arch-royalist military officers (Pravit December 24, 2008). Ultimately, in 2008–2014, the monarchy (aided by the military and Privy Council) overshadowed Thailand's political system to such an extent that elected administrations were unable to achieve the effective power to govern.

During this period, the intensifying and divisive instability between the aforementioned demonstrator groups either supporting Thaksin (UDD) or opposing him (PAD, PDRC) brought the country to a political standstill. Various chaotic efforts by these groups in 2008, 2009, 2010 and 2013–2014 – such as cordoning off parliament, occupying ministries, forcing reshuffles or new elections, shutting down the government or encouraging military coups – achieved the objective of destabilizing the elected governments. At the same time, the refusal of the military to put an end to anti-Thaksin demonstrations in 2008 and 2013–2014 prolonged democratic instability, while the military's repressive stanching of UDD protests in 2009 and 2010 led it to commit numerous human rights violations.

From 2008 until 2014, Thailand was not only split in terms of protest groups but also with regard to the arch-royalist military versus the more pro-Thaksin police. While elections (partial regime A) were generally respected and Thais seemed to enjoy many political rights, at least on paper (partial regime B), in terms of civil liberties (partial regime C), Thais could not expect fair and proper treatment from the police or military because both institutions had become politicized and divided.

Such instability was favourable to the parallel state because no elected prime minister seemed strong enough to challenge its clout. However, in 2013, the Yingluck government used its elected dominance in parliament to pass a 'blanket amnesty', which would absolve Thaksin of criminal convictions and amended the constitution to make the political system more democratic (e.g. re-establishing a fully elected senate). The parallel state saw these moves as a new challenge to its re-established hegemony and 'the final straw' in its toleration of any accommodation with democratic forces. In 2014, the arch-royalist military (as endorsed by the king and Privy Council) carried out another coup. The result was yet another collapse of Thai democracy, the entrenchment of military rule and the embedding of military-royalist hegemony. To the parallel state, the demise of democracy meant the end of democratic challenges to the parallel state.

THE LINK BETWEEN WELL-DEVELOPED STATENESS AND FRAGILE DEMOCRACY

It has been argued elsewhere (e.g. Linz and Stepan, 1996) that a sufficient level of stateness is necessary for democratic stability and consolidation. As such, where a state's degree of monopoly of force, administrative effectiveness and control over citizenship agreement are all well-developed, democracy should be able to flourish. This is certainly valid where political forces controlling stateness support democracy or where the forces controlling stateness and democracy are one and the same. But this is not always the case. Meanwhile, democracies can affect the evolution of stateness. This section queries to what extent stateness in Thailand has influenced the evolution of democracy and, also, what the effects of democracy have been on the formation of stateness. There are three types of conclusions: first, the sequentiality of state-building has impacted democracy building; second, stateness has affected the quality of Thai democracy; and third, the impact of democracy has affected the formation of stateness.

THE SEQUENTIALITY OF WELL-DEVELOPED STATENESS AND FRAGILE DEMOCRACY

For Thailand, a well-developed or solid level of stateness has not contributed to democratic consolidation but rather has perpetuated the power of the country's monarch-led parallel state with the military as its junior partner. The entrenched clout of the monarchy, the military and the Privy Council has prevented further democratization or simply rolled it back altogether. In essence, state-building in Thailand was carried out on each of the three dimensions of stateness under monarchical or military rule *prior to* the establishment of democracy in 1992. Because Thailand's level of stateness was well-developed *long before* 1932 and lasted until 1992, elected governments after that date only succeeded in gaining scarce, temporary or indirect control over the monopoly of force, administrative structures or citizenship agreement. Since the 1992 advent of democracy, these three dimensions remained under the overall control of the monarch, with elected governments seen as temporary managers or 'jockeys' for the king (Yoon, 2006). The parallel state could maintain its clout over Thailand because it was reluctant to part with the pre-1992 political monopoly it had amassed and thus simply reorganized its continuing domination over the post-1992 democratic regime.

THE IMPACT OF WELL-DEVELOPED STATENESS ON FRAGILE DEMOCRACY (1992–2014)

In Thailand, democracy has thrived only when elected civilians have not resisted tutelage by the monarchy and military, bowing down to an ineffective power to govern. Democratization could not have happened in 1992 without the acquiescence and approval of the state, as controlled by the parallel state.

In fact, only the state's upholding of moderate to high levels of capacity in coercion, extraction and administration allowed for the 1992–2006 stabilization and persistence of democracy. However, the state's support in guaranteeing the survival of democracy came at a price.

In the post-1992 period, the parallel state, through its control over stateness and state capacity, ironically guaranteed the survival of Thai democracy, but only as long as the quality of democracy remained constrained so that elected civilians could not threaten the institutional interests of the parallel state or the personal interests of the monarch, the Privy Council chairman (Prem) or arch-royalist senior military officials. Thus, the parallel state guaranteed that Thailand's well-developed state would sustain democracy. The overwhelming monopoly of force undergirded civilians' control over the following partial regimes of what Wolfgang Merkel describes as the embedded democracy (Merkel, 2004): (A) the electoral regime, (B) political rights, (C) civil liberties and (D) horizontal accountability. However, civilians eschewed any control over (E) effective power to govern.

The result was the aforementioned accommodation between the parallel state, which allowed the expansion of political space and democratic forces, which surrendered partial regime (E) – that is, the effective power to control the democratic polity. The arch-royalist civilian governments of 1992–2001 and 2008–2011 enjoyed longevity precisely because they acquiesced to the parallel state's political insulation and exclusive control over democracy.

In particular, after 1992, threats from the 1997 economic downturn, subsequent defence budget cuts and challenges from the post-2004 Deep South insurgency, all threatened to create problems for the stateness that was undergirding Thai democracy. The economic crisis diminished the amount of money available for security forces, which were ensuring the monopoly of force available to the state. The 1998–2001 security sector reforms were unpopular with most of the military. Nevertheless, reforms continued to be implemented because they were championed by the palace. The post-2004 Malay-Muslim counterinsurgency represented a new threat to the monopoly of force. The parallel state galvanized the dimensions of stateness in support of democracy to weather these political and economic storms.

However, when the democratically elected Prime Minister Thaksin and his allies tried to seek greater control over state-building through their own policies, the parallel state viewed this as a challenge to the accommodation. As a result, Thailand's well-developed stateness (as captured by the parallel state) wreaked havoc upon the country's democracy in two ways. First, anti-Thaksin demonstrations (allied with the parallel state) occupied state facilities in 2006, 2008 and 2013–2014, which weakened the pro-Thaksin governments' control over administrative effectiveness. Second, senior military officials (as part of the parallel state) increasingly acted independently of pro-Thaksin governments, which greatly diminished the latter's control over the monopoly of force. Nevertheless, most police tended to support

Thaksin. As a result, after 2008, as mentioned previously, control over stateness became highly disaggregated. The division eroded the state's singular monopoly of force and administrative effectiveness. Weaknesses in these dimensions directly influenced the rule of law and the effective power to govern – partial regimes of (C) and (E) of embedded democracy. When democratic (yet pro-Thaksin) prime ministers issued orders to the military to take legal actions designed to sustain the democratic regime (e.g. disbursal of anti-government protesters), the military routinely failed to enforce the law. The result was chaos.

In the end, there were two successive military coups backed by the parallel state and broadly supported by much of the state bureaucracy as well as the urban upper and middle classes. This, in turn, resulted in the 2014 democratic collapse followed by prolonged, direct state control by the arch-royalist military.

THE EFFECT OF FRAGILE DEMOCRACY ON THAI STATENESS

Despite the fragile quality of Thai democracy after 1992, it nevertheless succeeded in affecting the formation of stateness. In fact, it can be argued that democracy, however fragile, can strengthen stateness as well as state capacity. Evidence supporting this can be found in Thailand from 1992 until 2006 and 2008 until 2014, when elected governments were in office. Indeed, democratization in 1992 gave increased power over the bureaucracy to civilian capitalist-politicians and interest groups, paralleling their increasing economic status and access to state resources. Through their influence, from 1992 until 1996, democracy was beneficial to administrative and extractive capacity: it was elected civilians who oversaw the evolution of an efficient decentralized bureaucratic system while also managing robust economic growth. Though civilians were partly responsible for Thailand's 1997 economic downturn, they also oversaw the 1998–2001 efforts to improve military efficiency (thus improving the state's monopoly of force and coercive capacity). In addition, as a result of Thaksin's policy implementations, Thailand after 2001 witnessed a resurgence in its economy's extractive capacity as well as the advent of effective welfare programmes, improvements in administrative capacity and effectiveness through the restructuring of ministerial structures. Thaksin's ability to build mass support for his policies enhanced social support for state-building, which improved social acceptance of state authority, thus helping to increase state effectiveness.

From 2008 until 2014, though democracy was severely weakened, all four consecutive civilian governments worked to strengthen stateness by seeking to boost administrative effectiveness, economic development and welfare programmes. The apex of these efforts was reached under the 2011–2014 Yingluck government. Specifically, she sought to implement more welfare policies (similar to the earlier policies of her brother Thaksin). She also backed new education and economic growth policies. If there had been no coup in 2014, these reforms could well have sustained or improved Thailand's democratic institutions if they had been given the opportunity to become more thoroughly embedded.

CONCLUSION

Given Thailand's long history of monarchical absolutism, military autocracy and recurrent military coups, the monarchy and the military were, over time, able to construct a well-developed level of stateness across the country. They succeeded in maintaining control over stateness because, since 1980, they collaborated together with the Privy Council through the asymmetrical nexus of a parallel state to prevent any challenges to their supremacy. Democracy never stabilized or persisted because the parallel state, supported by the urban upper and middle classes as well as state bureaucrats, consistently opposed the consolidation of democracy. Thailand's political culture of obeisance and adulation of the monarchy helped to prevent popular opposition to coups – since all successful post-1977 putsches were endorsed by the monarchy. The persistent domination of the state by the monarchy and military facilitated the vicious cycle of coups because the parallel state continuously ousted any elected government that it perceived was attempting to strengthen democracy or competing with the parallel state's own influence over stateness.

Nevertheless, by the 1980s, amidst the erosion of bureaucratic polity and the increasing influence of civil society, pressures grew for Thailand to democratize. Defective democracy arrived in 1992 despite the continuing supremacy over the state by the monarchy and military because the parallel state felt sufficiently confident in its control over stateness to allow for democracy to exist – as long as it remained defective, allowing the parallel state to persist in exerting tutelage over it. Thus, from 1992 until 2006, there was to be a complete absence of partial regime (E) – that is, the effective power to govern. Until 2001, this accommodation worked. However, the parallel state began to perceive the 2001–2006 Thaksin government as a threat to its control over state-building. Moreover, the fact that the entrenched monarchy and military were so dominant across Thailand made the accommodation between elected civilians and the parallel state impossible to maintain. In the end, the parallel state overthrew Thaksin in a 2006 coup. In 2008, another elected pro-Thaksin government used its democratic sway over parliament to try to increase control over state resources. However, the arch-royalist judiciary forced it from power. Elected in 2011, yet another pro-Thaksin government (under Yingluck) used its democratic majority to again attempt to acquire influence over state-building. However, the parallel state perceived that Thaksin and Yingluck had again betrayed the post-1992 accommodation. The result was the 2014 coup and democratic collapse. As in 2006, given that the entrenched aristocracy (e.g. monarchy and military) was ultimately unwilling to share power with elected civilians, both agency and structure contributed to the demise of democracy in Thailand – a different path from the case of Indonesia.

In terms of the stateness-democracy connection, Thailand represents the case of a country where the sequential earlier entrenchment of a well-developed level of stateness under venal authoritarian actors before the much later establishment of democracy prevented elected governments from ever achieving effective control over stateness. In fact, the parallel state, through its control of stateness, ensured that the quality of democracy remained defective in order to protect monarchical and military interests. Nevertheless, evidence from the Thai case suggests that when democracy did exist from 1992 until 2006 and to a lesser degree from 2008 until 2014, elected governments were able to positively influence the formation of stateness.

Authoritarian rule by Thailand's military junta lasted from 2014 until 2019. Though the military returned to the barracks in July 2019, it left behind a palace-endorsed 2017 constitution which ensured the persistence of authoritarian influence given that the constitution, among other things 1) created a new Senate indirectly appointed by the junta and 2) enacted a new electoral formula which guaranteed that no party could obtain a Lower House majority. A March 2019 junta-organized and influenced election brought to office a junta-created party led by the ex-junta leader. In 2020 Thailand has become a pseudo-democracy whereby the parallel state more directly controls state-building behind a democratic facade. For the short term, any return to fuller democracy depends upon backing from the parallel state. But such support would only be conditional upon guaranteeing for the parallel state the resurrection of a form of democracy possessing no higher quality than the 1992–2006 defective democracy.

References

Albritton, R. B. (2006). Thailand in 2005: The Struggle for Democratic Consolidation. *Asian Survey*, 46(1), 140–47.
Andersen, D., Møller, J., and Skaaning, S. E. (2014). The State-Democracy Nexus: Conceptual Distinctions, Theoretical Perspectives, and Comparative Approaches. *Democratization*, 21(7), 1203–20.
Associated Press. (2012). Thousands Mark 'Red Shirt' Crackdown in Bangkok. AP. Available at: http://newsok.com/article/feed/384077 [Accessed 16 October 2011].
Bangkok Post. (2014). Cool Heads Must Prevail. *Bangkok Post*. Available at: www.bangkokpost.com/archive/cool-heads-must-prevail/410014 [Accessed 1 February 2016].
Beeson, M., and Bellamy, A. J. (2008). *Thailand: Military Rule, There and Back Again: Securing Southeast Asia – The Politics of Security Sector Reform*. Abingdon: Routledge.
BTI (Bertelsmann). (2006). Thailand Country Report. Available at: www.bti-project.org/fileadmin/files/BTI/Downloads/Reports/2006/pdf/BTI_2006_Thailand.pdf [Accessed 1 September 2017].

BTI (Bertelsmann). (2008). Thailand Country Report. Available at: www.bti-project.org/en/reports/country-reports/detail/itc/THA/ [Accessed 1 September 2017].
BTI (Bertelsmann). (2010). Thailand Country Report. Available at: www.bti-project.org/en/reports/country-reports/detail/itc/tha/ity/2010/itr/aso/ [Accessed 1 September 2017].
BTI (Bertelsmann). (2012). Thailand Country Report. Available at: www.bti-project.org/en/reports/country-reports/detail/itc/THA/ [Accessed 1 September 2017].
BTI (Bertelsmann). (2014). Thailand Country Report. Available at: www.bti-project.org/en/reports/country-reports/detail/itc/THA/ [Accessed 1 September 2017].
BTI (Bertelsmann). (2016). Thailand Country Report. Available at: www.bti-project.org/en/reports/country-reports/detail/itc/tha/ity/2016/itr/aso/ [Accessed 1 September 2017].
Bowornwathana, B. (2005). Administrative Reform and Tidal Waves from Regime Shifts: Tsunamis in Thailand's Political and Administrative History. *Asia Pacific Journal of Public Administration*, 27(1), 37–52.
Briscoe, I. (2008). *The Proliferation of the Parallel State, Working Paper, 71*. Madrid: Fundación para las Relaciones Internacionales y el Diálogo Exterior.
Case, W. (2015). *Routledge Dictionary of Southeast Asian Democratization*. Abingdon: Routledge.
Chachavalpongpun, P. (2011). Thai Democracy: Recessed, Regressed, Repressed. In Konrad-Adenauer Stiftung, eds., *Panorama: Insights into Asian and European Affairs Singapore: Konrad-Adenauer-Stiftung*, pp. 242–51. Available at: www.kas.de/wf/doc/kas_23467-1522-2-30.pdf?110804 [Accessed 3 March 2018].
Chaloemtiarana, T. (2007). *Thailand: The Politics of Despotic Paternalism*. Ithaca: SEAP Publications.
Chambers, P. W. (2008). Factions, Parties and the Durability of Parliaments, Coalitions and Cabinets: The Case of Thailand (1979–2001). *Party Politics*, 14(3), 299–323.
Chambers, P. W. (2009). Superfluous, Mischievous, or Mancipating? Thailand's Evolving Senate Today. *Journal of Current Southeast Asian Affairs*, 28(3), 3–80.
Chambers, P. W. (2010). U-Turn to the Past? The Resurgence of the Military in Contemporary Thai Politics. In P. W. Chambers and A. Croissant, eds., *Democracy under Stress: Civil-Military Relations in South and Southeast Asia*. Bangkok: ISIS, pp. 63–101.
Chambers, P. W., and Waitoolkiat, N. (2016). The Resilience of Monarchised Military in Thailand. *Journal of Contemporary Asia*, 46(3), 425–44.
Chattharakul, A. (2010). Thai Electoral Campaigning: Vote-Canvassing Networks and Hybrid Voting. *Journal of Current Southeast Asian Affairs*, 29(4), 67–95.
Croissant, A. (2007). *Electoral Reform and Party System in East Asian Democracies: A Comparative Analysis with Implications for Thailand*. Bangkok: Friedrich-Ebert-Stiftung.
Deep South Watch. (2009). An Interview on the Ongoing Southern Conflict with Abhisit & Thavorn. Available at: www.deepsouthwatch.org/node/371 [Accessed 8 May 2011].
Deep South Watch. (2017). Deep South Incident Database. Available at: www.deepsouthwatch.org/node/11053 [Accessed 1 January 2018].
Fenn, M. (2015). Thailand's Culture of Impunity. *The Diplomat*. Available at: https://thediplomat.com/2015/01/thailands-culture-of-impunity/ [Accessed 5 June 2016].

Fernquest, J. (2012). Government Spending: More to Provinces, Less to Bangkok. *Bangkok Post*. Available at: www.bangkokpost.com/learning/learning-news/292888/govt-spending-more-to-provinces-less-to-bangkok [Accessed 3 March 2017].

Ferrara, F. (2015). *The Political Development of Modern Thailand*. Cambridge: Cambridge University Press.

Freedom House. (1999). Thailand. Available at: https://freedomhouse.org [Accessed 2 September 2017].

Freedom House. (2000). Thailand. Available at: https://freedomhouse.org [Accessed 2 September 2017].

Freedom House. (2001). Thailand. Available at: https://freedomhouse.org [Accessed 2 September 2017].

Freedom House. (2002). Thailand. Available at: https://freedomhouse.org [Accessed 2 September 2017].

Freedom House. (2003). Thailand. Available at: https://freedomhouse.org [Accessed 2 September 2017].

Freedom House. (2004). Thailand. Available at: https://freedomhouse.org [Accessed 2 September 2017].

Freedom House. (2005). Thailand. Available at: https://freedomhouse.org [Accessed 2 September 2017].

Freedom House. (2006). Thailand. Available at: https://freedomhouse.org [Accessed 2 September 2017].

Freedom House. (2017). Thailand. Available at: https://freedomhouse.org [Accessed 2 September 2017].

Funston, N. J. (2008). *Southern Thailand: The Dynamics of Conflict*. Washington, DC: East-West Center Washington.

Girling, J. L. S. (1981). *Thailand, Society and Politics*. Ithaca: Cornell University Press.

Globalfirepower. (2017). Thailand Military Strength. Available at: www.globalfirepower.com/country-military-strength-detail.asp?country_id=thailand [Accessed 5 February 2019].

Greene, S. L. W. (1999). *Absolute Dreams: Thai Government under Rama VI, 1910–1925*. Banglamung, Thailand: White Lotus Press.

Haggard, S. (2000). *The Political Economy of the Asian Financial Crisis*. Washington, DC: Peterson Institute.

Hanson, J. K., and Sigman, R. (2013). Leviathan's Latent Dimensions: Measuring State Capacity for Comparative Political Research. Unpublished Manuscript.

Hewison, K. (2013). Thailand's Politicized Courts Fuel Protests. Available at: www.asiasentinel.com/politics/thailand-judiciary-politicized/ [Accessed 4 June 2017].

ICG (International Crisis Group). (2015). Southern Thailand: Dialogue in Doubt. Available at: www.crisisgroup.org/asia/south-east-asia/thailand/southern-thailand-dialogue-doubt [Accessed 5 August 2016].

INS (Isra News Service). (2016). Budgeting the Southern Fire Across the Era. Available at: www.isranews.org/isranews-scoop/item/43826-%E0%B8%B4%E0%B8%B5budget.html [Accessed 1 September 2017].

IOS (International Observatory on Statelessness). (2017). Thailand. Available at: www.nationalityforall.org/thailand [Accessed 30 December 2017].

ISI (Institute on Statelessness and Inclusion). (2015). *Thailand*. Available at: www.institutesi.org/ThailandUPR2015.pdf [Accessed 1 November 2016].

ISOC. (2016). Announcement 105/2016, Structure and Staffing the Forward Directorate of the Internal Security Operations Command Region 4. Available at: www.ratchakitcha.soc.go.th/DATA/PDF/2559/E/061/27.PDF [Accessed 3 January 2017].

Jitpiromsri, S., and McCargo, D. (2010). The Southern Thai Conflict Six Years On: Insurgency, Not Just Crime. *Contemporary Southeast Asia: A Journal of International and Strategic Affairs*, 32(2), 156–83.

Jukic, M. (2015). Measuring the Effectiveness of Government in Thailand's Provinces. DAI. Available at: http://dai-global-developments.com/articles/measuring-the-effectiveness-of-government-in-thailands-provinces/ [Accessed 29 November 2016].

Laungaramsri, P. (2015). *(Re) Crafting Citizenship: Cards, Colors, and the Politic of Identification in Thailand*. Cambridge: Harvard-Yenching Institute. Available at: https://harvard-yenching.org/sites/harvard-yenching.org/files/featurefiles/Pinkaew%20Laungaramsri_ReCrafting%20Citizenship.pdf [Accessed 4 July 2016].

Linz, J. J., and Stepan, A. (1996). *Problems of Democratic Transition and Consolidation: Southern Europe, South America, and Post-communist Europe*. Baltimore and London: Johns Hopkins University Press.

Maisrikrod, S. (1992). *Thailand's Two General Elections in 1992: Democracy Sustained*. Singapore: Institute of Southeast Asian Studies.

Maisrikrod, S. (2008). Civil Society, Accountability and Governance in Thailand: A Dim Case of Participatory Democracy. In T. Chong, ed., *Globalization and Its Counter-forces in Southeast Asia*. Singapore: Institute of Southeast Asian Studies, pp. 97–116.

Mann, M. (1984). The Autonomous Power of the State: Its Origins, Mechanisms and Results. *European Journal of Sociology/Archives européennes de sociologie*, 25(2), 185–213.

McCargo, D. (2005). Network Monarchy and Legitimacy Crises in Thailand. *The Pacific Review*, 18(4), 499–519.

McCargo, D. (2011). Informal Citizens: Graduated Citizenship in Southern Thailand. *Ethnic and Racial Studies*, 34(5), 833–49.

McCargo, D., and Pathmanand, U. (2005). *The Thaksinization of Thailand*. Yangpu: NIAS Press.

Mérieau, E. (2016). Thailand's Deep State, Royal Power and the Constitutional Court (1997–2015). *Journal of Contemporary Asia*, 46(3), 445–66.

Merkel, W. (2004). Embedded and Defective Democracies. *Democratization*, 11(5), 33–58.

Neher, C. D. (1992). Political Succession in Thailand. *Asian Survey*, 32(7), 585–605.

Pathmanand, U. (2008). A Different coup d'état? *Journal of Contemporary Asia*, 38(1), 124–42.

Pinyorat, R. (2006). PM Thaksin Accused of Criticizing the Thai King. *China Post*. Available at: https://chinapost.nownews.com/20060708-140317 [Accessed 4 September 2017].

Reuters. (2008). Thai Army Chief Balks at Protest Crackdown. b92. Available at: www.b92.net/eng/news/world.php?yyyy=2008&mm=09&dd=02&nav_id=53175 [Accessed 4 September 2008].

Reuters. (2017). Thailand's King Given Full Control of Crown Property. Available at: www.reuters.com/article/us-thailand-king-property/thailands-king-given-full-control-of-crown-property-idUSKBN1A2oOX [Accessed 18 July 2008].
Riggs, F. W. (1966). *Thailand: The Modernization of a Bureaucratic Polity*. Honolulu: East-West Center Press.
Rojanaphruk, P. (2008). Army Comeback through Soft, Silent Coup. *The Nation*. Available at: www.nationmultimedia.com [Accessed 1 January 2009].
Samudavanija, C. (1982). *The Thai Young Turks*. Farnham: Ashgate Publishing Company.
Samudavanija, C. (1997). Old Soldiers Never Die, They Are Just By-Passed. In K. Hewison, ed., *Political Change in Thailand*. London: Routledge, pp. 42–57.
SIPRI (Stockholm Institute for Strategic Studies). (2017). Available at: www.sipri.org, accessed [Accessed 2 December 2017].
Streckfuss, D. (2010). *Truth on Trial in Thailand: Defamation, Treason, and Lèse-Majesté*. New York: Routledge.
The Nation. (2007). Junta's Media War a Big Mistake. *The Nation*, 26 October, p. 1.
The Nation. (2011). Task Force 315 Not Linked to Politics: Army Spokesman. *The Nation*, 30 May. Available at: www.thaivisa.com/forum/topic/471077-task-force-315-not-linked-to-politics-thai-army-spokesman/ [Accessed 15 June 2011].
United Nations. (2016). Thailand. Available at: http://data.un.org/CountryProfile.aspx?crName=THAILAND [Accessed 10 October 2017].
USIP (United States Institute of Peace). (2014). Key Findings on Election violence Prevention: Thailand: February 2014 Elections. Available at: www.usip.org/sites/default/files/2017-02/Electing-Peace-Thailand-Preventing-Electoral-Violence.pdf [Accessed 16 May 2015].
Waitoolkiat, N., and Chambers, P. W. (2017). Arch-royalist Rent: The Political Economy of the Military in Thailand. In P. W. Chambers and N. Waitoolkiat, eds., *Khaki Capital: The Political Economy of the Military in Southeast Asia*. Copenhagen: NIAS.
Wilson, D. A. (1962). *Politics in Thailand*. Ithaca: Cornell University Press.
Winichakul, T. (2008). Toward the End of King Bhumibol's Era: The Historical Suicide of Royalist Democracy. Monarchies in Transition, Stanford University: Center on Democracy, Development and Rule of Law, 5–6 June.
Yoon, S. (2006). Old Soldiers Never Die; They Raise 'Career' Thoroughbreds. *The Star*, 23 July. Available at: www.thestar.com.my/opinion/letters/2006/07/23/old-soldiers-never-die-they-raise-career-thoroughbreds/ [Accessed 2 January 2019].

6

Weak State and the Limits of Democratization in Cambodia, 1993–2017

Kheang Un

INTRODUCTION

Democratic transition in Cambodia was not an outcome of domestic forces; rather, it was a product of external imposition through the 1991 Paris Peace Agreement. The accords authorized the United Nations through the United Nations Transitional Authority in Cambodia (UNTAC) in 1992–1993 to oversee the democratic transition by organizing multi-party elections and to assist in the drafting of a new liberal democratic constitution. Forced to comply with the mandate of the Paris Peace Agreement, Cambodian constitutional drafters fully incorporated all liberal elements of this document (Marks, 1994: 64). In other words, the constitution enshrines the partial regimes of embedded democracy – free and fair elections, political rights, civil rights, horizontal accountability and effective power to govern. Across the next two decades, Cambodia's democracy went through a period of electoral authoritarianism, where elements of authoritarianism co-existed with democratic elements. Regular multi-party elections occurred; however, electoral processes were not free and fair, and civil and political freedoms were curtailed (see, e.g. Schedler, 2006). By 2017, Cambodia plunged into de facto one-party authoritarianism. The Bertelsmann Transformation Index (BTI) scores for the partial regimes of the embedded democracy between 2006 and 2016 were low and declining (cf. Table 2 in the Introduction). This chapter investigates how Cambodia's stateness impacts the United Nations installed democracy, arguing that Cambodia's electoral authoritarianism and subsequent de facto one-party authoritarianism can be attributed to the country's low level of administrative and extractive state capacity, producing a low quality of governance, while the state retained effective coercive capacity against democratic forces. More specifically, the chapter contends that Cambodia's entrenched neo-patrimonialism kept the quality of governance low but coercive capacity strong. These conditions in turn undermine partial regimes of the embedded democracy.

THE CAMBODIAN STATE IN POST-UNTAC INSTALLED DEMOCRACY

It should be noted that state capacity in Cambodia prior to the introduction of democracy in 1993 was low for the following reasons. First, the destruction of the country by the ultra-Maoist Khmer Rouge regime dismantled existing state institutions and the market system and killed most of the educated class. Second, efforts to rebuild state institutions and the economy by the People's Republic of Kampuchea (PRK, 1979–1989)/State of Cambodia (SoC, 1990–1993) faced an international economic embargo and civil war. Furthermore, the PRK's low capacity was further exacerbated by entrenched patron-clientelism. The international community through the Paris Peace Agreement attempted to rebuild the Cambodian state by implanting a rational legal state in Cambodia; its efforts were overshadowed by the ruling Cambodian People's Party (CPP) determination to maintain its political domination and its entrenched patron-clientelism.

Although the CPP lost the 1993 United Nations sponsored elections to the National United Front for an Independent, Neutral, Peaceful and Cooperative Cambodia (FUNCINPEC), it muscled its way into a power-sharing arrangement wherein a coalition government with two prime ministers was created: Hun Sen of the CPP and Prince Norodom Ranariddh of FUNCINPEC. From 1993 to 1997, the Cambodian state was fragmented along the FUNCINPEC-CPP divide. This divide was based, in the words of political scientist Steve Heder (1995: 425), on the 'interlocking of pyramids of patron-client networks'. These networks, called *ksae* in Khmer, are in constant competition for supremacy or, at a minimum, interact in such a way as to maintain the status quo. These networks are linked to two other elements – corruption and the use of force – in a mutually re-enforcing triangular mechanism. This mechanism has impacted various dimensions of state capacity and consequently the partial regimes of embedded democracy through their re-enforcement of – to use Putnam et al.'s (1994) phrase – 'interminable vicious circles'.

The Cambodian state can be characterized as being composed of a number of *ksae* that constitute smaller networks whose patrons serve as backers, or *khnang* to their clients. These small networks, to use Eisenstadt and Roniger's (1984: 135) phrase, 'are mostly related to, and integrated into, large circles with a chain-to-centre structure'. Through these *ksae*, officials at local, provincial and national levels exercise personal control over the state apparatus, through which they and their clients monopolize a variety of economic activities through the non-transparent issuance of licenses, contracts and permits. Up until 1993, the networks that had a high impact on political and economic transformations were found within the ruling CPP. Following the formation of the coalition government in 1993, another *ksae* linked to Prince Norodom Ranariddh was created. Cambodian leaders' efforts to consolidate their power fuelled, as Gottesman (2003: 211) points out, 'a sprawling and heterogeneous network of ministries, agencies and provincial and local administrations whose members adhered to the rules of patronage'.

Patron-clientele relations, though not codified, Scott Mainwaring (1999: 178) points out, entail some degree of explicit or implicit bargaining on both sides. Other research has revealed that the power of clients to bargain derives from their ability to switch their allegiance if their former patrons lack the ability or the willingness to offer them access to resources or protection.[1] To shore up their power and to avoid the risk of alienating their clients and others within the network (upon which patrons' power rests), patrons often have to accommodate their clients' requests, tolerate their behaviour and protect their interests. This is the strategy that Hun Sen employs to balance the power of different sub-networks within his system. This strategy has evolved into path-dependency shaping Hun Sen's leadership, a style that has perpetuated a weak state.

Prince Ranariddh's *ksae* began to shrink and eventually became irrelevant following his ousting in a 1997 violent coup launched by Prime Minister Hun Sen. By the early 2000s, Prime Minister Hun Sen had become Cambodia's singular 'strongman'. Although he is often referred to colloquially as *Preah In* (God Indra) – without whose blessing nothing can be achieved – Cambodia is far from a personalist state as some scholars have suggested.[2] As a legacy of Cambodia's communist past (1979–1991), although the prime minister wields decisive power on many issues, he still needs to work through the CPP's structure to appoint senior government officials and adopt electoral strategies for the party. Its communist roots are also the reason the CPP has been intertwined with the Cambodian state. As such, the CPP extends state-based patronage into the electoral arena, which, as this chapter will explain, undermines the electoral process and choices.

COERCIVE CAPACITY

It might be a misperception to characterize the Cambodian state as weak overall. It is strong in terms of its ability to maintain social order and achieve a monopoly over violence within the Cambodian borders. Such complete territorial control under the unified armed forces followed the defeat of the remnants of the Khmer Rouge forces in 1998 and the FUNCINPEC military forces in the 1997 coup. However, the security forces also operate under the rules of

---

[1] For discussion on Indonesia and Thailand see Eisenstadt and Roniger (1984:127–38).
[2] For example, Morgenbesser, 2017.

patronage and corruption. Securing loyalty through promotions has led to a bloated military security sector, leading former King Norodom Sihanouk to once characterize the structure of the Cambodian army as a 'reverse pyramid' (Far Eastern Economic Review, 1994). Despite government efforts at military reform, factional politics and the regime's goal of maintaining electoral authoritarianism mean that this reverse pyramid structure lives on. By 2010, it was reported that the Royal Cambodian Armed Forces had over 2,200 generals in their ranks (some 1,500 more generals than in the entire US military), and in 2014, the government promoted an additional 29 officers to four-star generals (Radio Free Asia, 2014).

As the military is based on patronage and personal loyalty, it has been neither professional nor neutral. In other words, they serve as enforcers of the electoral authoritarian and then de facto one-party order. The military has been found to be involved in a range of human rights abuses. They suppress demonstrations by opposition party activists, human rights activists, labour organizations and protesters over land, fishing and forestry rights. Moreover, senior military officers openly declare their allegiance not to the state but to the CPP and Prime Minister Hun Sen. These officers have even gone as far as to identify themselves as an organ of the CPP and threatened to crackdown on any individuals or political parties who attempt to organize a 'colour revolution' against Hun Sen or the CPP (Radio Free Asia, 2015).

Furthermore, the politicization of the security forces is evident with the rise of the Prime Minister Bodyguard Unit. Following a 1994 failed coup against Hun Sen – allegedly organized by his own party comrades – the prime minister has built a well-equipped, well-funded and well-fed bodyguard unit numbering between 2,000 to 3,000 soldiers and a reserve unit known as Unit 70. Hun Sen's bodyguard unit was created to protect the prime minister and his government and is answerable only to him. For instance, investigation by human rights groups and the US Federal Bureau of Investigation implicated Hun Sen's bodyguard unit in the grenade attacks that killed sixteen people and injured over a hundred of Sam Rainsy Party's supporters. This bodyguard unit also played a leading role in the 1997 violence that toppled Prince Norodom Ranariddh, then Hun Sen's co-prime minister (Human Rights Watch, 2009). The role of Hun Sen's bodyguard unit was strengthened in 2009, when its functions were extended to include not only the prime minister's personal security but also national defence. The bodyguard unit's expanded role entitles it to possess the nation's most advanced modern arsenal.

Prime Minister Hun Sen has repeatedly stated that there are no other institutions or individuals who can control the armed forces other than himself. Consequently, his removal either by legitimate elections or other means would plunge Cambodia into civil war. Hun Sen uses this threat of political instability to suppress the democratic aspirations of Cambodians, many of whom are genocide survivors and who do not want to risk instability and potential violence by supporting opposition parties. Prime Minister Hun Sen's rhetoric also raises doubts over the possibility of a transfer of power in the event that his party loses a future election.

NEO-PATRIMONIALISM AND QUALITY OF BUREAUCRACY

Although the framework of a modern state bureaucracy existed, its substance was precariously weak. Legacies of past war, genocide, ongoing civil war and an international embargo under the PRK/State of Cambodia meant that the state bureaucracy faced poor funding, a low level of professionalism and widespread corruption. In many cases corruption was systematized as state actors and non-state actors collude in parallel economies in which state officials – to use Lemarchand's (1988: 163) phrase – act as 'privileged partners in the management of economic exploitation'. During this period, as Evan Gottesman's (2003: 335) observes: 'As long as the money flows, officials act with impunity – engaging in theft, extortion or worse'. Such corruption persisted and transformed in post-UNTAC Cambodia to accommodate the ruling party's efforts to perpetuate illiberal democracy. Corruption in post-UNTAC Cambodia therefore does not pertain only to officials' engagement in procedural, substantive and/or administrative behavioural patterns for private gain, gains for family members or a close private clique but also to illegal acquisition of resources to maintain the party's power.[3]

Payment becomes a condition of employment existing in a pyramid structure, as each tier purchases its positions from the one above it. Under these conditions, while low-ranking civil servants supplement their meagre incomes with petty corruption they impose on citizens and businesses they come into contact with, senior bureaucrats and party apparatchik enrich themselves through issuance of monopolistic licenses for business or the extraction of natural resources. As money changes hands via an informal payment system known as *sraom sambot chongkhae*, or 'the end of the month envelopes', there is little incentive for patrons to punish their clients for 'corruption' as long as the clients play by patronage rules.

It is undeniable that widespread corruption among civil servants is partially due to low salaries. For many years, the government had been unwilling and unable to raise civil servants' salaries. It was only because of the appeal for salary increases by the main opposition party, the Cambodia National Rescue Party (CNRP), in the 2013 national elections, the government decided to increase civil servants' salaries. Around that same time, the government also increased its rhetoric on fighting corruption. Ten years after it was drafted,

---

[3] For a detailed discussion of corruption, see Heidenheimer and Johnston (2011) and Rose-Ackerman (1999).

the anti-corruption law came into effect in 2010, enforced by a powerful yet politicized Anti-Corruption Unit (ACU). In the recent years, the ACU has charged a number of government officials, judges, prosecutors and members of security forces with corruption. The presence of the ACU has made people more cautious in engaging in bribery; as a senior official at a multi-lateral institution said, 'They know someone is watching over their shoulders'.[4] This might be an overly optimistic view of the effectiveness of the ACU and the ruling party's willingness to tackle corruption. Rather, the nature of corruption has transformed into a franchise system, wherein franchisers (top leaders/ruling party) license franchisees (top leaders' cronies) to collect rents. Within this context, while petty corruption has declined, grand corruption has persisted.[5] According to the World Bank Governance Indicators, Cambodia's score for control of corruption is low with an average score of −1.13.[6] Furthermore, corruption will live on so long as the system demands that government officials pay to retain their positions and the ruling party demands that government-cum party officials contribute to party campaign funding in the absence of laws on campaign financing.

Corruption affects the state's ability to mobilize revenue. These conditions, as the chapter later argues, permit the CPP to blackmail voters, claiming that its electoral defeat would result in the end of its patronage handouts. The government's low level of revenue mobilization is attributed to powerful vested interests embedded within patron-client networks. A World Bank report, after noting this problem, suggested that for the government to improve its revenue it 'will have to deal with vested interests and other obstacles to reform' (World Bank, 2003:xvi). The Cambodian government, through its public forums and policy papers, consistently acknowledges these problems and, with assistance from donors, has undertaken measures to reform public financial management (Hughes and Un, 2007). The results, however, have been mixed. Following the initial outset of reform, government tax collection increased from 8.3 per cent of gross domestic product (GDP) in 1999 to 12 per cent in 2006 (Donnelly, 2006), but it remains among the lowest in the world (IMF, 2007). Following the 2013 elections, there have been significant reforms in public financial management. A senior official of a multi-lateral financial institution said: 'Since the 2013 elections, the reforms in public finance amounted to the combined reforms of the

---

[4] Conversation with author, Phnom Penh, June 2012.
[5] Preap Kol, director of Transparency International-Cambodia, interview with the author, Phnom Penh, 2 August 2018.
[6] This score 'reflects perceptions of the extent to which public power is exercised for private gain, including both petty and grand forms of corruption, as well as 'capture' of the state by elites and private interests'. It ranges from −2.25 (weak) to 2.25 (strong). This average is calculated from the World Bank, Worldwide Governance Indicators. Available at: https://data.worldbank.org/data-catalog/worldwide-governance-indicators [Accessed 21 January 2018].

previous five years.'⁷ By 2016, revenue collection reached 17.37 per cent of GDP (World Bank, 2018). However, collusion between tax collectors and businesses and leakages at the Ministry of Economics and Finance (MoEF) persist. For instance, a typical government institution obtains only around 60 per cent of its allocated operational funds. Furthermore, 'tea money' is often required in order to receive funding approval or reimbursement from officials at MoEF.⁸

The interlocking of neo-patrimonialism and corruption extends to the national resource sector, such as logging and land. In the 1990s, the processes and actors involved in logging were decentralized wherein sub-national governments, power brokers and regional military leaders were those benefiting most directly. The government's unsuccessful management of the forest sector derived from the calculated subordination of rational legal management of resources to ending the civil war and maintaining peace and political stability in the 1990s through elite pacts. Such government calculations permitted the army, through networks of business tycoons, forestry bureaucrats, politicians and provincial authorities, to clear hardwood forests for personal enrichment, thereby depriving the state of much needed revenue (Le Billon, 2002: 570).

With the demise of the Khmer Rouge and pressured by donors, civil society and opposition parties, new laws and mechanisms were put in place, including mandatory forest management plans, socio-economic impact assessments of forest and land concessions and a total moratorium on logging (Technical Working Group Forestry and Environment, 2007: 4). The government subsequently introduced Economic Land Concessions in order to generate revenue and employment through agribusiness investment (Independent Forest Sector Review, 2004).⁹ However, the new law succumbed to the existing neo-patrimonial networks that linked political elites to economic elites. The consequences were twofold. First, as a 2007 Global Witness's report illustrates, the Economic Land Concession policies provided new opportunities for the 'kleptocratic [sic] elites' to collude with each other to fell tropical forest trees under the name of agribusiness investment within the government framework of Economic Land Concessions.¹⁰

Second, due to an ineffective and inefficient land registration system and weak enforcement of laws associated with a corrupt and politicized judicial system, the government has awarded vast land concessions to politically well-connected tycoons. Many of those awards were made in a non-transparent manner and exceed the 10,000 hectares per company limit specified by the

---

⁷ Conversation with author, Phnom Penh, October 2014.
⁸ Author's discussion with government officials and staff of multi-lateral institutions during his field research from January to May 2015.
⁹ On these issues, see also Verver and Dahles (2015) and Global Witness (2015).
¹⁰ This occurs, for instance, at the Tumring Rubber Plantation in Kampong Thom Province. See for example, Global Witness (2007).

2002 land law.[11] For instance, Pheapimex Company, a major sponsor of the CPP, holds land concessions equivalent to 7.4 per cent of the total land area of Cambodia (Global Witness, 2007: 10). Furthermore, many of the concessions have not been put into production, contrary to the land law, which stipulates that any concessions will risk cancellation if not put into productive use within twelve months. Such conditions have, in recent years, led to widespread land conflicts and human rights abuses affecting over 700,000 people and have deprived the poor and ethnic minorities of access to their land and non-timber forest products (Sloth et al., 2005: 4).[12]

Neo-patrimonialism also causes low state capacity as it affects the quality of the bureaucracy in three ways. First, recruitment of office holders is clientele-based. Thus, civil servants tend to be poorly skilled, inactive and politicized. Leaders gain confidence from subordinates through personal networks and not through formal bureaucratic channels. Therefore, loyalty is often prioritized over reliability and competency. Consequently, in each government ministry and agency, only a small number of senior bureaucrats command power and resources and conduct the affairs of their ministries and agencies.

Second, government institutions have high numbers of ghost employees or moonlighters (Jackson and Sokha, 2014). Both types of bureaucrats never, or irregularly, show up to work but remain on the government payroll. Third, similar to the pre-transition era, many ministers treat their ministries as their personal fiefdoms, appointing their children and relatives to key ministry positions. Clientele-based recruitment has bloated the state bureaucracy, which consumes most of a ministry's allocated budget, leaving little money for infrastructure development and programme implementation.[13]

NEO-PATRIMONIALISM AND ELECTORAL AUTHORITARIANISM

The low level of revenue and high levels of corruption has weakened the state's ability to provide public goods and other welfare programmes. These conditions permitted the ruling CPP to use its domination over state resources and its symbiotic relationships with tycoons to institutionalize machine politics.[14] This political machine has systematically permeated, superseded and, in some cases, operated parallel to state institutions to promote the CPP's propaganda and to organize and influence voters. Such working groups serve as mechanisms channelling the CPP's centrally controlled resources and personnel to local communities (Pak and Craig, 2011). These resources are mainly

---

[11] See UNHCHR (2007).
[12] For interactive map of land economic concessions and logging, please see LICADO, n.d.
[13] This information is based on the author's discussion with government officials and members of civil society organizations since the early 2000s. See also Sovuthy and Peter (2016).
[14] This information is drawn from the author's research on Chambers of Commerce in Cambodia in 2007 and 2010.

acquired through two sources. The first is from contributions from government officials, whose contribution amount depends on their access to rent-seeking (based their official positions). It is a CPP rule that across government ministries and agencies a portion of funds generated through rent-seeking has to be reserved for electoral campaigns. This is known as 'black box money' (Un, 2005). The second source is from contributions from private business. It is common practice that CPP ministers who are given responsibility for development in certain provinces or districts are linked to business tycoons whose companies are under the minister's jurisdiction.[15]

With financing from business tycoons and government officials, the CPP working groups have operated in a parallel system to the formal state structure. In most communities, the CPP working groups are seen as more effective than the state in promoting local development and in assisting local communities in times of crisis (Pak and Craig, 2011). The decentralization process, which began in 2002 with the election of commune councils, or *Sangkat* (cluster of villages), had the dual goal of improving local democratic and participatory government and fostering economic development. However, the decentralization's objective of alleviating poverty through local participatory development and service remains largely unrealized due to a lack of resources and the absence of real autonomy (Rusten et al., 2004).[16] In the midst of challenges facing local government, the CPP's development funds have reached local communities regularly, promptly and at almost double the amount provided by the state (Pak and Craig, 2011).

Furthermore, Prime Minister Hun Sen, the paramount patron of Cambodia's development, sponsors large visible projects such as schools, roads and inter-district irrigation networks. By 2003, Hun Sen had indeed built 2,232 schools. The *Cambodia Daily* reported that, 'with giant initials emblazoned in Khmer on the roof of each one, few Cambodians can miss the point: education came to their commune courtesy of their prime minister's generosity' (Stubbs and Sameun, 2003). According to statistics provided by Hun Sen's cabinet, the average cost for a school was US$20,000. Thus, an estimated US$44.6 million has been spent on school buildings alone (Stubbs and Sameun, 2003). Hun Sen's personal school building programme amounted to over half of the total 2003 government spending on education, which was around $75 million (World Bank, 2004: 147). By 2010, the total number of schools built by Prime Minister Hun Sen reached 17,931 (Strangio, 2014). Across the country, roads and bridges bear the signs: 'Gift from *Samdech* Prime Minister Hun Sen'.[17]

---

[15] Author's interviews with villagers and local authorities, Takeo Province, June 2007. This finding has been confirmed by author's subsequent research in 2014, 2015 and 2016. See also Pak and Craig (2011).

[16] See also Blunt and Turner (2005) and National Committee for Sub-National Democratic Development (2014).

[17] Author's observation during his trips across the countries over the past decades.

Prime Minister Hun Sen and the CPP use their control over resources to create a form of 'perverse accountability'[18] and have publicly threatened that the defeat of the CPP will mean the end of local development. Besides development projects, the CPP has also provided handouts to villagers, ranging from small amounts of cash to basic necessities during election campaigns.[19] Caroline Hughes's (2003) study shows that those small gifts offered by the CPP contained hidden threats. The risk of exclusion is high if voters are refused the gifts because it is not 'merely unprofitable but physically threatening' (Hughes, 2003: 76). The level of the CPP's real or perceived surveillance capability is strong, given its entrenched control of the Cambodian hinterland. Up until the early 2000s, with the strength of CPP's grassroots organization compounded by the relative geographical immobility of rural voters, where everyone seems to know everyone else in the village, rural voters were locked into complying with clientelistic exchange agreements or otherwise faced the risk of being excluded from the CPP' distribution of particularistic goods in the future.[20]

Over time, a number of factors have raised Cambodians' awareness of the negative impacts of the CPP's clientelistic politics. These include economic expansion, the deepening of decentralization, rising use of social media, inter- and intra-country migration, improved security and, most importantly, demographic changes. Increasingly, Cambodians have become aware of the gravity of cronyism, corruption and collusion in the extraction of natural resources and the perverse effects those phenomena have had on government's ability to provide public services and goods. Previously, when only minorities or people in remote areas were affected, most Cambodians may not have been aware or concerned, but nowadays, land issues and logging are common knowledge throughout the country. Additionally, the CPP's gifts are less valuable now given people's rising expectations and the extravagance displayed by Cambodia's political and economic elites. Although rural Cambodians remain cautious in their outward expression towards the CPP, many have become more tactically astute. When the party offered rural voters gifts in exchange for promises to vote for the CPP in 2013, voters took the gifts. However, to the shock of the CPP – when election day came – many cast their ballots against the ruling party (Un, 2015, 2019).

Despite its limitations, patronage politics has become path-dependent for the ruling CPP. Such path-dependence has curtailed its ability to strengthen state capacity. For instance, in light of its decreasing popularity in the 2013 national elections, instead of strengthening public services, the CPP has continued to rely on patronage to connect to voters, albeit with slight modifications. The CPP established 'social foundations' that provide financial assistance to

---

[18] For discussion of this concept, see Stokes (2005).
[19] Author's field notes 2013 and 2017.
[20] These conditions also found in patronage based electoral democracy in Latin America. See, for example, Stokes (2005).

families with newborn babies, members who have recently passed or newly married couples regardless of party affiliation. Again, funds for these foundations come from contributions by government officials and business tycoons. When increasingly large numbers of people demanded a more responsive state through the election of an alternative political party – the CNRP – the government resorted to the use of legal harassment and armed intimidation against the opposition party before eventually dissolving it in late 2017.

HORIZONTAL ACCOUNTABILITY

High democratic quality, theorists have long argued, requires the presence of democratic rule of law that grants all citizens political and legal equality and makes the state and its agents subject to the law (Diamond, 1999: 11).[21] Democratic rule of law requires an independent judiciary characterized by (1) party detachment and political insularity that ensures independence from other political institutions (Larkins, 1996: 606); (2) institutional strength such as adequate resources, salaries, trained personnel and strong intra-institutional co-operation (O'Donnell, 2004, see also Zakaria, 2007); and (3) insulation from patron-clientelism and patronage democracy (O'Donnell, 1992, 1996). Without those elements, the judiciary 'can be easily manipulated to prevent it from questioning the illegal or arbitrary acts of state actors' (Larkins, 1996: 606).

The current weakness of horizontal accountability is not a new phenomenon, but has its roots in earlier stages of political development. Throughout Cambodia's modern history, the legal system has regularly been shut down or twisted to serve the different regimes' political interests. From 1975 to 1979, the Khmer Rouge essentially abolished the entire judicial system (Donovan, 1993: 81–81, 90; Gottesman, 2003: 243–54). When the PRK came to power in 1979 en, following the fall of the Khmer Rouge regime, there was thus no legal system in place. The PRK, following Vietnamese and Soviet models, re-established a communist judicial system, thereby creating at least a pretence of legality. To address staff shortages, the PRK organized short-term training courses for would-be judges and prosecutors (Donovan, 1993: 181–82). However, because the regime wanted to establish the legal system as an integral part of the regime's communist party apparatus, the training emphasized Marxist-Leninist doctrines over legal subjects, and recruitment of prosecutors and judges was based on 'good biography', meaning that they had the correct political standing (Gottesman, 2003: 243–44).

Although the PRK slowly created a formal judicial system, party ideology subsumed legal procedures, resulting in frequent interference in the judicial process by government/party officials at both the central and provincial level. The party or powerful individuals, but not the law, determined the course of

---

[21] For detailed discussion on the rule of law in Cambodia, see McCarthy and Un (2017).

proceedings and the verdicts of trials. A former minister of justice complained during a meeting at the council of ministers in 1986: 'Sentencing depends on the influence of persons offering an opinion, not on the law' (Gottesman, 2003: 254). The previously outlined conditions have become path-dependent, impeding efforts at promoting rule of law and an independent judiciary in the post-international intervention era. After the 1993 UN-sponsored elections, Cambodia adopted a system of checks and balances wherein judicial independence became enshrined in the constitution. To safeguard the constitution and to protect citizens' fundamental rights, three tiers of courts were established: the courts of first instance, an Appeals Court and the Supreme Court.[22] Situated atop this system was the Supreme Council of Magistracy (SCM), whose constitutional role was to assist the king to ensure the independence of the judiciary and to recommend judges and prosecutors for royal appointment, dismissal and discipline. A Constitutional Council (CC) was also created to ensure the constitutionality of laws, rules and regulations through review and veto powers. Over time, these judicial institutions, however, failed to function appropriately, and many of the laws and regulations have not been systematically implemented. According to the World Bank Governance Indicators, the average score for rule of law between 1996 and 2016 is −1.11, based on a scale from −2.25 to 2.25.[23]

Despite its constitutionally enshrined independence, Cambodia's judiciary has been weak and politicized due to its embedding within the state's neo-patrimonialism system. The judiciary has experienced high levels of corruption among judges and prosecutors. Up until the late 2000s, one commonly noted factor underpinning corruption within the judiciary was the low salaries for judges and prosecutors. As part of judicial reform, the salaries of judges and prosecutors were substantially increased, rising from approximately US$20 per month to US$250 and even US$600, depending on seniority (World Bank, 2003: 25). However, this salary increase did not significantly diminish corruption within the judiciary or increase judicial independence. As seen in the context of other developing countries, if judges, prosecutors and clerks have to buy their positions and maintain kickbacks to retain them, they also have to re-coup their investment (Pepys, 2007: 4–5). Furthermore, judges and prosecutors in Cambodia are incorporated into the ruling party's political machine. Such politicization of Cambodian governance renders judicial neutrality impossible. Indeed, one prosecutor stated that 'the characteristics of politics determine the peculiarity of the court system' in Cambodia.[24]

---

[22] The government under the Council for Legal and Judicial Reform has since drawn up a blueprint for the creation of specialized courts.

[23] Rule of law measures 'perceptions of the extent to which agents have confidence in and abide by the rules of society, and in particular the quality of contract'. This average is calculated from the World Bank, Worldwide Governance Indicators (2016).

[24] Interview with Municipal Court prosecutor, 25 September 2002. Subsequent research has revealed that such remarks, though made several years ago, remain relevant to present day conditions.

Because judges and prosecutors owe their careers to their parties or patrons, in making any decision, they have to consider 'who offered them the seat'.[25] Consequently, in Cambodia 'it is unavoidable that court officials serve the interests of political parties and that the judicial system serves politics'.[26]

Because the judiciary can serve as a double-edged sword, the ruling party has made limited efforts to institute its independence. As mentioned earlier, the Cambodian constitution intends the SCM to be independent, serving as a pillar of checks and balances. Despite widespread and publicly known corruption within the judiciary, the SCM has failed to take any concrete actions to address the issue. Reform within the judiciary, if any, was designed only to strengthen the ruling party and the executive branch. For example, as part of the government's agenda for judicial reform in 2014, the National Assembly (though boycotted by the opposition party) passed three major laws: the Law on the Organization and Functioning of the Supreme Council of Magistracy, the Law on the Statue of Judges and Prosecutors and the Law on the Organization of the Courts. However, these laws offer broad power to the Ministry of Justice, including chairing the SMC, appointing the leadership of the SMC secretariat, management of the courts' budget and the appointment, promotion, transfer, suspension and removal of judges and prosecutors (Human Rights Watch, 2009; New York Times, 2014). This is to ensure that the courts are under state control.

With its control over the judiciary, the government has resorted to the application of the 'rule by law', wherein laws are selectively applied for political gain. Some key legislation passed since 2010 illustrate the government's application of rule by law. Despite government promises to lessen restrictions on freedom of expression, the new Criminal Code, which came into effect in December 2010, retains the criminalization of defamation and disinformation with detailed provisions along with penalties. Defamation and insult are covered in several sections of the Criminal Code (2007), most notably Articles 305–313, 445–447 and 511. Article 305 defines defamation as 'any allegation of slanderous charge that undermines the *honour* or the *reputation* of a person or an *institution*', while Article 511 defines insult as 'the use of words, gestures, writings, sketches or objects which undermine the *dignity* of a person'. Furthermore, the scope of defamation is extended to criminalize comments made not only against individuals but also against institutions of the state and public officials. These definitions of defamation and insult are very broad, providing the court wide-ranging room for interpretation as to whether the offending acts undermine a person's or an institution's honour, reputation or dignity.

---

[25] Interview with Municipal Court clerk, 20 November 2001.
[26] Interview with Municipal Court judge, 2 October 2002. Subsequent research indicates that this statement remains true.

The ruling CPP has increasingly used the judiciary to suppress civil and political liberties that are enshrined in the constitution. In recent years, the CPP government has systematically employed defamation and other legal tactics as a means to weaken opposition parties and suppress outspoken critics. This is evidenced by the increase in arrests, detention and lawsuits filed against non-governmental organization (NGO) leaders and journalists since 2005. More detrimental to Cambodia's democracy is the CPP's use of the courts to undermine the main opposition party through legal persecution and harassment and arrest of its leaders on charges commonly believed to be politically motivated, ranging from political insurrection, inciting social unrest, defamation, corruption and treason (Khy and Blomberg, 2015; Kouch, 2015). At the end, in 2017, when the ruling party faced the opposition party's increased popularity with an election on the horizon in 2018, it used the CPP-controlled judiciary to charge CNRP with plotting to overthrow the government. In November 2017, the Supreme Court issued a ruling that dissolved the NCRP and banned its members from participating in political activities for five years (Sokhean, 2017).

In 2015, with the objective to restrict civic space, the government passed the Law on Associations and Non-Governmental Organizations and the Law on Trade Unions. It is widely believed that these laws will restrict the constitutional rights of freedom of association for non-government organizations and trade unions. Of critical concern for NGOs is the requirement for the compulsory registration of all NGOs and vague provisions that could provide for the selective denial of registration applications.[27] In addition, there is a reporting requirement that could have potential negative effects on NGOs whose work focuses on sensitive issues like human rights violations, human trafficking and legal aid – all of which require confidentiality (The International Center for Not-for-Profit Law, 2017). The electoral reform law, which was passed in March 2015, also contains provisions (Articles 84, 137, 147 and 158) that restrict freedom of speech and are aimed particularly at NGOs. These provisions criminalize NGOs that issue any statement that is considered to be 'insulting' towards politicians or political parties in the period leading up to elections (The International Center for Not-for-Profit Law, 2017). Recently, the government also increased prosecution of trade unions and NGOs as well as community leaders (Khy and Wright, 2016).

Furthermore, to protect its power and interests, the CPP has also politicized the Constitutional Council, preventing it from exercising its constitutional rights to ensure a free and fair political process and to protect state's resources from illegal expropriation by members of the ruling elite. As far as electoral disputes are concerned, the CC serves as the last arbiter of complaints. However, the politicization surrounding the process of its establishment and its lack of independence means that the Council has been unable to

---

[27] See Cambodian Center for Human Rights (CCHR) and Article 19 (2011).

play the role of a fair, independent arbiter of electoral conflicts. Consequently, the Council, to use Hughes and Sopheap's phrase (2000: 152), has been 'perceived as a pawn of a political game' by opposition parties. This perception is re-enforced by the CC continuing to favour the ruling CPP when it comes to resolving electoral conflicts. In the end, opposition parties resorted to street demonstrations and/or boycott of the National Assembly as the only viable venues to challenge election results. The government responded to the opposition's strategies with force, threats, co-optation and, eventually in 2017, in the outlawing of the CNRP. These actions further exacerbated mistrust in the system and consequently compromised any efforts at promoting democracy.

The embeddedness of neo-patrimonialism within the Cambodian state also leads the executive branch to undermine the legislature. A United States Agency for International Development (USAID, 2008: 39) report notes that 'legislation is proposed by the government and almost always moves through the Parliament quickly with little opposition, debate or even discussion'. The consequence is that '… parliament's legislative power has become undermined as the government delivers sub-decrees without the approval of the National Assembly, which are subsequently applied as law' (Transparency International, 2006: 20). The lack of executive constraint is further exacerbated by a politically subordinated CC. The CC has the mandate to safeguard respect for the constitution and to interpret the constitutionality of executive orders and laws passed by the National Assembly. However, due to its lack of political independence, the CC has thus far not made any decisions that questioned government policies or served to protect the constitutional rights of the people.

The developments surrounding the classification of state land and government land concessions are a case *par excellence*. These developments reflect not only the negative impact of Cambodia's neo-patrimonialism and absence of inter-institutional accountability, and thus democracy, but also the rights and livelihoods of hundreds of thousands of families. Approximately 80 per cent of the land in Cambodia remains nominally state land. Legally, 'state land' is classified as either 'state private land' or 'state public land'. While the former can be transferred to private ownership, the latter is reserved for the public domain. However, under the neo-patrimonial state, classification of state land falls under the domain of executive decision: 'By executive fiat, state public land can be reclassified as state private land and legally sold or transferred to private hands by the state' (Un and So, 2011: 296). These conditions strengthen the crony relations between the state and big businesses, thereby filling the CPP's coffers (Beban et al., 2017).

CONCLUSION

Since its imposition over two decades ago, the quality of Cambodia's democracy remains low. These conditions are associated with Cambodia's weak state. This weakness, in turn, links to the country's persistent neo-patrimonialism, which came to be deeply entrenched in the Cambodian state with the imposition of internationally prescribed democracy. When it was forced to accept democracy, the CPP was determined to ensure that it would remain the dominant player. As Prime Minister Hun Sen remarked in anticipation of the imposition of multi-party democracy: 'If there is a political solution and if [opposition politicians] come [to Cambodia], there should be a mutual give-and-take. They repay us by recognizing us as the central leader. We repay them by recognizing them as a legal party' (Gottesman, 2003: 306). With this determination, the CPP has employed its networks of patronage to cement its internal cohesion and has extended this patronage into the state bureaucracy, legal institutions and the electoral arena. Such politicking has undermined state capacity, which in turn has adversely affected the quality of the partial regimes of embedded democracy.

Over the past few years, popular demand for deeper democracy has emerged, as evidenced by the CNRP's rising popularity in the 2013 elections and subsequent mass protests against alleged electoral fraud. Social discontent has prompted the CPP to undertake a number of governance reforms, such as strengthening the state's revenue collection, improving public service provision, and increasing civil servants' salaries. However, despite these reforms, the Cambodian state remains weak. State weakness is reflected in three key areas. First, bureaucratic quality continues to be extremely low. Second, the state still struggles to generate revenue, which means there is a significant lack of resources for public service provision and infrastructure development. These conditions, in turn, have allowed the CPP to use its political machine, which is funded through crony capitalism, to pressure and entice voters, thereby generating a form of perverse accountability. The third area is weak horizontal accountability, exemplified by the ruling party's utilization of the rule by law and violence – or threat of violence – to suppress its opponents and to protect the network of crony capitalism. Weak horizontal accountability, in turn, hinders the work of vertical accountability institutions – in particular, civil society organizations. This trajectory can partly be explained by the CPP's determination to preserve its interests but also by Hun Sen's goal to transform Cambodia into a developmental authoritarian state where economic growth takes precedence over liberal democracy. Hun Sen has had limited success in achieving his objective due to a clash with the CCP's strategies of power consolidation. While the presence of a developmental state requires a strong bureaucratic foundation, Cambodian rulers have focused on strengthening the party. The fusion of the party with the state has weakened the latter, which, in turn, has rendered the state unable to respond to people's needs – pushing many of them to rally behind the opposition party. As its grip on power was challenged, the CPP has used its control over the coercive apparatuses to dismantle the opposition, effectively creating a de facto one-party state.

References

Beban, A., So, S., and Un, K. (2017). From Force to Legitimation: Rethinking Land Grabs in Cambodia. *Development and Change*, 48(3), 590–612.

Blunt, P., and Turner, M. (2005). Decentralisation, Democracy and Development in a Post-conflict Society: Commune Councils in Cambodia. *Public Administration and Development*, 25(1), 75–87.

Cambodian Center for Human Rights (CCHR) and ARTICLE 19. (2011). Cambodia: Freedom of Expression and the Point of No Return, Press Release. scoop. Available at: www.scoop.co.nz/stories/WO1102/S00488/cambodiafreedom-of-expression-and-the-point-of-no-return.htm [Accessed 9 January 2014].

Chandra, N. (1994). Center Cannot Hold: Sihanouk Fears for the Future of His Country. *Far Eastern Economic Review*, 175 (20), 19–20.

Diamond, L. (1999). *Developing Democracy: Toward Consolidation*. Baltimore: Johns Hopkins University Press.

Donnelly, R. (2006). Cambodia-Risk Assessment. Available at: www.efic.gov.au/static/efi/cra/cambodia.htm [Accessed 15 January 2008].

Donovan, D. A. (1993). The Cambodian Legal System: An Overview. In F. Brown, ed., *Rebuilding Cambodia: Human Resources, Human Rights and Law*. Washington, DC: The John Hopkins Foreign Policy Institute, pp. 69–107.

Eisenstadt, S. N., and Roniger, L. (1984). *Patrons, Clients and Friends: Interpersonal Relations and the Structure of Trust in Society*. Cambridge: Cambridge University Press.

Global Witness. (2007). Cambodia's Family Trees Illegal Logging and the Stripping of Public Assets by the Cambodian Elite. Available at: www.globalwitness.org/documents/14689/cambodias_family_trees_low_res.pdf [Accessed 20 May 2016].

Global Witness. (2015). The Cost of Luxury: Cambodia's Illegal Trade in Precious Wood with China. Available at: www.globalwitness.org/en/campaigns/forests/cost-of-luxury/ [Accessed 8 February 2018].

Gottesman, E. (2003). *Cambodia after the Khmer Rouge: Inside the Politics of Nation Building*. New Haven: Yale University Press.

Heder, S. (1995). Cambodia's Democratic Transition to Neoauthoritarianism. *Current History*, 94(596), 425–29.

Heidenheimer, A. J., and Johnston, M., eds. (2011). *Political Corruption: Concepts and Contexts*. London and Oxford: Transaction Publishers.

Hughes, C. (2003). *The Political Economy of the Cambodian Transition*. London and New York: Routledge.

Hughes, C., and Sopheap, R. (2000). *Nature of Causes of Conflict Escalation in the 1998 National Election*. Phnom Penh: Cambodian Center for Conflict Resolution/Cambodian Development Resource Institute.

Hughes, C., and Un, K. (2007). *Cambodia Country Governance Analysis, March 2007 Report Commissioned by DFID*. Phnom Penh: Embassy of the United Kingdom.

Human Rights Watch. (2009). Cambodia: 1997 Grenade Attack on Opposition Still Unpunished: Suspects in Attack Have Been Promoted Instead of Prosecuted. Available at: www.hrw.org/news/2009/03/30/cambodia-1997-grenade-attack-opposition-still-unpunished [Accessed 2 September 2015].

IMF. (2007). Macroeconomic Development, Public Financial Management and Private Sector Development, Statement by Cambodia's Development Partners at the First Cambodia Development and Cooperation Forum, Phnom Penh. Available at: www.imf.org/external/np/dm/2007/061907a.htm [Accessed 31 December 2007].

Independent Forest Sector Review. (2004). Part I: Choices, Issues, and Options. Available at: www.forest-trends.org/wp-content/uploads/imported/Cambodia%20 Report%20New.pdf [Accessed 11 December, 2019].

Jackson, W., and Sokha, C. (2014). The Civil Service's Phantom Workers. *The Phnom Penh Post*. Available at: www.phnompenhpost.com/post-weekend/civil-service's-phantom-workers [Accessed 8 January 2018].

Khy, S., and Blomberg, M. (2015). Opposition Activists Convicted of Insurrection. The Cambodia Daily. Available at: www.cambodiadaily.com/archives/opposition-activists-convicted-of-insurrection-89103/ [Accessed 10 December 2017].

Khy, S., and Wirght, G. (2016). Government Slammed for Arrests of NGO Officers. The Cambodia Daily. Available at: www.cambodiadaily.com/news/government-slammed-for-arrests-of-ngo-officers-111973/ [Accessed 20 June 2016].

Kouch, N. (2015). Opposition Senator Arrested After Hun Sen's Order. The Cambodia Daily, 13 August 2015. Available at: www.cambodiadaily.com/archives/opposition-senator-arrested-after-hun-sens-order-91574/ [Accessed 11 November 2017].

Larkins, C. M. (1996). Judicial Independence and Democratization: A Theoretical and Conceptual Analysis. *The American Journal of Comparative Law*, 44(4), 605–26.

Le Billon, P. (2002). Logging in Muddy Waters: The Politics of Forest Exploitation in Cambodia. *Critical Asian Studies*, 34(4), 563–86.

Lemarchand, R. (1998). The State, the Parallel Economy, and the Changing Structure of Patronage Systems. In D. Rothchild and N. Chazan, eds., *The Precarious Balance: State and Society in Africa*. Boulder: Westview Press, p. 163.

LICADO. (n.d.). Static Map and Spatial Data. Available at: www.licadho-cambodia.org/land_concessions/ [Accessed 8 February 2018].

Mainwaring, S. (1999). *Rethinking Party Systems in the Third Wave of Democratization: The Case of Brazil*. Stanford: Stanford University Press.

Marks, S. P. (1994). The New Cambodian Constitution: From Civil War to a Fragile Democracy. *Columbia Human Rights Law Review*, 26(45), 45–110.

McCarthy, S., and Un, K. (2017). The Evolution of Rule of Law in Cambodia. *Democratization*, 24(1), 100–18.

Morgenbesser, L. (2017). Misclassification on the Mekong: The Origins of Hun Sen's Personalist Dictatorship. *Democratization*, 25(2), 1–18.

National Committee for Sub-national Democratic Development. (2014). *Is Governance Improving? A Comparison of the Results of the 2011 and 2013 IP3 Governance Perception Survey*. 6 April. Phnom Penh: Ministry of Interior. (hardcopy on file with author)

O'Donnell, G. (1992). Transitions, Continuities, and Paradoxes. In S. Mainwaring and G. O'Donnell, eds., *Issues in Democratic Consolidation: The New South American Democracies in Comparative Perspective*. Notre Dame, IN: University of Notre Dame Press, pp. 17–56.

O'Donnell, G. (1996). Illusions about Consolidation. *Journal of Democracy*, 7(2), 34–51.

O'Donnell, G. (2004). Why the Rule of Law Matters. *Journal of Democracy*, 15(4), 32–46.
Pak, K., and Craig, D. (2011). Learning from Party Financing of Local Investment Projects in Cambodia: Elite and Mass Patronage, Accountability and Decentralized Governance. In C. Hughes and K. Un, eds., *Reform and Transformation in Cambodia*. Copenhagen: NIAS.
Pepys, M. (2007). Corruption within the Judiciary: Causes and Remedies. In Transparency International, eds., *Global Corruption Report 2007: Corruption in Judicial Systems*. Cambridge: Cambridge University Press.
Putnam, R.D., Leonardi, R., and Nanetti, R. Y. (1994). *Making Democracy Work: Civic Traditions in Modern Italy*. Princeton: Princeton University press.
Radio Free Asia. (2014). Cambodian PM Promotes 29 to Four Star General. Available at: www.rfa.org/english/news/cambodia/promotion-02052014165509.html [Accessed 2 September 2015].
Radio Free Asia. (2015). Cambodia's Armed Forces 'Belong' to the Ruling Party. Available at: www.rfa.org/english/news/cambodia/military-07292015145855.html [Accessed 2 September 2015].
Rose-Ackerman, S. (1999). Political Corruption and Democracy. *Connecticut Journal of International Law* 14, 363–78.
Rusten, C., Sedara, K., Netra, E., and Kimchoeun, P. (2004). *The Challenges of Decentralisation Design in Cambodia*. Phnom Penh: Cambodia Development Resource Institute.
Schedler, A., ed. (2006). *Electoral Authoritarianism: The Dynamics of Unfree Competition*. Boulder: Lynne Rienner Publishers.
Sloth, C., Bottra, K., and Sreng, H. K. (2005). Non-timber Forest Products: Their Value to Rural Livelihoods. *Cambodia Development Review*, 9(4), 1–6.
Sokhean, B. (2017). Breaking: Supreme Court Rules to Dissolve CNRP. *The Phnom Penh Post*. Available at: www.phnompenhpost.com/national/breaking-supreme-court-rules-dissolve-cnrp [Accessed 29 December 2017].
Sovuthy, K., and Peter, Z. (2016). Corruption Czar's Sons Appointed as Assistants. *The Cambodia Daily*, 27 April, https://english.cambodiadaily.com/editors-choice/corruption-czars-sons-appointed-as-assistants-111794/ [Accessed 11 December 2019].
Stokes, S. C. (2005). Perverse Accountability: A Formal Model of Machine Politics with Evidence from Argentina. *American Political Science Review*, 99(3), 315–25.
Strangio, S. (2014). *Hun Sen's Cambodia*. New Haven, CT: Yale University Press.
Stubbs, F., and Sameun, Y. (2003). Ubiquitous Hun Sen School Raise Ethic Issues. *The Cambodia Daily*, 9 January.
Technical Working Group Forestry and Environment. (2007). Forest Cover Change in Cambodia 2002–2006. Cambodia Development Cooperation Forum, 19–20 June. Cambodian Rehabiliation and Development Board. Available at: www.cdc-crdb.gov.kh/cdc/first_cdcf/session1/forest_cover_eng.htm.
The International Center for Not-for-Profit Law. NGO Law Monitor: Cambodia. Available at: www.icnl.org/research/monitor/cambodia.html [Accessed 29 May 2015].
The New York Times. (2014). Cambodia's Subservient Judiciary. *The New York Times*, 7 July. Available at: www.nytimes.com/2014/06/07/opinion/cambodias-subservientjudiciary.html?_r=0 [Accessed 29 May 2015].

Transparency International. (2006). Country Study Report, Cambodia 2006. Available at: www.transparency.org/policy_research/nis/nis_reports_by_country [Accessed 2 September 2015].

Un, K. (2005). Patronage Politics and Hybrid Democracy: Political Change in Cambodia, 1993–2003. *Asian Perspective*, 29(2), 203–30.

Un, K. (2015). The Cambodian People Have Spoken: Has the Cambodian People's Party Heard? *Southeast Asian Affairs*, 2015(1), 102–16.

Un, K. (2019). *Cambodia: Return to Authoritarianism*. Cambridge: Cambridge University Press.

Un, K., and So, S. (2011). Land Rights in Cambodia: How Neopatrimonial Politics Restricts Land Policy Reform. *Pacific Affairs*, 84(2), 289–308.

UNHCHR. (2007). *Economic Land Concession for Economic Purposes in Cambodia: A Human Right Perspective*. Phnom Penh: UNHCHR.

USAID-Cambodia. (2008). *Political Competitiveness and Civil Society Assessment*. Phnom Penh: USAID-Cambodia.

Verver, M., and Dahles, H. (2015). The Institutionalisation of Oknha: Cambodian Entrepreneurship at the Interface of Business and Politics. *Journal of Contemporary Asia*, 45(1), 48–70.

World Bank. (2003). *Cambodia Enhancing Service Delivery through Improved Resource Allocation and Institutional Reform: Integrated Fiduciary Assessment and Public Expenditure Review*. Phnom Penh: World Bank/Cambodia.

World Bank. (2004). Cambodia at the Crossroads: Strengthening Accountability to Reduce Poverty. Available at: http://siteresources.worldbank.org/INTCAMBODIA/Resources/1-report.pdf [Accessed 20 May 2016].

World Bank. (2016). Worldwide Governance Indicators. Available at: http://info.worldbank.org/governance/wgi/index.aspx#home [Accessed 2 July 2016].

World Bank. (2018). Revenue, Excluding Grants (% of GDP). Available at: https://data.worldbank.org/indicator/GC.REV.XGRT.GD.ZS?view=chart [Accessed 6 January 2018].

Zakaria, F. (2007). *The Future of Freedom: Illiberal Democracy at Home and Abroad (Revised Edition)*. New York: W. W. Norton & Company.

7

The Institutional Roots of Defective Democracy in the Philippines

Erik Martinez Kuhonta and Nhu Truong

INTRODUCTION

The Philippines stands out from other Southeast Asian nations as the first democracy in the region and the one with the longest practice of democratic elections. Assessed strictly by a procedural conception of democracy, whereby elections have been regular, contested and free, the quality of democracy in the Philippines can be said to be *prima facie* satisfactory. However, despite the most extensive record of democratic elections throughout all of Southeast Asia, the Philippine electoral regime has been embedded in broader institutional weaknesses. Democracy in the Philippines in terms of other 'partial regimes',[1] namely political rights, civil rights, horizontal accountability and effective power to rule, has been remarkably mediocre.

Crucially, elections alone have not improved regime performance or substantive outcomes in the Philippines. This is most evident in the country's dismal economic record, both in terms of growth and equity, especially when compared to other countries in the region, including Singapore, Malaysia and Vietnam. If we expect democratic governments, on the basis of their roots in popular representation and concerns with the popular will, to be able to produce policy outcomes that yield benefits for the wider population, the results have been quite to the contrary.[2] Except for the holding of regular elections, the quality of democracy in the Philippines is unequivocally poor.

---

[1] See note on Wolfgang Merkel's (2004) model in the Introduction of this volume. Note that the way that Merkel uses 'regimes' is very different from its general usage within political science as a 'type of government'.

[2] For claims that there is something inherent in a democratic regime that should benefit the broader public, see Tocqueville (1945), Mill (1975), Frankel (1978) and Sen (1999); see also Acemoglu and Robinson (2006).

What explains the predicament of low quality or 'defective' democracy[3] in the Philippines? This chapter will argue that the poor performance of Philippine democracy can be explained by the weaknesses of the state and party system. As one of the key constitutive dimensions of stateness, a strong and functional bureaucracy is necessary to ensure the effective exercise of state power. However, the state bureaucracy of the Philippines has been predominantly captured by oligarchs since the heyday of American colonialism. Although some parts of the bureaucracy have functioned as 'islands of strength', for the most part, the Philippine state has been penetrated by social forces that have used its bureaus for purely electoral and personal interests.[4] Political elites and bureaucrats, who run the state, have shown little interest in the idea of the public good. In the most incisive analysis of the Philippine state, Paul Hutchcroft (1991) has accurately categorized it as 'neo-patrimonial'. As Hutchcroft writes: 'Political administration...is often treated as a personal affair. The state apparatus is choked continually by an anarchy of particularistic demands from, and particularistic actions on behalf of, those oligarchs and cronies who are currently most favored by its top officials' (Hutchcroft, 1991: 415). Whether under the post-war oligarchs, the Ferdinand Marcos dictatorship or the most recent presidency of Rodrigo Duterte, the same pattern of neo-patrimonialism remains deeply engraved in the Philippine state.

Furthermore, the Philippine party system is one of the weakest institutionalized party systems in all of Northeast and Southeast Asia. In fact, the Philippines has one of the highest levels of electoral volatility in the region. During 1992 to 2013, the electoral volatility score reached as high as 38.3.[5] The party system remains dominated by organizations that are largely clientelistic, personalistic and devoid of any substantive programmatic agenda.

The weak performance of Philippine democracy can therefore be attributed to its feckless political institutions. This is a fundamental dilemma that developing countries continue to face, which Samuel Huntington (1968) so forcefully pointed out in the mid-1960s. As a result of the significant lack of capacity of the Philippine state and parties as well as the lack an effective mechanism for ensuring performance accountability, the Philippines has not been able to

---

[3] Based on Merkel's (2004) conceptualization of 'embedded democracy', when a partial regime of an embedded democracy is impaired, the democracy is hence 'defective'. It is also important to note that defective democracies, defined as such, are not necessarily found only in incipient or transitional democracies. So long as the 'specific defects' are developed and sustained by political power, socio-economic and socio-cultural contexts within a 'mutually supportive coexistence of environment and partial regimes', the quality of democracy of the regime will remain defective (see Merkel, 2004: 48–52).

[4] For a list of these 'islands of strength', see Abinales and Amoroso (2017: 240–41, 264).

[5] In the pre-Marcos period, from 1946–1969, the electoral volatility score was significantly lower at 18.5 (see Hicken and Kuhonta, 2015: 12).

pursue an objective system of checks and balances or advance programmatic policies that are centrally concerned with the greater public good.

The contemporary weakness of institutions and its persistence throughout the modern history of the Philippines can be traced back to historical-structural factors. First, they have to do with the timing of the advent of electoral democracy vis-à-vis the building of the state.[6] Elections under the Americans were instituted soon after the new imperial power brutally ended Philippine resistance. Elections at the local, provincial and national level superseded efforts to build a functioning, autonomous and rationalized bureaucracy. Neither the Spanish nor the Americans were interested in state-building, since neither had a history of a strong bureaucracy – particularly when compared to other colonial powers such as the British.

The consequence of this was that the elites who gained office from elections were able to then dominate and penetrate the state in pursuit of their private goals. The state was unable to avoid becoming an instrument of the elite. There was neither a bureaucratic corps that possessed enough corporate coherence to resist such claims nor a political patron who had a deep interest in strengthening the state. Ultimately, then, this sequencing pattern of electoral democracy predating state-building has had the effect of ensuring that traditional oligarchs dominate the polity. Both state structures and party organizations are thus unable to pursue programmatic goals that would serve the public interest.

This chapter analyses the predicament of Philippine democracy in two parts: First, it empirically examines and evaluates the quality of democracy in the Philippines based on the six constitutive dimensions put forth by Merkel's conceptualization (cf. Introduction): elections; political rights; civil rights and horizontal accountability; effective power to govern; and economic outcomes. Second, the chapter analyses the formation of political institutions – especially the state and parties – and shows how their lack of rational-legal structures, corporate coherence, autonomous organizational structures and programmatic agendas has directly weakened the quality of democracy in the Philippines. The fecklessness of institutions has resulted in the inability of the democratic system to generate two key conditions of effective democracy: accountability and policy performance. Thus, the Philippine democratic regime has been deeply undermined by its historical-institutional conditions.

Although this chapter presents a very bleak picture of Philippine democracy, it should be stressed that this does not mean that there have not also been efforts to inject programmatic visions into the polity. Indeed, there have been some periods of state-building and effective policy making. A number of social groups and parties – such as the Sakdal movement in the 1930s, the

---

[6] The ontological emphasis given to historical timing and sequencing in explaining Philippine political development is evident in Anderson (1996), Sidel (1999) and Hutchcroft (2000).

Democratic Alliance in the 1950s, social-democratic coalitions in the 1980s and small leftist parties emerging out of the country's unique party-list system in the 1990s, as well as some reform-oriented individuals in the contemporary Liberal Party – have stood out as notable exceptions in the general trajectory of Philippine political development. Their status as outliers does not mean they should be ignored, for to do so would be to create an excessively black-and-white narrative of the country's political development.[7] Nonetheless, these initiatives have arguably not gained significant traction, and in the big picture, their effect is limited, like tiny reefs in a tidal wave.

PHILIPPINE DEFECTIVE DEMOCRACY: OPERATIONALIZING QUALITY OF DEMOCRACY

Reducing democracy to a singular dimension on the basis of elections is empirically and normatively problematic, lending minimal analytical and comparative value. Electoral procedures for measuring the quality of democracy are 'minimalist' relative to other conceptions of democracy. Democratic quality, as Larry Diamond and Leonardo Morlino (2005: x) suggest, resembles 'a system' with multiple dimensions in which 'improvement in one dimension can have diffuse benefits for others (and vice versa)'. Merkel (2004) stresses precisely this point in his root conception of democracy as the 'embeddedness' of internally complex institutional structures, termed 'partial regimes' and external spheres of enabling conditions.[8] In short, Merkel (2004: 37) states pointedly, 'A sufficient definition of democracy has to go beyond simple democratic electoralism'.

In this section, we apply Merkel's model of 'embedded democracy' to assess how the Philippines fares in terms of the model's five partial regimes: (a) electoral regime; (b) political rights; (c) civil rights; (d) horizontal accountability; and (e) effective power to govern. Although analytically distinct, each of the regimes is also interconnected and re-enforces the others. In this manner, deficits in one partial regime may very well also be symptomatic of shortcomings in other regimes. As the analysis demonstrates, Philippine democracy continues to be defined by electoral violence, fraud and dynastic influence and, hence, cannot be said to satisfactorily possess 'effective power to govern'. It can thus be seen that, except for procedural elections, democracy in the Philippines is of low quality and is aptly classified as a 'defective democracy'.

---

[7] This is the central point of Kerkvliet (1995) where he argues that, despite the generally elitist nature of Philippine politics, one should not ignore attempts, particularly at the local level, to pursue political and social reform. This is, in effect, an effort to stress the value of a micro, or lumpy, picture of the polity rather than a more macro big picture. For the latter, see the searing critique of Philippine democracy made in Anderson (1988).

[8] See Merkel (2004) and the Introduction chapter in this volume for a detailed theoretical discussion of this conceptual framework.

Electoral Democracy

The Philippines has the most extensive record of democratic elections in Southeast Asia. Elections were first held in 1901 under the auspices of American colonialism, interrupted by the Japanese occupation in 1941 and then restored in 1946 when the country gained independence. From 1972 to 1986, the Philippines was under the Marcos dictatorship. The 1986 People Power Revolution returned democracy to the Philippines. After seven coup attempts during the tenure of Corazon Aquino, the first stable turnover took place in 1998 to Aquino's loyal Defence Secretary Fidel Ramos, followed by four more presidential contests. In the post-independence era, the Philippines had accumulated by 2018 some fifty-eight years of electoral democracy. This is far more than its (few) democratic counterparts in Southeast Asia, namely the on-and-off democracy in Thailand and the relatively consolidated democracies of Indonesia and East Timor (see Chapter 8 and Chapter 9, respectively).

Since elections were first instituted in the Philippines, they have been described as a procedural style of 'dexterous manipulation' (Paredes, 1988: 7). Based on the description by Leonardo Quisumbing (1983: 30), elections were introduced as the 'new game' in town, bearing 'the meaning of victory' of 'the conquerors'. Even during Marcos' authoritarian rule, national elections were held between 1978 and 1986. Electoral procedures, in these cases, were part of 'an authoritarian electoral legitimation strategy', 'a thin veil for authoritarian elite efforts to reinforce undemocratic relations' (Franco, 2000: 80, 294). What R. H. Taylor has incisively said about the politics of elections in Southeast Asia, the same can be said of elections in the Philippines: 'Elections have been held regularly [...] Not only are elections held but they are taken seriously. Massive amounts of money are spent mobilizing voters and organizing polls when it is obvious to all that the election outcome has not shaken the formal position of the ruling authorities one iota.' (Taylor, 1996: 4). The regularity of procedural elections in and of itself is thus an insufficient measure of the quality of democracy in the Philippines.

Despite the country's extensive record of elections, electoral integrity in the Philippines has been questionable. According to survey results from the Perceptions of Electoral Integrity (PEI) project for the 2016 general election, the Philippines is ranked 101th out of 161 countries worldwide. On a standardized scale from 0 to 100 points, the Philippines has a PEI Index score of 51 (see Figure 7.1). Compared with other Southeast Asian countries, the Philippines has moderate electoral integrity like Thailand, but scores higher in the PEI Index than Malaysia and Vietnam.[9] The PEI Index is an overall

---

[9] Malaysia has a PEI Index score of 35, and Vietnam has a PEI Index score of 34. See variable 'PEI Index' of PEI-5.5, country-level dataset (Norris et al., 2017).

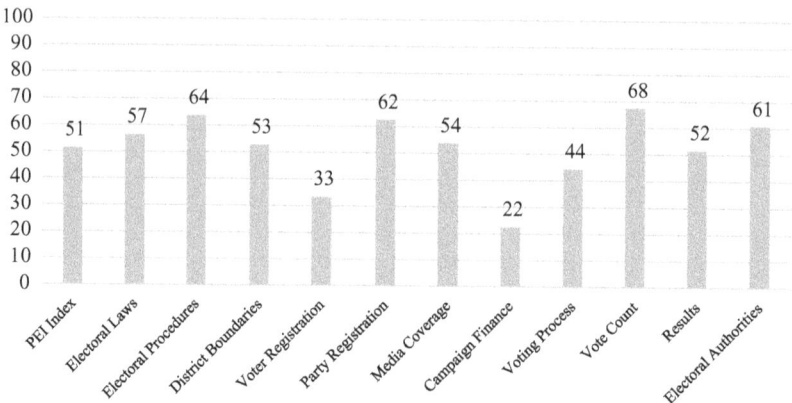

FIGURE 7.1. Perception of the Philippine electoral integrity and sub-dimensions, 2016.
Source: Perceptions of Electoral Integrity (PEI-5.5), Country-Level.
www.electoralintergrityproject.com.
Note: The Perceptions of Electoral Integrity (PEI) Index is an additive function of the forty-nine imputed variables which compose the eleven sub-dimensions in the electoral cycle. The values shown are imputed values, standardized to a 0–100-point scale. Higher values denote higher integrity based on the perception of experts surveyed (Norris, Wynter and Grömping, 2017).

summary evaluation of expert perceptions of the extent to which the election meets international standards and global norms based on eleven sub-dimensions. Particularly telling are the disaggregated variables of the two sub-dimensions of campaign finance and voting process. In particular, when asked if voters agree or disagree with the statement, 'rich people buy elections', on a scale from 1 to 5, 1 being strongly disagree and 5 being strongly agree, the mean value for the Philippines is 4.29.[10] Regarding the voting process, a mean value of 4.01 indicates that experts on average agreed with the statement, 'some voters were threatened with violence at the polls'.[11] Likewise, the Philippines has a mean value of 4.03 for 'fraudulent', meaning that experts on average agree with the statement, 'some fraudulent votes were cast' during the voting process.[12]

The perceptions of electoral integrity in the Philippines reflect the persistence and prevalence of corruption and violence in the country's elections. For instance, even the Commission on Elections, whose stated mission is to 'ensure the conduct of free, fair, and honest elections',[13] has been enwrapped in allegations of corruption and political scandals (see Patiño, 2002). In the infamous 'Hello, Garci' case in 2004, the former election commissioner

---

[10] Ibid. See variable 'rich' of PEI-5.5, country-level dataset.
[11] Ibid. See variable 'violence' of PEI-5.5, country-level dataset.
[12] Ibid. See variable 'fraudulent' of PEI-5.5, country-level dataset.
[13] See Commissions on Elections (n.d.).

Virgilio Garcillano was caught on wiretap conspiring with then president Gloria Macapagal-Arroyo for manipulating the 2004 election results. To date, none of those implicated in the scandal have been prosecuted (Crisostomo, 2014). Elections themselves are fraught with 'vote-buying, intimidation of voters, harassment of candidates, negative campaigning targeting militant groups, and the presence of military men and armed goons' (Aning et al., 2010). According to Freedom House, there were approximately 130 election-related deaths in 2010 and 80 elections-related deaths in 2013 attributed to local rivalries and clan competition during congressional, provincial, municipal and village-level elections (Freedom House, 2015). According to a news report, between January 10 and May 5 leading up to the recent general election in 2016, there were fourteen deaths in twenty-six 'validated election-related incidents'.[14] Thus, political violence, especially election-related violence, has not ceased.

Political Rights

On political rights, the Philippines has scored relatively high on the Worldwide Governance Indicators (WGI) for 'voice and accountability' between 1994 and 2014, at least compared to the more authoritarian regimes of Vietnam and (until recently) Malaysia (see Figure 7.2). As one of the six dimensions of governance for WGI, 'voice and accountability' is a composite indicator of citizens' perceptions of the extent to which citizens can participate in selecting their government, feel that they possess freedom of expression and freedom of association, and believe that there is a free media. Elections are also included in this dimension, illustrating the embeddedness of the partial regimes noted in Merkel's root conception of democracy. Point estimates for the Philippines over time ranges between 0.38 and −0.14.

Although the Philippines appears to fare much better than Vietnam and Malaysia, political rights in the Philippines, particularly freedom of the press, can be better assessed in the actual context of the country. Under democracy, the right to freedom of the press has paradoxically flourished and is without constitutional constraints; yet journalism has become a very dangerous profession in the Philippines. In the immediate independence period, along with elections, the press enjoyed a relatively unprecedented degree of freedom, a legacy of American colonial occupation. Prior to this, Article 256 of the Spanish Penal Code, for instance, defined 'word, deed, or writing [which] shall defame, abuse, or insult any Minister of the Crown or other person in authority' a punishable crime.[15] In *People of the Philippine Islands* v. *Gregorio Perfecto*, on October 4, 1922, the Supreme Court however acquitted

---

[14] 'Mayor candidate shot dead in Philippine election violence', May 2016.
[15] See Spanish Penal Code 1870 (*1870 Codigo Penal de España*).

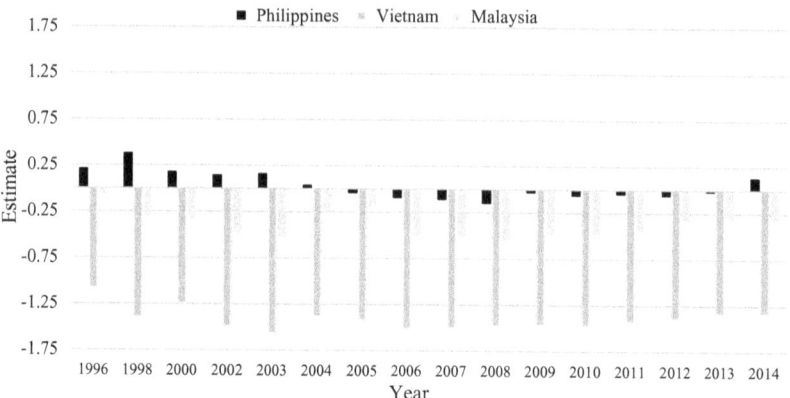

FIGURE 7.2. Voice and accountability estimate, 1996–2014.
Source: The Worldwide Governance Indicators (WGI). Available at www.govindicators.org.
Note: WGI reports the aggregate measures of the governance indicator in the standard normal units, ranging from around –2.5 to 2.5.

Mr. Perfecto, editor of the newspaper *La Nacion*, of committing *lése majesté* against members of the Philippine Senate.[16] The court also effectively repealed provisions of the *lése majesté* in the Spanish Penal Code. In an opinion by the Supreme Court, Justice George A. Malcom stated, 'No longer is there a Minister of the Crown or a person in authority of such exalted position that the citizen must speak of him only with bated breath'. It was cited that the crime of *lése majesté*, like ministers of the crown, had 'no place under the American flag' as well as 'the American conception of the interests of the public'. The Supreme Court then declared, 'Punishment for contempt of non-judicial officers has no place in a government based upon American principles. Our official class is not, as in monarchies, an agent of some authority greater than the people but it is an agent and servant of the people themselves'.[17]

The statement was indicative of the forceful shift following American colonial institutionalization in terms of both the legal right and the socio-political conception of the right to freedom of the press in the Philippines. This was later manifest in the proliferation of expression in the Philippine press after World War II. As Reynaldo Guioguio describes, 'Newspapers searched out every crack in the armour of officialdom, exposing, exposing, exposing. It was "Slam-Bang" Journalism...with hastily put, cropping-up-overnight, and independent newspapers pouncing on the government's least mistakes and making national issues out of them. The press sported an immoderate

[16] Gregorio Perfecto was previously found guilty of violating article 256 of the Spanish Penal Code by the municipal court of the city of Manila and again by the Court of First Instance of Manila before appealing to the Supreme Court.
[17] People v. Perfector, 1922.

TABLE 7.1. *Journalists killed in Southeast Asia, 2000–2015*

Year	Philippines	Burma	Cambodia	Indonesia	Thailand
2015	3	–	–	–	–
2014	3	1	–	–	–
2013	8	–	–	–	–
2012	4	–	1	1	1
2011	3	–	–	–	1
2010	4	–	–	1	2
2009	32	–	–	1	–
2008	6	–	1	–	3
2007	2	–	–	–	–
2006	6	–	–	1	–
2005	7	–	–	–	–
2004	6	–	–	–	–
2003	7	–	1	2	–
2002	3	–	–	–	–
2001	–	–	–	–	–
2000	–	–	–	–	–

Note: The table only lists Southeast Asian countries in which RSF reported journalists were killed. Countries with no reported deaths of journalists are hence not listed in the table.
Source: Reporters Without Borders (RSF). The data reported by RSF does not include journalists who were killed for reasons unrelated to their journalist work or for whom RSF was not able to establish the link with their work as the reason.

language; it was a natural aftermath borne out of being suddenly set free' (Guioguio, 1988: 8, cited in Guimary, 1989). While Guioguio's observation raises questions about the journalistic quality of the time, there was no question that the public sphere was opened for the exercise of freedom of the press.

Fast forward to the present day. Much of the euphoria has abated, replaced by more morbid sentiments. The National Union of Journalists of the Philippines (NUJP) questioned on World Press Freedom Day, for instance, if there was anything to celebrate. 'Not when media workers continue to be murdered, assaulted, threatened, harassed', the NUJP said in a public statement. Furthermore, the statement continued, 'the Philippines continues to mock its claim to being a democracy, unable to shake off the infamy of being the third most dangerous country for journalists, next to conflict-ridden Iraq and Somalia where most victims are casualties of war'.[18] According to data compiled by Reporters Without Frontiers (RSF), from 2000 to 2015, ninety-four journalists were killed in the Philippines as a result of their journalistic work (see Table 7.1). The most infamous incident was the Ampatuan massacre that occurred on the morning of November 23, 2009, when fifty-eight people,

---

[18] 'NUJP on World Press Freedom Day: "What's to Celebrate?"' 2012.

including thirty-two journalists, were killed. To date, not one person has been prosecuted for the Ampatuan massacre. In Southeast Asia, the Philippines has the highest number of reported deaths of journalists almost every year.

Civil Rights and Horizontal Accountability

Contrary to expectations about the rule of law under democracy, the WGI data show that the Philippines does not perform significantly better than Vietnam or Malaysia (see Figure 7.3). The WGI rule of law indicator captures the aggregate perceptions and confidence that individuals have in (and abide by) the rules of society, the quality of contract enforcement, property rights, the police and the courts, as well as the likelihood of crime and violence. With the exceptions of 1996, 1998, 2002, 2006 and 2013, point estimates show that Vietnam scored higher than the Philippines. On the other hand, Malaysia, ranging from 0.31 to 0.64, has outperformed both the Philippines and Vietnam.

Part of the reason that the Philippines ranks low on the rule of law is the widespread perception of corruption as well as the ineffectiveness or incompetence of the Philippine justice system. According to the Social Weather Stations 2007 survey of legal experts, practitioners and the Philippine public at large, 62 per cent of respondents cited 'my opponent would probably resort to bribery to win the case' as one of the problems they expect to encounter when taking a

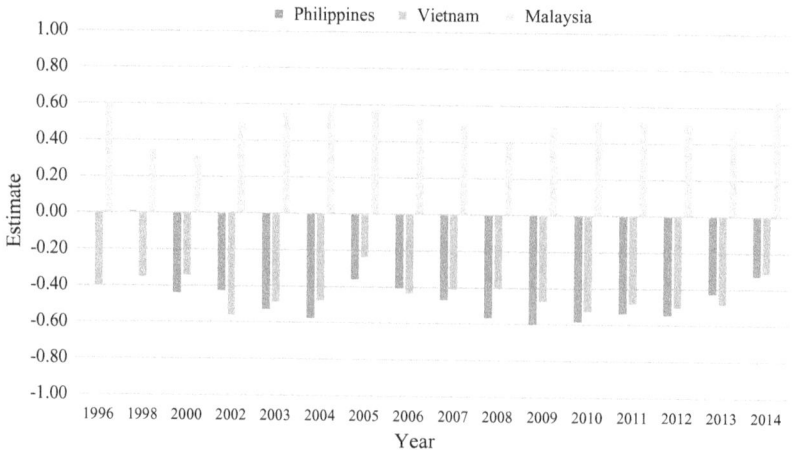

FIGURE 7.3. Country estimate on rule of law, 1996–2014.
Source: The Worldwide Governance Indicators (WGI). Available at www.govindicators.org.
Note: WGI reports the aggregate measures of the governance indicator in the standard normal units, ranging from around –2.5 to 2.5.

case to court. On the other hand, 69 per cent reported 'to take a case to courts takes more time than I can afford', while 70 per cent reported 'to take a case to courts cost[s] more than I can afford' among other problems that they would encounter.[19] An editorial published by the Philippine News in 2015 lamented,

> So what in heaven's name happened to our Philippine justice system where court cases usually take decades to be resolved? Compared to those in well-functioning democracies, our justice system appears to be little more than a joke at best. Here's how we see it: overseas Filipino workers are doing a herculean job of continually strengthening the Philippine economy—not just keeping it afloat. But their effort will be all for naught if Philippine courts continue to drag their feet dispensing justice. The Ampatuan massacre is now five years old and counting but the trial is barely past its preliminary stages. President Aquino was still a senator when the massacre happened. He'll soon be stepping down after six years as president but the court case has barely gotten off the ground.[20]

Calling the abuse of power and corruption the 'perennial demons' of Philippine democracy, Aries Arugay (2005) points, for instance, to the abortion of the impeachment trial of former president Joseph 'Erap' Estrada for blatant corruption and cronyism in 2001 as a manifestation of the 'accountability deficit' and the limitations of democratic institutions. From 1998 to 2001, Estrada pocketed around 545 million pesos in so-called *jueteng* money from illegal gambling syndicates for their protection and siphoned off 130 million pesos from tobacco taxes and more.[21] Such cases were not isolated incidents but occurred repeatedly over time, and each time, the court proved itself to be weak, partisan and not trustworthy to fulfil its institutional role as guardian of the rule of law and a constitutional check on the executive and other branches of power. On July 19, 2016, the Supreme Court voted 11–4 to acquit former president Gloria Macapagal-Arroyo ('GMA') of corruption charges and for plundering 366 million pesos (nearly US$8.8 million at the time) during her tenure from 2001 to 2010 (Whaley, 2016). GMA assumed the presidency after Estrada left office in 2001 in the midst of widespread corruption allegations. In 2005, GMA herself was part of the 'Hello, Garci' scandal. In 2007, GMA was accused of commanding Datu Andal S. Ampatuan, then governor of Maguindanao, where the massacre of 2009 later took place, to tinker with congressional election results in favour of her political party (Whaley, 2012). The fact that GMA was once again acquitted only further reinforced the public perception of a tarnished system of justice and rule of law. In sum, while the rule of law and a functional judiciary do exist in the Philippines to some extent, neither is sufficiently strong and independent to ensure that civil rights and horizontal accountability are safeguarded.

---

[19] 'Philippine Democracy Assessment. Rule of Law and Access to Justice', 2010.
[20] 'Will the Philippines Ever Speed Up Its Glacially Slow Judicial System?' 2015.
[21] See People of the Philippines v. Joseph Ejercito Estrada, et al., 2007.

Effective Power to Govern

The last partial regime in Merkel's model – effective power to govern – refers to the extent to which elected representatives are independent from ties to extra-constitutional actors and actually govern. Unlike Myanmar, the Philippines has not been dominated by the military, nor have there been recurring coup d'états like Thailand.[22] From this perspective, elected leaders in the Philippines can be said to enjoy relative political stability in terms of their power position as political elites and, hence, could be perceived as 'effective', in Merkel's terminology, to govern.

On the other hand, Philippine democracy continues to be defined by electoral violence, fraud and the persistence of dynastic influence. After Corazon Aquino defeated Ferdinand Marcos in a transition back to democracy following the People Power Revolution in 1986, Aquino was forced to make many concessions with political factions and rivals, which weakened and compromised the quality of Philippine democratic governance. For example, Aquino decided not to prosecute any police and security forces associated with Marcos, or adopt any deep structural reforms like land redistribution, but instead decided to preserve neo-imperialism by maintaining US military bases in the Philippines. These decisions were regarded as compromises that cast significant doubt on her actual power to govern. Such compromises further raised questions about whether the Philippine transition to democracy in 1986 was of deep substantive value or was ultimately superficial. On this question, Mark Thompson appears to have had a cautiously, optimistic assessment of Philippine democracy in 1996:

> Commitment to the restoration of electoral institutions finally prevailed as [Aquino's] popularity forced even her disloyal opponents into the electoral arena and each round of balloting peeled off another layer of the antisystem opposition. After the military rebels were finally defeated and the Communist insurgency weakened, elections remained the only political game in town. (Thompson, 1996: 192)

However, to date, it is evident that the electoral political game in town is one of contested personalities and political dynasties, as well as of personal militias and prevalent fraud, rather than programmatic differences and substantive goals. A recent study found that dynastic rule in the Philippine House of Representatives has had 'deleterious effects' on public goods provision. Empirical results show that, from 2001 to 2003, provinces dominated by family clans were significantly less likely to receive public goods. Overall, areas dominated by family dynasties experience poorer governance compared to non-dynastic areas. These areas have poorer infrastructure development,

---

[22] During the Corazon Aquino presidency, there were seven attempted coups, but this was a relative exception in Philippine democracy. The last coup attempt was in July 2003 against the Gloria Macapagal-Arroyo administration.

lower spending on health, less effective crime prevention and lower public sector employment rates (Tusalem and Pe-Aguirre, 2013).

SUBSTANTIVE OUTPUTS: RESPONSIVENESS AND REPRESENTATION IN THE PHILIPPINES – SOCIO-ECONOMIC DEVELOPMENT WITH EQUITY OR WITH INEQUITY

What are the consequences of the Philippines' defective democracy for socio-economic development and distributive outcomes? Does democracy in the Philippines result in actual representation of, and responsiveness to, popular demands for the provision of public goods? Responsiveness, that is, democracy with actual representation, can be assessed by the extent that a government's actual policies and outcomes reflect the preferences of its citizens. Daron Acemoglu and James Robinson (2000) as well as Carles Boix (2003) argue that where democratization entails the extension of actual political representation, pressures from the poor will lead to redistributive policies and greater income equality. Likewise, 'the qualities of democratic responsiveness' for Pippa Norris (2012: 8) mean that leaders are accountable to citizens, downward electoral accountability is strong, multiple horizontal and vertical checks and balances ensure leaders' responsiveness to public concerns and the provision of public goods meet social needs.

On these substantive aspects, the Philippine record has been dismal. Philippine economic performance and poverty alleviation are significantly lower than those of neighbouring countries, including Vietnam, Malaysia and Thailand (see Kuhonta, 2011). At multiple intervals, the country even experienced negative growth rates, plunging to −9.8 per cent in 1985 during the Marcos dictatorship, −3 per cent in 1991, −2 per cent in 1992, −2 per cent in 1993, −2.7 in 1998 and −0.5 per cent in 2009 (see Kuhonta, 2011).

The distribution of income in the Philippines has also been highly unequal, showing very little to no improvement from 1961 to 2015 (see Figure 7.4). Income inequality, as measured by the Gini coefficient, dropped by a minimal margin from 0.486 in 1961, to 0.478 in 1971 (just before martial law) and to 0.447 in 1988. However, inequality increased to 0.468 in 1991, to 0.498 in 1997 and to 0.482 in 2000. By 2009, the Gini coefficient marginally declined again to 0.448 (see Kuhonta, 2011). According to the latest data, as of 2015, income inequality in the Philippines has shown no improvement.

Reports from the National Statistical Coordination Board on the official poverty statistics of the Philippines in 2012 estimated that one out of five Filipino families lives below the per capita poverty threshold, that is, the minimum income required for a family or individual to meet the basic food and non-food requirements. Although the proportion of poor families in 2012 (19.7 per cent) has declined from 20.5 per cent in 2009 and 21.0 per cent in 2006, the decrease is found to be largely insignificant (National Statistical Coordination Board, 2013). These statistics provide a broad assessment of

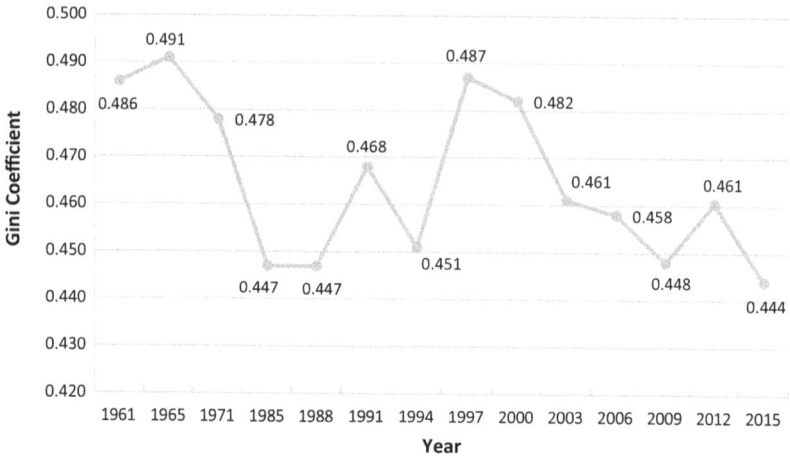

FIGURE 7.4. Philippine trend in income inequality, 1961–2015.
Source: Philippine Statistics Authority, Family Income and Expenditure Survey.

the actual performance and provision of public goods in terms of the country's economic development and poverty alleviation. They coincide with the overall trend of sluggishness and/or stagnancy previously associated with the Philippines. In short, 'the remarkable aspect of these statistics is not just that they show no improvement in the distribution of income over the long run but that there is little indication that the restoration of democracy has had any positive effect on growth and equity' (Kuhonta, 2011: 201). Thus, procedural democracy in the Philippines has not resulted in the representation of popular demands or responsiveness to social needs.

STATE AND PARTY FORMATION AND THEIR RELATIONSHIP TO DEMOCRACY[23]

What explains the deficiency of Philippine democracy? We argue that the low quality of Philippine democracy is rooted in the historical process of institutional development, especially in terms of state and party formation. The weaknesses of Philippine stateness are evident in the absence of a rational, functional and capable bureaucracy, as well as the lack of any programmatic distinction between political parties in response to citizen policy preferences. State institutions and political parties in the Philippines have been captured by particularistic interests that largely advance and perpetuate the interests of the caciques and oligarchy, as well as entrench corruption and patron-client

---

[23] The argument in this section draws partly from and builds on Kuhonta (2011).

politics. They do not function as effective mechanisms for performance-accountability or deepening the quality of democracy. The absence of institutional capacity means that the state lacks both the ability to constrain its elites through accountability and, in tandem with weak parties, a foundation for developing and executing programmatic policies. Without accountability and programmatic policies, democracy will inevitably remain a shallow and incomplete project.

Historically, the state in the Philippines, conceived under the Spanish colonial regime, was based on a very superficial structure of authority. The Philippines was seen by the Spanish primarily as a link in the galleon trade between Mexico and China. In that sense, the Philippines was peripheral to any real abiding Spanish interest in its lands. The colonial authorities had no interest in developing state institutions rooted in rational-bureaucratic capacities that might establish national policy across the archipelago. What mattered was trade across the Pacific and then religious conversion.

The weakness of the state began with the seat of the governor-general. The governor-general had extensive powers in Manila, but since the position was based on patronage, it was often filled by individuals who were there for personal enrichment. 'It was clearly understood, if rarely articulated, that the governor was to profit personally, provided he did not plunder too grossly', writes David Steinberg, 'the whole system was predicated on a presumption of graft' (Steinberg, 1994: 58). Furthermore, the minimal skeleton of the bureaucracy was riven between petty officials and provincial bureaucrats who followed their own interests and refused to work closely with the governor-general.

A crucial structural weakness of the colonial regime was that it did not possess a foundation for institutional continuity. Governor-generals could not hold tenure for more than two years and later for only one year, while middle-ranking civil servants could be removed arbitrarily.[24] The short time horizon of the governor-generalship resulted in 'fecklessness of long-range planning' and efforts by the governor-general to 'enrich himself in office in the shortest possible time' (Agoncillo, 1969: 61). In the long-run, this meant that the colonial regime lacked any distinct administrative agenda separate from the particularistic interests of its temporary office-bearer.

Compared to its other colonies in Latin America and to other colonial empires, such as those of the Dutch and the British, the Spaniards made barely an attempt to extend their authority beyond the capital. The reach of the Spanish colonial state was largely limited to Manila, with the countryside under the domineering presence of the religious friars. The friars acted as a second arm of government – indeed, 'in much of the Philippines, the friars were the state' (Abinales and Amoroso, 2005: 67) – establishing themselves as

---

[24] Between 1835 and 1898, there were fifty governors-general (Steinberg, 1994: 61).

the virtual rulers of life beyond Manila and blocking any minimal attempts at reform. Overall, the Spanish colonial regime did not develop any rational-legal foundations for the formation of a strong and capable state.

The American colonial period reproduced the same structural problems of Spanish colonial rule in terms of institutional incapacity but added into the mix political participation. Similar to the Iberian imperialists, the Americans made very little effort to build up a bureaucracy while buttressing the provincial elite. Like the Spaniards, the Americans did not seek to populate the bureaucracy with their own colonial civil servants. Governor-General Harrison's desire to speed up the Filipinization of the bureaucracy, in accordance with Woodrow Wilson's sympathies for national autonomy, was one important factor in constraining the staffing of the bureaucracy with Americans (Hayden, 1942: 95–101). By contrast, the Japanese in South Korea made a major effort to develop the bureaucracy, heavily populating it with their own forces (Kohli, 2004: 34–35).

The most significant contribution of American imperialism to Philippine political development was the establishment of elections. The American institutionalization of elections in the Philippines has all the elements of a defining critical juncture for the quality of democracy in the Philippines. It was precisely the nature in which elections were established that enabled oligarchs to cement their power without any circumventing autonomous bureaucracy to champion the public interest. Elections thus came early in the Philippines, but they were nested in a state structure that lacked bureaucratic coherence and autonomy. This ensured that power in the incipient democracy would lie in the hands of rural oligarchs and local bosses rather than government officials, whether elected or appointed, who might be imbued with a sense of public purpose.

Further moving democracy away from the public interest were a series of US colonial policies that tilted the playing field heavily in favour of the rural elites. With the defeat of the Spanish, the US authorities controlled some 400,000 acres of friars' lands. Instead of pursuing land reform, they sold the land at prices only the provincial elites could afford, thereby handing over even more social and economic power to the oligarchs. The Payne-Aldrich Act of 1909 then granted exporters of agricultural commodities entry into the US market without tariffs. The social and political basis for the dominance of an oligarchic democracy was thus in place: electoral office married to vast landed estates.

With the birth of electoralism, political parties also emerged to contest public office. However, party formation was not grounded in social movements, as was the case in Malaysia, Indonesia and Vietnam. Rather, parties were formed as vehicles to pursue narrow elite interests. The fact that the franchise in the first national elections was only 1.4 per cent of the population made it even more likely that elites would be so dominant.[25] The larger

---

[25] In terms of the male adult population, this was about 6 per cent (Cullinane, 2003: 315). In the 1940s, the voting population was still very low at 14 per cent (Anderson, 1996: 21).

problem that deeply shaped party development in the Philippines was the fact that the party system lacked a basis in social cleavages.[26] The complete defeat of the revolutionary movement that had fought for independence against the Spanish (1896–1898) and the Americans (1899–1902) was the fundamental cause for the failure of social cleavages to gain traction in the party system. Although the Filipino revolutionary movement had shown initial promise, it was deeply riven from within and lacked broad support across the country. Annihilated by the sheer brutality of US military power – perfectly exemplified by General Jacob Smith's notorious order to create a 'howling wilderness' on the island of Samar – the Philippines fell under American dominion without a radical oppositional force.[27]

Instead, the conservative Filipino elite, who had always been ambivalent and distrustful of the revolutionary nationalist cause, gained ascendance and showed themselves to be extremely willing to co-operate with the Americans. This same elite, represented by the *ilustrados* (enlightened ones), had withheld support for the Katipunan during the fight against the Spanish. Proponents of radical change found themselves constantly incapable of convincing members of the upper class from joining their cause. In this context, the incipient parties led by these conservative elites would have no interest in programmatic policies rooted in social and economic development. The long-term prospects for a democracy built upon public interest and the advancement of citizen rights were thus decisively bleak.

The party system was thus incubated within American imperialism as a conservative structure whose roots were based in gradual, evolutionary nationalism rather than a radical, revolutionary form. In 1900, the Partido Federal (Federalist Party) was established. Its platform emphasized recognition of American sovereignty, establishment of peace with the Americans and eventual statehood of the Philippines within the United States. The Partido Federal consisted of conservative members of the upper class who were committed to the status quo. In its own quest for power, this party saw American rule as a form of benevolent democracy and sought to create strong ties with the colonial administration. The colonial administration then appointed many members of this party to positions in government. The elite therefore thought of American colonialism as an ideal way of accessing power as well as securing economic wealth.[28]

---

[26] This argument addressing the lack of social cleavages in the Philippines (in comparison with Singapore and Thailand) and its implications for political development draws on and is elaborated more fully in Kuhonta (2016).

[27] A searing critique of American actions in the Philippines was made by Mark Twain. See, among others, 'Mark Twain on American Imperialism', *Atlantic Monthly* (April 1992): 49–65.

[28] When President McKinley's Philippine Commission conferred in 1900 with Filipino notables, their response was to testify that they needed 'American sovereignty in this country for the good of these ignorant and uncivilized people' (Abinales and Amoroso, 2005: 117–18).

In 1907, opposition to the Federalist Party (which in that year of national elections changed their name to Partido Nacional Progresista) coalesced into the Nacionalista Party. The main difference with the Federalistas was the Nacionalistas' push for immediate independence, which better expressed larger preferences in society. The Nacionalistas were divided among three factions that reflected in part different views on the immediacy of independence but were really riven over power struggles among ambitious elites. Despite the contrast between the Federalistas and Nationalistas, the parties were in fact very similar: they stood for a tiny sliver of the Filipino population – a sliver distinguished by wealth. 'In most provinces and municipalities, conservatism was a value shared by all the elites', notes Michael Cullinane, '... politics was concerned primarily with the struggle for control. The national victory or defeat of the Nacionalistas or Progresistas was of little concern to most....' This pattern of parties run by elites with no social base and with minimal ideological value set the early foundations for the Philippine party system.

A view of the socio-economic background of the first national assembly gives a good sense of the conservative roots of Philippine legislative and national politics. Of the eighty assemblymen from both parties, not one of them was involved in the revolutionary movement. Some three-fourths of the assemblymen were urban and provincial holders of land or major commercial interests, while one-fourth were from the urban middle sectors, principally journalism and law. Notably, seventy-eight of the eighty assemblymen had studied at major universities in the Manila area, while ten had gained their education in Spain. In addition, more than thirty assemblymen had received a significant part of their education at regional *colegios* (colleges), indicating a strong provincial element (Cullinane, 2003: 314–16).

Once in power, the Nacionalistas clashed at times with the American administration, but mostly they were able to work with the occupying power. The Americans made clear that they did not intend to rule the Philippines in perpetuity, making it easier for the Partido Nacionalista to accept the minimalist democracy. The consequence of accommodation between Philippine elites and American forces was that political parties became insular institutions. They were never forced to take the needs of the masses seriously because their economic and political control was so tightly secured. Parties were devoid of linkages with social movements and did not seek to represent any mass constituency. Indeed, indicative of how the national legislature would operate throughout Philippine political development, on the very first day of the 1907 legislature, the newly minted Assemblymen voted to increase their per diem allowances. (Constantino, 1975: 320).

In the post–World War II period of democracy, rather than competing to represent the demands of the broader electorate and expand their popular constituency, the Nacionalista Party and a newly formed Liberal Party exchanged resources during the 1950s–1960s under collaborative schemes to marginalize third parties and dominate the political system (Thompson, 1995: 20–24). Similar to the commonwealth period, there was little substantive difference between the parties. Both the Nacionalistas and the Liberals lacked any institutional value, whether in terms of a distinct ideology or a complex organization. Rather, they were parties formed simply for their elite office-bearers to take over the presidential residence, Malacañang Palace.

What is contested in the Philippine party system is not ideology, but rather spoils, access to contracts and licenses and familial accumulation of wealth. For the very reason that ideology has no meaning and that parties are concerned mainly with private wealth, violence has been especially rampant during elections. Murders of political figures have been a hallmark of democratic elections, such that many maintained bodyguards, arsenals and even private armies for their protection (Jackson, 1989: 238). In the 'heyday of cacique democracy' (1954–1972), Benedict Anderson (1988: 15) noted that along with the growth of new private armies, 'armed gangs financed by their hacendado masters', the oligarchy remained virtually uncontested.

The post-war bureaucracy also continued down a path of institutional hollowness. The neo-patrimonial structure that had been established under the Americans sank more deeply into the crevices of the state. The civil service was particularly vulnerable to the excesses of patronage politics and patrimonial influence. Bureaucrats' decisions were often based on personal favours for either politicians or friends and family members. One study of the bureaucracy in 1960 notes:

When vacancies occur in a particular agency, hordes of job seekers, bearing letters of recommendation from senators and congressmen flock to it. Some well-connected applicants are even accompanied by these politicians personally, or initial letters of recommendation are followed by telephone calls. With all these pressures, administrators have to be especially adept and tactful if they do not want to antagonize these politicians. While they may be really desirous of recruiting the best people, they are most of the time forced to compromise by accommodating protégés of politicians having considerable power and influence over the affairs of the agency. (Francisco, 1960: 193)

Civil servants have had very little incentive to stick to a more rational form of decision-making. Between 1940 and 1956, the cost of living increased by 350 per cent, but the salaries of middle- and upper-level civil servants did not even go up twofold (Wurfel, 1988: 79). Under such conditions, it is not surprising that personal favours and other forms of corruption were rampant in the bureaucracy. A larger problem in the Philippine bureaucracy was that entry into the civil service could bypass competitive examination. In the post-war period, more and more civil servants gained their positions through personal relationships rather than merit. In 1964, more than 80 per cent of national government employees and 57 per cent of high-ranking civil servants had *not* taken an admissions exam (Wurfel, 1988: 80).

Under Marcos, the bureaucracy became even more rooted in problems of patrimonialism, patronage, corruption and complete lack of legal-rational planning. Ministries and bureaucratic institutions were exploited for the sole purpose of supporting the lives of luxury of the first family or were created to give Marcos family members and cronies bases of power. The creation of a super government of Metro Manila was given to Imelda Marcos in order to establish her own fiefdom. Later, Imelda exerted influence through control of the Ministry of Human Settlements. The tentacles of the Marcos' family and cronies were all over the state. 'Imelda's favorite brother, Benjamin "Kokoy" Romualdez, controlled the Bureau of Customs, the General Auditing Commission and the Bureau of Internal Revenue', writes Mark Thompson, 'Imelda's sister, Alita Martel, was the "franchise holder" of the Central Bank and the Department of Agriculture. The president's brother, Pacifico Marcos, ran the Medicare Commission, which was plagued by corruption. Even Marcos's elderly mother had her sphere of influence, the Rice and Corn Administration'[29] (Thompson, 1998: 221).

It is notable that virtually all Philippine post-war governments have sought to reorganize or reform the bureaucracy. These included significant initiatives by presidents Quirino in the 1950s, Marcos in the 1970s, Aquino in the 1980s and Estrada and Macapagal-Arroyo in the 1990s and 2000s (Brillantes and Fernandez-Carrag, 2016: 152–53). Even President Duterte emphasized bureaucratic reform in his first State of the Nation address in July 2016. Despite such efforts, a recent study of the Philippine bureaucracy observes that 'civil service appointments continue to be made according to political pressure. This destroys the principle of merit, undermines security of tenure and demoralises [sic] career civil servants.... Over the years, various presidents, particularly Macapagal-Arroyo, have exercised presidential privilege and circumvented the merit and fitness stages of civil service appointment by installing 10,000 civil personnel' (Brillantes and Fernandez-Carrag, 2016: 172).

Thus, a bureaucracy lacking in rational-legal norms and skills, as well as corporate coherence and principles of meritocracy, has been central in the failure of the Philippine democracy to pursue the public interest or to serve as an institutional check on politicians. This problem of weak rational-legal norms, meritocracy and corporate coherence has persisted throughout Philippine modern history and has overshadowed the nature of the contemporary state.[30]

---

[29] Under Marcos, the audacity of government officials apparently had no bounds. Amazingly, Marcos's secretary of tourism had no qualms building a sub-regional tourism office in his small hometown that was significantly larger than any regional office (Richter, 1987: 59–60).

[30] Although space prevents a full discussion of the so-called Moro conflict, it bears emphasizing briefly here that a clear indication of the Philippine state's weak capacity has been rooted in its inability to end insurgencies and provide stability, especially in the deep south of Mindanao. Both the communist New People's Army (NPA) and numerous Islamic and Islamist insurgencies have consistently challenged the state's authority over far-flung

Without a bureaucracy trained in developing, managing and executing policy, the state lacks a foundation for policy advancement and reform. A bureaucracy rooted in personal relations can only be concerned with its own particularistic and material interests and not with broader institutional norms and goals. Under such conditions, democracy is quite simply unable to fulfil the basic functions of accountability and policy performance.

CONCLUSION

The quality of democracy in the Philippines is deeply defective. It is undermined by substantive weaknesses: fragile institutions, corruption, violence and poor socio-economic performance. This chapter has argued that these problems stem from the country's colonial heritage, in which state-building was given low priority, elections were established early and social cleavages failed to take root in the party system. An elite democratic system thus developed without a bureaucratic centre to tame or channel democratic participation. Like the Spanish regime, the American authorities never made an effort to develop a more robust bureaucratic core that would be insulated from elected officials and have the capacity to supervise these officials and act as a check on their behaviour. Elections were a central mechanism through which social elites could extract economic resources from their constituencies as well as from the centre. Without any entrenched centralizing structure to guide the direction of national policy, elections at every level of the state have allowed for the capture of the state rather than the state's penetration of the periphery. Thus, the larger problem of Philippine political development, including the quality of democracy, can be understood in terms of an unfortunate pattern of historical sequencing. Instead of a strong institutional core capable of pursuing a national agenda, the legacy of Spanish and especially American colonial rule has been the entrenchment of the private accumulation of power.

Most recently, Philippine democracy received a powerful jolt when Davao Mayor, Rodrigo Duterte, was elected president by a landslide in May 2016. In a crowded field of five candidates, four of whom were serious contenders, Duterte clinched the presidency with 39 per cent of the vote. Duterte's election sets in stark relief the central dilemma of Philippine political development: weak institutions and therefore weak accountability. Since winning executive

---

territory. Although the NPA had its heyday during the Marcos dictatorship and is today a relatively spent force, it has never given up its struggle against the state. More critically, Muslim discontent in Mindanao, dating from the American colonial period, has never been adequately addressed. The proliferation of groups that have risen up calling for a separate nation, including the Moro National Liberation Front and the Moro Islamic Liberation Front, is indicative of the failure of numerous administrations to quell discontent over rights, autonomy and development. The most recent battle over the city of Marawi, Lanao del Sur, which lasted five months under the Duterte administration, is yet another symptom of the weakness in the Philippine state's monopoly of violence.

power, problems of accountability, rule of law and human rights violations have characterized Duterte's presidency.

The centrepiece of Duterte's presidential campaign has been his war on drugs – a continuation of his proven ability to bring some semblance of order to the city of Davao for over two decades. His drug campaign has been rife with extra-judicial killings and massive human rights violations. Duterte bluntly advocated killing as a means to get rid of drugs. 'All of you who are into drugs, you sons of bitches, I will really kill you', Duterte warned before his election.[31] The day after his inauguration, Duterte told the police: 'Do your duty, and if in the process you kill 1,000 persons because you were doing your duty, I will protect you' (Iyengar, 2016; see also Peel, 2016). Within months after his election, the Senate held hearings on the killing spree that was emerging as part of the anti-drug campaign. The figures provided at these Senate hearings indicate that more than 2,000 people were killed in less than three months of his presidency.[32] By the fourth week of November 2016, the number of killings had risen to 4,942, of which 3,001 were victims of extra-judicial or vigilante-style killings.[33] At the end of 2017, estimates of human rights groups put the tally of deaths from the drug war at over 12,000.[34] Duterte dismissed these criticisms with colourful curse words. The United Nations, Human Rights Watch, the International Criminal Court and the United States government have all criticized the killing spree.[35] Any prospects of democratic strengthening in the Philippines thus remains caught in a precarious trajectory.

Despite the fact that Duterte's violent regime attracts such shocking and lurid headlines, the strongman from Davao arguably fits right into the mould of Philippine defective democracy. His government, like the dictatorship of Marcos, simply elevated to a higher level the extent of impunity that the state is able to get away with. Given a history of weak institutions, both within the state and the party system, Duterte has had great leeway to execute people and policy as he so desires. Indeed, the most important textbook on Philippine politics notes that 'Duterte represents a distillation of the major features of over one hundred years of state and society relationship, dating back to when the United States began to turn over colonial governance to Filipino leaders after the 1907 elections, to the Philippine Commonwealth, to today's "cacique democracy"' (Abinales and Amoroso,

---

[31] 'Full Speech: Rodrigo Duterte's speech during his miting de avance', [n.d.], video clip, YouTube, www.youtube.com/watch?v=I2ujrIjHSaM. 7 May 2016. Also see, report by Human Rights Watch (2017), 'License to Kill: Philippine Police Killings in Duterte's "War on Drugs"'.
[32] Data from Senate hearings, ABS-CBN live streaming, September 2016.
[33] Data from the Philippine National Police, as reported by Rappler. See www.rappler.com/newsbreak/iq/145814-numbers-statistics-philippines-war-drugs (accessed 24 November 2016).
[34] Human Rights Watch, www.hrw.org/news/2017/12/07/smokescreen-justice-drug-war-deaths-philippines (accessed 18 January 2018).
[35] See, among others, the Human Rights Watch Statement of 16 September 2016.

2017: 337). Whether any real substantive change is possible to the trajectory of Philippine political development remains an open question. What is clear for all to see, though, is that Philippine democracy operates in a structural context devoid of checks and balances, as well as programmatic deliberation and dispensation, precisely because of the problematic history of state and party formation.

References

Abinales, P., and Amoroso, D. (2005). *State and Society in the Philippines*. Lanham: Rowman & Littlefield.
Abinales, P., and Amoroso, D. (2017). *State and Society in the Philippines*. Lanham: Rowman & Littlefield, Second Edition.
Acemoglu, D., and Robinson, J. A. (2000). Why Did the West Extend the Franchise? Democracy, Inequality, and Growth in Historical Perspective. *Quarterly Journal of Economics*, 115(4), 1167–99.
Acemoglu, D., and Robinson, J. A. (2006). *Economic Origins of Dictatorship and Democracy*. Cambridge: Cambridge University Press.
Agoncillo, T. (1969). *A Short History of the Philippines*. New York: Mentor Books.
Anderson, B. R. (1988). Cacique Democracy in the Philippines: Origins and Dreams. *New Left Review*, 169, 3–33.
Anderson, B. R. (1996). Elections and Participation in Three Southeast Asian Countries. In R. H. Taylor, ed., *The Politics of Elections in Southeast Asia*. Cambridge: Cambridge University Press, pp. 12–33.
Aning, J., Cabrera, A., and Ruiz, D. B. (2010). People Heroes in Poll Success, Say Foreign Observers. *The Philippine Daily Inquirer*. Available at: http://newsinfo.inquirer.net/inquirerheadlines/nation/view/20100514-269837/People-heroes-in-poll-success-say-foreign-observers [Accessed 1 September 2015].
Arugay, A. A. (2005). The Accountability Deficit in the Philippines: Implications and Prospects for Democratic Consolidation. *Philippine Political Science Journal*, 26(49), 63–88.
Boix, C. (2003). *Democracy and Redistribution*. Cambridge: Cambridge University Press.
Brillantes, A. B., and Fernandez-Carag, M. T. (2016). Building Executive Capacity in the Public Service for Better Governance: The Philippine Civil Service. In A. Podger and J. Wanna, eds., *Sharpening the Sword of State: Building Executive Capacities in the Public Services of the Asia Pacific*. Canberra: Australian National University Press.
Commissions on Elections (COMELEC). (n.d.) Available at: www.comelec.gov [Accessed 22 June 2019].
Constantino, R. (1975). *A History of the Philippines: From the Spanish Colonization to the Second World War*. New York: Monthly Review Press.
Crisostomo, S. (2014). Comelec Asked to Tell Truth on 'Hello, Garci'. *The Philippine Star*, 16 May. Available at: www.philstar.com:8080/headlines/2014/05/16/1323650/comelec-asked-tell-truth-hello-garci [Accessed 3 September 2015].
Cullinane, M. (2003). *Ilustrado Politics: Filipino Elite Responses to American Rule, 1898–1908*. Quezon City: Ateneo de Manila University Press.

Diamond, L., and Morlino, L. (2005). *Assessing the Quality of Democracy*. Baltimore: Johns Hopkins University Press.

Francisco, G. A. (1960). *Higher Civil Servants in the Philippines*. Philippines: College of Public Administration, University of the Philippines.

Franco, J. C. (2000). *Campaigning for Democracy: Grassroots Citizenship Movements, Less-than-Democratic Elections, and Regime Transition in the Philippines*. Quezon City: Institute for Popular Democracy.

Frankel, F. (1978). *India's Political Economy, 1947–1977: The Gradual Revolution*. Princeton: Princeton University Press.

Freedom House. (2015). The Freedom House Report. Available at: https://freedomhouse.org/report/freedom-world/2015/philippines#.Veil9CvF-So [Accessed 21 June 2019].

Full Speech: Rodrigo Duterte's Speech during His miting de avance (n.d.) YouTube video, 7 May 2016. Available at: www.youtube.com/watch?v=I2ujrIjHSaM [Accessed 5 February 2018].

Guioguio, R. (1988). The Philippine Press: Reorienting the Message. *The Journalists Journal*, 2(2). Manila: Philippine Press Forum, the Philippines Press Institute. Cited in D. L. Guimary. (1989). The Philippine Press after Marcos: Restored Freedoms and New Problems. Annual Meeting of the Association for Education in Journalism and Mass Communication. Washington, DC, 10–13 August.

Hayden, J. R. (1942). *The Philippines: A Study in National Development*. New York: MacMillan.

Hicken, A., and Kuhonta, E. M. (2015). Introduction: Rethinking Party System Institutionalization in Asia. In A. Hicken and E. M. Kuhonta, eds., *Party System Institutionalization in Asia: Democracies, Autocracies, and the Shadows of the Past*. Cambridge: Cambridge University Press, pp. 1–24.

Human Rights Watch. (2017). License to Kill: Philippine Police Killings in Duterte's 'War on Drugs'. Available at: www.hrw.org/sites/default/files/report_pdf/philippines0317_web_1.pdf [Accessed 22 June 2019].

Huntington, S. P. (1968). *Political Order in Changing Societies*. New Haven: Yale University Press.

Hutchcroft, P. D. (1991). Oligarchs and Cronies in the Philippine State: The Politics of Patrimonial Plunder. *World Politics*, 43(3), 414–50.

Hutchcroft, P. D. (2000). Colonial Masters, National Politicos, and Provincial Lords: Central Authority and Local Autonomy in the American Philippines, 1910–1913. *Journal of Asian Studies*, 59(2), 207–306.

Iyengar, R. (2016). Inside Philippine President Rodrigo Duterte's War on Drugs. *Time*, 25 August. Available at: https://time.com/4462352/rodrigo-duterte-drug-war-drugs-philippines-killing/ [Accessed 20 June 2019].

Jackson, K. D. (1989). The Philippines: The Search for a Suitable Democratic Solution, 1946–1986. In L. Diamond, J. Linz, and S.M. Lipset, eds., *Democracy in Developing Countries: Asia*. Boulder: Lynne Rienner Publishers, pp. 231–68.

Kerkvliet, B. J. T. (1995). Toward a More Comprehensive Analysis of Philippine Politics: Beyond the Patron-Client, Factional Framework. *Journal of Southeast Asian Studies*, 26(2), 401–19.

Kohli, A. (2004). *State-Led Development*. Cambridge: Cambridge University Press.

Kuhonta, E. M. (2011). *The Institutional Imperative: The Politics of Equitable Development in Southeast Asia.* Stanford: Stanford University Press.

Kuhonta, E. M. (2016). Social Cleavages, Political Parties, and the Building of Legitimacy in Southeast Asia. In N. Bermeo and D. Yashar, eds., *Parties, Movements, and Democracy in the Developing World.* Cambridge: Cambridge University Press, pp. 61–92.

Mayor Candidate Shot Dead in Philippine Election Violence, Video. Channel News Asia, 7 May. Available at: www.channelnewsasia.com/news/asiapacific/mayor-candidate-shot-dead-in-philippine-election-violence-8049826 [Accessed 26 November 2017].

Merkel, W. (2004). Embedded and Defective Democracies. *Democratization*, 11(5), 33–58.

Mill, J. S. (1975). *On Liberty.* New York: Basic Books.

National Statistical Coordination Board (NSCB). (2013). 2012 Full Year Official Poverty Statistics of the Philippines. Available at: www.nscb.gov.ph [Accessed 20 June 2019].

Norris, P. (2012). *Making Democratic Governance Work: The Impact of Regimes on Prosperity, Welfare and Peace.* New York: Cambridge University Press.

Norris, P., Wynter, T., and Grömping, M. (2017). Perceptions of Electoral Integrity, (PEI-5.5), Harvard Dataverse, V2. Available at: doi:10.7910/DVN/EWYTZ7 [Accessed 21 June 2019].

NUJP on World Press Freedom Day: 'What's to Celebrate?' (2012). InterAksyon.com. Available at: http://interaksyon.com/article/30983/nujp-on-world-press-freedom-day-whats-to-celebrate [Accessed 10 October 2015].

Paredes, R., ed. (1988). *Philippine Colonial Democracy. Southeast Asia Studies Monograph 32.* New Haven: Yale University Southeast Asia Studies.

Patiño, P. I. (2002). COMELEC: Reform or Deform. *Conjuncture*, 14(1), 29–33.

Peel, M.P. (2016). President Duterte Says He Hunted Down Drug Suspects. *The Financial Times*, 14 December. Available at: https://www.ft.com/content/a5a946ae-c1da-11e6-9bca-2b93a6856354 [Accessed 5 December 2019].

People of the Philippines v. *Joseph Ejercito Estrada*, et al. (2007). Criminal Case No. 26558. The LawPhil Project. Available at: www.lawphil.net/courts/sandigan/sb_26558_2007.html [Accessed 21 June 2019].

People v. *Perfector.* (1922). G.R. No. 18463. The LawPhil Project. Available at: www.lawphil.net/judjuris/juri1922/oct1922/gr_l-18463_1922.html [Accessed 19 June 2019].

Philippine Democracy Assessment Rule of Law and Access to Justice. (2010). Stockholm: International Institute for Democracy and Electoral Assistance https://www.idea.int/sites/default/files/pictures/SoD-Philippines-long.pdf.

Quisumbing, L. (1983). Elections and Suffrage: From Ritual Regicide to Human Rights? *Philippine Law Journal*, 58, 28–43.

Richter, Linda K. (1987). Public Bureaucracy in Post-Marcos Philippines. *Southeast Asian Journal of Social Science*, 15(2), 57–76.

Sen, A. (1999). *Development as Freedom.* New York: Anchor Books.

Sidel, J. (1999). *Capital, Coercion, and Crime: Bossism in the Philippines.* Stanford: Stanford University Press.

Steinberg, D. J. (1994). *The Philippines: A Singular and a Plural Place.* Boulder: Westview Press.

Taylor, R. H. (1996). *The Politics of Elections in Southeast Asia*. New York: Cambridge University Press.

Thompson, M. R. (1995). *The Anti-Marcos Struggle: Personalistic Rule and Democratic Transition in the Philippines*. New Haven: Yale University Press.

Thompson, M. R. (1996). Off the Endangered List: Philippine Democratization in Comparative Perspective. *Comparative Politics*, 28(2), 179–205.

Thompson, M. R. (1998). The Marcos Regime in the Philippines. In H.E. Chehabi, and Juan J. Linz, eds., *Sultanistic Regimes*. Baltimore: Johns Hopkins University Press, pp. 206–30.

Tocqueville, A. (1945). *Democracy in America*. New York: Vintage.

Tusalem, R. F., and Pe-Aguirre, J. J. (2013). The Effect of Political Dynasties on Effective Democratic Governance: Evidence from the Philippines. *Asian Politics and Policy*, 5(3), 359–86.

Whaley, F. (2012). Former Philippine President Denies Election Fraud Charge. *The New York Times*, 24 February. Available at: http://nyti.ms/2cV2cUQ [Accessed 10 September 2015].

Whaley, F. (2016). Philippines Clears Gloria Macapagal Arroyo, Ex-President, of Graft Charges. *The New York Times*, 20 July. Available at: www.nytimes.com/2016/07/20/world/asia/philippines-gloria-arroyo-corruption-dismissed.html?_r=0 [Accessed 10 September 2015].

Will the Philippines Ever Speed Up Its Glacially Slow Judicial System? (2015). Philippine News. Available at: www.philnews.com/2015/13a.htm [Accessed 10 September 2015].

Wurfel, D. (1988). *Filipino Politics: Development and Decay*. Ithaca: Cornell University Press.

8

Stateness and State Capacity in Post-Authoritarian Indonesia: Securing Democracy's Survival, Entrenching Its Low Quality

Marcus Mietzner

INTRODUCTION

In recent years, political scientists have increasingly debated the nexus between stateness (and more specifically, state capacity) and the strength of democracy in post-authoritarian polities. As shown in the introduction to this volume, 'sequentialist' scholars argue that strong levels of stateness are a precondition for establishing democratic rule (Melville and Mironyuk, 2016). Their critics, however, insist that enhanced stateness can be the result of rather than the prerequisite for democracy (Carbone, 2015). Others again, mostly concerned democracy scholars, highlight that it is precisely excessive state capacity that poses the biggest threat to democratization (Holmes, 1995). The difficulty, then, of analysing the state-democracy relationship lies in the character of strong stateness (and the state capacity drawing from its various dimensions) as a 'two-edged sword: it can both be the guarantee of democratic rights and a tool that can be used to suppress such rights' (Andersen et al., 2014: 1203). This insight is reflected in and complicated by the fact that a similar debate exists about the degree to which state capacity enables *autocratic* rule (Slater and Fenner, 2011; Seeberg, 2014; Croissant and Hellmann, 2018). In this discussion, there is general agreement that strong levels of stateness are one of the most solid foundations of authoritarianism. Given these inherent complexities in the stateness-democracy question, it appears that it is not simply one of whether the level of stateness is low or high, or which one comes first. Rather, as this chapter demonstrates, it requires focusing on the *conditions* under which stateness is generated, the extent to which its capacities were developed under pre-democratic rule, and what price young democracies have to pay to the operators of stateness in order to stabilize democratic rule.

This chapter discusses the stateness-democracy linkage in Indonesia's post-1998 democratization process. For a number of reasons, Indonesia is an exceptionally suitable case study to illuminate the broader dynamics of this linkage. To begin with, Indonesia had developed relatively high levels of stateness under authoritarianism between the late 1960s and late 1990s. With Suharto's fall amidst a devastating economic crisis, however, the capacity inherent in this stateness seemed to have severely diminished. Indeed, there were fears that the nation itself might disintegrate. But democracy stabilized, and today, it is one of the most robust in Southeast Asia – albeit one with serious defects. This surprising outcome raises the question of what the precise role of stateness and its related capacities was in establishing and maintaining the democratic regime after 1998. Did the capacity developed under Suharto survive the collapse of the authoritarian regime in 1998 and help to create the conditions under which democracy was entrenched, together with its deficiencies? Or did democracy develop new state capacities that allowed the country to consolidate? There is convincing evidence, this chapter argues, that the core of Indonesian state capacity entrenched under Suharto endured during the transition, assisting in the creation of a formal, electoral democracy. Yet the deals that post-authoritarian rulers had to enter in order to access that state capacity trapped Indonesia in low-quality democratic rule. There is also evidence that although low in quality, Indonesia's democracy strengthened some of the state's capacities while it failed to impact others. Although both the sequentialists and their opponents capture elements of these dynamics, neither grasps the nuances inherent in the Indonesian case.

This chapter develops these nuances and the overall argument in six sections. The first assesses levels of stateness and state capacity under Suharto's authoritarian regime. The second evaluates how much of this state capacity survived the transition and which elements were strengthened during democratization. In the third segment, the depth of post-Suharto democracy is measured against the indicators of the five dimensions of embedded democracy (see Introduction in this volume). The section concludes that, while Indonesia developed a nominal democracy, it suffers from a host of ongoing weaknesses. The fourth part focuses on the impact that state capacity has had on the quality of democracy. It demonstrates that state capacity was crucial in securing the *survival* of democracy but that conservative actors nesting in key areas of state capacity were responsible for keeping the *quality* of that democracy at low levels. In the fifth section, the ways in which democratization influenced state capacity is examined, showing that democratic opening and competitiveness boosted some of the state's capacities but made the state overall a less egalitarian dispenser of services. The conclusion, finally, connects the Indonesian case to the debate on linkages between stateness, state capacity and democracy. Some young democracies, it seems, draw much of their staying power from state capacity grown under pre-democratic regimes, but they tend to experience continuously low levels of democratic quality as a result.

INDONESIA'S STATE CAPACITY UNDER AUTHORITARIAN RULE

In order to assess the ways in which Indonesian stateness shaped democratization outcomes after 1998, it is necessary to first establish the levels of stateness and state capacity that the new democratic polity inherited from its predecessor, namely Suharto's military-backed autocracy between 1966 and 1998. There has been much debate about how to best measure stateness and state capacity and – in particular – which sectors of the state need to be investigated. But generally, scholars of stateness focus their analytical attention on the strength of the state in four main arenas of its organization and legitimacy: coercive capacity (i.e. the state's possession of and ability to use resources to uphold its monopoly on violence); extractive capacity; administrative capacity; and the dimension of citizenship agreement (i.e. the public's acceptance of the nation-state and its body politic as legitimate) (Hanson and Sigman, 2013; and Croissant and Hellmann in the introduction to this volume). State capacity, then, is the ability of state institutions to implement official goals and policies, drawing from the resources built up in the four dimensions of stateness mentioned previously. It is against these four indicators that Indonesia's stateness and state capacity are measured throughout this chapter.

In the first dimension of stateness, that of *state coercion*, Suharto's authoritarian New Order regime left a mixed legacy. On the one hand, the Indonesian armed forces had developed much of their coercive capacity *before* grabbing power from long-time president Sukarno by military intervention in 1966. Between the early 1950s and 1965, the military and police had grown from around 300,000 to 505,000 troops (Crouch, 1978: 198). This enhanced coercive capacity facilitated Suharto – the leader of the military – to ascend to power and to transform the polity into a personal autocracy from the early 1980s onwards (Lowry, 1996). But while the coercive power of the state remained high throughout Suharto's rule, the president actually reduced – in relative terms – the size of his security forces as he feared an expanding army might turn against him. In 1997, the military and police forces remained at 505,000 troops (White Paper, 1997), while the population sized had doubled since 1965.[1] Thus, the troops-to-population ratio declined from around 1:198 to 1:396 – in roughly the same period, the Burmese military regime had boosted its ratio from 1:265 to 1:122 (Mietzner and Farrelly, 2013: 346).[2] By the 1990s, believing that coercion was no longer as crucial to his regime as in previous years and that

---

[1] While the overall numbers remained the same, there were significant internal shifts: The number of army troops declined from 300,000 to 243,000, while the police increased from 125,000 to 192,000. I am grateful to Robert Lowry for providing me with these numbers.

[2] Suharto also cut the military's budget from above US$2.5 billion in 1980 to around US$1.5 billion in the early 1990s (Lowry, 1996: 24).

continued economic growth was now the main source of his power, Suharto commanded a still significant, but at best stagnating, security apparatus when the protests against him escalated in 1998. Arguably, a larger military could have convinced Suharto to cling on for longer than he did – instead, he left without putting up much opposition.

Under Suharto's regime, the state developed moderately strong *extractive capacities*. At the end of his rule, the tax revenue to gross domestic product (GDP) ratio stood at 16 per cent, almost double that of India or Mexico (although the number of Indonesian taxpayers remained low). Similarly, the entrenchment of the regime from the early 1970s to the mid-1980s was fuelled by the state's ability to extract significant oil revenues – oil exports increased from US$641 million in 1973 to US$10.6 billion in 1980 (Hill, 1994: 99). This revenue was re-distributed to elites Suharto had to integrate into his regime and to the population, whose increasing welfare was a key pillar of the later New Order narrative to justify its rule. After the global oil crisis in the mid-1980s, the Indonesian state increasingly extracted revenues from foreign direct investment (FDI). Between 1981 and 1996, FDI grew from US$133 million to US$6.2 billion (in 2015 US$). But as important as taxes, oil and FDI was the informal extractive apparatus that funded the state and its officials. While much of this informally extracted money ended up in private pockets, substantial sums were also used to fund and support state services. This informal extraction system came in the form of a patrimonial pyramid (Crouch, 1979). State officials, from the president down to the lowest civil servant, all got a cut from state projects, investments, permits and other state licenses and services, creating a parallel system of taxation. Ross McLeod (2000, 2010) describes this 'better class of corruption' under Suharto as a 'franchise system'. Echoing this, Keith Darden (2008: 35) asserts that 'where graft is informally institutionalized in this way, it provides the basis for state organizations that are effective at collecting taxes [and] maintaining public order'. Arguably, Suharto's Indonesia was a case in point.

Strengthening the state's *administrative capacity* was one of Suharto's key priorities. In 1963, three years before the New Order came to power, there had been 608,000 civil servants; this number grew to 1.6 million in 1974, 2.7 million in 1984 and around 3.5 million at the time of Suharto's fall (Bresnan, 1993: 105; Tjiptoherijanto, 2008: 42). From Suharto's perspective, it seems, the enhanced bureaucracy counter-balanced the reduced size of the security forces, with civil servants holding coercive powers that rivalled those of the military and police. Deciding over who was to benefit from public services and who was excluded from them, bureaucrats – who since the early 1970s were required to support the government party, Golkar – possessed a crucial instrument of reward and punishment vis-à-vis the population. But the bureaucracy was more than just an instrument of control. While deeply corrupt and politically biased, it did deliver significantly improved public services to the broad citizenry, especially if compared to the period of Sukarno's Guided Democracy (1959–65). For instance, school enrolment rates were high by international standards, community health facilities were expanded and relatively efficient and the management of food production and distribution was professional (Hill, 1994). In the World Economic Forum Global Competitiveness Survey of 1996, Indonesia recorded an aggregate score of 0.48 in government effectiveness, drawing from a number of indicators (World Bank, 2015). As it would turn out, this was a level of effectiveness the post-Suharto state would initially struggle to match.

The extent of *citizen agreement vis-à-vis the body politic* – the fourth arena of state capacity – is typically difficult to measure in authoritarian regimes, given the absence or unreliability of opinion polls. But it is widely accepted that – for all of its repression – the New Order regime enjoyed a significant decree of performance legitimacy (Hill, 1994; Mietzner, 2009). Its economic achievements formed the basis of a social contract of sorts between Suharto and the majority of Indonesian citizens, suggesting that as long as his regime produced increasing levels of prosperity, the citizenry would accept limitations on democratic rights. Suharto also benefited from and further extended the relatively successful Indonesian nation-building project. Of course, this did not include the territories of Aceh, Papua and East Timor, where armed insurgencies challenged the legitimacy of Jakarta's rule. Otherwise, acceptance of the Indonesian nation-state was surprisingly solid for such a vast and young archipelagic state. Thus, while society's support for the body politic was contingent on its ability to deliver economic welfare, the core citizenry's endorsement of the nation-state as such strengthened over time and independently of politico-economic fluctuations.

But while Suharto had developed a state with comparatively high levels of capacity – lower than South Korea's or Malaysia's, but higher than the Philippines' or Burma's – this was not enough to save him. The Asian Financial crisis of 1997–98 devastated the Indonesian economy (Booth, 2002), depriving state institutions of the fuel they needed to thrive: Massive capital outflow left the extractive apparatus with very little to extract; the elite lost its patronage opportunities that underpinned the patrimonial pyramid; and the population no longer received the benefits that had made it acquiesce to the New Order's brutal rule. In other words, the Indonesian state in 1998 resembled an otherwise functional car robbed of its gasoline. This constellation harboured good *and* bad news for Suharto's post-authoritarian successors. On the one hand, the state apparatus itself was largely undamaged and thus ready to be reactivated should the economy pick up again. On the other hand, the extent of the economic crisis was so grave that nobody could predict how long the economic recovery might take. And even if it did occur faster than expected, the key executors of stateness and its capacity (security forces, extractive institutions, the bureaucracy) were almost exclusively made up of actors whose loyalty to the new democratic order was questionable at best.

THE MAINTENANCE AND EXPANSION OF STATE CAPACITY IN THE DEMOCRATIC POLITY

When Indonesia's democratic transition began in May 1998, the degree of Indonesian stateness was profoundly diminished by the severe economic crisis. Indonesia's GDP contracted by 13.1 per cent in 1998 – an economic collapse with few precedents in modern history. GDP per capita more than halved between 1997 and 1998, from US$1,078 to US$470 (in 2015 US$); it would take the post-authoritarian state until 2003 to reach the income levels the population had enjoyed before Suharto's fall. Obviously, the crisis had a particularly significant impact on the state's ability to extract resources, but the trickle-down effect of this reduced extractive capacity hit other sectors of state organization as well. It is no coincidence that Indonesia's lengthy political transition – which only ended with the introduction of direct presidential elections in 2004 – coincided with the protracted period of economic recovery. Communal conflicts were widespread, the bureaucracy was weakened and social indicators stagnated. But once the economy had stabilized and important political reforms were put in place, state capacity was not only restored to pre-transition levels but began to exceed them. By the mid-2010s, more than one and a half decades after Suharto's resignation, the Indonesian state was arguably stronger than under authoritarian rule.

To begin with, after a period of initial weakness, the Indonesian state gradually gained in coercive capacity. Suharto had left the new democratic state a numerically reduced and politicized security apparatus. As a result, the military and police were unable – and unwilling – to control the myriad of conflicts that sprang up after 1998, from ethnic wars in Kalimantan and religious clashes in Maluku to separatist campaigns in Aceh and Papua (Bertrand, 2004). But two developments were crucial in increasing the state's coercive capacity from the early 2000s onwards. First, both the military and the police realized that the democratic regime, dependent as it was on effective coercive apparatuses, was not going to seriously investigate their involvement in Suharto's repression (Honna, 2003; Muradi, 2014). Second, and related to that dependency, the size of and the budget for the security forces were significantly increased, boosting their capacity. By 2014, the military and police had a combined strength of 899,000 troops,[3] improving the troops-to-population ratio to 1:280. Simultaneously, the military's budget more than quadrupled from US$2 billion in 2001 to US$8 billion in 2015 (SIPRI, 2019).

---

[3] The military had 476,000 (Global Firepower, 2015) and the police 423,000 troops (Markas Besar Polri, 2014). I am grateful to Sidney Jones for providing me with the data on the police.

This enhanced coercive capacity showed: There was no large-scale communal or separatist violence in the decade after the signing of the 2005 Aceh peace accord (Jones, 2015). And while paramilitary groups associated with religious and corporate interests proliferated in the 2000s and often challenged the state's monopoly on violence, the military and police mitigated this problem through a mixture of occasional prosecution and co-optation.

Similarly, while the state's extractive capacity was weakened during the transition as a consequence of the economic meltdown, it was sufficient to carry Indonesia through the crisis and was strengthened once that crisis was over. Between 1997 and 2002, the tax-to-GDP ratio fell from 16 to 11.8 per cent, indicating that even though the extractive apparatus itself may have been intact, there were limited resources to pull from crisis-ridden citizens and businesses. Importantly, however, the state obtained additional operating capital through a US$25 billion loan from the International Monetary Fund (IMF), leading to an explosion in gross debt from 30.8 per cent of GDP in 1995 to 83.8 per cent in 2000 (de Mello, 2008: 18). Thus, despite its diminished revenue extraction capacity, the Indonesian state was able to keep public expenditure levels stable. Moreover, beginning in the mid-2000s, Indonesia benefitted from a new global commodity boom, which drove up the prices of its main export products of coal, gas and palm oil. By 2007, the debt ratio was back to pre-crisis levels, and the state's extractive institutions could again draw primarily from domestic revenue. Under the rule of President Susilo Bambang Yudhoyono (2004–2014), GDP growth averaged around 6 per cent, similar to the levels Indonesia had seen under Suharto (Hill, 2014). The extracted revenues were re-redistributed to pay for generous public subsidies and development programmes – between 2006 and 2015, fiscal expenditure quadrupled to almost US$200 billion.

In addition to external loans and the commodity boom, another factor in the sustenance of extractive state capacity during the transition was Indonesia's still thriving informal extraction machine. While the state's official extraction institutions struggled to function, the corrupt system of informal taxation and rent extraction continued to operate. Indeed, at the height of the crisis – with the state forced to sell off state-owned enterprises and the informal sector assuming primacy in economic life – opportunities for patronage exchanges mushroomed (Winters, 2011). However, the foundation of this informal extraction system was no longer the patrimonial pyramid that had dominated the Suharto era. Instead, a much more dispersed web of neo-patrimonial structures developed at all levels of state organization (Hadiz, 2010). Through this web, resources were extracted and circulated, complementing the state's official functions in this arena. Obviously, it is tempting to view this system as damaging to the democratic state's formal extractive apparatus. But as Darden (2008) points out, institutionalized systems of informal taxation and graft can stabilize states with weak institutions. Indonesia during the crisis was such a state; the day-to-day exchanges of rents kept the economy running and state officials materially satisfied at a time of official austerity. Of course, as we shall see later, this system – while steadying otherwise feeble states – also obstructs a polity's development towards higher levels of democratic quality.

The administrative capacity of the Indonesian state declined somewhat during the crisis, stabilized in the immediate post-transition period and has since been significantly expanded. Immediately after Suharto's downfall, the Indonesian bureaucracy was in a comparable situation to the security forces. It was uncertain about its place in the democratic regime and anxious about possible investigations into its transgressions (in its case, corruption). Hence, it worked only half-heartedly for the new rulers, focusing instead on its own profit maximization (Kristiansen and Ramli, 2006). But as was the case with the military and the police, bureaucratic leaders soon discovered that the democratic polity was not necessarily detrimental to their interests and that democratic leaders depended on their support. In fact, the new democratic competitiveness opened up new avenues of political power for state administrators. For example, many candidates in the post-2005 elections for governors, district heads and mayors were career bureaucrats (Mietzner, 2005; Buehler, 2010: 275). Indeed, state bureaucrats emerged as key actors in the post-Suharto polity, especially at the local level. Furthermore, the expansion of the civil service begun under Suharto in the 1970s was continued. By the early 2010s, the bureaucratic apparatus had grown to 4.5 million members.[4] Slowly but steadily, then, bureaucrats endorsed the post-Suharto state and worked towards its effective management.

These ups and downs in the state's administrative capacity are reflected in the ratings of the World Economic Forum Global Competitiveness Survey. From a New Order high of 0.48 in 1996, Indonesia's score dropped to 0.27 in 2000. In 2004, the score slightly exceeded Suharto era levels, and in 2010, Indonesia achieved a new record of 0.53 (World Bank, 2015). These numbers refuted previous fears that democratization and – since 2001 – decentralization would undermine the state's long-term bureaucratic effectiveness. Instead, the state expanded, both in capacity and in size. Between 1998 and 2012, the number of provinces rose from 27 to 34; districts from 249 to 399; subdistricts from 4,028 to 6,793; and villages from 67,925 to 79,075 (Mietzner, 2014: 58). In all of these cases of decentralization-induced proliferation, new government buildings were erected, new civil servants hired and thus far unpenetrated areas opened for the Indonesian state. This was accompanied by an unprecedented redistribution of funds, with around 40 per cent of government revenue now flushed into local bureaucracies and their projects. In many cases, local leaders invested increasing central government transfers into additional civil servants and other state employees,

---

[4] This number was provided by the then deputy minister for administrative reform, Eko Prasojo, in December 2013.

Stateness and State Capacity in Post-Authoritarian Indonesia 187

although they already had reached the limit of what they reasonably required. But hiring new personnel was a welcome instrument for local politicians to dispense patronage and consolidate loyalties, creating excess bureaucratic capacities in many areas as a result.

Nonetheless, the quality of public services has not increased proportionally to the expansion of the state apparatus. Health, infrastructure and education indicators have moderately improved (Schulze and Sjahrir, 2014: 203), but not as much as the increased investment would suggest. In addition, the quality of public services has become more uneven than under the highly centralized Suharto regime. While Suharto's central government put great emphasis on uniform state organization and service delivery, in the democratic and decentralized state, 'financially better-endowed districts provide significantly better services than poorer ones' (Schulze and Sjahrir, 2014: 204). This is particularly true for resource-rich districts in parts of Kalimantan and Sumatra, where coal, gas or palm oil extraction allowed local governments to spend considerably more than other districts. Some of these expenditures have been used for local health care plans or education scholarships that supplement national schemes. These local programmes in resource-rich areas have led to better services in those districts, increasing the gap to districts without such additional budgets. In other words, the post-1999 state in Indonesia is an administratively stronger but also a less egalitarian entity than its authoritarian predecessor.

Similarly, the level of public attachment to the state and its body politic was initially unstable and then consolidated over time. Clearly, the performance of the state in the first three areas of state capacity partially determined how it fared in the fourth, the field of citizen agreement vis-à-vis the state. Measuring this support can be analytically complex. While regime type and the state within which it operates are conceptually different categories, public support for the former typically indicates similar support for the latter (the reverse, however, is not true: citizens might reject a particular incumbent form of government while still supporting the existence and legitimacy of the state). Thus, we can use – for the purposes of this study – public support for the post-1998 democracy as a proxy for citizenship agreement with the state's body politic. At the beginning of the democratization process, support for democracy was still relatively low. While there was a great deal of enthusiasm after the fall of Suharto (which expressed itself in high voter turnout in the 1999 elections), it was mixed with anxiety and a sense of uncertainty. When opinion polling began in 1999, support for democracy stood at 55 per cent, indicating continued volatility. But by 2004, the proportion of Indonesians endorsing democracy in principle had grown to 85 per cent, and it remained stable at 76 per cent in 2017 (Mujani et al., 2012: 47; LSI, 2017: 104). The numbers of support for the way democracy was practiced within the Indonesian state was only slightly lower at 69 per cent in 2017 (LSI, 2017: 14).

Post-authoritarian citizen endorsement of the nation-state as such (as opposed to the regime through which the state delivers its services to the public) developed along similar lines. Two decades after democratization began, endorsement is high, but this was different at the beginning of the transition. During the early transition, which was marked by the secession of East Timor in 1999, the nation-state seemed fragile, and dissatisfaction with Jakarta's continued centralism was widespread. But after the onset of decentralization in 2001 and the settlement of the conflict in Aceh in 2005, centrifugal tendencies in Indonesia today are arguably at their lowest level since independence, with only Papua still exhibiting serious – but thus far controllable – separatist tendencies. Underlining this point, a 2017 survey found that 65 per cent of Indonesians were 'very proud' and 34 per cent 'somewhat proud' to be citizens of the Indonesian state (LSI, 2017: 106).

INDONESIA'S LOW-QUALITY DEMOCRACY

Having established the level of stateness and state capacity of post-Suharto Indonesia, we now have to assess its democratic quality – before then discussing the correlation between the two. Following Merkel's model of embedded democracy (2014), this section evaluates the quality of Indonesian democracy in five arenas: electoral regime; political liberties; civil rights; horizontal accountability; and effective power to govern. Overall, Indonesia has created a functional yet low-quality electoral democracy. In this polity, high levels of formal political competitiveness go hand in hand with serious defects in sectors such as rule of law, civil rights, equality and transparency. This democracy has now persisted longer than the country's only previous experiment with democracy (1950–57), and it is approaching an endurance level that comparative political scientists would view as an important safeguard against democratic reversal (but, importantly, not against democratic erosion or deconsolidation). Kapstein and Converse (2008: 59) found that 84 per cent of democratization attempts fail within the first ten years – Indonesia is now well beyond that. Nevertheless, Indonesian democracy has stagnated, and in some areas even eroded, since the mid-2000s.

In terms of its formal-institutional design, Indonesia's electoral regime is highly competitive (Aspinall and Fealy, 2003). This is because electoral rights were gradually expanded between 1999 and 2009, with the country introducing direct presidential elections in 2004, direct votes for governors, mayors and district heads in 2005 and a fully open party list system for parliamentary elections in 2009. But while the electoral regime is competitive as far as its institutional set-up is concerned, its effectiveness is undermined by substantive weaknesses. First, electoral management remains defective, with the voters list largely drawn from a questionable citizen registry (Schmidt, 2010). Second, the level of vote buying has increased as the system of parliamentary elections progressively moved from a closed party list in 1999 to a partially open list in 2004 and, finally, fully open list in 2009. While voters can now directly pick their preferred party candidates, this move has also facilitated unprecedented electoral clientelism (Aspinall and Sukmajati, 2015). And third, the absence of a credible party and campaign financing system produced increasing levels of oligarchization in parties and among candidates, with affluent entrepreneurs or bureaucrats buying themselves party posts or candidacies (Mietzner, 2015). Having said that, incumbency turnovers have been high, indicating a significant degree of contestation. In five national elections between 1999 and 2019, only twice was a ruling party and its presidential candidate returned to power, and incumbency turnover in parliament has been high as well (more than 50 per cent in 2014).

In the area of political liberties, Indonesia has achieved moderately high levels of democratic quality. For Merkel (2014: 15), the key political liberties are 'the freedom of speech and the right to associate, demonstrate, and formulate petitions'. Indeed, Freedom House upgraded Indonesia frequently, and rapidly, in this sector – from a score of 7 in 1997 to 6 in 1998; to a 3 in 1999; and a 2 in 2006.[5] Many political rights were quickly introduced by President B. J. Habibie after succeeding Suharto in May 1998: He lifted restrictions on media freedom; granted the right of free association; allowed political parties to form freely (with the only exception being communist parties); generally did not curb demonstrations; and largely upheld freedom of speech. In combination with continuously expanding electoral rights, this massive socio-political liberalization provided Indonesians with a catalogue of political freedoms they had last enjoyed in the 1950s. This does not mean that this register of rights has been safe from threats, however. Beginning in the late 2000s, the state tried to restrict some of the freedoms it had granted earlier. For example, freedom of speech was limited by the Information and Electronic Transaction Act of 2008, which imposed severe penalties for expressing 'damaging' opinions on social media or even through email, with dozens of citizens having since landed in jail (Hamid, 2015). Similarly, legislation was passed in 2013 (and further tightened in 2017) that put the operations of civil society organizations under greater state control. Thus, while political rights have largely been maintained, some state actors have aimed to re-limit them.

By contrast, civil rights registered a noticeable regression in the mid-2010s, following some initial post-1998 improvements. Merkel (2014: 15) asserts that 'individual rights grant legal protection of life, liberty and property, as well as protection against illegitimate arrest, exile, terror, torture, or unjustifiable intervention in personal life'. Reflecting Indonesia's uneven record in this regard, Freedom House upgraded Indonesia's score in civil liberties from 5 to 3 between 1998 and 2006, before downgrading it again from 3 to 4 in 2014. The initial upgrades echoed Indonesia's granting of more rights to its ethnic Chinese minority, the ratification of numerous international treaties on civil liberties and a

---

[5] Freedom Houses grants scores from 1 to 7, with 1 indicating the highest levels of freedom and 7 the lowest.

significant reduction in human rights violations. But in the mid-2000s, conservative elements in both the state and society began to push back against what they saw as Indonesia's excessive liberalization (Berger, 2015). Within the state, former security officers prevented the creation of a truth and reconciliation commission as well as the ratification of the Rome Statute, which would have obliged Indonesia to further investigate human rights violations. As a result, the impunity of the security forces was consolidated. Outside of the state, but with its cooperation, conservative Islamic leaders worked towards limiting the civil rights of religious minorities, especially Ahmadis and Shiites. Both Muslim minority sects suffered from increasing mob attacks and state-sanctioned closures of their places of worship. By the mid- and late 2010s, Indonesia's acquiescence towards these abuses earned it worldwide condemnation (Bush, 2015), and its erosion of civil rights was picked up by most democracy indexes, such as the civil liberties index of Freedom House (2019) and the democracy status index of the Bertelsmann Transformation Index (Bertelsmann Stiftung, 2018).

Formally, Indonesia's post-authoritarian polity has acquired high levels of horizontal accountability, but its actual effectiveness remains low. 'Horizontal accountability', Merkel (2014: 15) explains, 'concerns the mutual checking of constitutional powers [...] in terms of a balanced mutual interdependence and autonomy of the legislative, executive, and judicial branches'. While the pre-democratic constitution was heavily centred on the presidency, the 2002 constitutional amendments created a level playing field between a strong president, a powerful parliament and a nominally independent judiciary (Sherlock, 2015). Yudhoyono even referred to this arrangement as a 'semi-parliamentary, semi-presidential system' (Aspinall et al., 2015: 7). But while this executive-legislative balance should have increased accountability, some scholars have argued that instead of scrutinizing each other, Indonesia's political organs have engaged in 'promiscuous powersharing' (Slater and Simmons, 2013). In other words, they share the political spoils among each other and collectively escape accountability. While this 'cartel' thesis remains controversial, there is a broad consensus that the third constitutional branch, the judiciary, is deeply corrupt. Although now free of the dictate of authoritarian rulers, judges have often commercialized their decision-making, with many of them issuing verdicts in favour of the party offering the biggest bribe (Butt and Lindsey, 2011). With such weak rule of law, horizontal accountability cannot operate effectively.

Indonesia's democratic leaders mostly have had effective power to govern, but questions remain over the informal influence of some actors. For Merkel (2014: 16), effective power to govern requires 'that only individuals, organizations, and institutions that have been legitimized by free and general elections are entitled to make authoritatively binding political decisions'. According to some authors, oligarchs have become exceedingly powerful in post-Suharto Indonesia (Winters, 2011; Hadiz and Robison, 2014). In their view, omnipotent oligarchs steer weak politicians by making them dependent on external payments and demanding policy concessions in return. While overstated in its scope, the oligarchy theory has accurately captured the fact that Indonesia's dysfunctional political finance system has opened space for wealthy entrepreneurs to meddle in policy-making processes. Similarly, while the security forces no longer have the political might they had during authoritarian rule, democratic governments have been reluctant to intervene in their internal affairs, fearing their opposition (Baker, 2015). The continued legal impunity for security officers is a result of this anxiety. Finally, conservative Islamic groups have forced governments to adopt policies directed against religious minorities, with executive leaders fearful that they could lose electoral support in case of non-compliance. Thus, while holding formal power, leaders have had to make compromises with both state and non-state actors to exercise it.

In sum, the assessment of these areas of democratic quality produces the picture of a stable yet unconsolidated electoral democracy. This is in line with assessments of most democracy indexes. The Economist's Democracy Index has classified Indonesia consistently as a 'flawed democracy'; Freedom House ranked the country 'partly free' between 2014 and 2019 (after rating it 'free' between 2006 and 2013); and in the 2018 Bertelsmann Transformation Index, Indonesia was ranked 42th (out of 129) in terms of its 'democracy status', sandwiched between Peru and Bhutan above it and Liberia and Sri Lanka below it.

STATENESS, STATE CAPACITY AND THEIR IMPACT ON INDONESIAN DEMOCRACY

Before assessing how the extent of stateness and state capacity influenced the *quality* of Indonesian democracy after 1998, it is essential to point out how it helped to secure its *stability* or, more fundamentally, its *survival*. Arguably, Indonesian democracy could not have survived the immediate post-1998 transition without the state upholding moderate levels of capacity in coercion, extraction, administration and – as a consequence – in citizen recognition. Moreover, democracy would have found it difficult to subsequently stabilize had it not been for increasing levels of stateness and state capacity. However, while stateness, state capacity and the actors executing it made a positive contribution to the *stabilization* of Indonesian democracy, the same cannot be said about their impact on democratic *quality*. Indeed, it is precisely because key executors of state capacity were so crucial for the survival of democracy that they could negotiate compromises that negatively influenced its quality. These facilitators of stateness and state capacity – the security forces, economic extractors and distributors as well as bureaucrats – had been leftovers from the New Order regime and now settled into a new arrangement with the democratic polity. At its core was, it seems, a tacit agreement with the new power holders. Based on this arrangement, the state's capacity would be used to sustain the democratic regime, but democracy was to be constrained in ways that would not threaten the institutional and personal interests of the managers of state capacity.

The coercive power of the state, diminished as it was by Suharto's policies towards the security forces and the destabilizing impact of the crisis, played an important role in defending Indonesia, and the democracy operating in it, from the threat of breakdown and disintegration. After the New Order's fall, observers had expressed concern about the possible balkanization of Indonesia (Richburg, 1998), and the many communal and separatist conflicts erupting across the archipelago initially seemed to confirm this suspicion. The secession of East Timor in 1999 appeared to some as the first step in an inevitable process of state fragmentation (Tiwon, 1999). But while the security forces were weakened and disoriented about their new role in the post-Suharto regime, they still managed to contain transition violence to a number of hot spots and otherwise maintain stability. To be sure, under the chaotic presidency of Abdurrahman Wahid (1999–2001), Indonesian democracy came close to a security breakdown, with multiple conflicts stretching the capacity of the military and police (Klinken, 2007). But after President Megawati Sukarnoputri (2001–2004) granted concessions to the security apparatus (Mietzner, 2006, 2009) and began to expand its troops, security conditions stabilized. Presidents Yudhoyono and Joko Widodo (since 2014) both continued the concessions and the expansion strategy (Schreer, 2014), ensuring that democracy could develop without major security disturbances.

The extractive apparatus of the state was also important in sustaining the democratic system. With the exception of the year 2000, the state was able to mobilize enough resources to secure growing year-to-year government expenditure, despite the economic crisis. While initially a significant proportion of this extracted revenue had its origins in IMF loans, the size of the latter shrank over time and dissipated completely by the late 2000s. With the extracted resources, the state could distribute benefits to the population that helped it through the crisis. Most importantly, by distributing food aid and subsidizing key staples, the government succeeded in controlling inflation. According to Kapstein and Converse (2008), young democracies with high levels of inflation have a much reduced chance of survival compared to those with lower inflation (by contrast, GDP growth levels are not a determinant of democratic persistence). In Indonesia, inflation fell from over 80 per cent in the second half of 1998 to below 0 per cent in early 2000 and subsequently stabilized at normal levels. As mentioned earlier, the informal and long-entrenched parallel extraction regime, fuelled by patronage and corruption, also stabilized the mobilization and circulation of revenues in a society unsettled by major socio-economic and political upheaval.

Similarly, the state's administrative capacity assisted in creating a public service environment in which democracy could stabilize. While weakened by the fall of its long-time patron and confused by the suddenly severed ties between the civil service and the regime party, the bureaucracy continued to deliver public services that kept the democratic state functional. Certainly, the growth of Indonesia's Human Development Index (HDI) slowed down amidst the crisis, indicating that public service delivery in the health and education sector was experiencing some constraints. Between 1998 and 2003, the HDI index grew by only 3.6 basis points, while it had expanded by 5.2 basis points between 1992 and 1997 (UNDP, 2019). Nevertheless, public service delivery was far from the disaster that many had expected as a result of the economic downturn. A massive collapse of public services, it must be assumed, would have created widespread dissatisfaction with the existing order and, therefore, posed a serious threat to the survival of the democratic polity. The stability of the state's administrative capacity was all the more remarkable as it was maintained during the most substantial transformation of the civil service since 1945. Starting in 2001, the decentralization project shifted millions of civil servants from the supervision of the central government to that of local administrations (Aspinall and Fealy, 2003). Many sceptics had predicted that public services would deteriorate as a result, but they did not. As during the crisis, they were maintained at effective levels (for a low- to middle-income country, that is) and later even improved.

In combination, the state's post-authoritarian capacity in coercion, extraction and administration ensured that the state's most principal capacity, namely the legitimacy of public authority, was held initially at modest and later even reached comparatively high levels. In 2017, 58 per cent of Indonesians viewed the quality of state services as 'very good' or 'good', 30 per cent as 'average' and only 9 per cent as 'bad' (LSI, 2017: 11). Similar numbers were achieved if disaggregated by area (i.e. security and law enforcement, the economy and administrative services, such as health and education facilities). Without this citizen endorsement of the state and its body politic, democracy would not have been sustainable. Indeed, post-Suharto leaders were well aware of the centrality of public support for the continuation of the democratic project, putting pressure on them to secure continued coercive, extractive and administrative functionality in order to maintain public trust. This, in turn, forced leaders into stabilizing but risky deals with the executors of those key instruments of state capacity.

It is evident then, that democracy was able to take root in Indonesia to no small measure due to the continued existence of moderately strong levels of stateness and state capacity during the volatile transition and beyond. It is also clear that this state capacity was drawn – at the beginning almost exclusively – from the apparatus developed under the Suharto regime. However, the price the young Indonesian democracy paid for the continuation of state services was high. In order to access these pre-democratic repositories of state capacity, the post-1998 polity had to accommodate the predatory interests that nested within them, producing low levels of democratic *quality* as a consequence.

For instance, the loyalty of the security forces was obtained in exchange for significant concessions. Among them was, as indicated previously, the continued impunity for senior military and police officers; not a single high-ranking army officer has been imprisoned for human rights violations that occurred under Suharto's rule or afterwards (Hirst and Varney, 2005). Lower ranking personnel, who did get sanctioned, often continued to prospering careers. In 2015, the military's main academy was led by an officer who had overseen the killing of Papuan independence leader Theys Eluay after attending a party at the unit's headquarters in 2001. Similarly, when the Anti-Corruption Agency (*Komisi Pemberantasan Korupsi*, KPK) was established in 2003, the military was excluded from its jurisdiction. While the police were subject to KPK jurisdiction, it typically found ways to escape it. In response to the very few occasions in which the agency indicted police officers, their colleagues in the force simply fabricated cases against KPK leaders, leading to their temporary or permanent removal from office.[6]

In the area of the state's extractive capacity, the state had to rely on the former regime's notoriously corrupt tax agency, and other equally questionable extraction bodies, to supply funds. One of the reasons that Indonesia's tax base was, and remains, below that of more advanced democracies is that tax officials often take a cut from the sum they negotiate with taxpayers (Pramudatama, 2012). This practice continues under the democratic regime, and the government appears to silently accept it as the only way to keep revenue streams stable. The head of the tax agency, Hadi Poernomo, grew famously rich while in office between 2001 and 2006, and he used his wealth to fund his successful campaign to chair the country's Financial Audit Agency (*Badan Pemeriksa Keuangan*, BPK) between 2009 and 2014. The KPK arrested Hadi on the day of his retirement from the BPK, but he has so far evaded a permanent sentence with the help of a top-notch legal team. In the same vein, successive democratic governments have done little to dismantle the parallel apparatus of revenue extraction that continues to fuel Indonesia's informal universe of patronage-driven socio-economic relationships. This reluctance to disturb long-entrenched rent-seeking practices has provided stability to the polity (Webber, 2006), but it has obviously undermined the quality of democracy.

The quality of Indonesian democracy has also been undermined by bureaucrats discharging the state's administrative capacity. Indeed, the bureaucracy has been widely identified as the least reformed post-1998 actor (Sherlock, 2015: 106). Although carrying out administrative tasks that guarantee democracy's functionality, the bureaucracy has made this service delivery conditional upon the protection of its own interests. Whenever these interests come under attack, the bureaucracy has threatened to obstruct government. For instance, when Yudhoyono considered a new civil service law in the early 2010s, the head of the state bureaucracy mobilized massive opposition against it. The law envisaged the creation of an independent civil service agency to manage

---

[6] In 2015, both the head and vice-chairman of the KPK were removed from their positions after indicting a senior police general. The senior police general was subsequently appointed as deputy police chief.

all senior-level bureaucratic appointments. Such a move would have ended, or at least limited, the 'sale' of bureaucratic positions in ministries and local governments, which one senior government official estimated to be worth US$1 billion a year.[7] Vice-presidential staffers overseeing the bill's deliberation conceded that the government feared a 'rebellion' by the bureaucracy if the bill was passed in its initial form.[8] Ultimately, the civil service agency was established in 2014 but with much reduced powers. The authority to appoint bureaucrats has remained in the ministries and various levels of government, securing the continuation of intra-bureaucratic patronage. Thus, the bureaucracy has maintained significant veto powers that, in turn, has undermined the democratic quality of the post-1998 polity.

In combination, members of the security forces, the extractive apparatus and the civil service used their centrality in the key areas of stateness to compete for and occupy leading positions in the new democratic polity. Exploiting the weaknesses in the electoral regime mentioned beforehand (ranging from high levels of vote buying to a lack of political financing and logistical deficiencies), representatives of these state-anchored elites have claimed the pole position in many electoral races. This was visible at the national level – Yudhoyono, for instance, was a former general – but was especially true at the local level. Data collected by Michael Buehler (2010: 275) showed that in the 2005–2008 period, 23 per cent of all candidates in local executive elections were bureaucrats; 17 per cent were incumbent state office holders; and 8 per cent were from the military and police. Another 23 per cent were parliamentarians, some of whom were former security officers or bureaucrats as well. While this data has not been collected systematically for more recent periods, this is largely because it is widely accepted that the pattern has not changed. In many cases, these state-linked office holders in the democratic polity have perpetuated patronage patterns developed under the authoritarian regime, undermining democracy's ability to move towards higher levels of accountability and transparency. Overall, many state-affiliated politicians of the post-1998 era helped to stabilize the young post-autocratic polity, but they only did so in exchange for continued privileges under democratic rule.

THE EFFECT OF DEMOCRACY ON THE
CAPACITY OF THE INDONESIAN STATE

While a solid basis of stateness – and the manner in which it was obtained – proved essential in determining both democracy's perseverance and its low-level stagnation, the state-democracy relationship in Indonesia has not been a one-way process of the former shaping the latter. Rather, some developments initiated by or occurring within the realm of Indonesian democracy also

---

[7] Confidential interview, Jakarta, 2 December 2013.
[8] Confidential interview, Jakarta, 3 December 2013.

impacted the extent and quality of state capacity. As in the reverse linkage, not all outcomes of the democracy-state nexus have been positive. In some cases, democratization has strengthened stateness and the state capacities linked to it. In others, it has led to a reduced capability of the state to offer equal access to services and infrastructure across the archipelago.

The clearest case in which democratization has strengthened the degree of stateness is, rather ironically, that of the coercive apparatus. There has been a widespread assumption that young democracies have weaker coercive capacities than autocracies (Alagappa, 2001: 61). In the Indonesian case, some doubted whether it was wise to depoliticize and thus 'weaken the armed forces [...] at a time when it was perhaps the only body capable of maintaining order?' (Robinson, 2001: 248). But while the armed forces' continued loyalty to the new government was ultimately secured through concessions, its post-1998 de-politicization has *increased*, not weakened, the state's coercive capacity. Under Suharto, the armed forces had over time degenerated into a 'palace guard' aimed only at keeping the autocrat in power. It was a domestic apparatus of repression rather than a modern defence force, famously unable to end the insurgencies in East Timor, Aceh and Papua. It was only after the democratic transition began, and the military was extracted from politics, that its professionalization and modernization was advanced (Schreer, 2014). With much higher budget allocations, the force was expanded and equipped with new technology. While the armed forces remain underdeveloped compared to their regional neighbours, 'access to modern technologies [...] and improved capacity to deploy troops within the archipelago means that the [Indonesian military] will be better placed to engage any hostile force' (Schreer, 2014: 9). In other words, the post-authoritarian military is a much stronger defence force than Suharto's inward-looking army.

Similar to the armed forces, the post-1998 police experienced an increase in their capacity. Under Suharto, the police were part of and subordinate to the armed forces, making them a servant of the security interests of the regime. At the beginning of the democratic transition in 1999, the police were separated from the military, increasing their independence and institutional strength (Muradi, 2014). Importantly, the police more than doubled in size from 192,000 to 423,000 troops between 1997 and 2015. While still deeply corrupt, the police have – since around 2005 – generally managed to respond quickly to occasional outbreaks of communal tensions and prevent their escalation into large-scale conflicts. As a result, contemporary Indonesia has been spared the kind of violence that had shaken the early and late phases of the Suharto regime as well as the first five years of the democratic transition. The police's special anti-terror unit, Detachment 88, has been especially praised both domestically and internationally for its mostly successful work against radical Islamist groups (ICG, 2008). To be sure, the police's overall popularity remains low, but there is no doubt that a significant upgrading of their capacity took place during democratization.

In other arenas of stateness and state capacity, the impact of democracy has been more complex, however. In some cases, stateness and state capacity increased after 1998 but not necessarily as a result of democratization. For example, while the extractive capacity of the post-Suharto state eventually exceeded pre-crisis levels, this was not due to democratic impulses. Rather, IMF loans and the commodity boom of the 2000s flushed the economy with resources that the extractive apparatus found easy to draw from. The extractive machine itself remains largely unreformed. In other cases, stateness and state capacity were heavily impacted by democratization, but that impact was not always positive. One case in point is the area of administrative capacity. Clearly, democratic decentralization facilitated the expansion of the bureaucracy into previously uncovered areas of the archipelago (Hill, 2014). But this expansion came – as indicated previously – at the cost of the state's formerly more equitable distribution patterns. Public service outcomes are no longer tightly supervised by a paternalistic central government. Instead, local governments now oversee much of the state's administrative services, making their quality dependent on the resources of each locality. This inequality in public service outcomes mirrored a more general trend towards sharper social contrasts under democratic rule: Indonesia's Gini coefficient rose from 29.0 in 1999 to 41.0 in 2013. Democracy, it seems, mobilized new sources of state capacity but distributed its benefits unevenly among the population.

Despite this rising inequality, however, democracy has strengthened the fourth arena of stateness, namely that of the state's popular legitimacy. While it can only be asserted that the majority of Indonesians supported Suharto's repressive but growth-producing rule, the public's endorsement of the body politic after 1998 can be established quantitatively. Two trends stand out from the available data. First, the legitimacy of public authority has grown during democratization, pointing to a link between democracy and stabilizing citizen recognition of the state. Second, support for the democratic status quo has been insulated from fluctuations in the satisfaction with specific details of governance or the performance of individual leaders. For instance, during a period of high inflation in 2015, 74 per cent of Indonesians thought that the state of the economy was stagnant or getting worse; but at the same time, 60 per cent were convinced that the country was moving into the right direction (SMRC, 2015). Satisfaction with democracy was even higher. Thus, while it is clear that democracy would neither have survived nor solidified without satisfactory state services, the majority of Indonesians evidently appreciate democracy as a value in itself. Moreover, the democratic opening in the regions – accelerated through decentralization – defused many anti-centralist sentiments and therefore strengthened the collective acceptance of the nation-state. In this context, democratic change made negotiations with separatist rebels a much more palatable option than under authoritarianism, leading to the settlement of the Aceh conflict. In short, democracy delivered a measurable boost to the legitimacy of the state in the eyes of its citizens.

CONCLUSION: THE AMBIVALENCE OF STATE
CAPACITY IN YOUNG DEMOCRACIES

The examination of the Indonesian case has underscored the highly ambivalent nexus between stateness, state capacity and the quality of democracy in post-authoritarian polities (Carbone, 2015). On the one hand, the sequentialists are correct in that young democracies rely on the mobilization of stateness resources and the corresponding levels of state capacity in order to sustain the polity during what are usually very chaotic transitional periods. Without at least basic levels of stateness – and the deployment of its capacity – no transitional regime can survive. On the other hand, post-authoritarian leaders are often forced to compromise the quality of democracy by entering into pacts with the executors of state capacity. These executors, in turn, tend to be closely tied to the pre-democratic regime that the new government has, in most cases, vowed to dismantle. Indeed, the three key actors in managing stateness – security forces, resource extractors and bureaucrats – were more often than not the main pillars of autocratic rule. By offering them concessions – ranging from privileged participation in electoral competition to impunity from persecution to the promise of conservative, slow reforms – post-autocratic politicians secure the technocratic functionality of democracy but also predetermine its low quality. Thus, while accommodating the operators of state capacity is a *conditio sine qua non* for democratic survival, such accommodation can put young democracies on a path towards defective or 'illiberal' transition outcomes. In other words, the very state capacity that enables democracy can also seriously undermine its meaning – a fact that sequentialists tend to overlook.

In Indonesia, this accommodation went beyond a simple pact between the new democratic power holders, on the one side, and the executors of state capacity, on the other. In many cases, the managers of stateness and state capacity *became* the new power holders (Hadiz, 2010). Yudhoyono's presidency stood as a symbol for this reverse accommodation. At a time of great public uneasiness over the country's security conditions, the election of a former general as president signalled that the security forces and democracy had mutually endorsed each other. Yudhoyono not only embodied the guarantee that the military would not overthrow the new democratic order but also that the post-Suharto government would not harm the military's core interests. This interpenetration of the new democratic polity and the representatives of state capacity occurred on all levels of government. At the regional level, Suharto-affiliated state bureaucrats took the bulk of political leadership positions made available by the introduction of competitive elections. They typically built their campaign apparatuses by mobilizing the civil servants formerly under their control, perpetuating the patronage relationships that had developed under previous regimes. In the same vein, Indonesia's resource-extracting elite made peace with democracy after realizing that they could not only continue to operate within it but, in fact, occupy leadership positions in its key institutions (Winters, 2011).

While moderately strong degrees of stateness developed under authoritarian rule can both stabilize new democracies and keep their quality low, the impact of democracy on stateness and the ability to implement state goals is equally ambivalent. There is much evidence in the Indonesian case to suggest that democracy has the potential to strengthen stateness and its capacities, particularly by modernizing previously politicized security forces and solidifying citizen endorsement of the nation-state and its body politic. Decentralization, often seen as an initiative harbouring the risk of weakening the state, has strengthened it in Indonesia by increasing the level of bureaucratic penetration. But the principles of democracy and decentralization have also made it harder for the state to draw long-term plans for national development and distribute resources equitably among highly diverse regions. This element of Suharto's strong-state rule, widely praised by economists at the time (Hill, 1994), was not completely lost in the post-1998 polity, but it has taken a backseat to a new competitiveness between regions for resources and power.

Indonesian democracy's problem with stateness and state capacity, then, is not one of excessive weakness or strength. The post-1998 polity inherited a moderately strong state, and it has maintained these levels. Neither the Indonesian security forces nor the bureaucracy were particularly large by international standards when Suharto fell, and they are not oversized now. Countries with oversized, bureaucratized militaries such as Egypt, Pakistan, Thailand and Burma face much larger obstacles to democratization as they struggle to deal with excess military capacity and personnel. Indonesia, by contrast, experiences democratic quality challenges because it needed to procure the services of state capacity operators in order to stay afloat in the midst of an unprecedented economic-political crisis. This allowed key actors of the previous regime to transition into the new democratic order with many of their privileges intact. Once the worst of the crisis was over, the managers of state capacity had already settled in crucial positions of the new democratic regime, and they continued to remind reformist leaders that their services were still indispensable for democracy to function. It is difficult to see what Indonesia could have done differently during the transition – trying to 'cleanse' the security forces, the extraction bodies and the bureaucracy from their Suhartoist elements could have failed the democratic experiment early. As a consequence, post-authoritarian Indonesia has been forced to live with the 'irony of success' (Aspinall, 2010): The integration of the forces that secured democracy's survival is the very factor that continues to limit its chances of progressing to the next level of consolidation.

Indeed, the longer the drawbacks of this elite accommodation persist (especially the corrupt misappropriation of funds that could be used to fund better services), the more Indonesia will be exposed to the risk of democratic deconsolidation. There are signs that this deconsolidation may have already begun. The strong showing of Suharto's former son-in-law, Prabowo Subianto, in the 2014 and 2019 presidential elections (he gained more than 44 per cent of the votes each time with an openly articulated strongman platform) and the Islamist mobilization of 2016 (when Islamist populists gained much ground by challenging the pluralist foundations of the body politic), point to this increasing danger of democratic erosion and backsliding. The improved stateness and state capacity under democratization do not shield Indonesia from such a scenario; ironically, they could provide a populist or otherwise anti-democratic challenger with a solid foundation for governance should this challenge succeed.

References

Alagappa, M. (2001). Investigating and explaining change: An analytical framework. In M. Alagappa, ed., *Coercion and Governance: The Declining Role of the Military in Asia*. Stanford: Stanford University Press, pp. 29–68.

Andersen, D., Moller, J., and Skaaning, S. E. (2014). The state-democracy-nexus: Conceptual distinctions, theoretical perspectives, and comparative approaches. *Democratization*, 21(7), 1203–20.

Aspinall, E. (2010). Indonesia: The irony of success. *Journal of Democracy*, 21(2), 21–34.

Aspinall, E., and Fealy, G., eds. (2003). *Local Power and Politics in Indonesia: Democratisation and Decentralisation*. Singapore: ISEAS.

Aspinall, E., and Sukmajati, M., eds. (2015). *Politik uang di Indonesia: patronase dan klientelisme pada pemilu legislatif 2014*. Yogyakarta: PolGov.

Aspinall, E., Mietzner, M., and Tomsa, D. (2015). The moderating president: Yudhoyono's decade in power. In E. Aspinall, M. Mietzner, and D. Tomsa, eds., *The Yudhoyono Presidency: Indonesia's Decade of Stability and Stagnation*. Singapore: ISEAS, pp. 1–22.

Baker, J. (2015). Professionalism without reform: The security sector under Yudhoyono. In E. Aspinall, M. Mietzner, and D. Tomsa, eds., *The Yudhoyono Presidency: Indonesia's Decade of Stability and Stagnation*. Singapore: ISEAS, pp. 114–35.

Berger, D. (2015). Human rights and Yudhoyono's test of history. In E. Aspinall, M. Mietzner, and D. Tomsa, eds., *The Yudhoyono Presidency: Indonesia's Decade of Stability and Stagnation*. Singapore: ISEAS, pp. 155–74.

Bertelsmann Stiftung. (2018). BTI 2018: Indonesia Country Report. Available at: www.bti-project.org/en/reports/country-reports/detail/itc/IDN/ [Accessed 22 June 2019].

Bertrand, J. (2004). *Nationalism and Ethnic Conflict in Indonesia*. Cambridge: Cambridge University Press.

Booth, A. (2002). Growth collapses in Indonesia: A comparison of the 1930s and the 1990s. *Itinerario*, 26(3–4), 73–99.

Bresnan, J. (1993). *Managing Indonesia: The Modern Political Economy*. New York: Columbia University Press.

Buehler, M. (2010). Decentralisation and local democracy in Indonesia: The marginalisation of the public sphere. In E. Aspinall, and M. Mietzner, eds., *Problems of Democratisation in Indonesia: Elections, Institutions and Society*.

Bush, R. (2015). Religious politics and minority rights during the Yudhoyono presidency. In E. Aspinall, M. Mietzner, and D. Tomsa, eds., *The Yudhoyono Presidency: Indonesia's Decade of Stability and Stagnation*. Singapore: ISEAS, pp. 239–57.

Butt, S., and Lindsey, T. (2011). Judicial mafia: The courts and state illegality in Indonesia. In E. Aspinall and G. van Klinken, eds., *The State and Illegality in Indonesia*. Leiden: KITLV Press, pp. 189–213.

Carbone, G. (2015). Democratisation as a state-building mechanism: A preliminary discussion of an understudied relationship. *Political Studies Review*, 13, 11–21.

Croissant, A., and Hellmann, O. (2018). Introduction: State capacity and elections in the study of authoritarian regimes. *International Political Science Review*, 39(1), 3–16.

Crouch, H. (1978). *The Army and Politics in Indonesia*. Ithaca: Cornell University Press.

Crouch, H. (1979). Patrimonialism and military rule in Indonesia. *World Politics*, 31(4), 571–87.

Darden, K. (2008). The integrity of corrupt states: Graft as an informal state institution. *Politics & Society*, 36(1), 35–60.

De Mello, L. (2008). *Indonesia: Growth Performance and Policy Challenges, Working Paper*. Paris: OECD Publishing.

Freedom House. (2019). Freedom in the World 2019. Available at: https://freedomhouse.org/report/freedom-world/2019/indonesia [Accessed 22 June 2019].

Global Firepower. (2015). Indonesia's military strength. Available at: www.globalfirepower.com [Accessed 30 October 2015].

Hadiz, V. R. (2010). *Localising Power in Post-Authoritarian Indonesia: A Southeast Asia Perspective*. Stanford: Stanford University Press.

Hadiz, V. R., and Robison, R. (2014). The political economy of oligarchy and the reorganization of power in Indonesia. In M. Ford and T. B. Pepinsky, eds., *Beyond Oligarchy: Wealth, Power and Contemporary Indonesian Politics*. Ithaca: Cornell Southeast Asia Program, pp. 35–56.

Hamid, U. (2015). Social media and the quality of freedom of expression in Indonesia: Evidence from the field. Unpublished manuscript.

Hanson, J. K., and Sigman, R. (2013). Leviathan's latent dimensions: Measuring state capacity for comparative political research. Unpublished manuscript.

Hill, H. (1994). The economy. In H. Hall, ed., *Indonesia's New Order: The Dynamics of Socio-Economic Transformation*. St. Leonards: Allen & Unwin, pp. 54–122.

Hill, H. ed. (2014). *Regional Dynamics of a Decentralized Indonesia*. Singapore: ISEAS.

Hirst, M., and Varney, H. (2005). *Justice Abandoned? An Assessment of the Serious Crimes Process in East Timor*. New York: International Center for Transitional Justice.

Holmes, S. (1995). *Passions and Constraint: On the Theory of Liberal Democracy.* Chicago: The University of Chicago Press.
Honna, J. (2003). *Military Politics and Democratization in Indonesia.* New York: Routledge.
ICG (International Crisis Group). (2008). *Indonesia: Tackling Radicalism in Poso, Asia Briefing No. 75.* Brussels: ICG.
Jones, S. (2015). Yudhoyono's legacy on internal security: Achievements and missed opportunities. In E. Aspinall, M. Mietzner, and D. Tomsa, eds., *The Yudhoyono Presidency: Indonesia's Decade of Stability and Stagnation.* Singapore: ISEAS, pp. 136–54.
Kapstein, E. B., and Converse, N. (2008). *The Fate of Young Democracies.* New York: Cambridge University Press.
Klinken, G. (2007). *Communal Violence and Democratization in Indonesia: Small Town Wars.* London and New York: Routledge.
Kristiansen, S., and Ramli, M. (2006). Buying an income: The market for civil service positions in Indonesia. *Contemporary Southeast Asia,* 28(2), 207–33.
Lowry, R. (1996). *The Armed Forces of Indonesia.* St. Leonards: Allen & Unwin.
LSI (Lembaga Survei Indonesia). (2017). *National Survey on Radicalism, Corruption, and Presidential Election: August 16–22, 2017.* Jakarta: Lembaga Survei Indonesia.
Markas Besar Polri. (2014). *Laporan kekuatan personel Polri, triwulan IV T.A. 2014.* Jakarta: Mabes Polri.
Melville, A., and Mironyuk, M. (2016). 'Bad enough governance': State capacity and quality of institutions in post-Soviet autocracies. *Post-Soviet Affairs,* 32(2), 132–51.
Merkel, W. (2014). Is there a crisis of democracy, *Democratic Theory* 1(2), 11–25.
Mietzner, M. (2005). Local democracy. *Inside Indonesia,* 85, 17–18.
Mietzner, M. (2006). *The Politics of Military Reform in Post-Suharto Indonesia: Elite Conflict, Nationalism and Institutional Resistance.* Washington, DC: East-West Center.
Mietzner, M. (2009). *Military Politics, Islam, and the State in Indonesia: From Turbulent Transition to Democratic Consolidation.* Leiden: KITLV Press.
Mietzner, M. (2014). Indonesia's decentralization: The rise of local identities and the survival of the nation-state. In H. Hall, ed., *Regional Dynamics in a Decentralized Indonesia.* Singapore: ISEAS, pp. 45–67.
Mietzner, M. (2015). Dysfunction by design: Political finance and corruption in Indonesia. *Critical Asian Studies,* 47(4), 587–610.
Mietzner, M., and Farrelly, N. (2013). Mutinies, coups and military interventionism: Papua New Guinea and South-East Asia in comparison. *Australian Journal of International Affairs,* 67(3), 342–56.
Mujani, S., Liddle, R. W., and Ambardi, K. (2012). *Kuasa rakyat: Analisis tentang perilaku memilih dalam pemilihan legislatif dan presiden Indonesia pasca-Orde Baru.* Bandung: Mizan.
Muradi. (2014). *Politics and Governance in Indonesia: The Police in the Era of Reformasi.* New York: Routledge.
Pramudatama, R. (2012). RI loses trillions in taxes from systemic corruption. *Jakarta Post,* 14 March.
Richburg, K. B. (1998). Will Indonesia be balkanized? *Washington Post,* 4 June.

Robinson, G. (2001). Indonesia: On a new course? In M. Alagappa, ed., *Coercion and Governance: The Declining Role of the Military in Asia*. Stanford: Stanford University Press, pp. 226–58.

Schmidt, A. (2010). Indonesia's 2009 elections: Performance challenges and negative precedents. In E. Aspinall and M. Mietzner, eds., *Problems of Democratisation in Indonesia: Elections, Institutions and Society*. Singapore: ISEAS, pp. 100–21.

Schreer, B. (2014). *Moving beyond Ambitions? Indonesia's Military Modernisation*. Canberra: ASPI.

Schulze, G. G., and Sjahrir, B. S. (2014). Decentralization, governance and public service delivery. In H. Hall, ed., *Regional Dynamics in a Decentralized Indonesia*. Singapore: ISEAS, pp. 186–207.

Seeberg, M. B. (2014). State capacity and the paradox of authoritarian elections. *Democratization*, 21(7), 1265–85.

Sherlock, S. (2015). A balancing act: Relations between state institutions under Yudhoyono. In E. Aspinall, M. Mietzner, and D. Tomsa, eds., *The Yudhoyono Presidency: Indonesia's Decade of Stability and Stagnation*. Singapore: ISEAS, pp. 93–113.

SIPRI. (2019). Data for all countries, 1949–2018. Available at: www.sipri.org/databases/milex [Accessed 22 June 2019].

Slater, D., and Fenner, S. (2011). State power and staying power: Infrastructural mechanisms and authoritarian durability. *Journal of International Affairs*, 65(1), 15–29.

Slater, D., and Simmons, E. (2013). Coping by colluding: Political uncertainty and promiscuous powersharing in Indonesia and Bolivia. *Comparative Political Studies*, 46(11), 1366–93.

SMRC (Saiful Mujani Research and Consulting). (2015). *Kinerja Presiden Jokowi – Evaluasi Publik Nasional Setahun Pemerintahan, 6–15 Oktober 2015*. Jakarta: Saiful Mujani Research and Consulting.

Tiwon, S. (1999). *East Timor and the 'Disintegration' of Indonesia. NAPSNet East Timor Special Report*. Berkeley: Nautilus Institute for Security and Sustainability.

Tjiptoherijanto, P. (2008). Civil service reform in Indonesia. *Comparative Governance Reform in Asia: Democracy, Corruption, and Government Trust*, 17, 39–53.

UNDP. (2019). Human Development Data (1990–2018). Available at: http://hdr.undp.org/en/data.

Webber, D. (2006). A consolidated patrimonial democracy? Democratization in post-Suharto Indonesia. *Democratization*, 13(3), 396–420.

White Paper. (1997). *The Policy of the State Defence and Security of the Republic of Indonesia*. Jakarta: Department of Defence and Security.

Winters, J. A. (2011). *Oligarchy*. Cambridge: Cambridge University Press.

World Bank. (2015). Worldwide Governance Indicators – Indonesia, 1996–2013: Government Effectiveness. Available at: http://data.worldbank.org/data-catalog/worldwide-governance-indicators [Accessed 18 November 2015].

9

As Good as It Gets? Stateness and Democracy in East Timor

Aurel Croissant and Rebecca Abu Sharkh

INTRODUCTION

Since it gained independence on May 20, 2002, the Democratic Republic of Timor-Leste (RDTL, East Timor) has strived to create a democratic and effective state out of the ashes of colonial rule, armed conflict and foreign occupation. With the assistance of the United Nations Transitional Authority in East Timor (UNTAET, 1999–2002) and other international actors, East Timor has undergone enormous state- and democracy-building efforts since the turn of the century. As a case study, the country therefore reveals important insights into the complex and unique process of simultaneous state and democracy building.

As unique as this development has been, however, in other respects, East Timor faces challenges that plague many post-colonial states, post-conflict societies and least developed countries. Foremost among these is the emergence of a commodity export-based rentier economy, weak state capacity, a volatile security situation, organized crime and gang violence and challenging demographics.

Despite these challenges, democracy has been surprisingly resilient. With a combined freedom score of 2.5 (on a scale of 1–7 with lower scores indicting higher levels of freedom), Freedom House ranks East Timor higher than any other Southeast Asian country (Freedom House, 2018). East Timor therefore represents an unusual mix of fragile stateness but, given the circumstances, a relatively well-developed democracy. This chapter will investigate the reasons for and the implications of this unexpected combination. In doing so, the rest of the chapter is organized as follows: The next section provides an overview of the trajectories and legacies of Portuguese colonialism, Indonesian occupation and the United Nations (UN) interregnum for state-building and democratization in East Timor. The second and third sections examine East Timor's stateness and the quality of its democracy in the post-UNTAET period. We then consider how fragile stateness and low-quality democracy are intertwined in the specific context of East Timor. The final section presents the chapter's conclusions and discusses the relevance of the findings for the comparative research on stateness and democracy in Asia.

LEGACIES OF COLONIALISM, OCCUPATION AND THE INTERNATIONAL INTERIM ADMINISTRATION

Even though Portuguese merchants and Dominican friars had established permanent outposts on the eastern part of the island of Timor since the sixteenth century, the Portuguese exercised little territorial control beyond a few trading posts and mission stations. Due to this tenuous nature of Portuguese rule, the colonial state relied heavily on the co-optation of or co-operation with local rulers (*liurai*). It was only in the late nineteenth century that the state expanded its control through a series of military excursions meant to subdue local rulers and impose a unified and direct administration (Schlichter, 1996: 229–83; Taylor, 1999). When East Timor was granted the status of an overseas province with greater fiscal and administrative autonomy, the 'Timorization' of the colonial state in the 1960s opened up its civil administration and military service to locals. Yet this policy primarily benefited the 'latinized-creole' elite (see Gunn, 2001), while the majority of the population retained traditional Timorese customs, beliefs and languages (Guterres, 2006: 116). As such, the Timorese social structure was divided, and it limited the emergence of a coherent national identity. Moreover, Timorization did little to improve East Timor's rudimentary public services, weak state capacity and economic backwardness, resulting in living conditions that hardly differed from those at the beginning of colonization (Guterres, 2006: 116).

The 'Carnation Revolution' in Portugal in April 1974 triggered a wave of political mobilization in Portuguese-Timor. Several political parties were founded, of which the *Frente Revolucionária do Timor-Leste Independente* (Fretilin) was – and has remained – the most influential. Conflict between the left-nationalist Fretilin and other parties, most notably the pro-Portuguese *União Democrática Timorense* (UDT) and the pro-Indonesian APODETI, culminated in August 1975 in a brief civil war. Fretilin emerged as the victorious party (Lawless, 1976), subsequently declaring independence. This served the Indonesian government as a pretext for invasion in December 1975. Following the adoption of a petition for annexation by a hand-picked Timorese Assembly, East Timor was integrated into Indonesia as its twenty-seventh province (Taylor, 1991).

The Indonesian occupation bore a 'two-pronged strategy' in which the Indonesian state engaged in both accelerated economic and social development and brutal repression of the Timorese (Moxham and Carapic, 2013: 3118). On the one hand, Jakarta built up government services, improved infrastructure and invested in agriculture, health and education. While poverty was markedly higher than in other parts of Indonesia, these investments resulted in high annual average growth: 7.8 per cent between 1983 and 1990 and an average of 10 per cent during the 1990s (Chesterman, 2002; Moxham and Carapic, 2013; Traub, 2000). Moreover, the introduction of a comprehensive and wide-spread education system marked the first time a large section of the population gained access to formal education.

On the other hand, Indonesian rule was marked by harsh repression and gross human rights violations (Croissant, 2016: 337; Jones, 2010). Lacking local support and immediately met with fierce resistance, particularly from Fretilin and its military wing *Forças Armadas da Libertação Nacional de Timor-Leste* (Falintil), the occupation took on a distinctly coercive character. Although the exact figure is disputed, it is estimated that between 120,000 and 200,000 Timorese – effectively a quarter to a third of the population – died from violence, hunger and disease at the hands of the Indonesians (Cotton, 2000; Traub, 2000).

Despite conflicts among local factions and exiled Timorese elites in Portugal, Angola and Mozambique, the Indonesian occupation had the effect of propagandizing a common history and group identity, in turn engendering Timorese nationalism (Bishop, 2002). In an effort to unite the various factions, political parties continually called for national unity, basing its mobilization on 'Maubere consciousness', a shared history of repression and economic exploitation (Bishop, 2002; Hughes, 2009).[1] The role of the Catholic Church was also significant for Timorese identity building during the Indonesian occupation (Borgerhoff, 2006), transforming from a religious institution of Portuguese oppression into a symbol of cultural identity and faith-based resistance to Indonesian assimilation (Bishop, 2002; Borgerhoff, 2006; Guterres, 2006).[2] Moreover, the Church propagated the use of the native Tetum language, unifying and enabling a nationalist discourse (Bishop, 2002). Somewhat paradoxically, the Indonesian occupation thus created the basis for East Timorese citizenship, as mutual suffering proved to be an important aspect in overcoming vast ethnic and linguistic differences. Disagreements between the Timorese diaspora and members of the independence movement on the ground remained, yet the organizational separation of Falintil and Fretilin in the 1980s and the creation of a National Resistance Council (CNRT),[3] which included various political parties as well as religious and social groups, enabled the formation of a broad national movement (Guterres, 2006: 127).

---

[1] From *mau bere*, or 'my brother', a local greeting among the mountain people, which was used by the Portuguese as a derogative term for the primitive indigenous people of the interior, Maubere consciousness, or 'Mauberism', as invented by Fretilin and the Timorese government-in-exile, was an attempt to merge Marxist, nationalist and social democratic political strands under one unifying narrative and national identity (Hughes, 2009: 25; Shoesmith, 2003: 238).
[2] The share of Catholics rose from 27.8 per cent (1973) to 81.4 per cent of the population (1989, Simonsen, 2006: 577).
[3] Initially known as *Conselho Nacional da Resistência Maubere* (CNRM, 1986) and since 1998 as *Conselho Nacional da Resistência Timorense* (CNRT).

With the collapse of the New Order regime in Indonesia (see Chapter 8 by Mietzner in this volume), a new opportunity for independence arose. In January 1999, Indonesia's interim president B. J. Habibie proposed a referendum in which the Timorese could vote for autonomy within Indonesia or move towards independence (O'Rourke, 2002). In June, the United Nations Mission in East Timor (UNAMET) was created in order to conduct and oversee the referendum. While the Indonesian military was vested with the maintenance of law and order, UNAMET oversaw the referendum process with 600 international staff and an unarmed civilian police force. Although the ballot process was delayed twice because of internal disorder, and despite widespread violence and intimidation by pro-Indonesian militias (Beauvais, 2001; Jones, 2010), the UN-organized referendum on August 30, 1999, saw 78.5 per cent of voters opting against the Indonesian autonomy plan.

Yet even before the results were officially announced, local pro-Indonesian militias began 'Operation Clean Sweep' (Cotton, 2000; Croissant, 2008). Targeted killings of political activists and pro-independence voters were seen throughout the island, leaving between 1,500 and 3,000 Timorese dead and the majority of the population either displaced or forcibly removed to West Timor (Croissant, 2008; Huang and Gunn, 2004; O'Rourke, 2002: 256–80). Moreover, an estimated 70 to 80 per cent of East Timor's stock buildings and public and social infrastructure were destroyed (Beauvais, 2001; Croissant, 2008: 654).

On September 15, 1999, the International Force in East Timor (INTERFET) was ordered to restore peace and end the humanitarian crisis (Huang and Gunn, 2004: 22). Mandated to use all means necessary to do so by the UN Security Council, INTERFET began arriving on September 20, 1999, after which the Indonesian military and civil personnel as well as pro-Indonesian militias retreated to West Timor (Beauvais, 2001: 1103). While international fears of an emerging power vacuum may have been exaggerated (see Hohe, 2004), the sudden withdrawal of the Indonesian administration did leave East Timor in a precarious situation. Hence, on October 25, 1999, the UN Transitional Administration for East Timor (UNTAET) was launched, marking the beginning of a UN interim administration responsible for stabilizing the situation on the ground and establishing the necessary preconditions for the country's eventual sovereignty.

UNTAET's scope significantly exceeded previous UN peacekeeping mandates and was tasked with the threefold mandate of fostering political stability, ensuring economic development and creating administrative and democratic institutions. Unsurprisingly, this external state-building at the hand of UNTAET was multi-dimensional, diverse and, some have argued, a rather Herculean task (Butler, 2012). More specifically, the mission was given the responsibility to provide security and maintain law and order; establish an effective administration; assist in the development of civil and social services; ensure co-ordination and delivery of humanitarian assistance, economic rehabilitation and development aid; support capacity-building for self-government; and help establish conditions for Timorese self-government (UN Security Council, 1999, cited in Chesterman, 2002). UNTAET thus possessed full de jure and de facto legislative, executive and administrative powers (UN Security Council, 1999, cited in Chesterman, 2002) and marked the first time an international administration exercised full sovereignty over a territory (see Chopra, 2002).

The legacies of UNTAET are contested among scholars, yet many would agree that UNTAET suffered from 'an underlying tension between the mandate to govern East Timor and a longer-term, strategic objective of preparing East Timor for democratic self-government' (King, 2003: 745–46). This duality led the mission to overemphasize short-term visible gains and resulted in the lack of a long-term strategy, especially with regard to state-building and power-sharing arrangements with the Timorese (Beauvais, 2001; Butler, 2012). Whereas peacekeeping, institution building and the creation of a political environment in which free and fair elections could prosper required centralized control, democratization and local capacity building needed to be built upon pluralism and power sharing agreements (Beauvais, 2001). Yet the latter was not adequately addressed. This also manifested itself on the sub-national level: the UN-imposed timetable provided insufficient time for the Timorese to adequately debate and reach conclusions on the structures of local government and land administration (Farran, 2010). One legacy of the UN mandate has thus been limited investment in the state administration and bureaucracy, as UNTAET inadequately engaged in capacity building and in equipping the Timorese with solid building blocks for stateness (Butler, 2012).

Second, and relatedly, UNTAET is charged with failing to properly include local Timorese in its political process. Although the mission attempted to integrate Timorese at various levels of the administration, as the UN Security Council resolution 1272 (1999) stressed UNTAET should 'consult and cooperate closely with the East Timorese people', the transitional administration retained all responsibility for the design and execution of policy (Chesterman, 2002). Even UN administrator Sergio Vieira de Mello admitted they 'could not involve the Timorese at large as much as they were entitled to' (cited in Chesterman, 2002). Thus, UNTAET's project of 'Timorization' was ill-fated (Butler, 2012), especially because it did not recognize the CNRT as an official partner, while the locals regarded the umbrella movement as a legitimate power (Hohe, 2004). This resulted in 'lopsided' state-building, one more reliant on UN governorship than local self-government (Beauvais, 2001: 1177). Failure to involve the Timorese was also seen at the sub-national level, which struggled to reconcile elected government structures with local customs and power structures and more generally convert its hierarchical and centralized construction into decentralization and local empowerment (Hohe, 2004).

As Good as It Gets? Stateness and Democracy in East Timor

Lastly, authors argue that UNTAET's poor decisions regarding the reintegration of Falintil fighters into the security sector engendered tensions between political factions and within the security forces in the post-UNTAET period (Chopra, 2002; Croissant, 2008). The UN's lack of understanding of Timorese political cleavages and social structures also contributed to an unequal dispersion of government development funds between the eastern and western parts of East Timor, creating discrepancies between the regions in terms of administration and available public services. Moreover, while UNTAET organized free and fair general elections in 2001, it was unable to prevent Fretilin, who had won control over the newly elected Constituent Assembly, from pushing its own constitutional draft against almost universal opposition from the other political parties (Croissant, 2014).

STATENESS IN POST-UN EAST TIMOR

Due to these difficult background conditions, East Timor's nascent democracy has faced considerable challenges in establishing its stateness. Upon independence in 2002, the country faced particular difficulties in two of the three dimensions of stateness that the editors of this volume distinguish in their introduction: the monopoly of the legitimate use of physical force, henceforth monopoly of force; and the establishment of an effective and functioning, or 'usable', bureaucracy. The capacity measure developed by Hanson and Sigman (2013), shown in Figure 9.1, demonstrates this. It is a general-purpose measure of state capacity that draws from a variety of indicators (twenty-four) representing the three dimensions of extractive, administrative and coercive capacity.

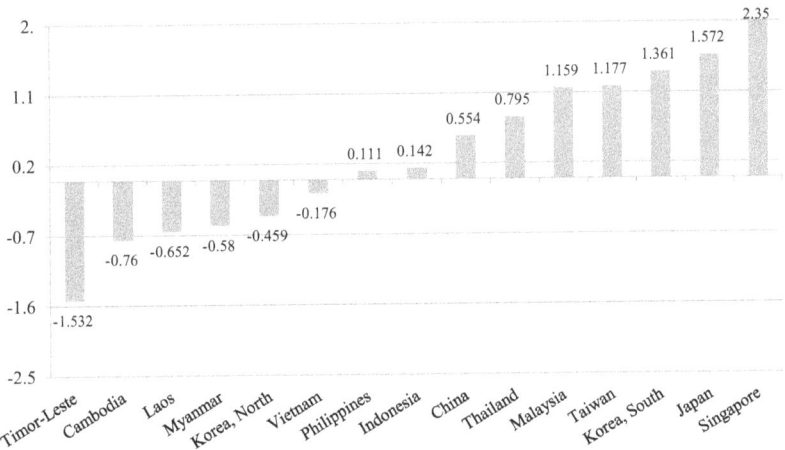

FIGURE 9.1. Average state capacity (capacity1 measure) in East and Southeast Asia, 2002–2010.
Note: State capacity is the value of the capacity1 measure developed by Hanson and Sigman (2013) in their State Capacity Dataset, version 0.95.

Considering these two factors, one observes very weak state capacity in the country, especially in regional comparison (cf. Figure 9.1). Although East Timor's stateness has remained diminished, one can also discern an improvement. Over the last years, the capacity1 measure has improved from −1.748 in 2002 to −1.252 in 2010 (most recent year available), representing the largest gain in state capacity in the region since the early 2000s. However, the measure does not include indicators that measure the strength of citizenship agreement and state identity – and it is precisely this third dimension of stateness that is relatively well-established in East Timor, for reasons discussed next.

Political Disorder and Monopoly of Force

The biggest challenge of East Timor's (re)creation of stateness after 1999 lay in the reorganization and enforcement of the state's monopoly of force. Aware of the difficulties of securing peace in a fragile post-conflict and post-occupation environment, the expiration of the UNTAET mandate was followed by the United Nations Mission of Support in East Timor (UNMISET). The UNMISET mission began on May 17, 2002, in order to provide assistance in securing political stability, providing interim law enforcement and maintaining the external and internal security of the country.

Initially, UNMISET confronted a number of security threats. Pro-Indonesian militias, which had retreated to West Timor, had not been disarmed by Indonesian authorities there and posed a potential danger. This risk waned quickly however, as the government in Jakarta lost interest in the conflict and withdrew its support for the militia. Deprived of financial means, the militia disbanded. Members either remained in Indonesia or returned to East Timor seeking political means to secure financial support by the government; others simply disappeared into the criminal milieu (Myrttinen, 2012).

Yet within East Timor itself, armed groups such as the Sagrada Família, Colimau 2000, the Committee for the Popular Defense of the Republic of Democratic Timor-Leste (CDP-RDTL), self-declared veterans, as well as so-called martial arts groups and youth gangs, posed security concerns (Myrttinen, 2012). Threats advanced by these groups were particularly acute because of the difficulty the UN and Timorese authorities faced in the disarmament, demobilization and reintegration (DDR) of a large number of Falintil fighters ('veterans') as well as the rebuilding of the security sector. Both during UNTAET and its successor mission UNMISET, the focus of UN efforts in security sector reform lay quite clearly on the police (*Polícia Nacional de Timor-Leste*, PNTL; see Myrttinen, 2012: 230). In contrast, the newly established F-FDTL (*Falinitil-Forças de Defesa de Timor-Leste*) was largely, and after 2002 almost entirely, controlled by the Timorese elite. As such, the officer corps of the F-FDTL was mainly recruited from Falintil veterans, whereas the PNTL was mostly comprised of former Timorese members of the Indonesian Police (POLRI) and only to a small part of former guerrilla fighters.

The haphazard DDR process and political interference in the establishment of the F-DTL are two major reasons for the continuing problems of the East Timorese security sector, which include a lack of civilian oversight of the military, a poorly disciplined police, regional cleavages and conflict between politicized military and police forces (Croissant, 2008; ICG, 2008, 2013; Kammen, 2011). The most significant setback so far was the near collapse of the F-FDTL and the PNTL in April 2006, during which fighting between the army and police, as well as civil unrest in the capital of Dili, resulted in more than 30 deaths and 150,000 internally displaced persons. The breakdown of public order could only be averted through the deployment of an approximately 3,000 troop strong International Stabilization Force (ISF) (Cotton, 2007: 476; Jones, 2010; Moxham and Carapic, 2013). The disorder eventually also led to the creation of the United Nations Mission in Timor-Leste (UNMIT).

Despite the failed assassination attempts by mutinous soldiers (so-called petitioners) on the then president Horta and Prime Minister Gusmão in February 2008, as well as recurring outbreaks of gang violence, the security situation has since relatively stabilized (Butler, 2012; Kingsbury, 2014). Since 2011, military and police forces have been responsible for policing throughout the territory, and 2012 saw the end of the ISF and UNMIT missions. Yet 'poor accountability, weak investigations, over reliance on large-scale special operations (generally featuring military backup), and weak crowd and riot control capacity' remain (IPAC, 2014:7). Since the early 2010s, a series of institutional reforms – including new laws on national and internal security, a defence law and the creation of a Ministry for Defence and Security that integrates military and the police – have been aimed at improving co-ordination and co-operation between police and armed forces. Still, occasional clashes between individuals from the police and the military suggest that there are problems of discipline, professionalism and impartiality of both the police and the army (Sahin and Feaver, 2013). Moreover, the conflict between political leaders and the 'neo-patrimonial'[4] character of the Timorese security forces, which are deeply factionalize by political networks and patronage politics, provide serious obstacles for further security sector reforms that could effectively strengthen both state and human security on the island (Croissant, 2018).

Basic Administration and Administrative Effectiveness

East Timor has also faced significant challenges in building up an effective administration, in large part due to a dearth of trained personnel (Goldfinch and Derouen, 2014) but also because of the prevalence of neo-patrimonialism as a key feature of Timorese politics and bureaucracy after 1999. The post-2006 period, mostly as a response to the April crisis, saw an

---

[4] For a definition of neo-patrimonialism, see Kheang Un's chapter on Cambodia (Chapter 6 in this volume).

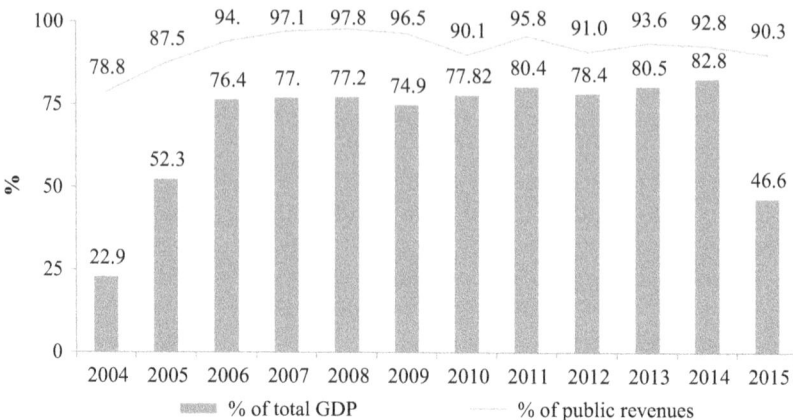

FIGURE 9.2. Petroleum sector in percentage (%) of total GDP and public revenues, 2004–2015.
Source: IMF (2009, 2013, 2016).

additional inpour of international experts, NGOs and institutions working to strengthen national capacity; yet the success of capacity and public service effectiveness building continues to be mixed (Goldfinch and Derouen, 2014). In addition to facing significant internal difficulties in building up its bureaucracy and administrative effectiveness, East Timor's administration is faced by challenges from without, most notably unfavourable demographics. East Timor has one of the world's highest birth rates and, as a result, a very young population (average age: 16.9 years; UNDP, 2011). With the share of the male population aged between 15 and 24 years at 44.2 per cent (2015) of the total male population over 14 years old, the country also constitutes the world's third largest male 'youth bulge' (UN Department of Economic and Social Affairs, 2015). Yet the country lacks the ability to provide such a large youth cohort with adequate employment opportunities, raising the potential of social conflict and contributing to social unrests and youth violence since 2002 (Curtain, 2006; Neupert and Lopes, 2006).

In this context, the boom in natural resources exports appears, at first glance, a welcomed development. However, East Timor has evolved into a rentier state, generating 90 per cent of its government revenue from the production of oil and natural gas (see Figure 9.2). The national economy is also largely dependent on the petroleum sector: only 23.6 per cent of East Timor's US$5.6 billion gross domestic product (GDP) is generated outside of the petroleum sector. Yet about half of this is due to state investments in public administration, procurement and infrastructure (Scheiner, 2015).[5]

---

[5] The recent fall in the proportion of the petroleum sector in the GDP reflects the slump in crude oil prices: from US$105 per barrel in 2012 to US$51 in 2015 (IMF, 2016). Mainly on account of this devaluation of global oil prices, petroleum revenue fell by 40 per cent in 2015.

The use of these revenues to fund generous severance packages for mutinous soldiers (the 'petitioners' of 2008) and the 'veterans' of the independence struggle, as well as creating jobs in the public sector and awarding contracts to companies with ties to key political actors, has sought to co-opt potential 'spoilers', prevent new outbreaks in violence and improve public service delivery (ICG, 2013: 3, 13; Leach, 2013: 160; Sahin, 2010: 356). The increased oil revenues between 2005 and 2013 reduced dependency on foreign aid. What has followed, however, is resource dependency, low investments in human capital and increasing public debt. The state budget approximately doubled from 2010 to 2015 (Scheiner, 2015), and public administration increased by 90 per cent from 2007 to 2013. However, infrastructure, governance and benefits (mostly for veterans), respectively, make up 35, 18 and 16 per cent of the state budget, and only 14 per cent is invested into education and health compared to 30 per cent in other developing countries (Scheiner, 2015). Lastly, only 2 per cent is invested into agriculture; although a large portion of Timorese engage in subsistence farming (about 27 per cent of the population) (Scheiner, 2015).

Citizenship Agreement

The shortcomings in the first two dimensions of stateness contrast with the strength of Timorese citizenship agreement and state identity. As Goldfinch and Derouen (2014) write, this is undoubtedly an outgrowth of the Timorese independence struggle: 'Timor-Leste is fortunate that it was borne out of an expressed will of its people, with broad support for the resistance and their role in government'. East Timor's strong citizenship agreement is made all the more remarkable considering the challenges of integrating formerly pro-Indonesian integration fighters, many of whom were involved in the devastation following the 1999 referendum. Joint Assessment Missions in the country stressed the need for reconciliation between the former militants and pro-independence fighters (Hohe, 2004), leading UNTAET to set up the Commission for Truth Reception, Truth and Reconciliation (*Comissão de Acolhimento, Verdade e Reconciliação de Timor-Leste*, CAVR) in March 2002, the first so-called truth commission in Asia. Huang and Gunn argue that local participation in the adjudication of crimes formed an integral part of the state-building process and contributed to increased citizen agreement (Huang and Gunn, 2004).

Nonetheless, while the Timorese state is recognized by its people as legitimate – reflected in the absence of secessionist movements or conflicts over citizenship – this should not be confused with the existence of a universally accepted conception of national identity.

As mentioned previously, the Timorese national identity emerged from anticolonial struggle and mutual suffering, yet as Arnold notes, 'While this form of nationalism may have been useful during the resistance era as a consolidating dynamic, interpreting that resistance history since independence has proven to be a divisive exercise' (Arnold, 2009: 444; see also Myrttinen, 2013). Tensions

TABLE 9.1. *Regional differences and inequalities*

	Percentage (%) of total population (2010)	Male youth bulge (2010)	Most frequently spoken language in percentage (%) of total population (2010)	Percentage (%) of population in poverty (2007)[a]	Infant mortality per 1,000 births (2011[b])
Western districts (Loro Munu)					
Aileu	4.1	36.9	Tetum (49.3)	68.6	94
Ainora	5.5	30.4	Mambei (61.5)	79.7	111
Liquiçá	5.9	34.8	Tokodede (61.7)	44.9	81
Manufahi	4.5	31.4	Tetum (56.9)	85.2	85
Ermera	10.9	35.0	Tetum (48.1)	54.6	98
Bobonaro	8.6	30.6	Kemak (43.7)	54.5	109
Cova Lima	5.5	32.6	Bunak (48.6)	49.1	97
Oekussi	6.0	27.1	Baikenu (96.1)	61.0	106
Eastern districts (Loro Sae)					
Baucau	10.5	31.1	Makasai (56.6)	22.3	99
Lautém	5.6	31.2	Fataluku (61.4)	21.3	83
Viqueque	6.5	26.1	Makasai (39.5)	43.4	103
Dili	21.9	39.4	Tetum (88.1)	43.3	60
Manatuto	4.0	32.7	Galoli (31.0)	73.7	79

Source: NSD and UNFPA (2011, 2012); World Bank (2007).

between the various resistance factions, former collaborators and self-declared veterans, as well as between older and younger cohorts, have emerged. Struggles over inequalities relating to resources, power and land disputes have likewise sprung up (Jones, 2010). These struggles have slowly taken on a regional character, revealing animosities between the west (*Loro Munu*) and the east (*Loro Sae*) of the country (Hohe, 2004; Jones, 2010). About half of the population lives in the western part of the country, but only approximately a quarter in the eastern.[6] Measured by the proportion of those living under the national poverty line and the infant mortality rate – indicators often used to measure socio-economic status and access to health care – the east of the country, with the exception of Viqueque, fared better than the west (cf. Table 9.1).

However, there does not appear to be systematic economic, social or political discrimination of a particular ethnic or regional group. Conflict between the two regions are historically rooted (King, 2003: 753–55; Trindade and

---

[6] The assignment of the districts to the regions is not uniform. Sometimes Manatuto is assigned to Loro Sae, while Oekussi, Dili and, at times, Manatuto are not ordered to one of the two regions. Since Portuguese colonialism, inhabitants of Loro Munu and Loro Sae are also referred to as Kaladi ('westerners') or Firaku ('easterners'). See Sahin (2007).

Castro, 2007), but the current frictions have only recently been articulated in politics and are used as political weapons (Guterres, 2006; Rich, 2007: 14–15; Saldanha, 2008; Shoesmith, 2012).

Quality of Democracy

It is widely argued that post-civil war societies are inherently more inclined to becoming dictatorships than democracies because the creation of stable political order – and not promotion of a democratic process – is prioritized (Jung, 2008). Yet East Timor has not given way to authoritarianism. In fact, East Timor's democracy is remarkably resilient and has fared well given the fragility of its stateness and the aforementioned challenges. Indeed, out of the eighteen post-civil war countries in which UN peace-building operations attempted to establish democratic governance between 1988 and 2002, ten countries still retain some form of authoritarian regime as of 2016.[7] Moreover, East Timor is one of only three democracies in Southeast Asia (Freedom House, 2018).

The following assessment of the quality of Timorese democracy is based on Merkel's concept of embedded democracy (Merkel 2004, see Introduction) that differentiates five partial regimes: (A) electoral regime, (B) political rights, (C) civil rights, (D) horizontal accountability and (E) effective power to govern. As we will demonstrate, democratization in East Timor has created a stable yet low-quality democracy. Regular free and fair elections, effective political rights and a reasonably well-functioning horizontal accountability coexist with serious defects in the rule of law, civil rights and the effective power to govern.

Electoral Regime

The electoral regime is one of the better functioning partial regimes of Timorese democracy. Since the end of Indonesian occupation, five parliamentary elections (2001, 2007, 2012, 2017 and 2018) and four presidential elections (2002, 2007, 2012 and 2017) have taken place.[8] The sixty-five members of parliament are elected through a closed list proportional representation system in one national district. The president is elected in a majority two-round system for a single term of five years. Non-party ('independent') candidates are permitted in presidential elections but not in parliamentary elections.

---

[7] Those are Afghanistan, Angola, Cambodia, Central African Republic, Democratic Republic of Congo, Haiti, Rwanda, Somalia, Tajikistan and Mozambique. The democracies include East Timor, Bosnia-Herzegovina, Liberia, Sierra Leone, Croatia, El Salvador, Guatemala and Namibia (see Call and Cook, 2003; Freedom House, 2016).

[8] Parliamentary elections in 2017 had produced a hung parliament. While newly elected President Francisco Guterres (Fretilin) had appointed Marí Bin Amude Alkatiri (Fretilin) as prime minister, the minority government failed to ram its budget and government programme through the unicameral parliament. In January 2018, the president called for new elections, despite pressure from the opposition who demanded the right to build a government of its own.

Since 2012, responsibility for the organization and conduct of the elections has rested exclusively in the hands of national election management bodies (EMBs): National Electoral Commission (CNE in Portuguese) and Technical Secretariat for Electoral Administration (STAE). National and international observers concur that the 2012 election occurred without significant evidence of vote buying, intimidation or other forms of manipulative election practices. Isolated technical and capacity problems of the national EMBs, spotty regulations of party finance and campaign funding (EU Election Observation Delegation, 2012), sporadic post-election riots by disappointed voters and threats by defeated parties not to accept the election results were seen, but the election was generally regarded as free and fair (EU Election Observation Delegation, 2012; Freedom House, 2015; Kingsbury, 2014). The presence of international observers, the fact that development assistance is coupled to accepting democratic standards and the consensus among the political parties that a peaceful election was a prerequisite for the withdrawal of the UN and the ISF all played a part in this (Beuman, 2016). While the last elections of May 12, 2018, had been highly contested, and the losing side claimed to have evidence for voter fraud and manipulation, the CNE rejected those claims. Finally, all political parties accepted the official results, and a new government under Prime Minister Taur Mata Rauk was inaugurated in June 2018.

The integrity of the electoral process coincides with a campaigning environment that allows for genuinely competitive elections. Although political parties of the coalition government enjoyed some incumbency advantages during the 2012 campaign – for example, disbursement of long-awaited veteran pensions and implementing a well-funded, nation-wide public works programme – East Timor is one of very few Southeast Asian countries with a level playing field. That is, ruling parties do not misuse their control over police, military or intelligence services in order to create an intimidating atmosphere for voters and candidates ahead of elections.

Public Arena

The overall positive assessment of the electoral regime largely holds for the partial regime of public arena. First, according to data from Freedom House and Reporters Without Borders, East Timor enjoys the freest press in Southeast Asia (see Table 9.2). This is the case even though the controversial media law of October 2014 created a government-sponsored Press Council that can fine journalists for 'undesirable' reporting, restrict foreign investment in Timorese media and request journalists to be accredited by the state and have minimum academic qualifications and professional experience (Freedom House, 2015).

Second, civil society groups (CSOs), non-government organizations (NGOs), professional organizations and labour unions operate in a relatively benign

TABLE 9.2. *Freedom of the press in East Timor and other Southeast Asian nations*

	World Press Freedom Index (Reporters Without Borders)		Freedom of the Press (Freedom House)	
	2002	2016	2002	2016
Brunei	38 (rank 111)	53.9 (155)	78 (not free)	76 (not free)
Indonesia	20 (57)	41.7 (130)	53 (partly free)	49 (partly free)
Cambodia	24.2 (71)	40.7 (128)	68 (not free)	69 (not free)
Laos	89 (133)	71.6 (173)	82 (not free)	84 (not free)
Malaysia	37.8 (110)	46.6 (146)	71 (not free)	67 (not free)
Myanmar	96.8 (137)	45.5 (143)	96 (not free)	73 (not free)
Philippines	29 (89)	44.7 (138)	30 (free)	44 (partly free)
Singapore	47.3 (144)[a]	53 (154)	68 (not free)	67 (not free)
Thailand	22.7 (65)	44.5 (136)	30 (free)	77 (not free)
East Timor	5.5 (30)[a]	32.0 (99)	21 (free)	35 (partly free)
Vietnam	81.25 (131)	74.3 (175)	92 (not free)	85 (not free)

[a] Data for 2003. Lower values in both indices indicate a higher degree of freedom of the press.
Source: Reporters Without Borders (2016), Freedom House (2016).

legal environment compared to the rest of Southeast Asia (see Table 9.3). Yet there are reports that public authorities have become more restrictive in issuing permits for demonstrations (US Department of State, 2015) and that individuals have been subject to harassment, detention or arrest because of membership to organizations recently declared illegal (Freedom House, 2015).

Moreover, the Internal Security Act of 2003 and the Demonstration Law of 2004 include provisions that, in principle, restrict the freedom of demonstration, information and expression (Guterres, 2006: 257–59). During the Fretilin government from 2002 to 2007, the 'friend-foe mentality' and the tendency to equate critique with opposition grew. However, pressure from international donors forced the institutionalization of national consultation mechanisms to allow for greater representation of civil society groups in a number of state planning and management units (Wigglesworth, 2010).

While the number of CSOs and NGOs expanded almost ninefold upon independence, and has enjoyed similar momentum since, much of this is induced by international donors and foreign NGOs. Domestic organizations still face many challenges, 'mostly related to weak institutional capacity, limited resources and centralized government decision-making' (Nur and Andersson, 2016). Moreover, not all of these organizations can truly be considered part of civil society, and some are of quite dubious character. These include a variety of 'veteran' associations that exert considerable influence on daily politics. Among these

TABLE 9.3. *Freedom of organization and association (Freedom House, 2006–2016)*

	2006	2007	2008	2009	2010	2011	2012	2013	2014	2015	2016
Brunei	3	3	3	3	3	3	3	3	3	3	3
Indonesia	8	9	9	9	9	10	9	9	8	8	8
Cambodia	6	6	6	5	5	4	4	3	3	3	3
Laos	1	1	1	1	1	1	1	0	0	0	0
Malaysia	6	6	5	6	6	6	5	5	6	6	6
Myanmar	0	0	0	0	0	0	2	4	4	4	4
Philippines	9	5	8	8	8	8	8	8	8	8	9
Singapore	4	3	3	3	3	3	4	4	4	4	4
Thailand	8	5	5	6	6	5	6	6	6	4	4
East Timor	8	7	7	7	7	7	7	7	7	8	8
Vietnam	2	2	2	2	1	1	1	1	1	1	1

Note: Freedom House measures the degree of freedom of organization and association in a country based on three indicators and sixteen key questions on a scale of 0–12. Higher values indicate a higher degree of realization of these liberties.
Source: Freedom House (2016).

are non-violent groups such as the *Associação dos Veteranos da Resistência*, *Fundação dos Veteranos das FALINTIL* (Falintil Veterans Foundation), the Association of Ex-Political Prisoners (ASSEPOL) and the Association of Veterans of the Resistance (AVR). The Falintil Veterans Foundation maintains close ties with Gusmão and President Ruak, whereas the Association of Ex-Combatants of 1975 is linked to Fretilin (see Rees, 2004; Simonsen, 2006: 592). There are also other organizations that purport to represent the interests of former resistance veterans. In reality, however, many of these organizations can be considered militarized armed groups or gangs, examples of which include *Sagrada Família*, *Colimau 2000* and CDP-RDTL (ICG, 2011; Simonsen, 2006: 593). As alluded to previously, such groups are immersed in criminal activities and more or less openly threaten violence in order to garner political participation and economic support. If anything, they symbolize the 'dark side' (Armony, 2004: 80) of social 'self-organization'.

Finally, East Timor has one of the most competitive political party systems in Southeast Asia. In the 2018 parliamentary elections, of the seventeen registered parties, all but four had formed party alliances. The main competitors, however, were, the Fretilin party and a four-parties alliance called *Allianca para Mudanca-e Progresso* (AMP). The Fretilin party under the leadership of Marí Bin Amude Alkatiri, a former secretary of state of the exiled government and prime minister of a short-lived minority government that had been formed after the 2017 general election, won twenty-three seats. The AMP was led by Xanana Gusmao, hero of the liberation war and prime minister of East Timor from 2007 to 2015. The alliance won thirty-four out of sixty-five seats and, thus, was able to build a new government. In one way or the other, these two individuals, and other former leaders of the liberation struggle such as Jose Ramos-Horta (Fretilin, president between 2007 and 2012) and Taur Mata Ruak (AMP, president from 2012 to 2017), dominated political competition on the island since 1999. The emergence of the Fretilin versus AMP party block conflict builds also around the conflict between Alkatiri and Gusmao (Aspinall et al., 2018). However, other political conflicts have also influenced party competition since and while political parties – and Timorese politics in general – are dominated by political strongmen, ideological and regional conflicts have a strong influence on the party system. This includes tensions between 'old' and 'new' elites, as well as between those who fought for independence in exile or on the ground (Guterres, 2006: 212–18; Myrttinen, 2008; Shoesmith, 2007, 2012). Nevertheless, it is notable that Fretilin's political stronghold lies is the eastern districts, where its residents, the so-called Firaku, claim that they suffered more under Indonesian occupation than the Kaladi of the western districts. Support for the ruling coalition government (since 2007), comprised of the *Congresso Nacional da Reconstrução Timorense* (CNRT) and other smaller parties, on the other hand, is particularly strong in the west, where the party is committed to the reintegration of those who collaborated with the occupying power or supported the Indonesian autonomy proposal (Croissant, 2016; Shoesmith, 2012).

The emergence of a competitive two-block system in East Timor contrasts with the experiences of other Lusophone countries, such as Mozambique, Angola, Cape Verde and Guinea-Bissau. Liberation parties in these countries – for example in Mozambique and in Angola – established post-colonial one-party systems. In contrast, Fretilin failed to establish itself as the hegemonic state-party. Fretilin won the elections to the Constituent Assembly of 2001, which enabled the party to create a semi-presidential system, even in the face of resistance from the other political parties and concerns by UNTAET. Nonetheless, Fretilin lost the presidential elections in 2002 and, since 2007, no longer possesses a majority in parliament.

Civil Liberties and Rule of Law

In contrast to the previous two partial regimes, civil liberties and rule of law constitute major weaknesses in East Timor's democratic quality. Frequent human rights violations include gender-based and domestic violence, insecure land rights and the excessive use of force and arbitrary arrests and detentions by PNTL members and military personnel (PDHJ, 2011). The judiciary is de jure independent, but many legal sector observers have expressed concerns about the de facto judicial independence of some judicial organs in politically sensitive cases (US Department of State, 2015). Deficits in the rule of law and the effective protection of human rights and civil liberties are also shaped by a lack of capacity and marginal accessibility to the formal judicial system. For example, the construction of a functioning justice system – a prerequisite for the establishment of the rule of law – is hampered by poor staffing. Until 1999, all prosecutors and judges originated from the other provinces of Indonesia. The lack of qualified local legal experts after the Indonesian withdrawal could not be compensated, and numerous senior positions are now occupied by lawyers from other Portuguese-speaking countries. This is also why Portuguese has been established as the de facto court language (Marriott, 2012). However, this impairs the population's access to the formal legal system. A 2009 study found that less than 10 per cent of respondents understand Portuguese; in contrast, Tetum is understood by more than 80 per cent (Asia Foundation, 2009). Moreover, the formal judicial system hardly extends beyond urban areas. Currently, there are courts in only four of the thirteen districts. Due to this lack of capacity and functional weaknesses, citizens are increasingly turning to informal dispute resolution mechanism. Yet such mechanisms are insufficient in guaranteeing human rights, especially those of women and other vulnerable groups (Asia Foundation, 2009; Marriott, 2012).

Moreover, the low prosecution rate, a large number of cases awaiting resolution and the political influence in 'sensitive' issues, such as dealing with mutinous soldiers, has engendered a culture of impunity and has damaged confidence in the system (Grenfell, 2011). Weak rule of law is also reflected in a low rule of law score in the World Bank's Worldwide Governance Indicators (WGI). The governance score for the rule of law indicator declined from −0.81 in 2004 (on a scale from −2.5 to 2.5, with higher values indicating better rule of law) to −1.17 in 2014. This score is significantly lower than the mean scores of other countries in the low-income group as well as the global average for democracies, and it is the second lowest in Southeast Asia (World Bank, 2016).

Horizontal Accountability

The partial regime horizontal accountability[9] reveals that accountability mechanisms in the country are generally weak, including legislature and prosecutorial agencies. Moreover, the abuse of public office remains a crucial obstacle for the consolidation of democracy in East Timor. Allegations of abuse of public office against high-ranking politicians and government members have increased following then prime minister Gusmão's strategy to 'buy' social peace after the social unrest of 2006 and the assassination attempts in 2008 (Grenfell, 2011; ICG, 2013; Wigglesworth, 2010: 233–35). Accordingly, Transparency International's Corruption Perception Index awarded East Timor a score of 28 (scores range from 0 (highly corrupt) to 100 (very clean)), ranking it 123rd out of the 168 reported countries (2015). Moreover, East Timor's Open Budget Index is rated 'minimal', suggesting little 'effective oversight provided by legislatures and supreme audit institutions, as well as the opportunities available to the public to participate in national budget decision-making processes' (Transparency International, 2015).

On the other hand, mechanisms of horizontal accountability have proven more effective than expected in restraining executive authoritarianism. The co-habitation of President Gusmão and Prime Minister Mari Alkatiri (Fretilin) from June 2002 to May 2006 contributed to political conflicts (Beuman, 2013; Shoesmith, 2003, 2007), yet the active role of the president as a watchdog of parliament and prime minister in the first turbulent years of democracy helped limit Fretilin's power. The following phase of a 'divided government' (June 2006–May 2007, with the Fretilin being the opposition majority party in parliament) was characterized by collaboration between president and prime minister. This resulted in strong alliances between president, prime minister and parliament, as well as the more restrained administrations of

---

[9] Horizontal accountability in accordance with O'Donnell, means 'the existence of state agencies that are legally enabled and empowered, and factually willing and able to take actions that span form routine oversight to criminal sanctions or impeachment in relation to actions or omissions by other agents or agencies of the state that may be qualified as unlawful' (1999: 38).

presidents Ramos-Horta and Taur Matan Ruak, which strengthened the institutional efficiency of the governmental system. After the 2007 election, the balance of power shifted in favour of the prime minister. The ruling coalition formed under Xanana Gusmão had the majority in the national parliament and supported presidents Ramos-Horta (2007–2012) and Taur Matan Ruak (2012–2017) (Beuman, 2013, 2016).

Although a more cooperative relationship between parliament and president has largely been a welcomed development in the country, from another perspective, it can be regarded as an obstacle for the consolidation of democracy, since measures to limit the power of the ruling party no longer exist (Croissant, 2016; Feijó, 2012, 2014). Notwithstanding this, parliament's ability to exercise supervisory and legislative functions is limited, and some analyses speak of a 'sleepy parliament' (ICG, 2013: 13–14). The national parliament's foci, however, do not lie in committee work, but in public debates. The president and opposition have since independence exercised their right to speak as a way to criticize and control the government (Beuman, 2016; Sahin, 2010).

Effective Power to Govern

Similar to other new democracies in Asia (see Croissant et al., 2013), East Timor also experiences substantial deficits in this last of the five partial regimes. While in many Asian countries this is due to legacies of military praetorianism, coup politics and military rule, in East Timor, effective power to govern has been marked by difficulties in establishing democratic governance over the security sector. In fact, the new democracy was poorly prepared to face the double challenge of developing solid institutions for the democratic control of the armed forces, the police and the intelligence agencies and also turning them into effective tools for the protection and security of its citizens. This resulted in a number of crises between the police and military, on the one hand, and the democratically elected authorities, on the other, reflected in the mutinies of 2006 and 2008. These conflicts, however, can be largely traced back to attempts by key political actors to manipulate factional conflicts inside and between the two main security services (ICG, 2008; Sahin and Feaver, 2013). Yet institutional reforms in recent years have contributed to a normalization of the situation and increased government oversight and civilian monitoring (Croissant and Lorenz, 2018). At the same time, the reorganization of the Timorese security sector has led to a notable personalization (instead of institutionalization) of political oversight. Many international and local observers also voice concern about the militarization of internal security and the nation-wide deployment of military troops for infrastructure projects, crime prevention, riot control and anti-gang operations (ICG, 2013: 15–25; Sahin, 2010: 351). Nonetheless, internal security has improved after 2013. While youth gangs, armed groups of self-declared veterans and rouge troops have in the past been able to resist the police and military and threaten the quality of democracy, there has not been a mutiny since 2008, and two prominent armed groups surrendered in March 2014 (Freedom House, 2015).

ON THE RELATIONSHIP BETWEEN STATENESS AND DEMOCRACY

In comparative democracy research, there is a consensus that functioning statehood is fundamental for the stabilization and consolidation of nascent democracies (Linz and Stepan, 1996). Weak, partial or ineffective stateness is commonly regarded as a disadvantage for successful democratization. This is because a state's limited monopoly of force hinders its ability to guarantee democratic rights and freedoms. Likewise, minimal administrative capacity complicates the performance-oriented legitimation of democracy. And lastly, a lack of citizenship agreement raises fundamental issues of the (im)possibility of the original constitution of the *demos* by democratic means. As Ivor Jennings (1956: 56) puts it: 'The people cannot decide until someone decides who are the people'. As the editors in their introduction to this volume argue, democratization may also have a causal effect on state-building, although there are contradictory views in the literature whether the introduction of democratic procedures is a driver for or a brake on state-building efforts.

So how has the process of stateness in East Timor influenced the development of democracy and, conversely, what have been the effects of democracy on the formation of stateness? The aforementioned descriptions of democracy and stateness in the country allow for three types of conclusions: (1) on the sequentiality of state- and democracy-building; (2) on the impact of democracy on the formation of stateness; and (3) on the effect of stateness on the quality of democracy.

THE SIMULTANEITY OF STATE-BUILDING
AND DEMOCRATIZATION

Unlike the sequentialism hypothesis (see the Introduction to this volume), the case study of East Timor shows that a coherent, functioning state is not a necessary precondition for democracy. As shown, state-building was carried out in two of the three dimensions of stateness (monopoly of force, usable bureaucracy) parallel to the development of democratic institutions. Only the dimension of citizenship agreement had been established beforehand. Nonetheless, although effective stateness may not be a precondition for democracy building, the case of East Timor does suggest that effective stateness may be precondition for a *well-functioning and consolidated embedded* democracy. It seems that democratic transitions under conditions of fragile, weak or precarious stateness lead – at best – to defective democracies, and at worst, to political chaos. This also applies to East Timor, although one can safely assert that the island nation would have been a candidate for the latter scenario if not for the international external assistance in virtually all key areas of stateness. Lastly, the case of East Timor also proves that even in micro-states and, with the help of immense and prolonged international efforts, the development of effective stateness is a lengthy and complicated process.

THE CAUSAL IMPACT OF DEMOCRATIZATION ON STATENESS

The impact of democratization on stateness is admittedly less established in current research, and the identification of causal relationships is more difficult to discern than the consequences of stateness on the development of democracy. Nonetheless, it can be argued – at least from an optimistic perspective – that democratization in the medium to long term strengthens state capacity in areas such as the rule of law, government legitimacy, welfare and security. This is supported, in principle, by the fact that state capacity did indeed improve in East Timor between 2002 and 2012. International comparative public policy research about the greater social-political efforts of democracies and the driving effect of democratization on welfare state policy in transitional states support such assumptions and are confirmed in the case of East Timor. At the same time, however, there are counter tendencies, which attest to the supposition that democratization exacerbates deficient or ineffective stateness, at least in the short term. Transparency International data and World Bank WGIs suggest that democratization until now has *not* resulted in stronger state institutions. Although there exists a somewhat higher degree of rule of law and protection of civil liberties now than during colonialism and occupation (i.e., until 1999), it must be noted that East Timorese 'illiberal democracy' (Merkel, 2004; Zakaria, 1997) has proven to be persistent and resilient.

Moreover, compared to the Indonesian occupation, democratization in East Timor has reduced the autonomy of the state bureaucracy from society. Democratization opened the bureaucracy to political actors and influential interest groups, giving them greater access to positions of power and the distribution of state resources. Coupled with weak accountability mechanisms, this increases the propensity of corruption and diminishes the bureaucracy's management and implementation capabilities. Nevertheless, it has also been shown that democratization can hinder state plunder. In contrast to authoritarian rentier states, such as Angola and Brunei, the government of East Timor cannot arbitrarily and freely – at least not without liability and accountability – decide over the use of oil rents. The use of the Petroleum Fund by the government is managed by budget laws and must be approved of by parliament, while CSOs and the media provide important watchdog functions. The coercive capacity, administrative effectiveness and bureaucratic quality of the East Timorese state are likely weaker than those of Indonesia. But the social acceptance of the monopoly of force is, most probably, significantly higher. In place of the strong yet illegitimate Indonesian Leviathan, a weaker but more legitimate state has emerged. East Timorese state bureaucracy may be less 'usable', but it boasts greater 'accountability'. Finally, democratization has introduced new opportunities for public participation in policy making, which in the long term improves the acceptance of state authority and helps strengthen state effectiveness.

THE EFFECT OF STATENESS ON THE QUALITY OF DEMOCRACY

The various facets of weak or limited stateness differ in their impact on the development of democracy in East Timor. Four causal relationships are notable. To start, a limited monopoly of force directly influences the rule of law and effective power to govern (partial regimes C and E) in an embedded democracy. Since state agencies routinely fail to enforce formal laws and regulations (crafted by democratically elected representatives), armed gangs, criminal organizations or local notables are able to implement their own informal rules at the local level – what Helmke and Levitsky (2004) call 'competing' institutions. Somewhat paradoxically, the participatory rights of democracy (partial regimes A and B) are respected, while the civil liberties (partial regime C) component of democracy is withheld from the local population: East Timorese can establish or join political organizations, vote freely and have their votes counted fairly, but they cannot expect proper treatment from the police or military. Evident also are the immediate effects of the lack of stateness on the quality of the rule of law. The rule of law guarantees citizens fundamental rights and the principle of isonomy of individuals, both against the state and from other citizens (Sunde, 2006). Yet these two protective functions are only possible when the state possesses both monopoly of force and sufficient institutional capacity (especially in the justice system). Yet it is precisely in this regard where considerable problems in East Timor exist.

Two further indirect effects of weak or failed stateness on the development of democracy are of note. First, the institutional capacities of states influence their ability to provide basic social services, particularly in areas such as health and education. Investments in health and education are positively correlated with economic development as well as the ability of the state to ensure property rights (Sunde, 2006). And in turn, higher education and social welfare are responsible for the emergence and sustainability of democratic institutions, again illustrating the two-way causal street of the two concepts (Boix and Stokes, 2003). Second, weak state capacity is associated with lower welfare benefit levels, a low ability to process socio-economic disparities and widespread poverty. The related problem of 'low intensity citizenship' (O'Donnell, 1999) thus holds a permanent destruction potential for democracy, as governments are exposed to the risk of losing the output-oriented, specific support of the population, until finally the democracy itself may no longer be regarded as legitimate.

CONCLUSION

Since the end of the UN mandate fifteen years ago, the quality of East Timor's stateness and democracy remains deficient. While defects in partial regimes C, D and E have persisted, democratic elections and the public arena (the 'core' aspects of polyarchy, cf. Dahl, 1971) are relatively robust and well-functioning. Yet, compared to the rest of Southeast Asia, the quality of democracy is clearly above average. As this chapter demonstrates, democratization in East Timor is more a surprising success story than acquiesced failure, given the difficult institutional and background conditions. Moreover, the defects of democracy in the country are associated with the nature of the Timorese state. The end of quasi-colonial rule in 1999 was accompanied by a near-complete collapse of state capacity – coercive, administrative, fiscal and symbolic. Even though clientelism, neo-patrimonialism and untamed politics upset Timorese politics, democracy as an abstract idea and democratic turnover of power have been accepted, both by the government and society more generally. This is the fact despite no prior experience of democratic governance, unfavourable demographics and economics and a history of twenty-five years of armed conflict.

At the same time, as a case study, East Timor speaks to the complex and multi-dimensional relationship between state and democracy building. Because of the unique simultaneity of these efforts, East Timor provides an important contribution to the 'state-democracy nexus debate', both theoretically and empirically. It has shown that stateness may not be a necessary precondition for stateness, but that stateness does – and in perhaps unexpected ways – shape the quality of democracy. Moreover, nascent democracy can have both welcome and unwelcome consequences for stateness, depending on the indicators and timeframe considered.

While scholars have noted neo-patrimonialism as the key element of Timorese politics and a main challenge of low-state capacity on the island (Aspinall et al., 2018), it is important to emphasize the success of democratization and state-building in East Timor compared to Cambodia, which is another prime example of externally led post-conflict reconstruction in Southeast Asia (see also Chapter 6 by Kheang Un in this volume). After all, democracy survived in East Timor but not in Cambodia. While state capacity is lower in the former compared to the latter, the development of state capacity in East Timor in the 2000s has been more positive than in Cambodia (Figure 9.1) – especially if we keep in mind that the higher state capacity score for Cambodia is mainly the result of the higher level of coercive capacity in Cambodia. Although a systematic comparison between the two cases is beyond the scope of this chapter, this study suggests that three factors seem to be particularly important. First, the differences in the nature of the conflict and the domestic constellation of involved factions might have played a role. While it is true that the main challenge in East Timor was to build a nation and a state from the ground up, the situation in East Timor differed from the conditions in Cambodia. In Cambodia, state and democracy had to be (re-)built after more than two decades of civil war; in East Timor, the struggle had been between a local liberation movement and an external occupation force. Within two months, INTERFET and UNTAET filled the power vacuum, which the Indonesians had left behind when they left in late 1999. Second, in contrast to Cambodia, there was one single interlocutor with which the UN interim administration was able to negotiate – the National Council of Timorese Resistance – rather than a number of hostile civil war factions as in Cambodia. Third, the comparison between East Timor and Cambodia suggests that simultaneous state-building and democratization can succeed if they are embedded in a comprehensive agenda for political, social and economic peace-building and Western governments and the UN accept long-term responsibility for guarding the development of stateness and democracy, even after the mandate of the UN interim administration expired. That had been the case in East Timor but not in Cambodia. Moreover, as the developments in post-UNTAC Cambodia and post-UNTAET East Timor suggest, if the international community ends too early, that is, before the roots of democracy are deep enough and before democratic institutions are strong enough to stand alone, then the entire endeavour of simultaneous state-building and democratization in post-conflict countries may fail.

Be this as it may, for the foreseeable future, and as the international community and the Timorese continue in their state- and democracy-building efforts, East Timor's stateness will likely remain diminished and its democracy largely illiberal. Considering not only the aforementioned challenges and tribulations but also that East Timor is Asia's youngest state, it might be as good as it gets.

References

Armony, A. (2004). *The Dubious Link: Civic Engagement and Democratization.* Stanford: Stanford University Press.
Arnold, M. (2009). Challenges Too Strong for the Nascent State of Timor-Leste: Petitioners and Mutineers. *Asia Survey,* 49(3), 429–49.
Asia Foundation. (2009). Law and Justice in Timor-Leste: A Survey of Citizen Awareness and Attitudes Regarding Law and Justice. Available at: https://asiafoundation.org/resources/pdfs/2008LawJusticeSurvey.pdf [Accessed 22 June 2019].
Aspinall, E., Hicken, A., Scambary, J. et al. (2018). Timor-Leste Votes: Parties and Patronage. *Journal of Democracy,* 29(1), 153–67.
Beauvais, J. C. (2001). Benevolent Despotism: A Critique of U.N. State-Building in East Timor. *New York University Journal of International Law and Politics,* 33(Summer), 1101–78.
Beuman, L. (2013). *Semi-Presidentialism in a New Post-Conflict Democracy: The Case of Timor-Leste.* Unpublished dissertation, Dublin City University, Dublin.
Beuman, L. (2016). *Political Institutions in East Timor: Semi-Presidentialism and Democratisation.* London and New York: Routledge.

Bishop, C. (2002). Constructing a Postcolonial Nation: The Case of East Timor, master thesis. American University, School of International Service.
Boix, C., and Stokes, S. C. (2003). Endogenous Democratization. *World Politics*, 55(4), 517–49.
Borgerhoff, A. (2006). The Double Task: Nation- and State-Building in Timor-Leste. *European Journal of East Asian Studies*, 5(1), 101–30.
Butler, M. J. (2012). Ten Years After: (Re) Assessing Neo-Trusteeship and UN State-building in Timor-Leste. *International Studies Perspectives*, 13(1), 85–104.
Chesterman, S. (2002). East Timor in Transition: Self-determination, State-Building and the United Nations. *International Peacekeeping*, 9(1), 45–76.
Chopra, J. (2002). Building State Failure in East Timor. *Development and Change*, 33(5), 979–1000.
Cotton, J. (2000). The Emergence of an Independent East Timor: National and Regional Challenges. *Contemporary Southeast Asia*, 22(1), 1–22.
Cotton, J. (2007). Timor-Leste and the Discourse of State Failure. *Australian Journal of International Affairs*, 61(4), 455–70.
Croissant, A. (2008). The Perils and Promises of Democratization through United Nations Transitional Authority – Lessons from Cambodia and East Timor. *Democratization*, 20(1), 649–68.
Croissant, A. (2014). Ways of Constitution-Making in Southeast Asia: Actors, Interests, Dynamics. *Contemporary Southeast Asia*, 36(1), 23–50.
Croissant, A. (2016). Ost-Timor. In A. Croissant, ed., *Die politischen Systeme Südostasiens*. Wiesbaden: Springer Fachmedien, pp. 335–82.
Croissant, A. (2018). *Civil-Military Relations in Southeast Asia*. Cambridge: Cambridge University Press.
Croissant, A., Kuehn, D., Lorenz, P., and Chambers, P. (2013). *Civilian Control and Democracy in Asia*. Basingstoke and New York: Palgrave.
Curtain, R. (2006). *Crisis in Timor-Leste: Looking Beyond the Surface Reality for Causes and Solutions*. Canberra: SSGM.
Dahl, R. (1971). *Polyarchy: Participation and Opposition*. New Haven: Yale University Press.
EU Election Observation Delegation. (2012). Legislative Elections in Timor-Leste, 5–9 July 2012. Available at: www.europarl.europa.eu/intcoop/election_observation/missions/2009-2014/2012_07_07_east_timor_en.pdf [Accessed 22 June 2019].
Farran, S. (2010). *Locating Democracy: Representation, Election and Governance in Timor-Leste*. Darwin: Charles Darwin University Press.
Feijó, R. (2012). Elections, Independence, Democracy: The 2012 Timorese Electoral Cycle in Context. *Journal of Current Southeast Asian Affairs*, 3(2012), 29–59.
Feijó, R. (2014). Timor-Leste in 2013: Marching on Its Own Feet. *Asian Survey*, 54(1), 83–88.
Freedom House. (2015). East Timor – Freedom in the World. Available at: https://freedomhouse.org/report/freedom-world/2015/east-timor [Accessed 22 June 2019].
Freedom House. (2016). Freedom of the Press 2016. Available at: https://freedomhouse.org/report/freedom-press/freedom-press-2016 [Accessed 22 June 2019].
Freedom House. (2018). Freedom in the World 2018. Democracy in Crisis. Available at: https://freedomhouse.org/report/freedom-world/freedom-world-2018 [Accessed 22 June 2019].

Goldfinch, S., and Derouen, K. (2014). In It for the Long Haul? Post-conflict Statebuilding, Peacebuilding, and the Good Governance Agenda in Timor-Leste. *Public Administration and Development*, 34, 96–108.

Grenfell, L. (2011). Promoting the Rule of Law in Timor-Leste. In V. Harris, and A. Goldsmith, eds., *Security, Development, and Nation-Building in Timor-Leste: A Cross-Sectional Assessment*. London/New York: Routledge, pp. 125–48.

Gunn, G. (2001). The Five-Hundred-Year Timorese Funu. In R. Tanter, M. Selden, and S. Shalmon, eds., *Bitter Flowers, Sweet Flowers*. Sidney: Rowman & Littlefield, pp. 3–14.

Guterres, F. (2006). Elites and Prospects of Democracy in East Timor. Dissertation, Griffith University, Brisbane.

Hanson, J. K., and Sigman, R. (2013). Leviathan's Latent Dimensions: Measuring State Capacity for Comparative Political Research. *APSA 2011 Annual Meeting Paper*. Available at: https://ssrn.com/abstract=1899933 [Accessed 22 June 2019].

Helmke, G., and Levitsky, S. (2004). Informal Institutions and Comparative Politics: A Research Agenda. *Perspectives on Politics*, 2(4), 725–40.

Hohe, T. (2004). Local Governance after Conflict: Community Empowerment in East Timor. *Peacebuilding & Development*, 1(3), 45–56.

Huang, R., and Gunn, G. C. (2004). Reconciliation as State-Building in East Timor. *Lusotopie*, 11, 19–39.

Hughes, C. (2009). *Dependent Communities. Aid and Politics in Cambodia and East Timor*. Ithaca: Cornell University Press.

ICG. (2008). Timor-Leste: Security Sector Reform. Asia Report No. 143. Brussels: International Crisis Group.

ICG. (2011). Timor-Leste: Reconciliation and Return from Indonesia. Asia Briefing No. 122. Brussels: International Crisis Group.

ICG. (2013). Timor-Leste: Stability at What Cost? Asia Report No. 246. Brussels: International Crisis Group.

IMF. (2009). Democratic Republic of Timor-Leste: 2009. Available at: www.imf.org/external/pubs/ft/scr/2009/cr09219.pdf [Accessed 22 June 2019].

IMF. (2013). Democratic Republic of Timor-Leste: 2013. Available at: www.imf.org/external/pubs/ft/scr/2013/cr13338.pdf [Accessed 22 June 2019].

IMF. (2016). Republic of Timor-Leste: 2016. Available at: www.imf.org/external/pubs/ft/scr/2016/cr16183.pdf [Accessed 22 June 2019].

IPAC. (2014). Timor-Leste after Xanana Gusmão. Available at: www.academia.edu/8005628/Timor-Leste_After_Xanana_Gusm%C3%A3o [Accessed 22 June 2019].

Jennings, I. (1956). *The Approach to Self-Government*. Cambridge: Cambridge University Press.

Jones, L. (2010). (Post-)Colonial Statebuilding and State Failure in East Timor: Bringing Social Conflict Back In. *Conflict, Security & Development*, 10(4), 547–75.

Jung, J. K. (2008). Mission Impossible? Democracy Building in Post-Civil War Societies. *Midwest Political Science Association Annual Meeting*. Chicago, 3–6 April.

Kammen, D. (2011). The Armed Forces in Timor-Leste. Politization through Elite Conflict. In M. Mietzner, ed., *The Political Resurgence of the Military in Southeast Asia: Conflict and Leadership*. London/New York: Routledge, pp. 107–26.

King, D. (2003). East Timor's Founding Elections and Emerging Party System. *Asian Survey*, 43(5), 745–57.

Kingsbury, D. (2014). Democratic Consolidation in Timor-Leste: Achievements, Problems and Prospects. *Asian Journal of Political Science*, 22(2), 181–205.

Lawless, R. (1976). The Indonesian Takeover of East Timor. *Asian Survey*, 16(1), 948–64.

Leach, M. (2013). Timor-Leste in 2012: Beyond International Statebuilding? *Asian Survey*, 53(1), 156–61.

Linz, J., and Stepan, A. (1996). *Problems of Democratic Transition and Consolidation: Southern Europe, South America, and Post-Communist Europe*. Baltimore and London: The Johns Hopkins University Press.

Marriott, A. (2012). Justice Sector Dynamics in Timor-Leste: Institutions and Individuals. *Asian Politics & Policy*, 4(1), 53–71.

Merkel, W. (2004). Embedded and Defective Democracies. *Democratization*, 11(5), 33–58.

Moxham, B., and Carapic, J. (2013). Unravelling Dili: The Crisis of City and State in Timor-Leste. *Urban Studies*, 50(15), 3116–33.

Myrttinen, H. (2008). Notizen zur Gewalt in Osttimor. In A. Borgerhoff and M. Schmitz, eds., *Osttimor am Scheideweg. Chaos oder Neuanfang?* Essen: Asienstiftung, pp. 27–31.

Myrttinen, H. (2012). Guerrillas, Gangsters, and Contractors: Reintegrating Former Combatants and Its Impact on SSR and Development in Post-Conflict Societies. In A. Schnabel, and V. Farr, eds., *Back to the Roots: Security Sector Reform and Development*. Münster: LIT Verlag, pp. 225–47.

Myrttinen, H. (2013). Resistance, Symbolism and the Language of Stateness in Timor-Leste. *Oceania*, 83(3), 208–20.

Neupert, R., and Lopes, S. (2006). *Demographic Component of the Crisis in Timor-Leste: Political Demography – Ethnic, National and Religious Dimensions*. London: London School of Economics.

NSD & UNFPA. (2011). Population and Housing Census of Timor-Leste, 2010, Volume 1–4: Population Distribution by Administrative Areas. Available at: www.statistics.gov.tl/category/publications/census-publications/ [Accessed 22 June 2019].

NSD, & UNFPA. (2012). 2010 Timor-Leste Population and Housing Census. Analytical Report on Education. Available at: www.statistics.gov.tl/category/publications/census-publications/ [Accessed 22 June 2019].

Nur, S., and Andersson, F. (2016). Free Access to Information and a Vibrant Civil Society as Cornerstones for Sustainable Development. Varieties of Democracy-Project Thematic Report. Available at: www.v-dem.net/media/filer_public/d6/9c/d69c4636-d0f6-4368-a307-04359e7456f6/v-dem_thematic_report_03.pdf [Accessed 22 June 2019].

O'Donnell, G. (1999). *Counterpoints: Selected Essays on Authoritarianism and Democratization*. Notre Dame: University of Notre Dame Press.

O'Rourke, K. (2002). *Reformasi: The Struggle for Power in Post-Soeharto Indonesia*. Crows Nest: Allen Unwin.

PDHJ. (2011). Joint submission from the Office of the Provedor for Human Rights and Justice and Civil Society organizations in Timor-Leste. Available at: www.laohamutuk.org/Justice/UPR/PDHJCSOSubMar2011.pdf [Accessed 22 June 2019].

Rees, E. (2004). Under Pressure. Falintil-forças de Defesa de Timor Leste. Three decades of Defense Force Development in Timor Leste 1975–2004. DCAF Working paper No. 134. Geneva: Geneva Center for the Democratic Control of the Armed Forces.

Reporters Without Borders. (2016). 2016 Press Freedom Index. Available at: https://rsf.org/en/ranking/2016 [Accessed 22 June 2019].

Rich, R. (2007). Introduction: Analysing and Categorising Political Parties in the Pacific Islands. In R. Rich, ed., *Political Parties in the Pacific Islands*. Canberra: ANU Press, pp. 1–27.

Sahin, S. (2010). Timor-Leste in 2009: Marking Ten Years of Independence or Dependence on International 'Assistance'? *Southeast Asian Affairs*, 2010, 345–64.

Sahin, S., and Feaver, D. (2013). The Politics of Security Sector Reform in 'Fragile' or 'Post-conflict' Settings: A Critical Review of the Experience in Timor-Leste. *Democratization*, 20(6), 1056–80.

Saldanha, J. (2008). Anatomy of Political Parties in Timor-Leste. In R. Rich, ed., *Political Parties in the Pacific Islands*. Canberra: ANU Press, pp. 69–83.

Scheiner, C. (2015). Can the Petroleum Fund Exorcise the Resource Curse from Timor-Leste? In S. Ingram, L. Kent, and A. McWilliam, eds., *A New Era? Timor-Leste after the UN*. Canberra: ANU Press, pp. 73–101.

Schlichter, M. (1996). *Portugal in Ost-Timor: eine kritische Untersuchung zur portugiesischen Kolonialgeschichte in Ost-Timor; 1850 bis 1912*. Hamburg: Abera.

Shoesmith, D. (2003). Timor-Leste: Divided Leadership in a Semi-Presidential System. *Asia Survey*, 43(2), 231–52.

Shoesmith, D. (2007). Timor-Leste. Semi-presidentialism and the Democratic Transition in a New, Small State. In R. Elgie and S. Moestrup, eds., *Semi-presidentialism Outside Europe*. London and New York: Routledge, pp. 219–236.

Shoesmith, D. (2012). Is Small Beautiful? Multiparty Politics and Democratic Consolidation in Timor-Leste. *Asian Politics & Policy*, 4(1), 33–51.

Simonsen, S. (2006). The Authoritarian Temptation in East Timor: Nationbuilding and the Need for Inclusive Governance. *Asian Survey*, 46(4), 575–96.

Sunde, U. (2006). Wirtschaftliche Entwicklung und Demokratie. Ist Demokratie ein Wohstandsmotor oder ein Wohlstandsprodukt? *Perspektiven der Wirtschaftspolitik*, 7(4), 471–99.

Taylor, J. G. (1991). *Indonesia's Forgotten War: The Hidden History of East Timor*. London: Zed Books.

Taylor, J. G. (1999). *East Timor: The Price of Freedom*. London: Zed Books.

Transparency International. (2015). Corruption by country: Timor-Leste. Available at: www.transparency.org/country/ - TLS_DataResearch_SurveysIndices [Accessed 20 June 2019].

Traub, J. (2000). Inventing East Timor. *Foreign Affairs*, 79(4), 74–89.

Trindade, J., and Castro, B. (2007). Rethinking Timorese Identity as Peace-Building Strategy. The Lorosa'e-Loromonu Conflict from a Traditional Perspective. DCAF (Geneva Center for the Democratic Control of the Armed Forces). Available at: https://issat.dcaf.ch/Learn/Resource-Library2/Policy-and-Research-Papers/Rethinking-Timorese-Identity-as-a-Peacebuilding-Strategy-The-Lorosa-e-Loromonu-Conflict-from-a-Traditional-Perspective [Accessed 22 June 2019].

US Department of State. (2015). Country Reports on Human Rights Practices for 2015: Timor-Leste. Available at: www.state.gov/j/drl/rls/hrrpt/humanrightsreport/index.htm?year=2015&dlid=252805 [Accessed 5 December 2019].

UN Department of Economic and Social Affairs. (2015). Population Division: World Population Prospects, the 2015 Revision. Available at: https://esa.un.org/unpd/wpp/ [Accessed 21 July 2016].

UNDP. (2011). About Timor Leste. Available at: http://hdr.undp.org/sites/all/themes/hdr_theme/country-notes/TLS.pdf [Accessed 22 June 2019].

Wigglesworth, A. (2010). Becoming Citizens: Civil Society Activism and Social Change in Timor Leste. Dissertation, Victoria University, Melbourne.

World Bank. (2007). Timor-Leste's Youth in Crisis: Situational Analysis and Policy Options. Available at: www.wds.worldbank.org/external/default/WDSContentServer/WDSP/IB/2008/05/07/000334955_20080507044213/Rendered/PDF/434800WP0ENGLI1hoinocrisis01PUBLIC1.pdf [Accessed 22 June 2019].

World Bank. (2016). Worldwide Governance Indicators. http://info.worldbank.org/governance/wgi/index.aspx – home [Accessed 22 June 2019].

Zakaria, F. (1997). The Rise of Illiberal Democracy. *Foreign Affairs*, 76(6), 22–43.

10

Stateness and Democracy: Evidence from East Asia and Cross-Regional Comparisons

Aurel Croissant and Olli Hellmann

INTRODUCTION

This concluding chapter offers reflections on the stateness-democracy nexus based on the Asian cases examined in this volume. We take up three themes that are central to the book. First, we synthetically discuss the state of democracy in the region. Is the glass half full or half empty, and how does the region perform in terms of democracy compared to other regions? Second, we discuss the state of the state in East Asia, again with a comparative view on other regions and the 'third-wave' democracies there. Third, what does the evidence from East Asia say about the debate between 'sequencers' and 'nexians'? Do we find tentative support for our main causal arguments, in Asia and in other regions?

THE STATE OF DEMOCRACY IN EAST AND SOUTHEAST ASIA

In sum, the seven case studies in this volume paint an inconsistent, even contradictory picture of the state of democracy in Asia. On the one hand, Asia has experienced a large number of democratic regime transitions since the mid-1980s, and the chapters on the new democracies that emerged in the Philippines (in 1986), Indonesia (1999) and in East Timor (2002) emphasize the resilience of democratic rule in the region. For all the setbacks, the third wave of democratization has made greater progress on democratization than previous waves, and there can be no doubt that the region is today much more democratic than thirty or forty years ago (Chapter 2 by Tuong Vu in this volume). Some of these regime transformations – especially South Korea and Taiwan – have made remarkable progress in consolidating democracy. Moreover, it is increasingly hard for regimes of any type to gain and exert political authority without at least some of the standard institutional trappings of representative democracy, such as regular elections and multi-party competition. With the exception of Vietnam, Laos, China, Brunei and North Korea, all Asian regimes commit themselves to the principle of popular accountability and political contestation. With the possible exception of Brunei, all claim to be realizations of popular sovereignty (Croissant and Lorenz, 2018). In authoritarian regimes such as Malaysia, Singapore, Cambodia and Thailand, incumbents and conservative extra-parliamentary forces may manipulate formal democratic rules and effectively deny the opposition a level-playing field, but they are not in a position to eliminate opposition forces.

On the other hand, the quality of some of these democracies is rather shallow. East Timor's democracy is classified as 'defective' by Croissant and Abu-Sharkh, and Marcus Mietzner's assessment of democratic quality in Indonesia produces the picture of a stable yet unconsolidated low-quality democracy, whereas the analysis by Kuhonta and Truong emphasizes the notorious weaknesses of Philippine democracy, despite the country's long history of competitive and (relatively) free elections. At the same time, authoritarian governments still outnumber democracies in East and Southeast Asia. And in the past two decades, the region experienced a number of autocratic reversals and democratic backsliders amidst the backdrop of economic crisis, contested national identities and deepening polarization. The consolidation of authoritarian rule in Thailand and Cambodia, the rise of religious extremism in Indonesia and Myanmar and the return of strongman rule in the Philippines and in other countries prompt reflection on how Asia serves as a laboratory of innovation for authoritarian practices (Dittmer, 2018; Morgenbesser, 2016).

While each country chapter uses a variety of approaches to examine the different partial regimes of the embedded democracy, they remain closely wed to the particularities of individual cases and are neither systematically linked to each other nor do they provide comparative assessments of the state of democracy on the cross-country or cross-regional level. For the purpose of this final chapter, which is to compare the development of democracy in the region and between Asia and other regions, we rely on data from the Bertelsmann Transformation Index (BTI). Updated every 2 years, the BTI provides numerical measures for 17 criteria and 49 individual indicators, which evaluate the quality of democracy, market economy and governance in 129 countries worldwide. Not included are countries that were members of the Organisation for Economic Co-operation and Development (OECD) by the year 1989, political entities that are not recognized as sovereign states, as well as, with few exceptions, countries with a population of less than three million (Bertelsmann Stiftung, 2018).[1] The BTI's democracy index is based on the

---

[1] Therefore, the BTI does not provide data for Japan, Brunei and East Timor. However, for the upcoming BTI 2020, the population threshold was lowered to 1.5 million, which means that the next round of the BTI will cover 137 countries, including East Timor for the first time.

TABLE 10.1. *BTI criteria, indicators and the partial regimes of embedded democracy*

Criterion	Indicators	Partial regime
2. Political participation	Q2.1 Free and fair elections	A
	Q2.2 Effective power to govern	E
	Q2.3 Association/assembly rights	B
	Q2.4 Freedom of expression	B
3. Rule of Law	Q3.1 Separation of powers	D
	Q3.3 Prosecution of office abuse	D
	Q3.2 Independent judiciary	C
	Q3.4 Civil rights ensured	C

Source: Croissant and Thiery (2009); Croissant and Merkel (2019).

model of embedded democracy (as described previously), although the project also provides scores for other indicators including 'stateness'.

Table 10.1 depicts the relationship between the criteria and indicators employed by the BTI and the five partial regimes of an embedded democracy, presented in the introductory chapter and employed as the conceptual framework in all seven country studies in this volume. The five partial regimes map onto the two criteria of 'political participation' and 'rule of law' and eight indicators. All indicator values are based on expert surveys and assign scores ranging from 1 (lowest) to 10 (highest).

Because the BTI indicators and criteria are highly compatible with the concept of embedded democracy, we refer to them in the following comparison of democracy trends in Asia and beyond. For methodological reasons, the data from the first BTI in 2003 cannot be compared with the data from subsequent reports. At the time of writing this chapter, the BTI 2020 data was not yet available. We therefore compare the results of the BTI 2006–2018.[2]

The BTI 2018 included 75 (out of 129) countries that had made a transition to democracy during the third wave of democratization, of which 14 (18 per cent) had reversed into authoritarian rule ('reversers') in 2017. Out of the remaining sixty-one democracies, only 14 (21 per cent) were considered democracies in consolidation ('consolidators'), mostly post-communist member states of the European Union plus three new democracies in Latin America as well as Taiwan and South Korea. The BTI classifies the remaining forty-seven cases as (highly) defective democracies (see Table 10.2).

---

[2] The observation period for each BTI usually begins on 1 February of the penultimate nominal year until 31 January of the year before the year shown in the title of the BTI. This means, for example, that the BTI 2018 covers the period from 1 February 2015 to 31 January 2017. The BTI data are therefore not recorded for individual country years but for time intervals that extend over three calendar years.

TABLE 10.2. *Third-wave democracies and current regime category (BTI, 2018)*

	Sub-Sahara Africa	East-Central and Southeast Europe	Latin America and Caribbean	Asia and Oceania	Middle East and Northern Africa	Post-Soviet Eurasia
Democracy in consolidation ('Consolidators')	–	Bulgaria, Croatia, Czech R., Estonia, Latvia, Lithuania, Romania, Slovak R., Slovenia	Argentina, Chile, Uruguay	S Korea, Taiwan	–	
Defective democracy	Benin, Cote d'Ivoire, Ghana, Guinea, Kenya, Lesotho, Liberia, Madagascar, Malawi, Mali, Namibia, Niger, Nigeria, Senegal, Sierra Leone, South Africa, Zambia	Albania, Bosnia & Herzegovina, Hungary, Macedonia, Montenegro, Poland, Serbia	Bolivia, Brazil, Dominican R., Ecuador, El Salvador, Guatemala, Honduras, Mexico, Panama, Paraguay	Bhutan, Indonesia, Nepal, Philippines, Sri Lanka, East Timor	Turkey Tunisia	Georgia, Moldova, Ukraine, Mongolia
Authoritarian regime ('Reversers')	Burkina Faso, Burundi, Sudan, Uganda		Haiti, Nicaragua	Bangladesh, Cambodia, Pakistan, Thailand	Lebanon	Armenia, Russia, Kyrgyzstan

Note: The table shows cases of democratization between 1974 and 2012, with at least three or more consecutive years of democracy. Regime and regional categories based on BTI 2018. Some countries experienced more than one transition towards democracy and democratic breakdown during the third wave (i.e. Thailand, Niger, Mali, Guinea, Nepal).

Source: The authors based on data from the BTI starting from 2006, www.bti-project.org/en/home/ accessed 20 July 2018.

A glance at the five partial regimes of embedded democracy in East and Southeast Asia shows that the gap between consolidators and defective democracies is smallest among the indicators of 'free elections' (partial regime A) and 'effective governance' (partial regime E), as well as 'freedom of association and assembly' and 'freedom of expression' (partial regime B). In contrast, defective democracies perform significantly worse on those indicators that measure the enforcement of civil liberties or the independence of the judiciary (partial regime C) and on ensuring horizontal accountability (partial regime D). Thus, it is, above all, limitations in the regimes of 'civil rights' (partial regime C) and 'horizontal accountability' (partial regime D) that characterize the defective democracies in Asia (and elsewhere). The gap between the electoral components of embedded democracy in partial regimes A and B – or what Robert A. Dahl terms 'polyarchy' – on the one hand, and partial regimes C and D (the 'liberal' in liberal democracy), on the other hand, correlates with the findings of other studies (Shin and Tusalem, 2009; Croissant and Bünte, 2011). In other words, in spite of long-term positive advances of democracy in the region (compared to the decades from 1950 to 1990), East Asian democracies remain weakly institutionalized and 'illiberal' (see Table 10.3).

A second finding from the BTI data is also consistent with the results of the case studies: the quality of democracies (measured over the BTI scale) has declined significantly over the past ten years or so. The partial regimes B and D appear to be particularly fragile and prone to backsliding. Unsurprisingly, the already weaker democracies in the Philippines and Indonesia exhibit stronger losses in democratic quality than South Korea and, especially, Taiwan, which Kharis Templeman described in Chapter 4 as 'one of the resounding success stories of the third wave of democratization'. The relatively low and declining scores of Korean democracy, especially in the partial regime of horizontal accountability, reflect what Olli Hellmann in Chapter 3 describes as 'hyper-presidential government' and 'imperial presidency' (Hellmann in this volume). The partial regimes A and C, on the other hand, are relatively stable. Interestingly, this profile also applies to the authoritarian regimes in Asia. In the area of effective governance (partial regime E), even a weak improvement can be observed in both democracies and autocracies, which probably has to do with the declining role of the military in the politics of most countries (Croissant et al., 2013; Croissant, 2018).

How is the state of democracy in Asia compared to other regions worldwide? In the BTI 2018, there were six countries (Bhutan, Kosovo, Lesotho, Liberia, Montenegro and Serbia) that were not yet classified as democracies in the BTI 2006; conversely, eight of the democracies from the BTI 2006 were listed as autocracies in the 2018 report (Armenia, Bangladesh, Lebanon, Nicaragua, Russia, Thailand, Uganda and Venezuela). Furthermore, from 2006 to 2018, the BTI records a total of twenty-nine autocratic reversals and twenty-four democratic transitions, which corresponds to 6.5 per cent of all regime classifications in that period (Figure 10.1).

TABLE 10.3. *BTI scores for the partial regimes of the embedded democracy in East and Southeast Asia*

	2006 BTI Scores						2018 BTI Scores				
	Electoral Regime (A)	Political Rights (B)	Civil Liberties (C)	Horizontal Accountability (D)	Effective Power to Govern (E)		Electoral Regime (A)	Political Rights (B)	Civil Liberties (C)	Horizontal Accountability (D)	Effective Power to Govern (E)
Consolidating democracies											
South Korea	10	8.5	9	8.5	10	South Korea	9	7	8.5	8	10
Taiwan	10	10	9.5	10	10	Taiwan	10	9.5	10	10	10
Defective democracies											
Indonesia	9	7.5	6	5	6	Indonesia	8	6.5	5.5	7.5	7
Philippines	7	9	5.5	6.5	7	Philippines	7	7	5.5	5.5	6
Thailand	7	6.5	7	6	7						
East Timor	–	–	–	–	–	East Timor	–	–	–	–	–
Authoritarian regimes											
Cambodia	5	5	3.5	2.5	5	Cambodia	3	3	2	2	2
China	1	1.5	2.5	2	1	China	1	2	2	2.5	2
Laos	1	1	2.5	2	1	Laos	1	1	2	1.5	1
Malaysia	5	5	5.5	5	2	Malaysia	4	4	4.5	3.5	3
Myanmar	1	1	1	1	1	Myanmar	7	4	3	3	5
North Korea	1	1	1	1.5	1	North Korea	1	1	1	1	1
Singapore	5	4	5.5	6.5	2	Singapore	5	3	5.5	6	3
Thailand						Thailand	1	2	3	3	1
Vietnam	1	2	2	2.5	1	Vietnam	2	1.5	3	2.5	2

Source: The authors' calculations based on data from the BTI, www.bti-project.org/en/data/.

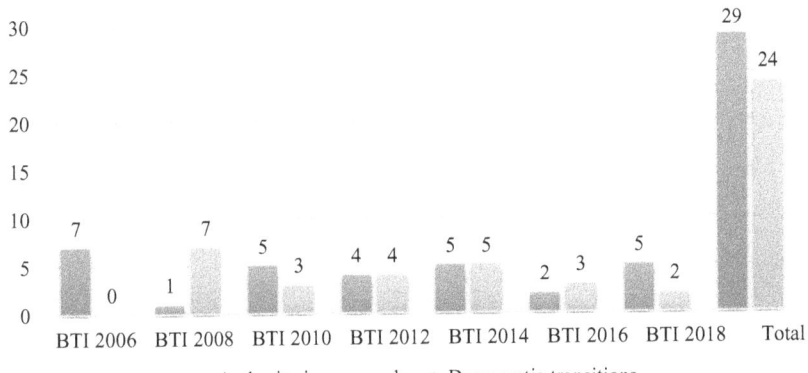

FIGURE 10.1. Autocratic reversions and democratic transitions according to BTI, 2006–2018.
Source: From the authors based on data from the BTI starting from 2006, www.bti-project.org/en/home/ accessed 20 July 2018.

The relatively high number of autocratic reversions is striking in comparison to the study by Haggard and Kaufman (2016), which for the years 1980–2007 finds a total of 73–79 transitions and 25–27 reversions. However, the authors themselves find that the number of reversions already increased significantly since 1994 compared to the period 1980–1993 (Haggard and Kaufman, 2016: 219). Apparently, this trend has intensified: fourteen of the twenty-nine re-autocratizations (48.2 per cent) recorded in the BTI took place during 2009–2017. Moreover, regime changes during this period tended to cluster among a fairly small group of countries: the twenty-none reversions are distributed among twenty-three countries, fifteen of which also experienced at least one transition towards democracy during the period under study. Thailand occupies the 'top position' (three reversions, two transitions), followed by Burkina Faso and Nepal (two transitions and two reversions each). In other words, such developments occur mainly in countries where political regimes of any type are likely to be unstable. While democracies in East and Southeast Asia do not appear more fragile or prone to autocratization than democracies in most other regions, a case like in Thailand, where democracy twice collapsed in a military coup d'état, is exceptional. The dominant mode of autocratic reversion in the early twenty-first century is through 'actions on the part of nominally democratic incumbents' (Haggard and Kaufman, 2016: 1–2; see also Bermeo, 2016; Huq and Ginsburg, 2018).

Unsurprisingly, defective democracies and democratic backsliders can be found in many regions. In fact, with the exception of post-communist East-Central and Southeast Europe, defective democracies are the rule in all regions for which the BTI provides data. Moreover, in all regions, the quality of democracy has noticeably deteriorated in recent years. In post-communist

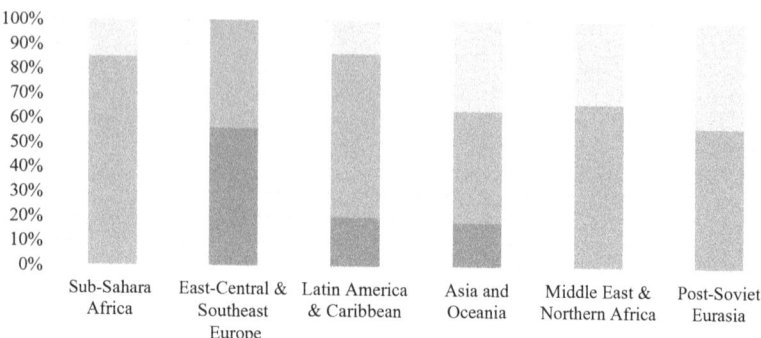

FIGURE 10.2. Consolidating, defective and failed democracies worldwide.
Source: From the authors based on data from the BTI starting from 2006, www.bti-project.org/en/home/ accessed 20 July 2018.

Europe, eight out of fifteen new democracies are consolidating, whereas in Latin America only three (Argentina, Chile and Uruguay) of the fifteen third-wave democracies are consolidating and two have already collapsed, whereas there are no 'consolidators' in the other regions (Figure 10.2).

From a comparative, cross-regional perspective, continuing difficulties and often deepening weaknesses of democracy, such as in East and Southeast Asia, are the rule rather than the exception. According to the BTI data, about half of all 'new' democracies in the BTI sample experienced a decline in one or more partial regimes of embedded democracy from 2006 to 2018. Prominent cases of democratic backsliding in post-communist Europe include Poland and Hungary; in Sub-Sahara Africa, most new democracies qualify as backsliders; the same is true for the Middle East and North Africa and post-Soviet Eurasia, the two least democratic regions in the BTI, and South Asia. In fact, at the aggregated level, all regions saw an erosion of political rights, civil liberties and horizontal accountability (see Table 10.4).

This includes tightening constraints on freedom of speech, media and assembly, often involving the concentration of power in the executive at the expense of the courts and the legislature, similar to what Guillermo O'Donnell (1994) and Wolfgang Merkel (2004) called 'delegative democracy'. In contrast, most regions perform best on indicators of 'free elections' (partial regime A) and 'effective governance' (partial regime E). Exceptions from this rule are Latin America and South Asia, where the effective power to govern of democratically elected governments and parliaments is often limited due to organized crime (Central America), armed insurgencies and religious extremists (South Asia) or other anti-democratic 'veto powers'.

TABLE 10.4. *BTI scores for five partial regimes of the embedded democracy by region, 2006 and 2018*

Region	BTI	Electoral Regime (A)	Political Rights (B)	Civil Liberties (C)	Horizontal Accountability (D)	Effective Power to Govern (E)
East-Central and Southeast Europe	2006	9.3	9.4	8	8.1	9.4
	2018	8.6	8.3	8	7.4	8.9
Sub-Sahara Africa	2006	6.7	6.9	5.5	5.2	5.7
	2018	6.6	6.2	5.3	4.7	6.4
Latin America and Caribbean	2006	8.5	7.6	6.1	6.2	7.8
	2018	7.6	7.4	5.7	6	7.3
East and Southeast Asia	2006	8	7.7	6.9	6.2	7.5
	2018	6.5	5.8	5.7	5.9	6
South Asia	2006	4.7	6.2	5.2	5.2	4
	2018	6.5	5.3	4.2	4.3	4.5
Post-Soviet Eurasia	2006	7	6.5	6	5	6.5
	2018	6.5	6.6	5.8	5.2	5.3

Source: From the authors based on data from the BTI starting from 2006, www.bti-project.org/en/home/ accessed 20 July 2018.

THE STATE OF STATENESS

States in Asia – while often as old as empires, civilizations and societies – are relatively new as modern states (Alagappa 1995: 36). As elsewhere, they vary substantially in terms of their stateness and capacity. As the chapters in this volume demonstrate, a high capacity, strong developmental state can be found only in a small number of Asian countries, such as South Korea and pre-2004 Taiwan. As evidenced in Chapter 4 on Taiwan by Kharis Templeman, the role of the state is changing in many ways, in part as a response to globalization and economic integration and partly because of changes in state-society relations as well as a shift from government to governance with active participation of civil society and the private sector.

In order to compare the levels of stateness and state capacity and the ways in which stateness shaped democratization outcomes in Asia (and elsewhere), we are utilizing data from the State Capacity Dataset v. 0.95 (Hanson and Sigman, 2013; Hanson, 2018). Hanson and Sigman provide annual estimates of the levels of state capacity along the three key dimensions of administrative, extractive and coercive capacity for up to 163 countries from 1960 to 2009.

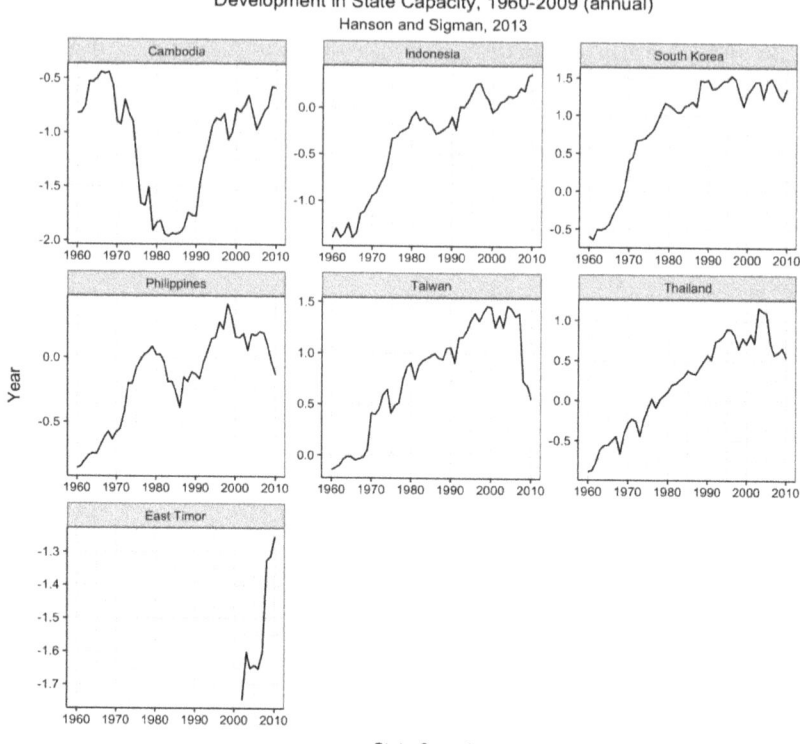

FIGURE 10.3. Development in state capacity in seven Asian societies, 1960–2009. *Source:* Hanson and Sigman (2013). We thank Jonathan Hanson for sharing their data with us.
Note: State capacity is the value of the capacity 1 measure.

This data indicates a steep increase in state capacity in Taiwan, South Korea, Indonesia and Thailand from the 1960s to the 1990s (see Figure 10.3). In contrast, Cambodia and the Philippines experienced a crisis of state capacity because of civil war and patrimonial dictatorship. And even as we are lacking reliable data for East Timor under Portuguese and Indonesian rule before 1999, it is clear that when the Indonesians withdrew in 1999, the administrative machinery was left in ruins due to the complete destruction of basic state institutions and the wholesale departure of Indonesian bureaucrats (see Chapter 9 by Croissant and Abu-Sharkh in this volume).

Further, as can be seen in Figure 10.3, the adoption of democracy correlated with a positive development of the state capacity in all seven societies, though this does not necessarily reflect a positive relationship in the sense of the 'sequencing' argument. As Templeman and Hellmann argue in their analyses, Taiwan and South Korea democratized not because of but despite strong state capacity, which gave authoritarian leaders the coercive, extractive and administrative means to manipulate politics and control society. Even though the data indicate a decline of state capacity in Taiwan and continuously high levels of state capacity in Korea, it is precisely the shift in the relative balance of power between state and society in favour of the later that explains why democracy in Taiwan is of better quality and more mature than in South Korea.

In Indonesia, a temporary crisis of state capacity, induced by economic collapse, paralyzed the Suharto Regime and kindled mass protests in favour of democracy, which the authoritarian regime then was too weak to suppress (see Chapter 8 by Mietzner in this volume). The resurgence of state capacity in Indonesia after the tumultuous period of authoritarian regime collapse and transition to democracy in 1998–2000 was perhaps a pre-condition for the survival of the post-authoritarian democracy. At the same time, however, it perpetuated the shortcomings of Indonesian democracy (see Chapter 8 in this volume). Similarly, the weakening of an already weak state in the final years of the Marcos presidency in the Philippines eventually led to the overthrow of the dictatorship. In contrast, factors of stateness and state capacity played a minor (if any) role in Thailand's transition to electoral democracy in the 1990s. Later on, however, relatively strong coercive, extractive and administrative capacities of the Thai state became associated with democratic failure because of the control of these capacities by the anti-democratic forces of the parallel state, as Paul Chambers explains in this volume. Finally, in Cambodia and East Timor, at least, it seems plausible to ascribe spiking state capacity in the 1990s and 2000s to the end of internal armed conflict and the state-strengthening efforts of the United Nations and international donors and development agencies.

The concepts of state capacity and stateness overlap to a considerable extent but are not identical. As we have argued in the introduction to this volume, state capacity specifically concerns the ability of state institutions to implement official goals and policies (Skocpol, 1985). Based on the literature on the stateness-democracy nexus, we highlighted three key dimensions of stateness: (1) political order and the monopoly on violence; (2) basic administration and administrative effectiveness; and (3) the dimension of citizenship agreement – that is, the attachment of citizens to the state. With the BTI data, we also have a valid and useful measurement of the degree to which stateness exists in modern states. The BTI data can be utilized to compare levels of stateness in democratic and non-democratic states in East Asia and across different regions of the world. To account for key aspects of stateness, we extrapolate three distinct indicators from the BTI's stateness criterion or the degree to which 'there is clarity about the nation's existence as a state with adequately established and differentiated power structure' (BTI Codebook, 2016: 16). The first indicator concerns political order ('To what extent does the state's monopoly on the use of

TABLE 10.5. *Cross-regional comparison of three BTI stateness indicators, 2006 and 2018*

		Monopoly on the Use of Force	State Identity	Basic Administration
East-Central and Southeast Europe	2006	9.4	8.6	9.1
	2018	9.6	8.4	9.2
Sub-Sahara Africa	2006	6.7	8.4	5.4
	2018	6.9	7.8	5.1
Latin America and Caribbean	2006	7.2	8.8	6.6
	2018	7	8.6	6.7
East and Southeast Asia	2006	7.6	8.1	7.5
	2018	7.8	8.1	7.6
South Asia	2006	5.2	6.2	5.2
	2018	6.4	6.4	5.8
Post-Soviet Eurasia	2006	6.3	8.1	5.8
	2018	7.1	8.3	7.0

force cover the entire territory?'), whereas the second indicators address issues of administrative capacity ('To what extent do basic administrative structures exist?'). The third indicator assesses citizenship agreement ('To what extent do all relevant groups in society agree about citizenship and accept the nation-state as legitimate?'; BTI Codebook, 2016: 16). Again, indicator values are based on expert surveys and scores can range from a low of 1 to a high 10.

Based on the BTI indicators, Table 10.5 shows the aggregated stateness scores for third-wave democracies (consolidating, defective and failed) in six different regions, including East and Southeast Asia. In contrast to the findings concerning the quality of democracy in the previous section, the new democracies in Asia perform much better (on average) than in other regions: only post-communist Europe exhibits, on average, a better monopoly on the use of force and basic administration. The extent to which the state's monopoly on the use of force cover the entire territory and the extent to which basic administrative structures exist are also highly correlated, at both the regional and the cross-regional level.[3] On the other hand, state identity and lack of

---

[3] Using average scores for the BTI 2006–2018, the two indicators 'monopoly on the use of force' (MoF) and 'basic administration' (BA) are strongly associated ($r = 0.8411; p \leq 0.01$). Since unchallenged domination over the means of coercion largely goes hand in hand with a firm administrative presence, we combine the two indicators by multiplying the country scores for each indicator and taking the square root (to make sure that low scores for the first indicator are not substituted by high scores for the second indicator). We then plot this composite MoF/BA index against the BTI indicator for citizenship agreement. The statistical relationship between the indicators for the three dimensions of stateness is still strong and significant ($r = 0.669; p \leq 0.01$).

citizenship agreement appear to be the weak spots of stateness in the region. This reflects the fact that, in a number of states, the dominant concepts of the nation-state are shared by large sections of the majority population but not by all minority groups. This is often accompanied by violent conflicts between the central government and ethnic-national minorities. Moreover, tensions between religious and secular norms and the influence of religious dogmas or their adherents on state and political institutions are often a source of conflicts over national identity.

However, regional averages cover the considerable variances within the region. Table 10.6 therefore compares the scores of the BTI 2006 and BTI 2018 for the individual Asian cases. Three broad categories of cases can be identified: first, states with high or very high scores in all three dimensions (South Korea, Taiwan, China, Malaysia and Singapore); second, (authoritarian) political systems with strong stateness on two dimensions but significant deficits with respect to state identity or administrative structures (Laos, North Korea, Vietnam); third, countries at a medium-strength level of stateness such as Indonesia, the Philippines, Cambodia and Thailand. Here, some groups question the legitimacy of the nation-state, the state's monopoly on the use of force is challenged in territorial enclaves and the territorial scope and effectiveness of bureaucratic structures is somewhat limited. In the region we are concerned with, Myanmar is somewhat of an outlier because stateness is clearly inferior to all other countries, regardless of the indicator.

Finally, neither in Asia nor in the full sample of 129 countries do democracies and autocracies divide neatly in two coherent groups. Rather, there is a lot of variation for each indicator within and across different types of political regimes. However, what can be found is that China, Taiwan, South Korea, Singapore and, though with a significantly weaker administrative capacity, North Korea and Vietnam exhibit similarly high levels of stateness. This group is almost identical to what American sinologist and historian Edwin O. Reischauer (1974) calls the 'Sinic world'.

At a first glance, the empirical evidence from the BTI data seems to support the view that state identity problems were and still are an obstacle for successful democratization in Southeast Asia. In fact, Indonesia (1998–2000), Thailand (since 2004) and East Timor (in 2006) experienced sudden outburst of ethnic violence and armed unrest during or shortly after the (incomplete) transition from authoritarianism to (electoral) democracy. Yet one can argue that outbursts of armed conflicts in democratizing nations of Southeast Asia are actually not caused by political liberalization and democratization but are triggered by the same set of factors as democratization – that is, destabilization of the 'iron-glade' authoritarian order, the failure of old nationalisms and economic crisis. Furthermore, anti-Chinese pogroms and communal unrest in Indonesia in 1998–2000 and the deepening of armed unrest in southern Thailand and southern Philippines has also been a by-product of competition between branches of a state's security apparatus for power and resources in the emerging

TABLE 10.6. *BTI stateness indicators in East and Southeast Asia*

	2006 BTI Scores			2018 BTI Scores		
	Monopoly on the Use of Force	State Identity	Basic Administration	Monopoly on the Use of Force	State Identity	Basic Administration
Consolidating democracies						
South Korea	10	10	10	10	10	10
Taiwan	10	10	10	10	10	10
Defective democracies						
Indonesia	6	7	6	7	7	7
Philippines	6	7	6	5	7	7
East Timor						
Thailand	7	7	8			
Authoritarian regimes						
Cambodia	7	8	5	7	8	5
China	9	7	8	7	7	7
Laos	8	8	7	9	8	8
Malaysia	9	9	9	8	8	7
Myanmar	4	3	3	9	8	9
North Korea	10	10	7	4	3	3
Singapore	10	10	10	10	10	6
Vietnam	9	7	7	10	10	10

regime (e.g. Gledhill, 2012). In fact, according to the BTI expert survey, the majority of Indonesians share a strong sense of nationalism and enthusiastically support the nation-state, though there are important exceptions (i.e. Papua). Unlike the authoritarian regime, the current democratic regime does not deny any particular groups (i.e. ethnic Chinese) access to citizenship. As a state with around 87 per cent Muslim inhabitants, Indonesia has traditionally struggled to maintain a balance between promoting Islamic values and the rights of non-Muslim minorities. In recent years, Islamist organizations such as the Islamic Defenders Front (FPI), who insist that Islamic scripture is of higher value than the constitution, have been able to inject their view into the national mainstream. The more liberal media environment, inter-party competition and the formation of new 'identity coalitions' comprising religious, non-government, security and party elites helped drive this development (see also Ziegenhain, 2018).

Similarly, a large majority of Filipinos accept the nation-state as legitimate and identify with the Filipino nation, though many Muslims in Mindanao see themselves more as *Moro* (the Spanish word for Moor, the Reconquista-period term used for Muslims) than Filipino. Therefore, they adhere to the idea of *Bangsamoro* (*Moro* nation). Following the transition to democracy in 1986–87, the government has made concessions in a multi-culturalist direction to offer significant autonomy both to indigenous cultural communities, whose rights are explicitly recognized in the 1987 constitution, and to the Mindanao Muslims (Abinales and Amoroso, 2005). While several peace agreements between the government of the Philippines and insurgent groups have been settled, implementation has typically been complicated by Philippine politics and political resistance within Congress (Hernandez, 2016).

In the case of East Timor, the limits of anti-colonial visions of the nation were exposed after independence in 2002 as new fissures and tensions developed (Croissant and Abu-Sharkh in this volume; see also Henick, 2014; Leach, 2017). However, some of these developments, for example, the 2006 political crisis that began when a section of the East Timorese armed forces claimed they had been treated less favourably than those soldiers and officers from the eastern part of the country, turned out to be temporary. The 2006 crisis and the tensions between the western districts (*Loro Munu*) and the eastern part (*Loro Sae*) of the country had more to do with rivalries between dominant political leaders, rather than the failure of national identity formation and lacking citizenship agreement.

Traditionally, Khmer identity manifests by separating itself from Vietnamese influences. Most Cambodians are Buddhists, though there are smaller ethnic minorities such as Muslim Cham, ethnic Vietnamese and Montagnard minorities living in Cambodia's northeastern provinces. The long-standing enmity between Cambodia and Vietnam and the Vietnamese occupation from 1979 until 1985 fostered strong anti-Vietnamese resentments among Cambodians. From 1979 to 1991, the ruling Cambodian People's Party (CPP) was dependent on military and economic patronage by Vietnam, while a strong

'Anti-Vietnamism' was one of the few things that had held the fragile opposition alliance together. Today, anti-Vietnamese sentiment is omnipresent among opposition politicians and even in civil society. Especially during election times, the competition between the CPP and the opposition, who accuses the government of collusion with Hanoi, fuels hostile sentiments against the *Yuon* (a derogative term used for Vietnamese in general) (Millar, 2016; Chapter 6 in this volume).

As mentioned by Paul Chambers in Chapter 5, the state-sponsored conception of national identity in Thailand is based on a constructed notion of Thainess, which has both assimilated (forcefully) and integrated other minorities into the mono-ethnic state. Although the legitimacy of the Thai nation-state is questioned by few, the biggest challenge to the legitimacy of the Thai nation-state continues to come from the Malay-Muslim insurgencies in the four southernmost provinces of Satun, Pattani, Yala and Narathiwat. While the conflict had been described as 'waning' and 'relatively quiet' in the 1990s, it re-emerged when in the early 2000s the government of Prime Minister Thaksin Shinawatra tried to impose greater central control over a region traditionally dominated by his main opponent, the Democratic Party (Croissant, 2005). From 2004, when the insurgency recently intensified, to late 2016, almost 7,000 people were killed and at least 12,000 were wounded due to violence in the region (International Crisis Group, 2017). The southern conflict in Thailand is perhaps the most impressive Southeast Asian example of the relationship between incomplete democratization, unsolved national identity problems and the onset of domestic armed conflict.

By comparison, the open contestation over Taiwanese identity for three decades after democratization has led to a newly consolidated identity on the island that is more Taiwanese than Chinese. As Templeman explains in Chapter 4, after the lifting of martial law in 1987, residents of Taiwan began a long debate over their national identity. Eventually, a 'new Taiwanese' identity emerged, which is defined less in terms of ethnicity and more as a commitment to the island's new civic values and democratic institutions. Finally, in South Korea, state identity had long been shaped by anti-communism (on the Right or in the conservative spectrum of society) and anti-colonialism (i.e., anti-Americanism) on the Left or liberal/progressive side of the political spectrum. Since the 1990s, however, North Korea has become less an identity concern than a security and economic one (Rozman, 2012: 68–69).

THE STATENESS-DEMOCRACY NEXUS: REFLECTING
ON PATTERNS AND MECHANISMS

As argued in the introduction to this volume, the stateness-democracy nexus is too complex to be comprehensively explained on the basis of statistical analyses. Specifically, we made the case that both stateness and democracy are multi-dimensional concepts that cannot be captured by single quantitative indicators. Based on our methodological critique of the existing literature on the stateness-democracy nexus, the different contributions to this volume have applied qualitative methods of inquiry, drawing on empirical evidence from East Asian countries that embarked on processes of political liberalization during the third wave of democratization. East Asia lends itself to a small-N comparative analysis, as political systems in the region display great variation on the two variables in question: stateness and the quality of democracy. For one, we find high-capacity 'developmental' states (South Korea and Taiwan) next to low-capacity 'predatory' states (e.g. Cambodia, East Timor), with a number of intermediate states positioned between the two extremes (e.g. Thailand, Indonesia). Moreover, in terms of democratic transition processes, we can observe three different outcomes across political systems in East Asia: consolidated democracies, defective democracy and autocratic reversal. By comparing these different outcomes, we are able to develop a number of conclusions that will further our understanding of the stateness-democracy nexus not only in East Asia but more generally in the developing world.

DEMOCRATIC CONSOLIDATION: NOT A LINEAR PROCESS

The sample of third-wave democracies analysed in this volume contains two outstandingly successful cases of democratic consolidation: South Korea and Taiwan. Compared with other parts of the developing world, only three other countries – Chile, Uruguay and Argentina – have performed at similarly high levels when scrutinized through the 'embedded democracy' framework (see Table 10.2). As the chapters by Hellmann and Templeman as well as the BTI indicators (see Table 10.3) show, all partial regimes display a high degree of consolidation – even though there remain problems with horizontal accountability (both Korea and Taiwan) as well as civil society (Korea) and the civil rights regime (Taiwan).

Moreover, both South Korea and Taiwan stand out from other late democratizers in the developing world in that their political systems are based on strong foundations of stateness. Specifically, in both countries, the state exercises high levels of coercive and administrative capacity, and there is (almost) unanimous agreement among citizens that the state possesses legitimate authority. Taken together, then, the cases of South Korea and Taiwan seem to support the sequentialist argument: higher levels of stateness facilitate the deepening of democratic rule. This conclusion is further evoked by the fact that Chile, Uruguay and Argentina – the only other cases of successful democratization in the developing world – also feature comparatively high levels of stateness.

As the case studies in this volume have shown, however, there is by no means a linear relationship between stateness and the quality of democracy. Certainly, high degrees of coercive capacity, administrative capacity and citizen agreement helped state authorities – both in South Korea and Taiwan – to enforce policies and legal regulations that were key to the consolidation of the different partial regimes of democracy. Yet, by taking an empirically rich historical perspective, the case studies also reveal how, initially, the introduction of free and fair elections led to a decline in stateness – in particular, on the dimension administrative capacity. While Hellmann outlines how, in South Korea, the exploding demand for political finance created strong incentives for politicians to engage in corrupt behaviour and grow their collusive relationships with private business, Templeman explains how the Kuomintang (KMT) – facing mounting electoral pressure – expanded its vote-buying networks and increasingly resorted to the misuse of public resources to support its campaign activities. It was only when vertical accountability mechanisms – boosted by greater media freedom and widening space for social activism – became more effective that these particularistic practices were placed under public scrutiny. This, in turn, increased the risk for politicians and parties, thereby strengthening state organizations' ability to fend off particularistic demands. In other words, the case studies demonstrate that the stateness-democracy nexus has to be understood in cyclical terms, not in linear terms.

Perhaps even more importantly, the Korea and Taiwan case studies provide evidence that processes of democratic consolidation can be constrained by path-dependent effects – effects that will retain their strength irrespective of high levels of stateness. As Hellmann and Templeman show, state-building processes in Korea and Taiwan – even though they resulted in equally strong developmental states – unfolded in very different ways: whereas in KMT-ruled Taiwan state-building was closely intertwined with party building processes, Korea's military-bureaucratic regime refrained from building intermediate state-society organizations and relied almost exclusively on repression as an instrument of social control. These differences still haunt the two democracies today. In Taiwan – because the KMT had, for decades, 'colonized' the state through a dense network of party cells and civil service appointments – the development of the civil rights regime and judicial independence continues to be stymied. Korea's democracy, in contrast, suffers from the opposite problem: political parties lack organizational structures, do not provide institutionalized channels for bottom-up participation and are easy prey for ambitious politicians. This, in turn, facilitates 'hyper-presidential' politics and encourages civil society to engage in militant behaviour.

Similar path-dependent effects can also be observed in other consolidated democracies of the third wave. In Chile, up until 2017, parliamentary elections were held using a unique 'binomial' electoral system – a system that had been put in place by the Pinochet regime after it lost the 1988 plebiscite, carefully designed to produce a moderate two-party system under the new democratic rules. This electoral system has been blamed for creating disincentives for political parties to develop organizational roots in society and creating opportunities for citizen participation (e.g. Luna and Altman, 2011). As a result of these organizational weaknesses, and similar to the case of South Korea, growing parts of Chilean society have deep apathy towards party politics – reflected, for example, in dramatically declining electoral turnout rates – and increasingly participate in extra-institutional, contentious collective action to have their voices heard (e.g. Morgan and Meléndez, 2016).

Democracy in Argentina, on the other hand, continues to be plagued by what O'Donnell calls 'brown areas'. These sub-national areas can be described as 'democracy of low-intensity citizenship': political rights – such as the right to vote in elections – are respected, but citizens 'often are unable to receive fair treatment in the courts, or to obtain from state agencies services to which they are entitled, or to be safe from police violence, etc' (O'Donnell, 1993: 1361). Specifically, in Argentina, scholars have observed that, while democratic processes at the national level are relatively well consolidated, democratization has proceeded unevenly at the sub-national level. Behrend, for example, argues that, democratic politics at the sub-national level often resembles a 'closed game', whereby 'a family, or a reduced group of families, dominates politics in a province, controlling access to top government positions, the provincial state, the media, and business opportunities' (2011: 153). Different explanations abound as to why these 'brown areas' persist; however, one factor that is commonly highlighted is the design of Argentina's federal system, central features of which date back to the mid-nineteenth century (e.g. Giraudy, 2015; Ardanaz et al., 2014; Gibson, 2012). Essentially, Argentina's federalism turns provincial actors (especially provincial governors) into key players in national politics. To secure the support of provincial actors, national politicians not only tolerate undemocratic practices at the sub-national level, but they further fuel these practices with national tax money.

In short, what cases of successful democratic consolidation in East Asia and other parts of the developing world show is that there is no linear relationship between stateness and the quality of democracy. First, the arrow of causality also points the other way – in particular, the introduction of democratic institutions may have negative effects on the state's capacity to enforce laws and regulations. Second, processes of democratic consolidation can be subject to path-dependent effects. That is to say, defective characteristics of democracy may reproduce themselves over time despite high levels of stateness.

AUTOCRATIC REVERSAL: STATENESS IS NOT A SUFFICIENT SAFEGUARD

The cases of South Korea and Taiwan show that, while high levels of stateness certainly support the consolidation of democratic process, stateness is by no means a sufficient condition for the successful consolidation of new democracies. The case of Thailand (Chapter 5 by Chambers in this volume) provides even stronger support for this conclusion. The Thai state, despite problems on the dimension of citizen agreement, is comparatively strong. In fact, when measured quantitatively (see Figure 10.3), Thailand displays a degree of state capacity that is similar to Taiwan. Yet, irrespective of the fact that Thai state organizations are characterized by the strong ability to enforce laws and regulations, Thailand witnessed a return to autocratic rule. For the sequentialist approach to the state-democracy nexus, Thailand is thus a deeply puzzling case.

To explain the collapse of Thailand's democratic regime, Chambers places the focus on the Thai 'parallel state' – an 'informal power structure embedded in Thai society, economy, bureaucracy' that 'consists of a certain set of political actors (bureaucratic, military and royalist elites such as the member of the Privy Council), controlling and employing the coercive, bureaucratic, and extractive capacities of the state', even though democratically elected governments should formally be in charge. As Chambers explains, this 'parallel state' was established under Thailand's semi-democratic regime in the 1980s, as conservative factions in the military tried to form an effective counter-balance to progressive political forces. When civilian politicians implemented institutional reforms in the early 1990s, thereby considerably increasing the competitiveness of political competition and expanding the space for political participation, the 'parallel state' initially stood back. This, as Chambers argues, had largely to do with the fact that the fragmented multi-party system that emerged with the introduction of free and fair elections did not pose a serious threat to conservative interests harboured by the 'parallel state'. However, the rise of Thaksin Shinawatra – a populist politician with unprecedented electoral support among rural voters – and the subsequent concentration of the party system in the early 2000s set off alarm bells in conservative networks. The 'parallel state' consequently struck back, using its networked resources to oust Thaksin from power in 2006 and then orchestrate a silent coup against Thaksin's successor, his sister Yingluck, which culminated in the establishment of military rule in 2014.

The case study of Thailand thus demonstrates that informal networks – if they command sufficient resources and are subjected to centralized control – can be used to undermine democratic institutions and co-ordinate a return to autocratic rule. Interestingly, Un (Chapter 6 in this volume) arrives at a similar conclusion in his case study of autocratic reversal in Cambodia. As Un illustrates, Cambodian politics is largely structured along patron-client networks, called *ksae* in Khmer. The most powerful *ksae* networks can be found in the CPP, with control over these networks monopolized by the party leadership under Hun Sen. According to Un, Cambodia under the CPP essentially operates as a neo-patrimonial regime, whereby governing elites exchange access to rent-seeking opportunities for political support. This neo-patrimonial regime reaches into all corners of the state and has allowed the CPP to considerably weaken the democratic regime that was forced on the party by the international community in the early 1990s. Specifically, neo-patrimonial networks have provided the CPP with the means to gain particularistic control over those public organizations put in charge of keeping a check on executive power and enforcing the political/civil rights regime. In addition, the neo-patrimonial machine gives the CPP an unfair advantage in elections, to the extent that Cambodia must now be regarded as an 'electoral authoritarian' regime.

We can therefore summarize that, when compared with each other, the cases of Thailand and Cambodia suggest that centralized informal networks – whether held together primarily by political beliefs or clientelistic exchanges – can be employed to engineer a shift from democratic to autocratic politics, provided that these networks control sufficient politically relevant resources.

In fact, other cases of autocratic reversal in the developing world (see Table 10.2) reveal similar mechanisms. Nicaragua, which implemented free and fair elections in 1990 after eleven years of autocratic rule under the *Frente Sandinista de Liberación Nacional* (FSLN), has slowly deteriorated into a system of electoral authoritarianism. Key to this turnaround were the strategic manoeuvres of President Daniel Ortega before and after winning the 2006 elections. Ortega had been the FSLN's candidate for the 1990 elections, which the party lost – a defeat that was completely unexpected. Subsequently, Ortega moved to deinstitutionalize the FSLN, turning it into a personalistic political vehicle that came to resemble the typical *caudillo* party in Nicaraguan politics, structured around family ties and other inter-personal relationships (Martí i Puig, 2010). Next, in a move that shook the political landscape, Ortega entered into a pact with Arnoldo Alemán, who had won the presidential elections in 1996 on an aggressive anti-Sandinista platform and was charged with corruption towards the end of his term. In *el pacto* (The Pact), Alemán gave the FSLN an almost equal number of seats on key constitutional agencies (including the Supreme Court and the Federal Electoral Council); in exchange, Ortega used his newly gained influence to keep Alemán out of prison. In addition, the two former enemies worked together to change the constitution. Perhaps most importantly, Alemán agreed to lower the threshold for election of the president to 35 per cent of votes.

Together, these agreements established a system of what Telleria calls *bicaudillismo* – 'a collusive power equilibrium in which political power is equally shared and uncertainty is controlled', granting each partner 'seemingly unlimited control over the four branches of government and the political system as a whole' (2011: 36). That is to say, similar to cartel arrangements in economic markets, the Ortega-Alemán pact severely undermined the competitiveness of the Nicaraguan electoral market. Crucially, the pact allowed Ortega to win the 2006 presidential elections (with a mere 38 per cent of the vote – the lowest winning percentage in Nicaraguan electoral history), after which he consolidated his networked control over democratic institutions and choreographed a transition towards an electoral authoritarian regime (see Thaler, 2017; Martí i Puig, 2016).

Comparable arguments about the role of informal networks in autocratic reversal have also been made about Bangladesh – even though the context is fundamentally different. Bangladeshi politics have, since the end of military rule in 1990, revolved around a highly polarized two-party system, with the Awami League (AL) and the Bangladesh Nationalist Party (BNP) being the main contenders for power. For many scholars of Bangladeshi politics, the main reason for the country's return to autocratic government is to be found in the major parties' extensive patronage networks that permeate the state, including judicial and law-enforcement agencies. For example, as Arfina Osman summarizes,

> Restoration of parliamentary democracy marked the emergence of an adversely competitive political system where the parties are merely committed to democratic practices. The party that wins the election monopolizes the state apparatus with "winner takes all" attitude, leaving little scope for the losing party to take part in the process of governance, which leads them to be violent, destructive and irresponsible. In the monopolization process, the ruling party exerts a strong control over all the key state institutions. Thus, a political culture of impunity, patronage and institutionalization of partisanship has been developed. The trend of monopolization of state apparatus by the winning party has impaired the functioning of the formal accountability mechanisms, which ultimately leads to a crisis in governance. (2010: 310–11)

Given that both major parties operate on the basis of centralized patron-client networks, which – once in government – are deployed to gain particularistic control over the state, Bangladesh has been described as a 'bipolar competitive neopatrimonial' regime (Islam, 2013). However, the competitive element of this system weakened considerably under the most recent AL government (since 2008), when the neo-patrimonial control of the state was pushed to new limits, with opposition harassment and political manipulation reaching unprecedented levels. The opposition BNP thus saw no other option but to boycott the 2014 elections – at which point is it was no longer possible to classify Bangladesh as a democracy (e.g. Diamond, 2015). One final example from the African continent – Burundi – further substantiates our argument about the role of informal networks. After years of ethnically charged civil war, Burundi held free and fair elections in 2005. The *Conseil National Pour la Défense de la Démocratie–Forces pour la Défense de la Démocratie* (CNDD-FDD), a rebel group turned political party, won these elections with almost 60 per cent of the vote. In its campaign to mobilize voters, the CNDD-FDD benefitted heavily from vertical command structures that it had established during the war. As Uvin and Bayer explain,

> In many regions a shadow CNDD-FDD administration existed in parallel to the official one [...] the CNDD-FDD in reality controlled much of the countryside and was awaiting the elections merely to confirm its hegemony. To this end, both the shadow organization and the official party set up informal local power networks to manage the electoral process and the transition into legitimate power. (2013: 207)

Moreover, not only did this shadow administration help the CNDD-FDD win the first elections, the party then subsequently merged its shadowy networks with formal state structures, thereby laying the foundation for a particularistic capture of the state. In the words of Van Acker (2015: 6), 'Since its electoral victory in 2005 [...] the CNDD-FDD party has exercised a quasi-monopoly over the state and its resources. As such, it has been able to build, from top to bottom, a system of patronage around its own party structures. On all scales and levels, affiliation to these structures has become the main factor for acquiring access to state resources'. Based on a firm control of the state apparatus, the CNDD-FDD has steadily been chipping away at the institutions of democracy, thereby turning Burundi into 'a textbook example of autocratization through elections' (Vandeginste, 2015: 636).

To sum up, evidence from other parts of the developing world supports the conclusion we drew from the East Asian cases. Whether termed parallel state, neo-patrimonialism or shadow administration, what the comparison has shown is that non-democratic elites can, through the strategic deployment of informal networks, 'hijack' the state and gain control of those public organizations tasked with enforcing democracy's partial regimes. What is especially puzzling – at least if the sequentialist approach to state-democracy nexus is applied – is that autocratic reversal through particularistic state capture can even occur in political systems that are characterized by comparatively high levels of stateness, such as Thailand or Nicaragua. However, as our discussion of defective democracies in the next sub-section will show, informal networks need to be organized in certain ways for such a scenario to play out.

DEFECTIVE DEMOCRACIES: STUCK IN A 'PREDATORY STATE' TRAP?

Having discussed cases of successful consolidation and cases of autocratic reversal, it needs to be noted these are exceptional outcomes of the third wave of democratization. Most countries that were hit by the third wave of democratization have subsequently developed into defective democracies (see Table 10.2) – including three cases analysed in this volume: the Philippines, Indonesia and East Timor. Moreover, most of these defective democracies display a similar pattern in the degree of consolidation across the different partial regimes: while the electoral regime (partial regime A) and the political rights regime (partial regime B) perform relatively well, the other partial regimes suffer from significant weaknesses. In other words, these political systems can be classified as minimalist democracies in the Schumpeterian sense, but they do not meet the more demanding definition of embedded democracy.

Nevertheless, the large number of minimalist democracies that was caused by the third wave of democratization presents a serious challenge to the sequentialist approach to the state-democracy nexus. Specifically, what is clear from the empirical evidence – both from East Asia and the cursory comparative overview at the beginning of this chapter – is that minimalist democracy can be sustained even under low levels of stateness. The case of East Timor is particularly informing in this respect: despite the fact the newly independent nation has greatly struggled to develop coercive capacity, administrative capacity and citizen agreement, the political system's electoral regime and deliberative arena are relatively robust in their functioning. The case of East Timor thus shows, as Croissant and Abu Sharkh (Chapter 9) summarize, 'that stateness may not be a necessary pre-condition for democracy'.

However, the analysis of minimalist democracies in East Asia does not just blow a hole in the sequentialist argument but it also offers an insight into the causal mechanisms that explain the reasonable performance of basic democratic institutions under conditions of low stateness. At the most fundamental level, the cases of the Philippines, Indonesia and East Timor support the argument that state-building plays out as a conflict between public organizations and formal regulations, on one side, and particularistic networks and informal norms, on the other side (see North et al., 2009; Mungiu-Pippidi, 2015; Rueschemeyer, 2005). In all three countries, informal networks are key vehicles in the political process: family clan networks in the Philippines, networks controlled by henchmen of the former Suharto regime in Indonesia and command-style networks that developed under Indonesian occupation in East Timor. In a manner that resembles what Johnston terms 'oligarchs and clans' or 'official moguls' corruption (2005), these networks seek to gain control over the state's resources as a means to increase their power vis-à-vis competing networks, thereby establishing greater certainty over the outcomes of political and economic activities.

As the respective chapters in this volume show, elites in control of these particularistic networks support minimalist democracy, as it provides an institutionalized mechanism that regulates access to rent-seeking opportunities. Put differently, minimalist democracy – characterized by functioning partial regimes A (elections) and B (political rights) – ensures competition between networks and prevents monopolization of the particularistic extraction of public resources. This mechanism is perhaps most readily observable in the Philippines, where powerful family clans already realized the benefits of minimalist democracy during the final stages of American colonial rule in the mid-twentieth century. As Kuhonta and Truong (Chapter 7) summarize, 'What is contested in the Philippine party system is not ideology but rather spoils, access to contracts and licences and familial accumulation of wealth'. Similarly, in the chapter on Indonesia's new democracy, Mietzner outlines how key elements of the outgoing Suharto regime – in particular, military and bureaucratic elites – came to understand that the resources and networks they controlled would allow them to retain their rent-seeking opportunities even under free and fair elections. As Mietzner observes, 'representatives of these state-anchored elites have claimed the pole position in many electoral races' and have thus 'helped to stabilize the young post-autocratic polity'. Finally, in East Timor, political parties are rooted in clandestine resistance networks. As in the Philippines and Indonesia, elections serve as a means for leading elites to share access to the particularistic goods of the state – as illustrated, for example, by the bloated size of the government cabinet (Scambary, 2015; also see Chapter 9 by Croissant and Abu Sharkh in this volume).

In short, under these systems of 'competitive clientelism' (Mungiu-Pippidi, 2015), democracy's partial regimes A and B work relatively well. Other partial regimes, in contrast, are severely impaired – in particular, partial regimes C (civil liberties) and D (horizontal accountability). The reason being that particularistic networks seek to maximize their rent-seeking profits, unconstrained by institutional checks and balances. Of relevance are findings by the general literature on corruption showing that particularistic practices are more likely to flourish in environments of insufficient judicial independence and separation of powers (e.g. Rose-Ackerman, 2007; Herzfeld and Weiss, 2003). The Philippines, again, offers the clearest illustration of this mechanism: still under colonial rule, Filipino elites designed the state in such a way that public organizations – including judicial authorities and law enforcement agencies – could easily be subordinated to particularistic interests. Likewise, in Indonesia and East Timor, democratically elected politicians have done very little to strengthen public organizations that are responsible for enforcing constitutional principles and the rule of law. Both political systems continue to be plagued by widespread public office abuse and a culture of legal impunity.

While it is thus clear that minimalist democracies – specifically, their ability to survive in contexts of low stateness – pose a challenge to sequentialism, it needs to be pointed out that they are also problematic for the nexian approach to the state-democracy nexus. This is because the nexian approach puts great emphasis on elections as a state-building mechanism. Specifically, nexians have argued that electoral competition creates incentives for politicians to mobilize voters through the provision of public goods, which in turn requires an investment in the state's bureaucratic apparatus (see Carbone, 2015: 13). However, the empirical evidence from East Asia demonstrates that this mechanism does not work in minimalist democracies.

Certainly, the analyses in this volume suggest that elections can help to build citizen agreement and thereby, indirectly, increase the state's coercive capacity (in particular, see the contributions by Vu and Mietzner). Administrative capacity, in contrast, remains largely unchanged in minimalist democracies. Despite the introduction of free and fair elections, states in the Philippines, Indonesia and East Timor continue to be burdened by corruption, patronage and other particularistic practices. The failure of electoral competition in strengthening states' ability to fend off particularistic demands can be linked back to the weaknesses of other elements of embedded democracy and problematic features of the contextual embedding. First, systemic legal impunity – facilitated by the malfunctioning of partial regimes C (civil liberties) and D (horizontal accountability) – allows politicians to mobilize voters through illicit means, such as vote buying and patronage, thus creating disincentives to develop policy platforms based on the promise to deliver public goods.

Second, if civil society is weak, the freedom for politicians to employ illicit methods of voter mobilization is further enhanced. Third, the socio-economic context matters: voters from low-income groups are much more susceptible to the distribution of private goods through vote buying and clientelism than high-income voters. In other words, widespread poverty undermines the effectiveness of elections as a state-building mechanism.

Overall, what this suggests is that minimalist democracies can get stuck in a 'predatory state' trap: when democracy's partial regimes A (elections) and B (political rights) are merely implemented to provide an institutionalized mechanism for particularistic networks to compete over access to the state's resources, elections will not have a strengthening effect on the bureaucratic quality and autonomy of the state. This is because political elites will actively work towards undermining partial regimes C (civil liberties) and D (horizontal accountability), which enables them not only to engage in unconstrained rent-seeking behaviour but also to mobilize voters through illicit means, thereby weakening elections as a vertical accountability tool. Reform-oriented politicians and parties face significant challenges in such an environment, as the analyses of the Philippines and Indonesia in this volume show.

This 'predatory state' trap is not only observable in Southeast Asia but can also be witnessed in other part of the developing world. The list of case studies that illustrate how the institutions of minimalist democracy have been hijacked by particularistic interests is long, ranging from Peru (Crabtree and Durand, 2017) to Kenya (D'Arcy and Cornell, 2016), from Mexico (Morris, 2018) to Nigeria (Kendhammer, 2015). Policy-oriented parties have, generally, only played a marginal role in these minimalist democracies. And even where such parties succeeded in challenging particularistic contenders, they have been forced to play by the 'rules of the game', failing to significantly reduce the extent of corruption and other forms of public office abuses – for example, illustrated by the case of the Brazilian Workers' Party (*Partido dos Trabalhadores*) whose time in government (2003–2016) was marred by rampant corruption (Ribeiro, 2014).

SUMMARY

By comparing the different regime outcomes of the third wave of democratization – both across East Asia and other parts of the developing world – this section has produced a number of findings regarding the relationship between stateness and the quality of democracy. First, against the theoretical predictions of the sequentialist approach to the state-democracy nexus, we have demonstrated that stateness is neither a sufficient nor a necessary condition for democratic consolidation. Our analysis of consolidated democracies shows that these systems can continue to suffer from path-dependent deficits, irrespective of high levels of stateness. Moreover, the investigation of autocratic reversal reveals that high levels of stateness are not a guarantee that political systems will continue on the path of democratization. When centralized particularistic networks – regardless of whether these are termed parallel state or shadow administration – have infiltrated key public organizations, non-democratic elites can use these networks to co-ordinate a return to autocratic rule. In addition, defective democracies – specifically, Schumpeterian minimalist democracies that display adequate performance only in the partial regimes A (elections) and B (political rights) – can be sustained even under very low levels of stateness. This, as we have argued, has to do with the organization of particularistic networks at the systemic level: when control over these networks is fragmented, elites will institutionalize political competition as a mechanism to share the particularistic spoils of office. Second, through our comparative analysis, we have been able to demonstrate that the nexian argument about the state-democracy nexus only holds when elections are embedded in other well-functioning partial regimes and a favourable socio-economic context. In other words, only consolidated democracies will have a strengthening effect on all three dimensions of stateness; defective democracies, while they can certainly improve citizen agreement and coercive capacity, do not create incentives for political elites to invest in administrative capacity. Taken together, these findings suggest that minimalist electoral democracies – which is the predominant outcome of the third wave of democratization – can be caught in a 'predatory state' trap.

References

Abinales, P. N., and Amoroso, D. J. (2005). *State and Society in the Philippines*. New York/Oxford: Rowman & Littlefield.
Alagappa, M. (1995). The base of legitimacy. In M. Alagappa, ed., *Political Legitimacy in Southeast Asia: The Quest for Moral Authority*. Stanford: Stanford University Press, pp. 31–53.
Ardanaz, M., Leiras, M., and Tommasi, M. (2014). The politics of federalism in Argentina and its implications for governance and accountability. *World Development*, 53, 26–45.
Arfina Osman, F. (2010). Bangladesh politics: Confrontation, monopoly and crisis in governance. *Asian Journal of Political Science*, 18(3), 310–33.
Behrend, J. (2011). The unevenness of democracy at the subnational level: Provincial closed games in Argentina. *Latin American Research Review*, 46(1), 150–76.
Bermeo, N. (2016). On democratic backsliding. *Journal of Democracy*, 27(1), 5–19.
Bertelsmann Stiftung. (2016). BTI 2016 Codebook for Country Assessments. Available at: www.bti-project.org/fileadmin/files/BTI/Downloads/Zusaetzliche_Downloads/Codebuch_BTI_2016.pdf [Accessed 22 June 2019].
Bertelsmann Stiftung. (2018). BTI – Bertelsmann Transformation Index 2018. Available at: www.bti-project.org/en/home/ [Accessed 22 June 2019].
Carbone, G. (2015). Democratisation as a state-building mechanism: A preliminary discussion of an understudied relationship. *Political Studies Review*, 13(1), 11–21.

Crabtree, J., and Durand, F. (2017). *Peru: Elite Power and Political Capture*. London: Zed Books.
Croissant, A. (2005). Unrest in South Thailand: Contours, causes, and consequences since 2001. *Contemporary Southeast Asia*, 27(1), 21–44.
Croissant, A. (2018). *Civil-Military Relations in Southeast Asia*. Cambridge: Cambridge University Press.
Croissant, A., and Bünte, M., eds. (2011). *The Crisis of Democratic Governance in Southeast Asia*. Basingstoke and New York: Palgrave.
Croissant, A., and Lorenz, P. (2018). *Comparative Politics of Southeast Asia: An Introduction into Government and Politics*. Heidelberg: Springer.
Croissant, A., and Merkel, W. (2019). Defective democracy. In R. Kollmorgen, W. Merkel, and H.-J. Wagener, eds., *Handbook of Political, Social, and Economic Transformation*. Oxford: Oxford University Press, pp. 437–46.
Croissant, A., and Thiery, P. (2009). Erosion der Demokratie oder Beharrlichkeit defekter Demokratien? Eine Analyse des Verlaufs demokratischer Transformation. In Bertelsmann Stiftung, ed., *Bertelsmann Transformation Index 2010*. Gütersloh: Verlag Bertelsmann Stiftung, pp. 110–29.
Croissant, A., Kuehn, D., Lorenz, P., and Chambers, P. W. (2013). *Civilian Control and Democracy in Asia*. Basingstoke and New York: Palgrave.
D'Arcy, M., and Cornell, A. (2016). Devolution and corruption in Kenya: Everyone's turn to eat? *African Affairs*, 115(459), 246–73.
Dahl, R. A. (1971). *Polyarchy*. New Haven: Yale University Press.
Diamond, L. (2015). Facing up to the democratic recession. *Journal of Democracy*, 26(1), 141–55.
Dittmer, L. (2018). Asia in 2017: Return of the strongman. *Asian Survey*, 58(1), 1–9.
Gibson, E. L. (2012). *Boundary Control: Subnational Authoritarianism in Federal Democracies*. Cambridge: Cambridge University Press.
Giraudy, A. (2015). *Democrats and Autocrats: Pathways of Subnational Undemocratic Regime Continuity within Democratic Countries*. Oxford: Oxford University Press.
Gledhill, J. (2012). Competing for change: Regime transition, intrastate competition, and violence. *Security Studies*, 21, 43–82.
Haggard, S., and Kaufman, R. R. (2016). *Masses, Elites, and Regime Change*. Princeton: Princeton University Press.
Hanson, J. K. (2018). State capacity and the resilience of electoral authoritarianism: Conceptualizing and measuring the institutional underpinnings of autocratic power. *International Political Science Review*, 39 (1), 17–32.
Hanson, J. K., and Sigman, R. (2013). Leviathan's latent dimensions: Measuring state capacity for comparative political research. Unpublished Manuscript.
Henick, J. (2014). Nation building in East Timor: National identity contests and crisis. Dissertation, Honolulu: University of Hawai'i.
Hernandez, C. G. (2016). The Philippines in 2015: A house still not in order? *Asian Survey*, 56(1), 115–22.
Herzfeld, T., and Weiss, C. (2003). Corruption and legal (in) effectiveness: An empirical investigation. *European Journal of Political Economy*, 19(3), 621–32.
Huq, A., and Ginsburg, T. (2018). How to lose a constitutional democracy. *UCLA Law Review*, 65, 78–169.

International Crisis Group. (2017). *Jihadism in Southern Thailand: A Phantom Menace. Report No. 291*. Brussels: International Crisis Group.

Islam, M. M. (2013). The toxic politics of Bangladesh: A bipolar competitive neopatrimonial state? *Asian Journal of Political Science*, 21(2), 148–68.

Johnston, M. (2005). *Syndromes of Corruption: Wealth, Power, and Democracy*. Cambridge: Cambridge University Press.

Kendhammer, B. (2015). Getting our piece of the national cake: Consociational power sharing and Neopatrimonialism in Nigeria. *Nationalism and Ethnic Politics*, 21(2), 143–65.

Leach, M. (2017). *Nation-Building and National Identity in East Timor*. Abingdon: Routledge.

Luna, J. P., and Altman, D. (2011). Uprooted but stable: Chilean parties and the concept of party system institutionalization. *Latin American Politics and Society*, 53(2), 1–28.

Marti i Puig, S. (2010). The adaptation of the FSLN: Daniel Ortega's leadership and democracy in Nicaragua. *Latin American Politics and Society*, 52(4), 79–106.

Marti i Puig, S. (2016). Nicaragua: Desdemocratización y caudillismo. *Revista de Ciencia Política*, 36(1), 239–58.

Merkel, W. (2004). Embedded and defective democracies. *Democratization*, 11(5), 33–58.

Millar, P. (2016). Race to the bottom: How Cambodia's opposition is targeting ethnic Vietnamese, *Southeast Asia Globe*, 21 October. Southeast Asia Globe. Available at: http://sea-globe.com/cambodia-opposition-cnrp-vietnamese/ [Accessed 20 June 2019].

Morgan, J., and Meléndez, C. (2016). Parties under stress: Using a linkage decay framework to analyze the Chilean party system. *Journal of Politics in Latin America*, 8(3), 25–59.

Morgenbesser, L. (2016). *Behind the Façade: Elections under Authoritarianism in Southeast Asia*. New York: State University of New York Press.

Morris, S. (2018). Corruption in Mexico: Continuity amid change. In B. Warf, ed., *Handbook on the Geographies of Corruption*. Cheltenham/Northampton: Edward Elgar, pp. 132–53.

Mungiu-Pippidi, A. (2015). *The Quest for Good Governance: How Societies Develop Control of Corruption*. Cambridge: Cambridge University Press.

North, D., Wallis, J. J., and Weingast, B. R. (2009). *Violence and Social Orders: A Conceptual Framework for Interpreting Recorded Human History*. Cambridge: Cambridge University Press.

O'Donnell, G. (1993). On the state, democratization and some conceptual problems: A Latin American view with glances at some postcommunist countries. *World Development*, 21(8), 1355–69.

O'Donnell, G. (1994). Delegative democracy. *Journal of Democracy*, 5(1), 55–69.

Reischauer, E. O. (1974). The Sinic world in perspective. *Foreign Affairs*, 52(2), 341–48.

Ribeiro, P. F. (2014). An amphibian party? Organisational change and adaptation in the Brazilian workers' party, 1980–2012. *Journal of Latin American Studies*, 46(1), 87–119.

Rose-Ackerman, S. (2007). Judicial independence and corruption. In Transparency International, eds., *Global Corruption Report 2007: Corruption in Judicial Systems*. Cambridge and New York: Cambridge University Press, pp. 15–23.

Rozman, G. (2012). Introduction. In G. Rozman, ed., *East Asian National Identities: Common Roots and Chinese Exceptionalism*. Washington, DC and Stanford: Woodrow Wilson International Press and Stanford University Press, pp. 1–15.

Rueschemeyer, D. (2005). Building states – inherently a long-term process? An argument from theory. In M. Lange and D. Rueschemeyer, eds., *States and Development*. New York: Palgrave Macmillan, pp. 143–64.

Scambary, J. (2015). In search of white elephants: The political economy of resource income expenditure in East Timor. *Critical Asian Studies*, 47(2), 283–308.

Shin, D. C., and Tusalem, R. (2009). East Asia. In C. Haerpfer, et al., eds., *Democratization*. Oxford: Oxford University Press, pp. 356–74.

Skocpol, T. (1985). Bringing the State Back in: Strategies of analysis in current research. In P. B. Evans, D. Rueschemeyer, and T. Skocpol, eds., *Bringing the State Back In*. Cambridge: Cambridge University Press, pp. 3–38.

Telleria, G. M. (2011). A two-headed monster: Bicaudillismo in Nicaragua. *Latin American Policy*, 2(1), 32–42.

Thaler, K. M. (2017). Nicaragua: A return to Caudillismo. *Journal of Democracy*, 28(2), 157–69.

Uvin, P., and Bayer, L. (2013). The political economy of statebuilding in Burundi. In M. Berdal and D. Zaum, eds., *Political Economy of Statebuilding: Power after Peace*. Abingdon and New York: Routledge, pp. 263–76.

Van Acker, T. (2015). *Understanding Burundi's predicament: Africa Policy Brief No. 11*. Brussels: Egmont Royal Institute for International Relations.

Vandeginste, S. (2015). Burundi's electoral crisis: Back to power-sharing politics as usual? *African Affairs*, 114(457), 624–36.

Ziegenhain, P. (2018). Islam and nation-building in Indonesia and Malaysia. *ASIEN: The German Journal on Contemporary Asia*, 146 (January), 78–96.

Index

Note: Page numbers in italic and bold refer to figures and tables, respectively.

absolutism, 32, 33, 107, 127
abuse of power, 27, 163
accountability, 14, 80, 120, 142, 154, 155, 159, 160, 163, 167, 173, 174, 190, 195, 211, 221, 224, 225, 234, 254
   horizontal, 3, 11, 15, 16, 18, 19, 73–74, 237, 240, 249, 257, 258
      Cambodia, 133, 143, 147, 148
      East Timor, 215, 221
      Indonesia, 188, 190
      Philippines, 153, 155, 156, 163
      South Korea, 47, 62
      Taiwan, 73, 76, 77, 91, 92, 93, 94
      Thailand, 118, 120, 125
   vertical, 15, 20, 250, 258
      Cambodia, 148
      Philippines, 165
      Taiwan, 82
Aceh, 30, 39, 183, 184, 188, 196, 197
Africa, 13, 20, 240, 254
Alliance of Hope, 41
Aquino, Beningno III, 41
Aquino, Corazon, 41, 157, 163, 164, 172
Argentina, 240, 249, 251
armed forces, 9, 106, 107, 108, 109, 110, 111, 112, 114, 122, 135, 136, 181, 196, 211, 222, 247. *See also* military
Asian financial crisis (of 1997), 2, 110, 116, 183
Asian puzzle, 9
Association of Southeast Asian Nations (ASEAN), 40

Aung San Suu Kyi, 40
authoritarian regime, 2, 3, 8, 12, 16, 26, 39, 47, 48, 109, 159, 180, 183, 195, 215, 234, 237, 243, 247, 253
authoritarianism, 3, 4, 6, 9, 10, 13, 16, 17, 18, 38, 48, 56, 60, 62, 63, 66, 108, 109, 110, 133, 179, 180, 191, 197, 198, 215, 221, 245, 252, 253, 259. *See also* authoritarian regime; autocracy
   in Bangladesh, 254
   electoral authoritarianism, 253
      Cambodia, 133, 136
   in Indonesia, 179, 181, 184, 198
   in Korea, 48, 56, 59, 60, 62, 63, 64, 66
   military regime, 15, 48, 49, 50, 55, 56, 61, 63, 65, 66, 104, 106, 108, 121, 181, 250. *See also* dictatorship, military; military, regime
   (one-) party regime, 2, 133, 154
   personalist regime, 135
   in Taiwan, 71, 73
   in Thailand, 104, 109, 116, 121, 127
autocracy, 10, 15, 16, 71, 73, 104, 121, 127, 181, 184
autocratic reversal, 3, 4, 17, 18, 19, 234, 237, 239, 249, 252, 253, 255, 258. *See also* autocratization
autocratization, 4, 19, 123, 128, 239, 255
   in Asia, 3, 4, 10, 19, 239
   third wave of, 10

263

autonomy, 57, 62, 65, 72, 74, 77, 79, 80, 105, 141, 168, 173, 190, 205, 207, 220, 247
state autonomy, 6, 53, 56, 57, 62, 80, 85, 94, 224, 258

backsliding, 4, 200, 237. *See also* autocratization; democratic backsliding
Bangladesh, 237, 253, 254
Barisan Nasional (BN), 4
Bertelsmann Transformation Index (BTI), 3, 47, 71, 104, 119, 190, 191, 234, 235, 236, 237, 239, 243, 245, 247, 249
citizenship agreement, 8, 16, 104, 243, 244, 245
Brazil, 258
British colonial rule, 35, 36
brown areas, 251
Brunei, **217**, 224, 234
Buddhism, 30, 113
bureaucratic capacity, 51, 85
bureaucratic polity, 108, 109, 110, 117, 127
Burma, 13, 29, 30, 34, 35, 36, 37, 38, 39, 40, 41, 42, 43, **161**, 183, 199
Augn San Suu Kyi, 40
civil war, 40, 43
ethnic minorities, 36
Karen, 36
Ne Win, 36
state-building, 30, 34, 35, 36, 39, 41, 42
Tatmadaw, 4
Burundi, 254, 255

Cambodia, 2, 3, 4, 13, 14, 16, 17, 18, 19, 29, 30, 38, 39, 40, 41, 42, 43, 71, 108, 133, 134, 135, 136, 137, 138, 140, 141, 142, 143, 144, 145, 146, 147, 148, **161**, 211, 215, **217**, 218, 226, 227, 234, 242, 243, 245, 247, 249, 252
accountability, 148
horizontal, 133, 143, 147, 148
perverse, 142, 148
anti-corruption unit (ACU), 138
black box money, 141
bodyguard unit, 136
business tycoons, 139, 141, 143
Cambodia National Rescue Party (CNRP), 40, 137, 143, 146, 147, 148
Cambodian People's Party (CPP), 18, 19, 134, 135, 136, 138, 140, 141, 142, 146, 147, 148, 247, 248, 252
working group, 140, 141
campaign financing in, 138
civil service, 137, 140, 148
civil society in, 139, 148
coloured revolution, 136
constitutional council of, 144
decentralization, 141, 142
defamation, 145, 146
democratic transition, 133
demographic change, 142
economic land concessions, 139
effective power to govern in, 133
elections in, 133, 134, 136, 137, 138, 142, 144, 146, 148
electoral authoritarianism in, 133, 136
electoral regime in, 133, 136
forest sector, 139
FUNCINPEC, 134, 135
human rights in, 136, 140, 146
Hun Sen, 134, 135, 136, 141, 148
judicial system, 139, 143, 145
communist judicial system, 143
judicial reform, 144, 145
rule of law, 143, 144
law on associations and non-governmental organizations, 146
National Assembly, 145, 147
neo-patrimonialism, 135, 136, 137, 138, 139, 140, 142, 144
and bureaucracy, 137, 140, 148
and electoral democracy, 135, 143
Paris Peace Agreement (PPA), 134
patron-clientelism in, 134, 135, 138, 143. *See also* ksae
personal fiefdoms, 140
personalist state, 135
political machine, 140, 144, 148
politicization of security forces, 136
public financial management, 138
revenue mobilization, 138
Sam Rainsy (party), 136
Supreme Council of Magistracy (SCM), 144, 145
United Nations Transitional Authority in Cambodia (UNTAC), 133, 137, 227
Cambodian People's Party (CPP) working group, 141
campaign finance, 15, 56, 57, 158
in Cambodia, 138
in Indonesia, 189
in South Korea, 15, 56
in Timor-Leste, 216
Central America, 240

Index

chaebol, 54, 55, 57, 83
Chakri dynasty, 32
Chile, 240, 249, 250
China, 25, 29, 30, 31, 32, 33, 38, 39, 40, 41, 42, 43, 49, 75, 76, 77, 78, 79, 80, 81, 82, 84, 87, 91, 93, 167, 234, 245
   communist party of, 49, 79, 81
   cross-strait relations with, 85
   empire, 29, 78
   Qing dynasty, 32, 78
   Republic of, 76, 78, 79, 80, 81, 82, 87, 91, 93. *See also* Taiwan
   revolution, 32
   Sun Yat-sen, 32
Chulalongkorn, king, 32
Chun Doo-hwan, 54
church, 28, 55, 83, 206
citizenship agreement, 113, 114, 124, 187, 223, 247
   Bertelsmann Transformation Index (BTI), 8, 16, 104, 243, 244
   definition, 7
   stateness, 106, 110, 113, 124, 181, 210, 213, 223
city-states, 30
civil liberties, 3, 10, 11, 16, 18, 37, 72, 73, 93, 94, 117, 119, 123, 125, 189, 190, 220, 224, 225, 237, 240, 257, 258
civil rights, 73
civil society, 12, 15, 18, 36, 38, 47, 53, 241, 248, 250, 258
   in Cambodia, 139, 148
   in Indonesia, 189
   in Korea, 53, 59, 60, 61, 62, 65, 66, 249
   organizations, 61, 64, 65, 75, 82, 83, 86, 216, 217
   in Philippines, 167, 168, 171, 172
   in Taiwan, 72, 75, 82, 85, 94
   in Thailand, 118, 119, 127
   in Timor-Leste, 217
civil war, 26, 27, 215
   in Burma, 40, 43
   in Burundi, 254
   in Cambodia, 40, 43, 134, 136, 137, 139, 227
   in Indonesia, 39, 42
   in Philippines, 42–43, 242
   in Taiwan, 79
   in Timor-Leste, 40, 205, 227
civil-military relations, 11, 13
   in Burma, 13
   in Cambodia, 13, 136
   in East Timor, 205, 211, 220, 222
   in Indonesia, 13, 20, 182, 184, 186, 196, 198
   in Laos, 13
   in Myanmar, 4
   in Philippines, 33, 37, 164
   in South Korea, 13, 15, 48, 49, 50, 51, 53, 55, 56, 61, 62, 63, 65, 66
   in Taiwan, 72, 76, 86, 90, 93
   in Thailand, 32, 105, 106, 107, 108, 109, 110, 112, 113, 114, 116, 117, 118, 121, 122, 123, 124, 127, 128
clientelism, 8, 16, 257, 258
   in Cambodia, 134, 135, 138, 143
   and democracy, 20
   in Indonesia, 189
   in Korea, 62
   in Philippines, 166–67, 171, 172
   in Taiwan, 94
   in Thailand, 105
   in Timor-Leste, 226
colonial rule
   in Burma, 35, 36
   in Korea, 50, 51, 53, 56, 62, 66
   in Malaya, 35
   in Philippines, 16, 33, 157, 167, 168, 169, 173, 256, 257
   in Taiwan, 78
   in Timor-Leste, 204, 224, 226
colonialism, 16, 30, 33, 35, 36, 50, 51, 53, 62, 78, 157, 167, 169, 173, 204, 214, 224, 226, 248, 256, 257
communism, 34, 35, 36, 42, 49, 51, 79, 81, 93, 135, 143, 240, 244, 248
   communist insurgency, 37, 109, 164. *See also* insurgency
   stalinist-maoist model, 42, 49
comparative historical analysis, 17
conflict, 17, 26, 28, 39, 40, 42, 48, 65, 140, 147, 161, 184, 188, 192, 197, 210, 211, 212, 214, 219, 226, 245
   armed, 204, 226, 243, 245, 248
   civil war, 26, 27, 39, 40, 43, 79, 134, 136, 137, 139, 205, 215, 227, 242, 254
   intra-state, 243, 248
consolidated democracy, 1, 6. *See also* democratic consolidation
constitutionalism, 11
constitutional court
   in Cambodia, 146
   in Taiwan, 75, 92
   in Thailand, 120
constitutional democracy, 10, 11, 32, 33, 56, 74, 91, 133, 190

corporatism, 38, 54, 55. *See also* corporatist system
corporatist system, 31, 38, 54, 55
corruption, 8, 18, 27, 257
　in Brazil, 258
　in Cambodia, 134, 136, 137, 138, 139, 140, 142, 144, 145, 146
　in Indonesia, 182, 186, 192, 194
　in Korea, 55, 56, 58, 62
　in Nicaragua, 253
　in Philippines, 158, 162, 163, 166, 171, 172, 173
　in Taiwan, 75, 76, 77, 84, 94
　in Thailand, 109, 110, 113, 120
　in Timor-Leste, 221, 224, 256
coup d'état. *See also* military, coup
　in Burma, 36
　in Korea, 51
in Thailand, 103, 110, 116, 118, 123, 126, 127, 164, 239

Dahl, Robert A., 3, 26, 237
defective democracy, 19, 104, 116, 121, 127, 128, 156, 165, 174, 249
delegative democracy, 240
democracy, 1, 12, 13, 14, 15, 17, 18, 19, 20, 25, 26, 27, 31, 32, 33, 34, 35, 37, 38, 39, 40, 41, 47, 49, 57, 63, 65, 66, 72, 73, 75, 76, 77, 79, 80, 81, 83, 86, 87, 88, 89, 90, 91, 93, 94, 103, 104, 105, 108, 114, 115, 116, 118, 120, 121, 122, 123, 124, 125, 126, 127, 133, 134, 143, 146, 147, 148, 153, 154, 155, 156, 157, 159, 161, 162, 163, 164, 165, 166, 168, 169, 170, 171, 172, 173, 175, 179, 180, 187, 192, 193, 194, 195, 197, 198, 199, 204, 209, 215, 221, 222, 223, 224, 225, 226, 227, 233, 234, 239, 240, 242, 243, 245, 247, 250, 251, 254, 255, 256, 257, 258
　consolidation, 4, 6, 14, 15, 16, 17, 18, 19, 25, 27, 28, 31, 33, 34, 37, 38, 39, 47, 62, 65, 71, 73, 84, 103, 104, 117, 124, 127, 157, 197, 221, 222, 223, 233, 235, 237, 240, 244, 249, 250, 251, 255, 258, 259. *See also* consolidated democracy
　defective, 3, 4, 10, 17, 19, 74, 104, 116, 117, 118, 121, 128, 154, 156, 165, 166, 173, 174, 198, 223, 226, 234, 235, 237, 239, 244, 249, 251, 255, 259
　definition, 10, 12, 26, 73, 156, 255
　delegative, 240
　embedded, 10, 12, 19, 62, 73, 74, 104, 117, 118, 126, 133, 134, 148, 156, 180, 188, 215, 223, 225, 234, 235, 237, 240, 249, 255, 257
　essentially contested concept, 10
　illiberal, 43, 137, 198, 224, 227, 237
　liberal, 3, 10, 11, 12, 31, 37, 43, 47, 73, 77, 89, 148, 237
　measurement, 1, 3, 5, 27, 71, 156
　　Bertelsmann Transformation Index (BTI), 47, 71, 104, 121, 190, 191, 234, 237
　　economist intelligence unit (EIU), 191
　　Freedom House, 47, 75, 104, 121, 190, 191
　　Varieties of Democracy (V-Dem), 71, 74
　quality of, 4, 5, 6, 9, 10, 12, 14, 15, 43, 48, 62, 66, 71, 72, 77, 93, 94, 103, 117, 118, 121, 122, 125, 126, 128, 147, 153, 155, 156, 157, 167, 168, 173, 180, 188, 191, 194, 198, 205, 215, 223, 226, 234, 239, 243, 244, 249, 251, 258. *See also* democracy, measurement
democratic backsliding, 3, 4, 10, 103, 118, 188, 234, 237, 239, 240. *See also* autocratization; backsliding
democratic consolidation, 6, 14, 16, 18, 19, 38, 47, 62, 65, 73, 124, 249, 250, 251, 258
democratization, 4, 10, 12, 13, 14, 15, 17, 19, 20, 25, 26, 27, 28, 29, 30, 31, 32, 33, 39, 41, 42, 43, 223, 227, 233, 249, 251, 259
　in Asia, 1, 3, 4, 17, 25, 38, 42, 43, 241, 245
　in Burma, 35, 39, 40, 41
　in Cambodia, 2, 4, 39, 40, 41
　in China, 32, 42
　first wave, 1, 6, 35
　in Indonesia, 2, 35, 179, 180, 181, 186, 187, 188, 196, 197, 199, 200
　in Japan, 31
　in Korea, 2, 50, 52, 56, 59, 65
　in Malaya, 35
　in Philippines, 2, 33, 37, 41, 165
　second wave, 1, 37, 38
　in Siam, 33
　in Taiwan, 2, 71, 72, 81, 82, 86, 90, 94, 248
　in Thailand, 2, 37, 41, 103, 105, 116, 117, 118, 121, 124, 126, 127, 248

Index

third wave, 1, 2, 4, 6, 10, 17, 20, 38, 41, 42, 71, 233, 235, 237, 240, 244, 249, 250, 255, 258, 259
  in Timor-Leste, 2, 4, 39, 40, 41, 204, 208, 215, 223, 224, 225, 226, 227
  in Vietnam, 42
developmental state, 9, 15, 18, 19, 49, 148, 241, 250
  in Korea, 47, 49, 50, 52, 53, 54, 65, 66
  in Taiwan, 49, 78
dictatorship, 32, 33, 37, 42, 109, 154, 157, 165, 174, 215, 242, 243
  military, 1, 15, 34, 48, 49, 50, 55, 56, 61, 63, 65, 66, 104, 106, 108, 121, 181, 250
  personalist, 34, 135
Duterte, Rodrigo, 5, 154, 173, 174

East Timor, 71. *See also* Timor-Leste
  administrative effectiveness, 212, 224, 243
  Association of Ex-Political Prisoners, 219
  Association of Veterans of the Resistance, 219
  and Cambodia (in comparison), 227
  Catholic Church, 206
  civil liberties in, 220, 224, 225, 237, 240
  clientelism in, 226
  colonialism (Portuguese), 204, 224, 226
  Democratic Republic of Timor-Leste, 204
  effective power to govern in, 215, 222, 225
  elections in, 208, 209, 215, 216, 219, 220, 226
  electoral regime in, 215, 216
  Falintil, 206, 209, 210, 219
  Fretilin, 205, 206, 209, 217, 219, 220, 221
  gender-based violence, 220
  horizontal accountability in, 215, 221
  illiberal democracy in, 224, 227
  Indonesian occupation, 204, 205, 206, 215, 219, 224
  international donors, 217, 243
  International Force in, 207
  land rights, 220
  Maubere, 206
  National Council of Timorese Resistance, 227
  nationalism in, 206, 213
  peace-building, 215, 227
  post-colonial, 204, 220
  post-conflict, 204, 210, 226, 227
  power-sharing, 208
  referendum, 207, 213
  Tetum, 206, 220
  Timor-Leste, 183
  UNAMET, 207
  UNTAET, 204, 205, 207, 208, 209, 210, 213, 220, 227
  West Timor, 207, 210
Economist Intelligence Unit, 3
Egypt, 104, 199
elections, 10, 13, 15, 16, 18, 19, 20, 27, 41, 62, 74, 234, 237, 240, 250, 256, 257, 258
  in Argentina, 251
  in Bangladesh, 254
  in Burma, 36
  in Burundi, 254, 255
  in Cambodia, 40, 133, 134, 136, 137, 138, 142, 144, 146, 148, 253
  in Chile, 250
  in East Timor, 208, 209, 215, 216, 219, 220, 226
Election Commission
  Philippines, 158, 159
  Taiwan, 74
  Thailand, 120
electoral laws, 62
electoralism, 10, 156, 168
  in Indonesia, 20, 34, 184, 186, 187, 188, 189, 190, 195, 198, 200, 256
  in Japan, 31, 38
  in Korea, 34, 51, 53, 57, 61
  majority two-round system, 215
  in Malaysia, 4
  in Myanmar, 4
  in Nicaragua, 253
  in Philippines, 33, 37, 41, 153, 155, 156, 157, 158, 159, 164, 168, 171, 173, 174, 234
  proportional representation, 119, 215
  in Taiwan, 71, 72, 73, 74, 75, 76, 80, 81, 82, 83, 84, 87, 88, 89, 90, 92, 94
  in Thailand, 41, 116, 117, 119, 122, 123, 252
electoral authoritarianism, 133, 136, 253
Electoral Integrity Project, 74
electoral regime, 10, 15, 16, 65, 74, 87, 93, 94, 118, 119, 125, 153, 156, 188, 195, 215, 216, 255, 256
embedded democracy, 19
  partial regime, 12, 15, 19, 65, 74, 76, 77, 87, 88, 93, 133, 134, 148, 156, 215, 234, 235, 240, 249, 250, 255
  civil liberties, 11, 16, 18, 19, 20, 73, 75, 77, 118, 123, 125, 126, 133, 153, 156, 215, 220, 225, 226, 237, 257, 258

embedded democracy (*cont.*)
    effective power to govern, 11, 74, 94, 120, 125, 126, 127, 133, 156, 164, 215, 222, 225, 226, 237, 240
    electoral regime, 10, 15, 16, 19, 73, 77, 94, 118, 123, 125, 133, 156, 159, 215, 216, 225, 237, 240, 255, 256, 257, 258, 259
    horizontal accountability, 11, 15, 16, 18, 19, 20, 73–74, 77, 94, 118, 125, 133, 153, 156, 215, 221, 226, 237, 257, 258
embedding, social, 7, 8
Estrada, Joseph, 41, 163, 172
ethnic cleavage, 26, 36, 42
ethnic diversity, 8, 29
    in Burma, 35, 36
    in Cambodia, 247
    in Indonesia, 189, 190, 247
    in Philippines, 37
    in Taiwan, 84
    in Thailand, 113, 248
ethnic minorities, 36, 113, 114, 140, 142, 189, 190, 245, 247, 248
ethno-religious violence, 184, 245
    secessionist revolt, 37, 111, 213
Evans, Peter, 49
export-oriented industrialization, 53, 54
external intervention, 27, 29, 43

factionalism
    in Cambodia, 40, 227
    factions, local, 15, 39, 40, 51, 80, 84, 107, 164, 170, 206, 209, 214, 226, 252
    in Korea, 39, 51
    in Philippines, 164, 170
    in Taiwan, 15, 39, 80, 84
    in Thailand, 107, 252
    in Timor-Leste, 206, 209, 214, 226
federalism, 251
foreign intervention. *See* external intervention
Freedom House, 3, 47, 71, 74, 77, 104, 119, 121, 122, 159, 189, 190, 191, 204, 216, 217, 218
    civil liberties, 119, 189, 190
    political rights, 74, 75, 119, 189
freedom of association and assembly, 119, 237
freedom of expression, 119, 145, 159, 237
French Revolution, 31
Fukuyama, Francis, 12

governance, 16, 26, 51, 61, 105, 133, 134, 144, 159, 164, 174, 197, 200, 213, 215, 221, 222, 226, 234, 237, 240, 241, 254
guided democracy, 35, 183

Habibie, B. J., 189, 207
Han dynasty, 29, 30
historical institutionalism
    comparative historical analysis, 17
    historical experience, 6, 26
    historical turn, 1
    historical-institutional conditions, 155
    historical-structural factors, 155
    legacies, 18, 30, 38, 56, 72, 77, 78, 107, 137, 204, 208, 222
    path-dependency, 4, 6, 15, 18, 48, 56, 66, 72, 94, 135, 142, 144, 250, 251, 258
horizontal accountability, 3
    in Cambodia, 133, 143, 148
    in East Timor, 215, 221
    in Indonesia, 188, 190
    in Korea, 47, 62, 249
    partial regime of embedded democracy, 11, 15, 16, 18, 19, 20, 73–74, 94, 118, 125, 133, 153, 156, 215, 221, 226, 237, 240, 257, 258
    in Philippines, 153, 155, 163
    in Taiwan, 73, 76, 77, 91, 92, 93, 94, 249
    in Thailand, 118, 120, 125
Human Development Index (HDI), 192, 193
human rights
    in Cambodia, 136, 140, 146
    human rights commission (of Thailand), 119
    in Indonesia, 39, 190, 193, 206
    in Philippines, 174
    in Thailand, 112, 118, 119, 120, 123
    in Timor-Leste, 220
Hun Sen, 18, 19, 40, 134, 135, 136, 137, 141, 142, 148, 252
Huntington, Samuel, 26, 154

identity
    in Indonesia, 35
    national, 35, 43, 105, 205, 206, 213, 245, 247, 248
    state, 110, 210, 213, 244, 245, 248
    in Taiwan, 43, 248
    in Timor-Leste, 205, 206, 210, 213
illiberal democracy, 43, 137, 198, 224, 227, 237
India, 30, 36, 182

Index

Indonesia
  Aceh, 30, 39, 183, 184, 185, 188, 196, 197
  administrative capacity, 181, 182, 186, 192, 193, 194, 197
  Ahmadis, 190
  Anti-Corruption Agency (KBK), 194
  armed forces, 196. See also military
  armed struggle against Dutch rulers, 34
  army, 181, 193, 196
  Chinese minority, 189
  citizenship agreement, 181, 187
  civil liberties, 188, 189, 190
  civil society, 189
  coercive capacity, 181, 184, 185, 196
  decentralization, 186, 188, 193, 197, 199
  democratization, 179, 180, 186, 187, 188, 196, 197, 199, 200
  economic inequality, 197
  effective power to govern, 188, 190
  elections in Indonesia, 20, 34, 184, 186, 187, 188, 189, 190, 195, 198, 200, 256
  electoral regime, 188, 195
  ethnic diversity, 189, 190
  extractive capacity, 181, 182, 184, 185, 194, 197
  Financial Audit Agency (BPK), 194
  foreign direct investment (FDI), 182
  Gini coefficient, 197
  governance, 197
  guided democracy, 183
  Habibie, B. J., 189, 207
  horizontal accountability, 188, 190
  human rights, 190, 193
  International Monetary Fund (IMF), 185
  Kalimantan, 184, 187
  Maluku, 184
  nation building, 197
  new order (regime), 181, 182, 183, 186, 191, 192, 207
  oil exports, 182
  Papua, 183, 184, 188, 194, 196
  parliament, 188, 189, 190, 195
  party and campaign finance, 189
  police, 181, 182, 184, 185, 186, 192, 193, 195, 196
  political rights, 189
  presidentialism, 181, 184, 188, 190
  public services, 182, 183, 186, 187, 192, 193, 197
  Rome Statute, 190
  Shiites, 190
  Suharto, 19, 20, 35, 39, 180, 181, 182, 183, 184, 185, 186, 187, 188, 189, 190, 192, 193, 194, 196, 197, 198, 199, 200, 243, 256
  Sumatra, 187
  Susilo Bambang Yudhoyono, 192
  Theys Eluay, 194
inequality, 86, 165, 197
  Gini coefficient, 165, 197
  income inequality, 165
institutionalism, historical, 1, 6, 15, 17, 18, 26, 30, 38, 48, 56, 66, 72, 77, 80, 94, 107, 135, 137, 142, 155, 204, 208, 222, 250, 251, 258
insurgency, 111, 112, 113, 114, 115, 119, 125, 248
  communist, 36, 37, 109, 110, 164
interest groups, 11, 15
  in Korea, 48, 60, 61, 65, 66
  in Thailand, 126
  in Timor-Leste, 224
intermediate state, 249, 250
International Monetary Fund (IMF), 192, 197
Islam, 30, 190, 191, 196, 200, 247

Japan
  developmental state, 49, 78
  Liberal Democratic Party (LDP), 49
  Meiji (restauration), 31, 32
  Taisho (democracy), 31, 38
judicial independence, 3, 144, 220, 250, 257
judiciary, 19, 237
  in Cambodia, 143, 144, 145, 146
  in Indonesia, 190
  in Philippines, 37, 163
  in Taiwan, 73, 75, 76, 85, 90, 92, 94
  in Thailand, 117, 118, 120, 127
  in Timor-Leste, 220

Kenya, 258
Khmer Rouge, 134, 135, 139, 143
Kim Dae-Jung, 57
king monarchy (in Thailand), 122
Korea
  agriculture in, 54
  anti-corruption measures, 56
  campaign finance, 56, 58, 64
  chaebol, 54, 55, 57, 83
  Chun Doo-Hwan, 54
  civil society, 47, 53, 59, 60, 61, 63, 65, 66
  coercive capacity, 48, 53, 62

Korea (cont.)
  colonialism, 50, 51, 53, 56, 62, 66
  corporatism, 54, 55
  corruption, 55, 56, 58, 62
  developmental state, 47, 49, 50, 52, 53, 54, 65, 66
  Economic Planning Board (EPB), 52, 53, 54
  effective power to govern, 62
  elections in, 51, 53, 57, 61, 62
  electoral regime, 65
  Evans, Peter, 49
  extractive capacity, 52
  Federation of Korean Trade Unions (FKTU), 55
  horizontal accountability, 47, 62, 249
  industrialization, 50, 52, 53, 54, 55, 56, 66
  Kim Dae-Jung, 57
  Kim Young-Sam, 57
  Korean Central Intelligence Agency (KCIA), 51
  Korean parliament, 64
  Korean war, 34, 50, 51, 53, 79
  Kwangju uprising, 55
  labour and trade unions, 54, 55, 59, 60, 61, 65
  landholding class, 53
  landowners, 62
  Lee Myung-Bak, 64
  military
    civilian control over, 51, 62
    coup, 51
    factions, 51
  National Assembly, 62, 63, 64
  North Korea, 52, 53
  Park Geun-Hye, 64
  parliament, 66
  path-dependency, 48, 56, 66
  peasants, 53
  political parties, 48, 49, 57, 58, 59, 61, 64, 65, 66
    candidate selection, 58, 64
    funding, 57, 58, 61, 64
    institutionalization, 48, 58, 59, 64, 66
    local organizations, 49, 57, 58
    relations with civil society, 61, 65, 66
  presidentialism, 48, 51, 62, 63, 64
  Roh Moo-Hyun, 56, 58, 61
  Saemaŭl (New Village) Programme, 55
  working class in South Korea, 52, 55
  Yushin constitution, 55
ksae, 134, 135, 252

Kuomintang (KMT), 15, 49, 72–73, 74, 75, 78–86, 87, 89, 90, 91, 94, 250

land reform, 53, 79, 84, 168
Laos, 13, 29, 234, 245
late developer, 71
Latin America, 20, 167, 235, 240. *See also* Central America
Leftwich, Adrian, 49
legitimacy, 7, 8, 15, 18, 27, 39, 62, 193, 197, 224
  international, 26, 39–41, 42, 43
  of (nation) state, 8, 187, 197, 245, 248
  performance, 183
  in Thailand, 105–8, 248
  in Timor-Leste, 213, 224
Leviathan, 224
liberal democracy, 3, 10, 11, 12, 39, 43, 73, 77, 89, 148, 237
liberalism, 10

Macapagal-Aroyo, Gloria, 41
Mahathir, Mohammad, 36, 41
Malay, 36
  Malay-Muslims (of Thailand), 111–12, 113–14, 120, 125
Malaysia, 3, 4, 30, 34, 36, 38, 41, 114, 153, 157, 159, 162, 165, 168, 183, 234, 245
  Mahathir, Mohammad, 36, 41
  National Front, 41. *See also* Barisan Nasional (BN)
  Rajak, Najib, 41
Mann, Michael, 7, 104
  despotic power, 8, 13
  infrastructural power, 8, 13, 48
Maoism Maoist-model, 42
Marcos, Ferdinand, 154, 157, 164, 165, 172, 174, 243
mechanism, causal, 4, 6, 14, 19, 27, 256
media, 27, 34, 64, 71, 74, 75, 77, 86, 89, 90, 94, 119, 159, 224, 240, 247, 251
  freedom, 189, 250. *See also* press freedom
  journalists, 77, 146, 161, 162, 216
medieval institutions, 13, 28
Megawati Sukarnoputri, 192
Meiji (restauration), 31, 32
Merkel, Wolfgang, 10–12, 62, 73–74, 77, 87, 94, 118, 155, 156, 159, 164, 188, 189, 190, 215, 240
Mexico, 167, 182, 258
middle class, 31, 55, 117, 126, 127
Middle East, 240

Index

Migdal, Joel, 48
military, 1, 4, 9, 13, 37, 247
  in Cambodia, 135–37, 139
  civilian control over, 11, 51, 62, 110, 116, 118, 136
  coup, 36, 51, 103, 110, 116, 118, 123, 126, 127, 239
  factions, 51, 107, 252
  in Indonesia, 181–82, 184–85, 186, 192, 193, 195, 196, 198, 199
  in Korea, 15, 34, 49–50, 51–52, 53, 55–57, 62, 65, 250
  in Philippines, 33, 37, 164–65
  regime, 15, 48, 49, 50, 55, 56, 61, 63, 65, 66, 104, 106, 108, 121, 181, 250. *See also* military, rule
  role in politics, 48, 62, 252
  rule, 4, 9, 35, 36, 39, 40, 42, 103, 114, 115, 117, 122, 123, 124, 222, 252, 253–54
  in Taiwan, 39, 72, 76, 78, 86, 90, 93
  in Thailand, 18, 32, 33, 42, 104, 107, 111–12, 114–18, 120–23, 124, 125, 126, 127, 252
  in Timor-Leste, 205–7, 211, 216, 220, 222–23, 225
mobilization, 73, 200, 205, 206, 258
modernization, 31, 32, 34, 86, 103, 196
monarchy (in Thailand), 104, 108–10, 113, 114, 116–18, 121–23, 124, 127–28
  king, 106–7, 108, 113, 116, 118, 121, 123, 124
  palace, 105, 107, 108, 117, 121, 123, 125
monopoly on use of force, 7, 26, 124–26, 244, 245
  in East Timor, 209–11, 223, 224, 225
  in Philippines, 173
  in South Korea, 48
  in Thailand, 104, 107, 109, 110–12, 124, 125, 126
Weber, Max, 6, 7, 28
Myanmar, 4, 9, 29, 71, 114, 164, 234, 245. *See also* Burma

national building
  national identity, 35, 43, 105, 205, 213, 245, 247, 248
  nationalism, 169, 245
    in East Timor, 206, 213
Ne Win, 36
networks, particularistic, 6, 9, 15, 16, 19, 256, 257, 258, 259
New Order regime
  in East Timor, 207
  in Indonesia, 181, 183, 191
nexians, 12, 17, 26–27, 29, 32, 33, 37, 39, 41, 94, 233, 257. *See also* state-democracy nexus
Nicaragua, 237, 253, 255
Nigeria, 258
North Korea, 34, 52, 53, 234, 245

O'Donnell, Guillermo, 221, 240, 251
oligarchic rule, 31, 33, 37, 191
one-party regime, 2, 39, 133, 136, 148, 220

Pakistan, 199
parallel state (Thailand), 18, 103, 104, 108, 109, 112, 114, 116, 117, 118, 121–22, 123, 124–26, 127–28
Park Chung-hee, 50, 51, 53, 54, 55, 66
particularism, 8
  particularistic networks, 6, 9, 15, 16, 19, 256, 257, 258, 259
patrimonialism, 172
  neo-patrimonialism, 9, 18, 105, 133, 143, 144, 147, 154, 211, 255
    in East Timor, 211, 226
patronage, 8, 16, 33, 51, 84, 105, 136, 142, 148, 183, 253–55
patron-client relationship, 9, 18, 28, 135
personalism, 154, 253
  personalist regime, 135
personalization, 222
Peru, 121, 191, 258
Phibun Songkhram, 37
Philippines, 2, 5, 10, 14, 16, 17, 19, 31, 32–35, 37, 39, 41, 42, 71, 77, 94, 103, 108, 121, 153–75, 183, 233, 237, 242, 243, 245, 247, 255–58
  Alliance of Hope, 41
  American colonialism, 154, 157, 159–61, 168–69, 256
  Ampatuan massacre, 161, 162, 163
  Aquino, Benigno III, 41
  Aquino, Corazon, 41, 164–65, 172
  bureaucracy
    decentralization, 33
    effectiveness, 154
  civil rights in, 153, 155, 156, 162–63
  colonial powers, 155, 167, 169, 173
  colonial regime, 167–69, 173
  defective democracy in, 154, 156, 165, 166, 173, 174
  democratic quality in, 154, 156–65, 166, 173

Philippines (cont.)
  Duterte, Rodrigo, 5, 154, 172, 173–75
  electoral integrity, 157–59
  Estrada, Joseph, 41, 163, 172
  Federalist Party, 170
  income inequality, 165
  institutionalized party, 154
  Liberal Party, 156, 171
  Macapagal-Aroyo, Gloria, 41
  Marcos, Ferdinand, 37, 41, 154, 157, 164, 165, 172, 174, 243
  Marcos, Imelda, 172
  Marcos, Pacifico, 172
  Martel, Alita, 172
  Nacionalista Party, 170–71
  neo-patrimonialism in, 154
  oligarchs, 168
  oligarchy in, 154–55, 166, 171. *See also* oligarchic rule
  Partido Federal, 169
  party formation, 156, 166–73
  party institutionalization, 154
  patrimonialism, 172
  Payne-Aldrich Act of 1909, 168
  People Power Revolution, 157, 164
  political rights in, 159–62
  public interest, 155, 168, 169, 172
  Ramos, Fidel, 41
  responsiveness, 165–66
  Romualdez, Benjamin 'Kokoy,' 172
  social cleavages, 168–69, 173
  Spanish colonial regime, 167–68
  Spanish Penal Code, 159, 160
polarization, 2, 51, 82, 234
political cleavages, 26, 42
  in East Timor, 209
  in Taiwan, 82
political community, 7
political parties
  in Brazil, 258
  in Burma, 36
  in Cambodia, 16, 18, 40, 49, 134, 135, 136–38, 140–43, 145, 146–48, 247, 252
  in East Timor, 205, 215–16, 219–20, 221, 222
  in Indonesia, 34, 182, 188–89, 190, 192, 194
  institutionalization, 48, 58, 59, 60, 64, 66, 73, 81, 82, 154
  in Japan, 38
  in Korea, 53, 55, 57–61, 63–64
  National Front, 41. *See also* Barisan Nasional (BN)
  party organization, 49, 64, 79, 81, 155, 250
  in Philippines, 154, 156, 163, 166, 171, 173, 174, 256
  political party system, 15, 18, 59, 61, 63, 72, 73, 81, 82, 83, 89, 94, 119, 154, 169–71, 173, 174, 219, 220, 250, 252, 254, 256
  relations with civil society, 61, 65, 66, 82, 83, 248
  relations within civil society, 258
  in Taiwan, 18, 49, 71–73, 74, 76, 79–84, 86, 87, 88–89, 90–92, 94
  in Thailand, 112, 118–19, 120, 122, 123, 248
political rights, 10, 19, 73, 77, 88–89, 93, 94, 117, 118, 122, 123, 125, 133, 153, 155, 156, 162, 215, 237, 251, 255, 256, 258, 259
  Bertelsmann Transformation Index (BTI), 240
  Freedom House, 74, 75, 119, 189
polyarchy, 3, 10, 226, 237
post-communist Europe, 239, 240, 244
power
  despotic, 8, 13
  effective power to govern, 11, 74, 76, 93, 94, 118, 120, 123, 124–26, 127, 133, 155, 156, 164, 188, 190, 215, 222–23, 225, 226, 237, 240
  infrastructural, 5, 8, 9, 13, 15, 18, 20, 48, 50–56, 65
power-sharing, 27, 35, 36, 40, 118, 134, 208
predatory state, 20, 258, 259
presidentialism
  in East Timor, 220
  in Indonesia, 181, 184, 188, 189, 190
  in Korea, 48, 51, 62, 63, 64
  in Philippines, 243
  in Taiwan, 75, 91
press freedom, 10, 119, 120, 162, 216
protest, 13
  in Burma, 40
  in Cambodia, 148
  in Indonesia, 182, 243
  in Philippines, 41
  in South Korea, 48, 53, 55, 59, 64–65
  in Taiwan, 73, 76, 83
  in Thailand, 41, 110, 111, 112, 123

Index

Qing dynasty, 32, 78
quality
  of bureaucracy, 48, 81, 137–40, 173, 224, 258. *See also* bureaucratic capacity
  of democracy, 5, 6, 9, 10, 14, 15, 48, 62–66, 72, 77, 86, 94, 118, 121, 122, 125, 128, 143, 153, 154, 155, 156, 157, 167, 168, 180, 186, 188, 189, 191, 193, 194, 195, 198, 199, 215–23, 226, 234, 237, 239, 244, 249, 251, 258

Ramos, Fidel, 41, 157
Ranariddh, Norodom, 134, 135, 136
Red Shirts, 42, 111, 122
regime, political
  authoritarianism, 1, 3, 4, 6, 9, 10, 13, 16, 17, 18, 48, 49, 50, 55, 56, 59, 60, 62, 63, 64, 66, 71, 104, 108, 109, 110, 116, 121, 127, 133, 136, 179, 181, 184, 191, 197, 198, 215, 245, 250, 252, 253, 254, 259
  definition, 7, 10, 12
  military, 15, 48, 49, 50, 55, 56, 61, 63, 65, 66, 104, 106, 108, 121, 181, 250
rent-seeking, 12, 141, 185, 256
Reporters Without Borders, 71, 75, 216
revolution, 205
  from above in Japan, 32
  from above in Thailand, 108
  China, 32
  coloured, 136
  French, 31
  People Power, 157, 164
  Vietnam, 42
Rhee Syngman, 34, 50, 51, 53
rule of law, 11, 16, 27, 37, 235, 257
  in Cambodia, 143, 144
  in Indonesia, 188, 190, 215, 220–21, 224, 225
  in Philippines, 162, 163, 173
  in Taiwan, 71, 72, 73, 75, 84, 85, 89, 93, 94
  in Thailand, 118, 123, 126

secessionism, 188, 192, 213
  secessionist revolt, 37, 111
separation of powers, 257
  and horizontal accountability, 73, 91
  and presidentialism, 63, 64, 190
sequencing, 4, 47, 71. *See also* sequentialism
  debate, 25, 29, 31, 35, 37, 38, 94
  stateness first, 4, 6, 12–14, 17, 19

sequentialism, 6, 13, 12–14, 16, 223, 257
Siam, 29, 30, 31, 32–33, 34, 107, 108. *See also* Thailand
Singapore, 38, 41, 71, 114, 153, 169, 234, 245
South Korea. *See* Korea
Spanish colonial rule, 168, 173
Stalinist model, 42, 49
state, 109, 118, 125, 126, 155
  autonomy, 6, 53, 56, 57, 62, 80, 85, 94, 224, 258
  capacity, 5, 6–9, 12, 13, 14, 17–20, 40, 43, 47, 48, 50–52, 53, 56, 62, 66, 71, 73, 86–88, 93, 94, 103, 104, 106, 109, 110, 114–16, 117, 121, 125, 126, 133, 134, 140, 142, 148, 184–88, 191–200, 204, 205, 209, 210, 223, 224, 225, 226, 241–43, 252
  definition, 6–9
  state-building, 4, 5, 6, 10, 12–14, 15, 17, 18, 19, 43, 48, 51, 56, 62, 63, 66, 79, 103, 108, 109, 110, 116, 124, 127, 128, 155, 173, 204, 207, 208, 223, 226, 227, 250, 256, 257, 258
  state-democracy nexus, 1, 4–6, 9, 12, 14, 20, 26, 66, 226, 252, 255, 257, 258, 259. *See also* nexians
state capacity, 5, 6–9, 12, 13, 14, 15, 106, 252
  administrative, 6–9, 15, 16, 18, 20, 27, 48, 50, 51, 53, 56, 62, 85, 106, 110, 112–13, 114–16, 124, 125, 126–27, 133, 181, 182–83, 186, 192–93, 194, 197, 209, 211–13, 223, 226, 241–45, 249–50, 256, 257, 259. *See also* bureaucratic capacity
  coercive, 7, 9, 13, 15, 16, 18, 34, 48, 50, 51, 53, 62, 106–7, 108–9, 114–15, 126, 133, 135–37, 181, 182, 184, 185, 192, 193, 196, 209, 224, 226, 241–43, 249, 256, 257, 259
  extractive, 52, 53, 105, 106–7, 114–16, 126, 181, 182, 184–86, 192, 193, 194, 197, 209, 241–43
  power, despotic, 8, 13
  power, infrastructural, 5, 8, 9, 13, 15, 18, 20, 48, 50–52, 53, 65
state society relations, 9, 14
  in Korea, 56, 59, 61, 65, 66
  in Philippines, 174
state-democracy nexus, 1, 4–6, 19, 12, 14, 20, 26, 66, 226, 252, 255, 257, 258, 259
  sequencing, 4, 173, 242

stateness, 1–2, 4, 5–6, 9, 12–14, 17, 18, 19, 20, 47, 78, 87, 88–89, 103–4, 108–13, 117, 121, 124–28, 133, 154, 166, 179–80, 181, 184, 188, 191, 193, 195–200, 204, 205, 208, 209–10, 213, 215, 223–27, 233, 235, 241–45, 248–49, 250, 251, 255, 256, 257, 258–59
  definition, 6–7, 12
  first, 4, 6, 12–14, 17. *See also* sequencing
  scalar concept, 8
state-society relations, 5, 42
  in Korea, 48, 50, 52, 53, 55, 56, 63
  in Taiwan, 79, 241
Suchinda Kraprayoon, 41
Suharto, 35, 39, 180, 181–88, 189, 190, 192, 193, 194, 196–97, 198–200, 243, 256
Sukarno, 35, 181, 183
Sun Yat-sen (Sun Yatsen), 32

Taisho democracy, 31, 38
Taiwan, 2, 3, 4, 10, 14–15, 17, 18, 19, 38, 39, 40, 42, 43, 47, 49, 71–94, 233, 235, 237, 241, 242, 243, 245, 248, 249, 250, 251, 252. *See also* China, Republic of
  2–28 Incident, 79
  accountability in
    horizontal, 73–74, 76, 77, 91–92, 94
    vertical, 15, 72, 74, 80, 81, 82, 90
  authoritarian legacies, 72
  benshengren, 78, 79, 80, 84
  campaign regulation in, 89
  central government, 72, 80, 83, 91, 93
  Chen, Shui-bian, 85, 94
  Chiang, Kai-shek, 49, 79, 80, 93
  Chinese influence in, 75, 77
  civil society, 72, 75, 82–83, 85, 86, 94
  civil-military relations, 76, 86, 90, 93
  Control Yuan, 90, 91, 92
  Council of Grand Justices (constitutional court), 75, 76, 92
  democracy, consolidation of, 71, 73, 84
  democracy, deepening of, 94
  democracy, transition to, 71, 72, 73, 74, 79, 80, 81, 83, 84, 88–89, 90, 91, 93, 94
  Democratic Progressive Party (DPP), 74, 81–83, 85, 89, 94
  effective power to govern in, 74, 76, 93, 94
  elections in, 71, 72, 73–75, 76, 79–82, 83, 84, 87, 88, 89, 90, 92, 94
    election integrity, 74, 87
    electoral fraud, 88
    vote buying, 74, 76, 77, 84, 88
    voter intimidation, 88
  Examination Yuan, 91
  export-oriented industrialization, 79
  freedom of assembly in, 73, 75
  freedom of speech in, 73, 75, 89
  Heijin ("Black gold"), 84
  horizontal accountability in, 73–74, 76, 77, 91–92, 93, 94
  household registration system, 87
  industrial policy, 83
  Japanese colonial legacy in, 78
  judicial independence in, 75, 76, 92, 94
  Kuomintang (KMT), Chinese Nationalist Party, 72–73, 74, 78–79, 80–86, 87, 89, 90, 91, 94
    hegemonic party, 72, 91, 94
    Leninist party, 49, 81, 82
  labour unions, 82
  land reform, 79, 84
  legacies, 77, 84
  Legislative Yuan, 92, 93
  liberal democracy in, 73, 77, 89
  local factions, 80, 84
  local government, 72, 80–81
  local government, corruption of, 81, 88, 94
  local government, election to, 80, 81, 82
  Ma, Ying-jeou, 85–86, 90, 92
  mainlander, 39, 78, 79, 84, 93
  media freedom in, 71, 75, 77, 88, 89
  National Assembly in, 80, 84, 91, 93
  New Power Party, 83
  partisanship, 82
  party institutionalization in, 73, 82
  police administration, 88
  political party-civil society relations, 82, 258
  political polarization, 82
  prosecutoriate, 76, 90
  rule of law in, 71, 72, 73, 75, 84, 85, 89, 91, 93, 94
  separation of powers in, 73, 91
  small and medium enterprises (SMEs), 83
  sovereignty, 77
  state-business relations, 84, 85
  state-owned enterprise (SOE), 78, 83, 84, 85
  Sunflower Movement, 76
  Taiwan Garrison Command, 90
  United States, Taiwan's relations with, 77, 86
  in World War II, 78
taxation, 52, 182, 185
terrorism, 39

Index

Thailand, 2, 3, 4, 14, 16, 17–19, 29, 30, 33, 34, 37, 38, 41, 42, 71, 94, 103–28, 157, 164, 165, 199, 234, 237, 239, 242, 243, 245, 248, 249, 251–53, 255. *See also* Siam
accountability
  horizontal, 118, 120, 125
  vertical, 120
Administrative Court, 120
Adulyadej, King Bhumipol, 116
Anti-Money Laundering Office (AMLO), 120
(Asian) Financial crisis (of 1997), 110, 115, 116
Border Patrol Police, 115
Buddhism, 113
bureaucratic polity, 108, 109, 110, 117, 127
Chakri dynasty, 32
Chulalongkorn, reforms, 32
Computer Crimes Act, 123
constitution
  1997, 117, 119, 120, 122
  2006, 103, 108, 110, 116, 122
  2014, 103, 110, 116
coup d'état, 103, 104, 106, 109, 110, 111, 112, 114, 116, 118, 121, 122–23, 126, 127
Deep South, 111–12, 113, 115, 119, 120, 125
Democrat Party, 112, 123
effective power to govern in, 118, 120, 123, 125, 126, 127
Election Commission, 120
elections in, 116, 117, 119, 120, 122, 123
ethnic minorities, 114
experts of violence, 105
Human Rights Commission, 119
king, 32, 103, 105–8, 109, 110, 113, 116, 117, 118, 121, 122, 123, 124. *See also* monarchy (in Thailand)
lèse majesté, 107, 119, 120, 122
Malay-Muslims, 112, 113–14, 120, 125
monarchized military, 107
Mongkut, King, 32, 108
Nationality Act (of Thailand), 114
Navy, 115
Or Sor Volunteers, 115
parallel state, 18, 103, 104–8, 109, 110, 111, 112, 113, 114, 116, 117–18, 121–22, 123, 124–26, 127–28, 243, 252
People's Democratic Reform Committee (PDRC), 111, 123
Phibun Songkhram, 37
Red Shirt movement, 42, 111, 122, 123

Royal Thai Police, 111, 115, 116, 121, 123, 125
Suchinda Krapayoon, 41
Sundaravej, Samak, 111
Thai Rak Thai (TRT), 119, 120
Thaksin Shinawatra, 103, 117, 248, 252
Tinsulanonda, Prem, 107, 109
Vechachiwa, Abhisit, 112
Wongsawat, Somchai, 111
yellow shirt movement, 42, 111, 123
yellow shirt protest, 42
Yingluck Shinawatra, 111
Thaksin Shinawatra, 103, 117, 248, 252
Thanom Kittikachorn, 41
Timor-Leste, 4, 5, 14, 16, 17, 19, 39, 103, 157, 188, 192, 196, 204–27, 233, 242, 243, 245, 247, 249, 255–58. *See also* East Timor
Tocqueville, Alexis de, 153
transition to democracy, 82, 93

United Nations (UN), 133, 134, 204
  interim administration, 4, 207, 227
  Security Council, 207, 208
  United Nations Mission in East Timor (UNAMET), 207
  United Nations Transitional Authority in East Timor (UNTAET), 204, 205, 207–9, 210, 213, 220, 227
United States, 34, 39, 64, 77, 86, 92
  colonial rule, 16, 154, 157, 159, 160, 168, 169, 173, 174, 256
  occupation, 37, 38
US government, 174

Varieties of Democracy (V-Dem), 3, 71, 74
Vietnam, 29–30, 38, 40, 41, 42, 153, 157, 158, 159, 162, 165, 168
vote buying, 20
  in East Timor, 216
  in Indonesia, 188, 195
  in Philippines, 159
  in Taiwan, 74, 76, 77, 84, 88, 250
  in Thailand, 119, 120

Weber, Max, 6, 7, 8, 28, 51
Western Europe, 25, 30
working class, 52, 55, 56
World War II, 1, 13, 17, 35, 37, 51, 53, 78, 160, 170

Yingluck Shinawatra, 111
Yushin (constitution), 34, 55

Lightning Source UK Ltd.
Milton Keynes UK
UKHW010854050722
405332UK00007B/219